How to Succeed in Your Own Business

How to Succeed in Your Own Business

William R. Park

•

Sue Chapin–Park

A WILEY-INTERSCIENCE PUBLICATION

John Wiley & Sons • New York • Chichester • Brisbane • Toronto

Library of Congress Cataloging in Publication Data:

Park, William R

How to succeed in your own business.

"A Wiley-Interscience publication."

Includes bibliographical references and index.

1. Small businesses—Handbooks, manuals, etc.
I. Chapin-Park, Sue, joint author. II. Title.

HD2341.P393 658'.022 77-28955

ISBN 0-471-03189-5

Printed in the United States of America

10 9 8 7 6 5 4 3 2 1

Preface

We are firmly convinced that there are only three ways for a person to get smart: (1) by reading, (2) by listening to smart people, and (3) by personal experience. There is no denying the adage that "experience is the best teacher." In business, however, there is always the danger that the time required to acquire the necessary experience may exceed the funds available for its acquisition. Experience, although good, can also be a most expensive teacher.

Best of all is a combination of all three approaches, in the sequence listed: (1) learn as much as possible from published material; (2) clarify what is not covered or is not understood by talking to people who know and practice the subject; and then (3) do it. If you go through the necessary planning and then decide not to act on it, all that has been lost is the planning; however, if you go into a new business venture without having made adequate plans first, the action is apt to result in financial disaster.

The initial incentive for writing this book came shortly after we began our own small retail business and found that the available published material fell far short of what we really needed to cope with many of our day-to-day operating problems and failed to forewarn us of many of the longer-range planning requirements. If we had had access to the information contained in this book, our own small retail business would have been successful at least a year sooner. We are, therefore, confident that the material included in this book is worth a year's experience, and possibly a life's savings, to the person contemplating a new small independent retail or service business.

This book is about small retail and service businesses. It deals thoroughly with all the elements necessary for successfully establishing and profitably operating a small independent business, encompassing personal, market, environmental, and financial requirements.

Getting involved in a new business for the first time can be a bewildering and complex experience, presenting the new entrepreneur with a seemingly overwhelming number of things to do. This need not be the case.

The primary objective of this book is simply to remove much of the uncertainty from the small business venture by informing the reader of what is to be expected, whether he is an aspiring or practicing small business owner. The book serves two important purposes: (1) it presents, in clear and simple terms, the basic principles of getting into, operating, and succeeding in a small business; and (2) it contains specific, detailed financial and operating data for a wide variety of small business opportunities, along with the interpretation and application of the data.

The first part of the book covers the general principles of selecting, starting, and managing a small retail or service business; it includes a thorough description of the economics of small business operation and the techniques of financial analysis and money management especially applicable to small businesses. The second part presents specific financial and operating data on some 80 different types of businesses.

The "principles" sections of the book are of value to anyone who is either considering getting into his own business or is already engaged in a small business. They enable the reader to understand the relationships among the various factors necessary for business success.

The "data" section is invaluable to both the aspiring and practicing businessperson. It provides the aspirant with specific information on shop size, investment requirements, expected sales and costs, and other useful data. It provides the practicing businessperson with a reference and basis of comparison of his operations to others in his own or related lines of business.

In addition to imparting an overall understanding of business principles and an intimate familiarity with the economics of business operation, the book also covers a multitude of annoying little problems that confront the small business owner, ranging from all the federal, state, and local forms to be completed, licenses to be obtained, and taxes to be paid, to personal problems such as how to get away for a vacation. In between are helpful suggestions on such diverse subjects as how to advertise, decorate a window, control inventory, minimize costs, handle personnel problems, and develop the full sales potential of the business.

The primary emphasis throughout the book is on the practical economic and financial aspects of the small business. All the necessary techniques and data for making realistic estimates and projections of potential sales volume, cost of goods sold or services offered, operating expenses, and profits are clearly presented, with numerous illustrative examples drawn from actual small business experience.

The specific businesses for which financial and operating data are presented are representative of the types of businesses toward which most of the book is oriented. These are small but substantial retail and service businesses with permanent storefront locations—*not* the operate-out-of-your-home or get-rich-quick schemes prevalent in many books on small business.

Every subject has its "inside" books and its "outside" books. "Inside" books are written by people who actually work in the field they write about. "Outside" books are written about some subject by people who may be generally knowledgeable (such as consultants or academicians) but are not actively engaged in the activity about which they write.

In reviewing more than 50 different books on "how to be successful in your own small independent business," one point was alarmingly apparent: very few of the books were written by people who were directly involved in small business, and most were written by people who had *never* operated, let alone been successful in, their own small business.

There is nothing wrong with this objective outside look at business, although it seldom addresses the specific problems that confront the small businessman. It is important for the reader to realize that the "nationally recognized expert" has, quite likely, never experienced a dozen impatient customers demanding individual attention, several salesmen anxious to show their new product lines, a ringing telephone, and an urgent need to go to the bathroom, all at the same time. And, like love and war, if you haven't experienced it yourself, you just can't know what it's really like!

In this case, the authors have been there, and still are, every day. A large part of this book, in fact, was written in our own small retail shop, in between customers, phone calls, salesmen, and calls of nature.

As Ralph Waldo Emerson once said, "Commerce is a game of skill, which every man cannot play, which few men can play well." Small business today is so complex that by the time a person could learn all the rules through experience, he might be too old to play the game.

It is our sincere hope that this book will help both aspiring and practicing small businesspeople to play the game just a little better, or at least to understand better the rules by which the game is played.

Overland Park, Kansas
Kansas City, Missouri
December, 1977

William R. Park
Sue Chapin-Park

Contents

List of Tables

List of Illustrations

How to Succeed in Your Own Business

1

An Introduction to Small Business

> ***Whenever big business and little business are required to sleep in the same bed, big business steals all the covers.***

This chapter familiarizes the reader with the scope and characteristics of small business in the United States. We describe its competitive role in a big-business-oriented economy and emphasize the unique characteristics of both small businesses and small businessmen.

What is a "Small Business"?

The first difficulty encountered in talking about small business is one of definition: exactly what is meant by a *small* business? How small is small?

The Small Business Administration (SBA) defines a small business as one that is independently owned and operated, is not dominant in its field, and meets the criteria for SBA-sponsored loan programs listed at the top of the next page. The SBA does not specify the maximum annual sales allowable for a manufacturing firm to be classified as "small," but instead defines a small manufacturer as one whose average annual number of employees does not exceed 250 to 1500 people.

The specific size limitations vary by industry; this is why ranges are given for service, retail, wholesale, and manufacturing businesses.

Using the SBA definition, small business actually encompasses over 98 percent of all business firms in the United States, including the very largest firms in some fields.

What constitutes a small business depends on the type of business rather than its annual sales. A "small" lumber yard has larger sales than a "large" hardware store; a "small" supermarket has larger sales than a "large" donut shop; and a "small" department store's sales far exceed the

Type of Business	Annual Receipts Not Exceeding
Service	\$2.0–8.0 million
Retail	\$2.0–7.5 million
Wholesale	\$9.5–22.0 million
General construction	\$9.5 million
Special trade construction	\$5.0 million
Farming and related activities	\$275,000

annual sales of what would be considered a "large" family shoe store. Most "small" manufacturers have far greater sales than most "large" retailers.

Throughout this book a "small" business refers to one that is independently owned, either by an individual or a few partners or shareholders; is actively operated and managed by the owner or owners; usually has one, but may have several, shop locations, all in the same city or metropolitan area; and has a physical size (measured in square feet of shop space occupied) and annual dollar volume *less* than the average or median for that particular type of business. For the businesses covered here, this definition *excludes* businesses with more than a million dollars in annual sales and includes only a few with sales exceeding $500,000.

Characteristics of the Independent Businessman

There are two basic types of small, independent businessmen. One type is in business simply because he enjoys the challenge and independence of being in business for himself; the specific type of business makes little difference to him. His enjoyment comes from playing the game of business, and he would be equally happy regardless of the kind of business he is involved in, as long as he runs it himself.

The second type of small businessman is in his own business primarily because he likes that particular type of business. If his ambition were to have his own consulting engineering firm, for example, he would not be satisfied with owning a dry cleaning establishment. His enjoyment in being an independent businessman, then, comes from his enjoyment of the product or service that he offers, rather than from the feeling of independence and the excitement and challenge of business competition.

For either type of independent businessman, however, money is not usually his most important consideration; if it were, he would probably be working for a large corporation. Instead, money is simply a way of keeping score of how well he is playing the game. If he is a real professional, the independent businessman will play the game as well as he can.

By any standards, the independent small businessman is a unique individual. Many fit the description by Robert Service of "a race of men that don't fit in." The independent businessman is a person who is willing to risk his personal energy and financial resources to achieve unpredictable results. He is the true *entrepreneur*—the person who organizes, operates, and assumes all the risks for his business ventures.

Most entrepreneurs come from families with some tradition of independent work, with the trait of independence often surfacing early in life. If there are any character traits common to all successful entrepreneurs, they must include a strong desire for independence, a high degree of self confidence, and a highly practical outlook.

Some of the personal characteristics associated with this unique type of individual include:

- *Initiative*—He is ingenious, resourceful and alert to opportunities.
- *Attitude*—He must have a positive outlook toward people, showing a friendly interest in a pleasant and polite manner.
- *Leadership*—He should be able to inspire confidence and loyalty among his employees and business associates.
- *Responsibility*—The small businessman must be willing and capable to assume complete responsibility for the operation and success of his business.
- *Organizing Ability*—He must be capable of perceiving and arranging fundamentals in logical order.
- *Industriousness*—He must be capable of working hard for the long hours required in an independent business.
- *Decision*—He must be able to react quickly and accurately when decisions are required.
- *Sincerity*—He must maintain a reputation as one who is honest and fair in his dealings with others.
- *Perseverance*—He must remain steadfast in working toward his goals and not be easily discouraged by obstacles.
- *Physical Energy*—He must be well above average in terms of maintaining a high level of energy.

The entrepreneur's educational background is relatively unimportant in most cases, unless special technical skills are required. Business school graduates have no special advantage in an independent business;

their training equips them to be managers rather than entrepreneurs. Engineering training, on the other hand, may be an asset because of its emphasis on practicality. Best of all, though, is a combination of talents, encompassing the management, marketing, and technical skills needed to bring all the diverse elements of a business together—getting people, machines, money, and markets working together.

Characteristics of Small Businesses

The single most distinguishing characteristic of the small independent business is its *personal* nature. The customer or client deals, not with a company, but with an individual, a person. Each time the customer returns to the shop, he deals with the same few individuals, and a mutual feeling of personal warmth gradually develops.

The personal nature of the small independent business carries over into other areas, too. The owner/operator generally knows his merchandise, products, and services better than those involved in large corporations, because he is solely responsible for them. He selects the products to be handled and the services to be offered; he deals directly and personally with the sales representatives of his suppliers; he devotes his personal attention to all phases of the business.

The typical small business is characterized by far more than its "smallness." What it lacks in size, it must make up for in other areas; to compete effectively with big businesses, it must offer its customers and clients values that larger firms cannot duplicate. Personal service is the key to success—the one thing that big businesses so seldom can achieve.

Small Business in the United States

Just as "the Lord must have loved the little people, for he made so many of them" the same might be said of businesses. Out of some 13 million business firms in the United States, two-thirds have annual receipts totaling less than $25,000; less than two percent exceed a million dollars in yearly sales. Some 10 million businesses are conducted as sole proprietorships, another million as partnerships, and two million as corporations.

There are currently about 1.8 million retail businesses in the nation; Table 1 shows how they are distributed with respect to annual sales volume, and Table 2 breaks them down in terms of employment.

As shown in Table 1, some 30 percent of the retail firms do less than $30,000 per year in sales, whereas just over four percent have sales exceed-

TABLE 1
Size Distribution of Retail Firms

Annual Sales Volume	*Firms (%)*	*Total Retail Sales (%)*
Under $30,000	30.2	1.6
$30,000–50,000	11.0	1.7
$50,000–100,000	17.8	5.1
$100,000–300,000	26.3	18.2
$300,000–500,000	6.2	9.5
$500,000–1,000,000	4.2	11.4
Over $1,000,000	4.3	52.5
Total	100.0	100.0

ing $1 million. The "average" retail store has annual sales of around $250,000; however, the median store's sales are only about $75,000 annually, with half the establishments selling more than $75,000 and half selling less.

In terms of employment (Table 2), 64.6 percent of the retail firms employ three or fewer persons; 6.5 percent have 20 or more paid employees.

Although small businesses far outnumber big businesses, there is no doubt that big businesses dominate the retail market. Figure 1 shows the portion of total retail sales handled by firms of various size. As indicated, the largest five percent of the retail firms account for well over half of all retail sales, and 15 percent of the firms sell three-fourths of the merchan-

TABLE 2
Employment Characteristics of Retail Firms

Number of Paid Employees	*Firms (%)*	*Total Retail Employment (%)*
0–3	64.6	8.5
4–7	16.5	14.0
8–19	12.4	23.8
20 and over	6.5	53.7
Total	100.0	100.0

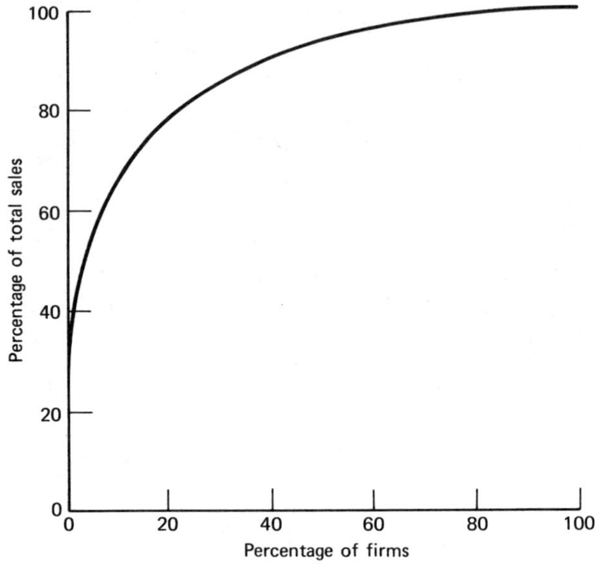

Figure 1. Distribution of retail sales among firms.

dise. In fact, the curve of Fig. 1 adheres roughly to the "20/80" rule that states in effect that the largest 20 percent of a firm's customers account for 80 percent of its sales. In this case, 20 percent of the retail firms handle 80 percent of all retail business.

Small Businesses are Different

The differences between small business and big business go far beyond matters of size and scale of operations.

The large business exercises a certain amount of clout over its suppliers and can influence market behavior through extensive advertising and promotional campaigns.

The small business has virtually no influence over either its suppliers or the markets for its products or services.

Perhaps the main difference between big business and small business is best illustrated by the organization charts shown in Figs. 2 and 3.

The president of a large business (see Fig. 2) generally reports to the corporation's board of directors; the board has set policies that the chief operating executive is expected to carry out. To assist him are a variety of highly paid, highly competent, highly specialized vice presidents, each responsible for certain well-defined management functions:

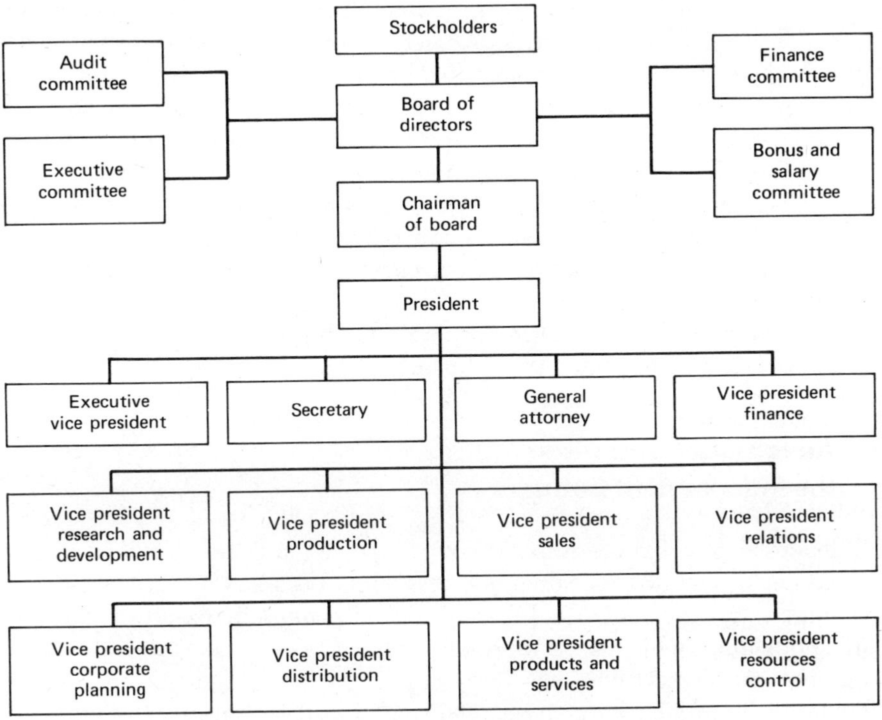

Figure 2. Organization chart for large corporation.

law, finance, research and development, production, sales, public relations, personnel relations, advertising, planning, distribution, products, services, and every other important phase of the business. Each of these vice presidents, in turn, has a large staff operating under his direction and reporting back to him.

In contrast, the small businessman (Fig. 3) *is* his business' legal, accounting, research and development, production, sales, planning, and distribution staff. His policies are the ones that he has established himself, he gets advice from no one but himself, he reports to no one but himself, and he gets a helping hand nowhere but from the end of his own arm. If things go wrong, he has no one to blame but himself. His is a lonely position.

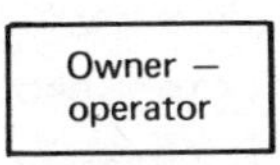

Figure 3. Organization chart for small independent business.

The big business, with its large research staff, can analyze and anticipate consumer demands for its products and services, but the small business, lacking the resources to *anticipate* market demands, is in a far better position to *react* to the demands of the marketplace. There are no cumbersome and time-consuming channels of communication to go through, no paperwork delays, and no executive or board approvals needed.

When an event occurs that requires action or reaction, the small businessman is in a position to act or react immediately. He is close to his market. He can offer service to his customers that the large company cannot.

For these reasons, a large corporation simply cannot compete effectively with a well-managed small business.

Advantages and Disadvantages of the Independent Business

Independence always requires certain sacrifices, and the sacrifices are not always easy. Having your own business offers both advantages and disadvantages, and the individual must decide for himself, based on his own sense of values, which are important to him.

For the person who has been employed in a large business all his life and is just embarking on his own small business venture, the first feeling is probably one of personal loneliness; this is followed shortly by a feeling of financial insecurity when the realization hits that there will be no monthly paycheck, the group medical and life insurance programs are no longer in effect, and there is no more pension program.

Still, the man who works for himself has a good boss. Here are some of the advantages and disadvantages of owning your own small independent business.

Advantages

- You are your own boss.
- You are doing something in which you are interested.
- You can choose (within limits) your operating schedule.
- You set your own policies and goals.
- You will not be fired or laid off.
- You can select the people you want to work with.
- You have the opportunity to meet lots of people.
- You are close to your business; you always know exactly where you stand.
- You can react quickly to the demands of the marketplace.

- You can offer services that large competitors cannot match.
- You do not need a large share of the market to succeed.
- Many of the annoying government regulations applying to larger companies do not apply to you.
- The small independent business has a relaxed environment; you can talk to your customers and get to know them.
- You do with the business whatever you want to make it work for you.

Disadvantages

- You are obligated to keep the business open during specified hours, whether you want to be there or not. You cannot call in sick if you are the only employee.
- It is difficult to take a vacation; you lose money twice if you have to close the shop while you are gone.
- If anything must be done, you have to do it.
- In a retail business, it is difficult to get away even for a few minutes to eat lunch or go to the bathroom.
- No one else cares whether your business succeeds or fails.
- You are risking your own personal and financial resources on a business that may fail.
- You have no influence with your suppliers and may be unable to match the prices of larger competitors.
- You have none of the personal benefits offered to employees of large corporations—sick leave, vacation pay, group health and life insurance, pension programs, and so on.
- The long hours often devoted to the business steal time away from family activities and may cause friction.
- There is a danger of becoming obsessed with the business, leading to serious physical and emotional problems.
- The small business is more sensitive to economic conditions and seasonal variations than big businesses.
- The likelihood of business failure is much greater for small businesses than for large ones and much greater for new businesses than for old ones.
- You must assume primary responsibility for *all* phases of the business and *all* functions of management, even the areas in which you lack any competence.

There is no way to explain or measure the personal satisfaction an individual obtains from starting and succeeding in his own business; the freedom, sense of achievement, and other noneconomic rewards of the successful independent business defy measurement, as do the potential penalties in time, risk, and disappointment should the venture fail.

Motivation for Going into Business for Yourself

Undoubtedly, the first question to be asked and answered when considering going into a small independent business is, "why?"

Why give up the security of employment, with a regular salary and a variety of fringe benefits, just to have a business of your own? Why assume all the risks and responsibilities of an independent business when you could probably make as much or more money working for a large corporation?

There are perhaps as many answers to these questions as there are people leaving the security of employment for the uncertainty of self-employment. The greatest single motivating factor is the desire for independence—to be one's own boss.

The motives most often cited by independent businessmen include:

- *Independence*—They wanted to be their own boss.
- *Ambition*—They felt that they could get further and achieve more by being in business for themselves rather than by working for others.
- *Investment*—They had the necessary financial and personal resources available and felt that their investment returns would be higher in their own business than elsewhere.
- *Control*—They felt that they would have better control over their lives and their futures by being in their own business.
- *Permanence*—Establishing their own business enables them to stay in the same locality, to settle down for as long as they wish.
- *Inheritance*—They took over the family business.

The Important Business Operations

The basic operation of a conventional retail business is to buy as little as possible from suppliers at the lowest possible price and sell as much as possible to consumers at the highest possible price. In other words,

> Buy it for a dime,
> sell it for a dollar,
> and make everybody think they need it.

If it were easy to do this, of course, there would be no unsuccessful retail businesses.

Actually, there are five basic business operations that must be carried out by any business, regardless of size: (1) buying, (2) pricing, (3) selling, (4) paying, and (5) pleasing.

Buying. Merchandise purchased for resale can be obtained directly from a manufacturer, through a manufacturer's representative, or from a distributor; the buying channels vary in different businesses, and some businesses may use all channels. The most important point is not *where* the merchandise is bought, but *what* is bought and *when* it is bought. The merchandise inventory should be kept as low as possible and turned over as rapidly as possible. Some sort of balance must be struck between the expected sales of particular items, the manufacturer's or distributor's discount schedules, and the penalties associated with having too much or too little of the merchandise in stock.

Pricing. Pricing policies vary widely among different merchandise lines. Some carry a manufacturer's list price, whereas pricing on others is left to the discretion of the seller. Competition is a key factor in product pricing, defining the upper limit at which an item can be sold (unless other valuable services are offered in lieu of price); the lower limit of price is established by the product's cost. Considerable thought must be given to the area between cost and price by management. Whether products are to be sold at list price, at some percentage below list price, or at some percentage above cost, the pricing decision is a most important one.

Selling. The selling operation encompasses a wide range of functions and must include merchandise planning, advertising, promotional activities, and, at the final point, closing the sale. Good selling technique requires that the businessman know his product, his market, and his customers. He must be able to attract attention to his merchandise, arouse the prospective customer's interest in it, create a desire on the part of the customer to own that merchandise, and then convince the customer to act on his desire by completing the sale.

Paying. Anything that is bought, regardless of how liberal the terms, must eventually be paid for. In the retail business, the businessman buys in lots of dozens, hundreds, or thousands of units at a time, even though he sells his products one unit at a time. This cannot help but create cash flow problems, since much of the merchandise must be paid for before payment is received for it. The retail business must operate on credit, and maintaining good credit relationships with suppliers is essential to ensure that open accounts will be kept open.

Pleasing. Customer goodwill is the only asset that competitors cannot undersell or destroy. Good merchandise will not come back, but the customers who bought it will; if you offer shabby merchandise, it will come back but the customers will not. Perhaps 80 percent of a retail firm's business is from regular, repeat customers, and the firm cannot be successful without them. The objective of good salesmanship is *not* to make a sale, but to gain a customer.

The Functions of Management

Management responsibilities are essentially the same in small businesses as in large businesses. The difference, as pointed out earlier, is simply that the large business has staffs of specialists trained and paid for handling each of the many management functions; the small businessman must handle them himself. Even if he is totally incompetent in certain phases of management, he must still assume primary responsibility for seeing that the necessary work is carried out. If he is incapable of doing the work himself, he has only two realistic choices: (1) train or educate himself to handle the job capably or (2) hire a specialist to do the job.

Effective management takes in four broad functions, each involving a number of specific activities: (1) planning, (2) organizing, (3) controlling, and (4) improving performance.

Planning. Management planning is the work done to lay out the business' future course. It involves looking ahead, foreseeing new opportunities, establishing goals and devising the specific steps for accomplishing them, setting company policies to provide standard answers to recurring questions, setting priorities and specifying the sequence of business activities, and scheduling and budgeting the business' available resources, both personal and financial.

Organizing. The "next week I'm going to get organized" type of individual is unlikely to be successful in his own independent business. Organizing the business means that all activities must be tied together under an individual so that specific goals can be accomplished. This involves total coordination of the "five Ms": markets, money, manpower, methods, and merchandise (or products or services). It also involves developing the organizational structure necessary to accommodate this coordination, delegating responsibilities where possible or appropriate. Even in what is essentially a one-person business, a sales clerk can be hired to relieve the owner/manager of this responsibility so that he can devote at least a part of his time to other management functions.

Controlling. Management control is required to make sure that the work being done conforms to the firm's objectives and plans, within the specified time and budget constraints. It involves measuring, evaluating and correcting performance—both personal and personnel. It requires a firm grip on the *present,* managing *today's* business in light of *yesterday's* business, with a view toward *tomorrow's* business.

Improving. Improving a business' performance implies making decisions based on the analysis of *past* performance, a complete understanding of the *present* situation, and the anticipation of *future* events. The probable impact of changes on the business' overall situation must be carefully assessed, recognizing that change for the sake of change is not good. Every important management decision may involve a change of some type; improving business performance requires that most of the changes be for the better.

The Foundations of a Successful Business

Regardless of the type of business—large or small, manufacturing, wholesale, retail, or service—the chances for success involve three basic elements:

1. The product, service, or merchandise
2. The market
3. The management

This basic truth can be visualized as a three-legged milking stool, with the seat representing the business as a whole (see Fig. 4). One leg represents the product or service offered; the second leg represents the market in terms of customers or clients; the third leg—the management leg—represents the business firm itself, providing the customers or clients access to the products or services.

All three legs are necessary. If even one leg is missing or deficient, the "stool" will not support the business adequately.

A retailer with merchandise for which there is no consumer demand, or an engineer with highly specialized talents and skills for which no

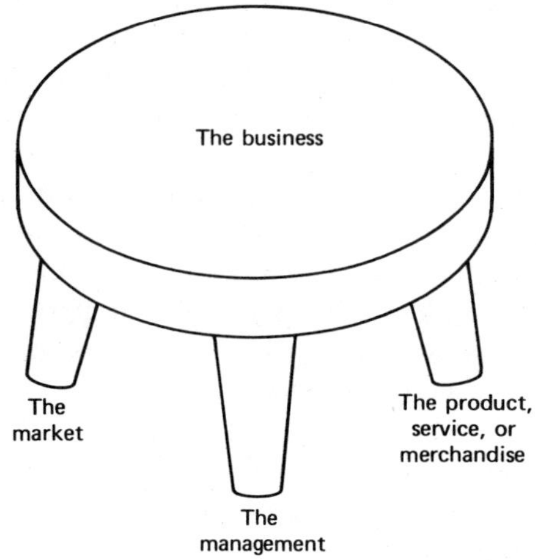

Figure 4. The foundations of a successful business.

projects are available, are in much the same awkward position; they end up with either unsold merchandise or unsold time. Similarly, if the retailer is not in a location that provides easy access for potential customers to buy his merchandise, or if the engineer is unable to make potential clients aware of their need for his talents or to make himself aware of the needs of his market, an equally unprofitable situation results.

Summing up, then: There must be quality merchandise, products, or services for which identifiable consumer demands exist and capable management that provides the facilities and accessibility for the supply and demand to get together.

Even a strong company cannot successfully sustain a market for a poor product or service, nor can a company with inadequate capabilities in marketing or an inaccessible location be competitively successful, even with a superior product. It is possible for a first-rate company to introduce or offer a service that is far superior to all others available and then find that there is inadequate consumer demand to support it.

Newly established small businesses are especially vulnerable to failure because of deficiencies in one or more of these three areas, particularly retail and service businesses. More than 40 percent of all failures in the retail field occur within the first three years of the firm's operation and more than 60 percent within five years. In service businesses, about 30 percent of the failures come during the firm's first three years, and just over half of the failures take place within five years of the time the business started.

About 40 percent of the failures in retail and service businesses are attributed to "inadequate sales," which in turn can reflect a weakness in any of the three "legs" of the business "stool": a poor product or service, inadequate market demand, or simply a business that is poorly located or unable to match supply and demand for some other reason.

"Competitive weakness" is blamed for another 20 percent of the business failures in the retail and service fields. This is evidence of an unhealthy market environment or, more likely, poor management.

Failing in business is easy, requiring only that one thing be done wrong; succeeding in business is difficult, requiring that everything be done right.

Mistakes Made by Small Businessmen

Building a successful small business requires that very many things be done right and very few things be done wrong. Although neglect, fraud, and disaster cause a few business failures, less than 10 percent of all failures can be attributed to these causes. Good management is what makes a business successful; bad management is what makes a business fail.

Bad management becomes evident in many ways: inadequate sales, heavy operating expenses, problems with accounts receivable, inventory difficulties, top-heavy investment in fixed or nonproductive assets, poor location, or competitive weaknesses. Still, they all boil down to the inability of management to match the merchandise or services to the market.

Here are some of the major management mistakes made by small businessmen.

- Failure to create customers; emphasis is on making the sale without regard to the customer's needs or wants.
- Failure to keep adequate records; if the businessman does not know where the business has been, he cannot know where it is going.
- Failure to view the business objectively; the businessman becomes so emotionally involved with the business that he fails to recognize its shortcomings.
- Failure to recognize who and where the customers are and why they are his customers.
- Failure to keep abreast of the competition; not knowing what competitors are doing.
- Failure to be thoroughly familiar with his own product lines and their strengths and weaknesses.
- Failure to keep in close touch with the market.

- Failure to keep alert to factors affecting the market for specific products and services, including seasonal and cyclical trends as well as technological factors.
- Failure to anticipate accurately the market for goods and services, resulting in overstocking on slow moving items (lost space and high inventory costs) or understocking on fast moving items (lost sales due to unavailability).

The list could go on ad infinitum, but every mistake on the list could be classified under one or more of the three basic headings: bad merchandise, bad market, or, by far the most likely, bad management.

This principle is so simple that it has been completely overlooked by many businessmen, from small entrepreneurs to large corporation executives. *Every business failure can be attributed to weakness in one or more of these three areas!*

These business failures are, in most cases, completely inexcusable. They occur simply because the management has failed to recognize the importance of maintaining strength and balance in the three areas.

2
Finding Your Own Business

Small opportunities are often the beginning of great enterprises.

Having decided to pursue a business of his own, the prospective entrepreneur faces a bewildering, almost overwhelming number of different courses of action in carrying out his plan. This chapter explains exactly what must be done prior to making any major personal or financial commitments.

Choosing the Right Business

There are at least several million people in the United States who would some day like to own their own independent small business. For most, the desire will remain only a desire; only for a few will it ever become a reality.

Regardless of the business in question, making the break from a relatively safe, secure, and well-paying salaried position to an independent business can be a frightening experience.

Before choosing any business, it is essential to decide what kind of business is most appealing, then to learn as much as possible about it. Professional and trade associations and publications abound in virtually every field imaginable, and a wealth of useful information can be obtained from these sources.

To "know thyself" is an essential step in choosing an appropriate type of business. Some of the important character attributes of the small businessman were discussed in the preceding chapter. Anyone who does not possess most of these characteristics should not become involved in *any* business of his own. The successful business person seems to think different thoughts and have different ideas from the average person. Successful entrepreneurs are able to see opportunities in their problems and to anticipate the problems associated with their opportunities.

The "right" business for an individual, then, depends on a combination of both personal and business factors.

The individual must consider his own personal characteristics, interests, abilities, needs, and desires; he must assess the "management" leg of the three-legged stool that supports any business, being completely honest and realistic in his assessment. Only then is the profit potential for his business important, based on the specific products or services to be offered, the market for these products or services, and the financial resources available and required. These elements comprise the other two legs (the market and the merchandise) of the stool.

The new business, whatever it is, should be one in which he has a definite *interest,* for which he has the necessary *ability* (both personal and financial), and that will return a *profit* on his investment of time and money.

The Steps to Finding Your Own Business

The preliminaries to getting into a new business venture involve essentially the same steps that must be taken in solving any complex problem. The standard approach consists of nine distinct steps:

1. Understand the problem
2. Define the objectives
3. Collect the data
4. Interpret the data
5. Devise alternative solutions
6. Evaluate the alternatives
7. Select the best alternative
8. Implement the best alternative
9. Monitor the results

Understand the problem. Get to know something about the business in question; visit similar types of operations in different locations, talking to the owners, employees, and customers. Find out what trade associations are active in the field and what journals and publications are available. Try to determine whether there is a need for another business of this type, and if so, where.

Define the objectives. The prospective businessman should have a good idea of exactly what he hopes to accomplish with the new business—how much profit he must generate from the business to provide himself with his short- and long-term income requirements and investment returns.

Collect the data. Obtain all types of economic and operating data on the business in question; find out who and where the customers are, what facilities are required to serve them, and what locational factors are important; for a retail business, determine the investment requirements and what can be expected in the way of sales; contact suppliers to obtain discount schedules, credit terms, and information on opening accounts.

Interpret the data. Put all the data together into an economic feasibility study, preparing financial statements and profit-and-loss projections. If possible, prepare a month-by-month cash flow projection for the first year and annual projections for the next several years. This step will define the financial requirements and potential financial returns of the business.

Devise alternative solutions. If the economic outlook for the proposed business is good, a plan of attack can be devised. Having already determined the important locational factors and physical requirements of the business, a general area can be selected. There are four ways to start the business: (1) start it yourself, from scratch, (2) buy an already established, going business, (3) buy a business franchise, or (4) start up on a part-time basis.

Evaluate the alternatives. All four options for starting a new business are seldom available; there may be no existing businesses of the type wanted in the area selected, or the business may not be one normally franchised. Look carefully at all investment, income, and expense aspects of each alternative. If you consider a franchise, decide whether the franchise name will pay for itself in additional sales; if you buy an existing business, look at its past and present performance to be sure the purchase price is justified.

Select the best alternative. The best alternative is the one that most nearly fits your objectives; most likely, it is the one that will, in the long run, offer the highest return on invested capital while satisfying the individual's personal objectives. Each of the four different ways of getting into business have different investment requirements and income opportunities; identification of the best alternative may not be easy. It is extremely difficult to be completely objective whenever a certain outcome is strongly desired, and subjective evaluations are both necessary and desirable when choosing one's own business future. However, a certain amount of objectivity must be maintained to avoid a possible personal financial disaster.

Implement the best alternative. The detailed analysis conducted up to this point provides a strong basis for obtaining the necessary financing, should outside funds be required. Legal help will be a necessity at this stage; all contracts should be examined by competent attorneys, and some legal form of business organization must be set up. This would also be a good time to seek advice on accounting procedures for the new business.

Monitor the results. Going into business for yourself is not an irreversible decision; if the business does not work out satisfactorily, it can be sold or abandoned if it cannot be improved. Watch the results closely, comparing them with the estimates made earlier and identifying the reasons for any significant variations. Most new businesses end up costing more than anticipated, selling less than anticipated, and taking longer than anticipated to become profitable.

Finding and Buying an Existing Business

Probably the easiest and best way to get into your own independent business is to buy an already existing business. The problem is in finding just the right business, in just the right location, at just the right price, at just the right time. It seldom happens, but occasionally it does; when it does, fast action is required.

Buying a going business offers a number of definite advantages over starting from scratch:

- There is less risk involved, since much information is already available. Sales, operating costs, and working capital requirements can be estimated accurately.
- Start-up time is eliminated; sales receipts will be continuous.
- Everything necessary to do business is already available.
- If the shop has regular customers, which it should, most of these customers can be kept, and sales should remain fairly steady.
- Lines of supply will already have been established; new accounts will be necessary and new credit established, but there will be

fewer problems encountered in obtaining credit than with a brand-new operation.

- Buying an existing operation means that one competitor has been eliminated.
- Owner financing may be obtained on more liberal terms than would be available from a bank.
- The old owner may stay on for a while to familiarize the new owner with the business, introducing him to customers and suppliers and making for an easy transition.

Before buying an existing business, there are several things that should be checked. An attorney is essential, and an accountant is desirable.

Find out why the present owner wants to sell his business. There are good reasons and bad reasons. A good reason, for example, is that he has made so much money that he is ready to retire. A bad reason is that the neighborhood is changing or has changed and will no longer support a business of that type. Other reasons for selling include ill health, a desire to relocate, or a desire to be free of the pressures and responsibilities of an independent business. If relocation is a reason, be certain that the sales contract prohibits the seller from opening a competitive shop nearby.

The price of a going business depends on how badly the buyer wants to buy. The lower limit of price for a retail shop is the value (at cost) of inventory and fixtures. A more common pricing arrangement is the value of inventory plus fixtures plus something extra for "goodwill" or "going value," with the extra amount depending on how profitable the operation is. The selling price of a going retail business seldom exceeds one year's sales volume. Another way to price a going business is by applying some multiple of the net profit before taxes; the multiple may be as low as three or as high as eight.

Finding an attractive existing business opportunity requires considerable persistence. There are only three ways to do it: (1) watch the "business opportunities" section in newspapers and trade publications, (2) check with business brokers on their available listings, and (3) pick the shop you want and approach the owner concerning its sale, either personally or through a broker or other representative.

Starting the New Business from Scratch

Starting a new business from nothing is the most difficult way to begin, especially if the businessman is not thoroughly familiar with all aspects of the business. Even if he is, the details can be almost overwhelming.

A brand-new business in a brand-new location does offer some advantages. It can be all new and fresh in appearance, a real asset in some locations and some types of businesses. It can be located wherever the owner wants and space is available; any name can be given to the new business, and the owner can hire whoever he wants and can afford.

The new business, then, offers a clean start from zero, with no carry-over values or liabilities.

There are disadvantages, too.

Raising capital may be a difficult task, lacking any operating data to present to investors or lenders. Start-up expenses may be high, with several months required to install fixtures and acquire inventory, much of it on a cash-with-order basis until credit is established with suppliers. The early months are high in cost, with no offsetting receipts from sales.

Once the business is ready to open, sales are apt to be slow until a solid clientele is built up, and it may be necessary to get by with little outside help until the business gains a solid base; this means the owner will be tied down, doing as much as possible by himself. He may have to start small, adding to inventory as his cash position improves and the specific characteristics of his customers and markets become more clearly identifiable. He will have to work out his own solutions for his own problems, with no one to call on for advice.

There is a great deal of personal satisfaction in starting a new business, a satisfaction that cannot be expressed in monetary terms. If the entrepreneur has done his homework prior to making his financial and personal commitment to the new business—assessing the market, the merchandise (or service), and his own managerial capabilities, interests, and abilities—he has a good chance of making a success of it. With a lot of hard work.

The Franchised Business

A franchised business offers a compromise between starting anew and buying an existing business.

There are good franchises and there are bad franchises. There are more bad ones than good ones. Good ones are seldom advertised—they do not need to; they already have long waiting lists. Bad franchises can be very persuasive—they have to be; their income is derived from selling franchises, not from sharing operating profits with franchises.

A good franchise is a profitable and effective way to do business. The chances of failure are much lower for franchise operations than for new independent businesses. Capital requirements may be lower, with financing available from the franchiser. It may be possible to establish credit more easily with a franchise, and the start-up time may be reduced. The franchiser may offer management training programs and provide advice in such areas as sales, advertising, marketing, buying, accounting, and technical operational problems, as well as assistance in selecting a location and training employees.

There are several areas that must be examined with extreme caution in evaluating the potential attractiveness of a proposed franchise. The first is that the franchise actually offers some real benefits over starting your own business and that the initial cost of the franchise package is not excessive. Many franchise names carry no weight with consumers, and in these cases there is no economic justification for paying extra for the franchise name. Before deciding on a franchise, its total cost should be weighed carefully against the total cost of a comparable independent operation.

Most franchises offer a source of supply for equipment, materials, and merchandise used in the business. This centralized buying power should be advantageous, but the prospective franchisee must make sure that the franchiser is not tying him into contracts for purchases that could be made under more advantageous terms elsewhere; some franchisers use this as another way to generate profits at the expense of their franchise operators.

Beware also of the franchiser who promises to refer or provide business for his franchise operators; some have been known to "foreclose" on operators who are unable to make payments because ample business was not provided as promised; these unfortunates end up forfeiting their up-front franchise fees and down payments.

Still, a good business is a good business whether it is franchised or independent. The economics of operation are comparable, and success depends, as always, on the market, the merchandise, and the management.

The Cost of Going into Business

Whether the new business has been started from scratch, purchased from a previous owner, or obtained from a franchiser, the basic operation and economics are similar. Investment requirements vary, depending on the type of business, its location, and a variety of other factors. However, in every case the business must give to its owner or owners a fair return on the invested capital.

Almost anyone with sufficient interest and determination *can* become an independent businessman, although only a real professional can become a *successful* independent businessman. Many, probably most, small businesses can be started with only modest capital and good credit.

An outside source of income, providing at least a minimum subsistence level of living, is not a bad idea. The knowledge that family needs can be met contributes greatly to overall peace of mind. Sufficient savings or investment income to cover living expenses for at least a year should allow the business to become established and come close to paying its own way.

The capital investment required to start a new retail business falls into several distinct categories, the most important of which include inventory, fixed (or depreciable) assets, and working capital; for a service business, inventory costs may not be significant.

Fixed Assets. Fixed assets include fixtures and equipment; the installation of fixtures and equipment and decorating and remodeling expenses may be lumped with the fixtures for accounting purposes, or they may be handled separately and charged off over a shorter period of time for income tax purposes. Sometimes at least a part of the redecorating and remodeling expenses are absorbed by the landlord. For retail businesses, the total cost of store fixtures and furnishings is generally between $5.00 and $15.00 per square foot of floor space.

Inventory. Inventory requirements vary widely among different types of businesses. If the business has been operating for some time or is a franchised operation, the inventory should be fairly complete when the new owner takes over; for a new business, inventory can be built up more gradually. The total inventory investment in retail businesses can range anywhere between $10.00 and $50.00 per square foot of floor space.

Working Capital. Working capital represents the cash available to run the business; however much it is, it is usually not enough in the new business. Working capital must cover the start-up expenses incurred prior to opening the business to the public and must be sufficient to carry the operating expenses of the business until sales can generate the necessary cash flow. Working capital should amount to at least three months' out-of-pocket cash expenses, and more would be highly desirable.

Specific information should be obtained regarding the magnitude of the various investment requirements. Data should be sought from other businesses, suppliers, contractors, landlords, bankers, lawyers, accountants, the Small Business Administration, and trade associations and publications. Putting together the information should give a fairly clear picture of the money involved.

As an example, suppose that a new retail business is to be started in a suburban shopping center, occupying 2000 square feet of space. The investment requirements might look like this:

Fixtures and equipment at $12.00/sq. ft.	$24,000
Inventory at $20.00/sq. ft.	40,000
Working capital at three months' expenses	32,000
Total investment requirement	$96,000

Even a rough estimate such as this enables the prospective businessman to evaluate his situation and decide whether he can afford to proceed further.

Analyzing a New Business Opportunity

The general procedure for analyzing the potential feasibility and economic attractiveness of a new or an existing business is simple and straightforward:

Total annual sales
− Cost of goods sold
= Gross operating profit
− Other costs and expenses
= Net profit before taxes
÷ Total investment
= Percentage return on investment

For a retail business, total annual sales are a function of the store size (measured in square feet) and the sales intensity (measured in dollars of sales per square foot per year). The cost of goods sold depends on the type of merchandise carried, the quantities ordered, and the suppliers' discount schedules. The major direct expenses are rent, utilities, and payroll costs. Other expenses include depreciation, interest, insurance, property taxes, licenses, professional fees, advertising, maintenance, and a variety of less significant items.

Many of the important elements of cost can be identified early, at least by a range of values. Sales per square foot, for example, can vary from less than $30 per square foot to more than $200 per square foot among different businesses and different locations, but variations are seldom so extreme for similar businesses or for different businesses with similar locations. The average and range of sales intensities for a particular shopping center location provide a guide for estimating what might reasonably be expected for a new shop; this estimate can be tempered by the typical range of values for the business in question.

Most retail merchandise carries a markup of from 20 to 60 percent of the retail price; the average, considering allowances for shipping costs, damage, theft, returns, and markdowns, is probably in the 30 to 40 percent range, leaving some 60 to 70 percent of the net sales volume as gross operating profit. A reasonably accurate figure can be obtained from suppliers.

Most expenses, too, can be pinned down in some detail. The rental expense—between $2.00 and $20.00 per square foot in most shopping centers—comes from the landlord, who can also provide information on utility costs.

Payroll costs depend on local conditions and prevailing minimum wages, but they seldom are less than $7500 per employee for a 2000-hour year by the time fringe benefits and associated payroll expenses are figured in. If the owner expects to function as the shop's sales staff as well as manager, he should include at least a sales clerk's wages for himself as an operating expense; any additional compensation for being the owner and manager can come out of profits.

There should also be an allowance for the many other expenses that will be incurred; until they can be specifically identified and estimated, they can be included as a percentage of total sales or total investment.

Here is an example of how a prospective new business might look in this initial economic study, using the investment figure ($96,000 for a 2000 square foot retail shop) from the preceding section.

Net sales (2000 sq. ft. at $80/sq. ft.)	$160,000
− Cost of goods sold (65% of sales)	−104,000
= Gross operating profit	= 56,000
− Expenses	
Rent and utilities ($5.00/sq. ft.)	10,000
Payroll (3 employees at $7500 each)	22,500
Fixed expense (8% of investment)	7,700
Misc. expense (5% of sales)	8,000
	− 48,200
= Net profit before taxes	= 7,800
÷ Total investment	÷ 96,000
= Percentage return on investment	= 8.1%

Using this approach and applying ranges of values to the different cost elements, it is not difficult to arrive at a reasonable estimate for virtually any condition. As better data becomes available, it is easy to plug them in and refine the estimate. After a few years of operating experience, the proprietor should know his entire economic situation down to the dollar.

Analyzing the Trade Area

In buying real estate as an investment, experts agree that there are three factors that far outweigh all others in importance. These are

1. Location
2. Location
3. Location

The same might be said for an investment in a new business. Regardless of the merchandise, product, or service, and regardless of how large a market exists for these products and services, the best management in the world cannot bring them together in a bad location.

The trade area of a business may encompass an entire major metropolitan area, or it may include just the residences within walking distance. In either case, the trade area defines the geographic area from which the business' customers come. The trade area determines the total market for any given product or service offered at a specific location. The trade area and the number of businesses offering those given products or services within the trade area, in turn, determine the potential sales volume for each business.

After a business has been in operation for some time, it is easy to identify its trade area simply by tabulating the zip codes of customers' addresses; until then, the prospective trade area can be roughly blocked out by plotting on a map the locations of competitive businesses and other shopping areas. Other things being equal, customers generally patronize the businesses closest to them.

A certain population or customer base is required to support any business, and the size of this base determines the size of the business, investment requirements, and operating characteristics.

Whatever the trade area, it is essential to study the competition. There may be enough dollar volume for a certain type of merchandise or service, for example, to allow two competitive businesses to prosper, but not enough to allow three competitors to break even. Consider a situation in which there are two businesses in operation within a single trade area; each has the characteristics described in the preceding sections. They share the area's $320,000 total sales.

	Shop A	*Shop B*	*Total*
Net sales	$160,000	$160,000	$320,000
Cost of goods sold	104,000	104,000	208,000
Gross operating profit	56,000	56,000	112,000
Costs and expenses	48,200	48,200	96,400
Net profit before taxes	7,800	7,800	15,600

In this situation, business is going along smoothly, with both Shop A and Shop B making a comfortable living. Now, suppose a third business, Shop C, enters the picture in the trade area already served by Shops A and B and succeeds in getting an equal share of the total market. The situation now looks like this:

	Shop A	*Shop B*	*Shop C*	*Total*
Net sales	$106,700	$106,700	$106,600	$320,000
Cost of goods sold	69,400	69,400	69,300	208,100
Gross operating profit	37,300	37,300	37,300	111,900
Costs and expenses	38,100	38,100	38,100	114,300
Net profit before taxes	(800)	(800)	(800)	(2,400)

Now instead of two shops operating profitably, there are three shops operating at a loss; instead of two businesses making $15,600 between them, three businesses are sharing a $2,400 loss. This assumes that each shop can reduce its payroll and some variable expenses to compensate for its decline in sales, but it still has the same rent, utilities, and investment-related expenses to pay.

This is an extremely important consideration: Opening a new shop within a given trade area does not necessarily generate additional business volume; it may simply redistribute the business that is already there.

Sometimes, however, a business may be justified in opening a new shop within a trade area on purely defensive grounds; if a new shopping center is built, it may be advantageous to redistribute the available business among one's own shops rather than to allow a new competitor to move in and capture a share of the already limited market.

Shopping Centers

Shopping centers are generally classified under four broad categories: (1) super regional centers, (2) regional centers, (3) community centers, and (4) neighborhood centers.

Super Regional Centers. These largest shopping centers are comparable to the central business districts of large cities, offering a wide selection of general merchandise, apparel, and home furnishings, and a wide variety of services and recreational facilities. They contain three or more major department stores occupying at least 100,000 square feet each. A super regional center averages about a million square feet of leasable space and generates sales of $80 million annually.

Regional Centers. Regional shopping centers have one or two major department stores as their main tenants; the scope of merchandise and services offered is similar to what might be expected in the central business district of a small city. Most regional centers offer between 500,000 and 600,000 square feet of space and have annual sales of $40 to $50 million.

Community Centers. The community shopping center offers convenience goods and a wide range of facilities for shopping such as apparel and home furnishings, and may include banks, professional services, and recreational facilities. A small department store or large variety store is usually the major tenant. The community shopping center occupies 150,000 square feet, with total sales of around $12 million.

Neighborhood Centers. Neighborhood shopping centers offer the convenience goods needed by nearby customers, such as food, drugs, hardware, and personal services such as beauty and barber shops. Usually the principal tenant of a neighborhood shopping center is a large supermarket. These centers are generally about 50,000 square feet in size, with sales of $4 million annually.

Selecting the right shopping center for a new business location is dictated largely by the type of merchandise or services to be offered. It is essential to study the types of businesses located in a center to identify the customer characteristics for that trade area. A jewelry store, for example, would not want to locate between a hardware store and a supermarket.

The intensity of sales—dollars per square foot—may not vary much for shops located in a neighborhood or super regional center, provided the shops are appropriate for the location in terms of their size and the types of merchandise and services offered. However, rental costs are usually higher in the large shopping centers—at least in the newer large shopping centers.

A proposed shopping center location for a new business should be examined closely, watching for traffic flow within the center. Wandering through shopping centers has become a major leisure time activity for many adults and teen-agers, and the number of people strolling through a mall is not necessarily indicative of its sales potential.

A prospective shop owner should look for packages, not people, in evaluating a shopping center location. If the people are not carrying packages, they have probably not bought anything; they are not customers, they are sightseers; they are lookers, not buyers.

Beware of high-traffic areas in the centers. Large numbers of people may congregate in certain areas for some reason that will be of little benefit to the new business; a post office branch or a rest room may attract a lot of people who have things other than shopping in mind.

3
Getting Started

Before everything else, getting ready is the secret of success.

Henry Ford

Once the personal commitment is made to pursue a career as an independent businessman, but before the new business opens its doors to the public, there are a few things that the entrepreneur must do, many things that he should do, and much that he should know before doing anything. This chapter discusses these aspects of the new business venture, defining the legal, financial, and physical requirements of a new business and describing specific preparatory techniques.

Starting a Business

Many details must be attended to in the process of starting a new business or acquiring an existing one. Finding out ahead of time exactly what is required can save considerable time, trouble, and expense later.

Listed here are 40 items. Not all apply to every business, but most do. The 40 items are arranged in a rough sequence, although the sequence may vary under different conditions. Some of the early items could be started as much as several years before the business actually opens; others must wait until certain preparatory steps have been completed.

Checklist for Starting a Business

Step No.	Activity Description	Refer to Page No.
1	Decide on the type of business.	17
2	Identify and consult sources of trade information.	33, 45

Checklist for Starting a Business (*Continued*)

Step No.	Activity Description	Refer to Page No.
3	Decide on a general city or suburban location for the business.	27, 35
4	Decide how to enter the business, whether by buying an existing business, starting a new one, or franchise.	19
5	Select a specific shopping center or building site location.	29, 35
6	Check zoning requirements if the business is to be located in other than an established commercial area.	38
7	Identify the trade area.	27
8	Analyze the competition within the trade area.	27
9	Identify customer characteristics in the trade area.	34, 47, 70
10	Prepare an economic analysis of the business.	25, 53, 95
11	Determine the appropriate shop size.	35, 90
12	Get a lawyer.	20, 36
13	Choose a business name.	22
14	Decide on the form of business organization: sole proprietorship, partnership, corporation, or Subchapter S corporation.	43
15	Establish a bank account for the business.	34, 42
16	Get an accountant	20, 65
17	Set up a bookkeeping system.	65, 103
18	Arrange for the building lease or construction.	35
19	Obtain the necessary federal, state, and local licenses and permits.	36
20	Make arrangements for utilities.	92
21	Obtain a listing in the classified telephone directory (Yellow Pages).	49, 79
22	Obtain general office supplies such as letterheads, business cards, order forms, etc.	39
23	Plan the merchandise line.	46
24	Design the store's interior.	81

Checklist for Starting a Business (*Continued*)

Step No.	Activity Description	Refer to Page No.
25	Develop sales, cost, and cash flow projections.	53, 130
26	Determine cash requirements.	38, 130
27	Make arrangements for whatever outside financing is necessary.	41
28	Identify and contact sources of supply.	45
29	Establish lines of credit with suppliers.	11, 58
30	Place initial merchandise orders with suppliers.	46, 57
31	Obtain store furniture and fixtures and complete necessary remodeling.	39
32	Obtain appropriate insurance coverage.	50
33	Establish the business' operating schedule.	84
34	Plan and initiate beginning promotional and advertising activities.	49
35	Obtain the merchandise.	57
36	Establish business policies concerning pricing, personnel, etc.	59, 74
37	Hire and train personnel.	47
38	Establish an inventory control system.	69
39	Stock the shelves.	82
40	Open for business.	49

The preceding checklist is aimed primarily at retail businesses; however, most of the steps are equally important to service businesses.

Sources of Business Information

The most important consideration in evaluating the advice offered by any source, whether individual, agency, business firm, or whatever, is to realistically consider the source and

> TRUST LEAST THE ADVICE OF THOSE WHO HAVE THE MOST TO GAIN IF YOU FOLLOW THEIR ADVICE.

It is also a good practice not to ask for advice from any source unless you have some intention of following it. Friends, especially, may be offended if you ask their advice and then ignore it, no matter how stupid it may be. Contrary to popular opinion, advice is not necessarily worth what you pay for it; it may be worth far less, even if it costs nothing. Some free advice, on the other hand, can be invaluable. Again, consider the source.

Unquestionably the first place to look for information before considering starting a new business is the nearest Small Business Administration (SBA) field office. The SBA is the only federal government agency specifically set up to assist and counsel the practicing or prospective small businessman. Any businessman who fails to avail himself of this opportunity is depriving himself of an extremely valuable business asset.

The SBA has an almost overwhelming variety of publications available, ranging from specific information on how to get started in a certain type of business to general information on business management and related areas. Some of these publications are cited in the references section of the appendix.

Among SBA's many services are financial assistance, management training and counseling, and help in getting a share of government contracts. Seminars are sponsored, frequently with the cooperation of local colleges and universities, on subjects of special interest to small business such as marketing, tax planning, and many other topics.

A unique SBA-sponsored program of exceptional value to small business incorporates the skills and talents of retired business executives who volunteer their time to assist small businesses without charge. The SCORE (Service Corps of Retired Executives) program is available free on request to all small businesses. On submission of a request, the local SBA office assigns a SCORE member to meet with the small businessman on a consulting basis. Although most SCORE representatives have backgrounds in big business, they offer a fresh and informed outside look at the business and may spot problem areas or opportunities for improvement that the small businessman, immersed in his business, has completely overlooked.

Banks, too, can be good sources of information regarding the characteristics of their trade areas and may be able to offer useful suggestions regarding the financial aspects of various businesses. A good banking relationship is necessary for the small businessman, and establishing an early acquaintance with bank officers will be mutually beneficial in the long run.

Other shopping center merchants can provide useful information concerning customers within the trade area, such as the type of people who shop there, where they come from, and what type of shopping they usually do.

Real estate agents who handle property in the area can also give the new business owner an idea of what types of people live in the area as well as the turnover and types of people who are moving in and out. This information is especially valuable, for example, for businesses handling home improvement products and home furnishings.

Other sources of information for the business owner include chambers of commerce, better business bureaus, credit bureaus, merchandise and equipment suppliers, the business section of libraries, trade associations, trade publications, and many reference books on all phases of small business. Many of these references are included in the appendix.

Location, Store Size, and Rent

A good location is the key to bringing together the market and the merchandise or service. According to consumer surveys, people average about seven shopping trips per month. The availability of goods, the convenience of locations, and the adequacy of parking facilities generally determine where the shopping is done.

There is no one best location for a retail or service business. Highly profitable businesses can be located in small neighborhood shopping centers that draw only customers within walking distance or in super regional centers whose customers come from throughout the metropolitan area. The important factors are that the business offer the goods or services in demand by those customers in its trade area and that the business be properly sized for its location. A store selling fine jewelry would obviously be out of place in a low-income trade area, as would a lawn and garden supply store in a shopping center oriented toward apartment dwellers.

A business located in a shopping center serving a small trade area does less total business than a similar business in a super regional center. Sales per square foot, however, do not necessarily vary significantly between large and small shopping centers.

The average intensity of sales for the retail occupants of shopping centers of all types—large and small, new and old—ranges between \$50 and \$150 per square foot per year, with a median value of between \$80 and \$90. Rental costs show far wider variations, with the cost per square foot of space occupied from as low as \$2.00 or \$3.00 per square foot per year in small, old neighborhood centers, to more than \$10.00 in new regional centers. In some fashionable locations in high-income areas, rentals may be over \$20.00 per square foot annually.

Whether a high rental cost is justified is strictly a matter of economics. Since rent constitutes a fixed cost, each additional dollar spent on rent must generate some additional sales volume to pay for itself. A business that operates with a variable cost rate of 0.80 (of 80 percent) needs $5.00 in sales to pay for each dollar of fixed cost. If the shop occupies 2000 square feet, each extra dollar spent on rent must produce $5.00 in sales; the difference between a $5.00 per square foot and $10.00 per square foot rental cost could be justified only by achieving total sales of $50,000 more at the high-rent location than at the lower-rent location. If this extra $25 per square foot per year is doubtful, the location cannot be justified economically.

Licenses, Permits, and Governmental Regulations

Licenses, permits, and other similar legal requirements are among the most annoying realities of the small independent business. Obtaining and maintaining them requires time, trouble, and money, involves considerable recordkeeping that might otherwise be unnecessary, and subjects the business to a variety of regulations and controls. However, without them the businessman is without an opportunity to do business.

At the very least, the business requires a federal identification number, a state retail sales license, a city occupational license, and perhaps a county merchant's license. In obtaining all the necessary licenses and permits and satisfying whatever additional legal requirements are in effect, it is probably a good idea to work with a local attorney; he knows the appropriate regulating agencies and has immediate access to the necessary application forms; he can complete the forms while the new businessman devotes his efforts to more productive pursuits. The lawyer is needed in any case to examine any purchase contracts and lease agreements arising during the business' formative stages.

The degree of regulation affecting a particular business varies according to the type and location of the business. If the operations are conducted entirely within one state (intrastate), the primary concern is with state and local licensing. If operations carry across state lines (interstate), federal regulations become increasingly significant. Most licenses require accompanying fee payments, and some (such as state sales tax licenses) may require posting a bond or making advance payments to cover future tax liabilities. A written application is almost always required, with the licenses usually issued on an annual basis. Again, consult with an attorney or contact state, municipal, and county authorities for complete information regarding license requirements and other pertinent regulations.

As soon as a business is formed, a federal taxpayer identification number should be applied for. An individual engaged in a trade or business is assigned an *employer identification number* that is used on all business returns, documents, and statements in connection with the trade or business. However, the individual's *social security account number* is still used on individual income tax returns, self-employment schedules, and declarations of estimated tax. Corporations are required to use the taxpayer identification number on all federal forms. If a proprietorship or partnership is incorporated, a new employer identification number must be obtained for use on the corporation tax returns.

To apply for a social security account number, Form SS-5 is used; Form SS-4 will get the business its employer identification number. These and many more forms are available from any Internal Revenue Service office, along with a great deal of useful information on tax planning for small businesses.

If the business is operating under a name other than that of the owner, the "fictitious" name may have to be registered with a local government agency. If the name is not registered and renewed regularly (often without notification), competitors may be free to use it.

In addition to licenses and permits, there are a number of other regulations of which the small businessman should be aware. Certain business practices are prohibited or restricted by federal and state legislation designed to encourage competition. These laws prohibit contracts, combinations, and conspiracies in restraint of trade; they prohibit discrimination in price between different purchasers of commodities similar in grade and quality that may injure competition; they make "unfair methods of competition" and "unfair or deceptive practices" unlawful. The term "deceptive practices" refers to false advertising, misrepresentation, simulation of competitive products, and "bad-mouthing" competitors. Even on violations by a manufacturer or distributor, the retailer may be considered equally guilty if he knowingly accepts an illegal concession offered by the vendor.

Some states allow a manufacturer to fix the retail price of certain brand-name products ("fair trade" laws), whereas others specifically prohibit the practice. A fairly common statute forbids the sale of any article at less than the seller's cost if the intent is to injure competitors. Other laws may deal with "bait and switch" selling, withholding appropriate refunds on deposits made by customers, misrepresenting warranties and guarantees, and the brand and quality of certain merchandise.

Because of the complexities and implications of these various regulations and the penalties imposed for their violation, a consultation with a lawyer is almost essential.

Zoning Restrictions

If the new business is to be located in an already existing shopping center or is purchased from a previous owner, zoning regulations should not be a problem. However, if a new facility is to be constructed, an existing building is to be used for a purpose different from that for which it was originally intended, or extensive remodeling is required, local building and zoning codes should be carefully checked. Restrictions on land use are becoming increasingly strict throughout the country, and many localities require strict adherence to specifications regarding occupational health and safety, facilities for the handicapped, and other factors not considered only a few years ago.

Although zoning may be (and has been) used for a great variety of purposes, it is essentially a way of ensuring that the land uses of the community are properly situated in relation to each other, that adequate space is available for each type of development, that the density of development in each area is held at a level that can be properly served by such governmental facilities as streets, schools, and recreational and utility systems, and that the development is sufficiently "open" to permit light, air, and privacy for persons living and working within the municipality. The overriding theory of zoning is that land must be zoned to its wisest and best use. Any restrictions considered unreasonable by the applicant for a zoning change must be appealed through the courts.

If the request for zoning is approved, a number of restrictions still apply. In addition to meeting all local building codes, there are probably certain requirements for minimum setbacks at the front, side, and rear of the structure, minimum total area requirements, minimum provisions for parking space, maximum building heights, and other factors. There can be no generalizations on this subject, since each government entity has its own specific policies. However, in any situation, if the proper zoning conditions cannot be met, there can be no business conducted.

Financial Requirements for the New Business

The amount of money required to bring a new business into operation is determined by the type, size, and location of the business, the kinds of merchandise handled, and the credit arrangements between the business and its suppliers and customers.

A detailed work sheet, itemizing all major cost and expense items, should be prepared during the early stages of the project, using whatever

Inventory

Office Furniture
- Desks
- Chairs
- Tables
- Filing cabinets
- Storage cabinets
- Book cases

Office Equipment
- Typewriter
- Calculator
- Adding machine
- Copy machine
- Postage meter
- Mailing equipment
- Coffee maker
- Duplicator

Store Interior
- Interior decorating
- Remodeling
- Painting
- Carpets
- Ceiling
- Lighting
- Windows
- Background music

Store Furniture and Fixtures
- Counters
- Display stands
- Display tables
- Storage shelves
- Storage cabinets
- Inside-display fixtures
- Window-display fixtures
- Inside signs
- Outside signs
- Security

Store Equipment
- Cash register
- Floor cleaning
- Imprinting machine
- Sign printer

Office and Store Supplies
- Record systems
- Stationery
- Business cards
- Mailing envelopes
- Purchase orders
- Sacks
- Boxes
- Wrapping materials
- Sales books
- Gift certificates

Other
- Delivery equipment
- Professional services
- Rent and utility deposits
- Promotional materials
- Licenses and permits
- Working capital

Figure 5. Checklist for estimating capital requirements for a new business.

data are available. Later, as firm prices are quoted by suppliers, the data can be refined. Figure 5 shows some of the major items that should be included on a capital requirements work sheet.

The major categories of capital required to start a business are

1. Inventory
2. Furniture, fixtures, and equipment

3. Start-up expenses
4. Working capital

The cost of inventory, furniture, fixtures, and equipment varies widely even among businesses of a similar kind. Start-up expenses may be similar for different types of businesses, since they entail roughly the same legal obligations, licenses, permits, and so on. Working capital must be sufficient to cover the out-of-pocket expenses of the business at least until it generates enough cash flow to pay the bills; thus the amount of working capital needed initially is based on a forecast of sales and expenses during the first few months of operation.

Generalizations about the costs associated with starting a new business are dangerous if too much credibility is placed on them. Some rules of thumb are useful nevertheless in helping to grasp the overall financial picture. Table 3 is offered for this purpose only; it shows the range of

TABLE 3
Total Capital Requirements for Retail Businesses

Total Capital Investment ($/sq. ft.)	*Businesses (%)*
10–15	4
15–20	18
20–25	10
25–30	18
30–35	18
35–40	8
40–45	0
45–50	16
Over 50	8
Total	100

total investment requirements (measured in dollars per square foot of floor space) for retail businesses. It can be seen that capital requirements for these retail businesses range from less than $15 per square foot to more than $50 per square foot. The median investment is $30 per square foot.

Of this $30, about half represents the investment in inventory; 20 percent is for furniture, fixtures, equipment, and other fixed assets; the remaining 30 percent provides for working capital and other obligations.

The total capital requirement for a "typical" 2000-square-foot retail store is broken down like this:

Inventory	$30,000
Fixed assets	12,000
All other	18,000
Total investment	$60,000

A manufacturing firm would be expected to have a higher capital requirement, especially in the fixed assets account; a wholesaler would probably require a larger investment in inventory; a service firm would need less total capital, especially in the inventory category.

In general, it is preferable for a new independent business to start small and grow gradually as profits can be put back into the business. The merchandise inventory should include a carefully selected but minimum variety of stable backstock merchandise and currently popular items; then, as the store becomes established and the market situation can be assessed with some accuracy, new lines can be added to accommodate specific customer needs. It is a serious mistake to try to start the business by offering everything to everyone.

Sources of Money for the Independent Business

Finding the money to finance a new business venture is always a problem, and in some cases it may be insurmountable. Most ideas for new businesses never become realities because of the lack of funds.

In some 60 percent of all new independent businesses, the initial source of funds comes from the cash and savings supplied by the owners themselves; about 25 percent is borrowed from financial institutions or the business' former owners; most of the rest comes from loans made by the owners' families and friends. According to a survey sponsored by the Small Business Administration, the sources of funds for initial capital investments in new independent businesses were

Cash and savings	53%
Previous ownership of stock and fixtures	8%
Loans from financial institutions	16%
Loans from family members	7%
Loans from friends	5%
Credit from suppliers	6%
Loans from previous owners	3%
All other sources	2%

The main outside source of capital is the commercial bank. To have even a modest hope of obtaining financial assistance from a bank for a venture as high in risk as a new business, it is necessary to present a complete and well-documented financial prospectus. This prospectus should include a detailed breakdown of the specific purposes for which the money will be used, along with the personal history and financial statement of the applicant and a complete description of the proposed business' operating economics. A statement of projected sales, costs, operating expenses, profits, and cash flows is necessary; preferably this statement contains monthly estimates for the first year of operation and annual estimates for at least the next few years or throughout the duration of the requested loan. Supporting market data should also be supplied.

Even with all this information neatly prepared and in perfect order, it is unlikely that a commercial bank will approve the loan as requested unless personal collateral valued at a substantial percentage of the loan amount can be offered. Banks are justifiably pessimistic about the chances for the success of a new business. The only way a bank can make a profit is to make good loans; it cannot afford to risk its depositors' funds unless it is reasonably certain of loan repayments being made in cash, *not* in unsold merchandise or used store fixtures and equipment. When dealing with banks, the businessman's chances of success are tied to his own personal financial resources.

If suitable financial arrangements cannot be made with local banks or other lending institutions, application can be made to the Small Business Administration for a direct or participation loan. Such loans can be made to small manufacturers, wholesalers, retailers, and service businesses to construct, expand, or convert facilities, purchase buildings, equipment, or materials, or obtain working capital.

To get an SBA loan, the applicant must first be refused financing by one or two local banks (depending on the size of the community in which the business is to be located), and he must

- Be of good character.
- Show ability to operate his business successfully.
- Have enough capital so that, with an SBA loan, he can operate on a sound financial basis.
- Show that the proposed loan is sufficiently sound or secured to reasonably ensure repayment.
- Show that the prospects of the business indicate the ability to repay the loan and any other debts out of profits.
- Be able to provide enough of his own funds to assume a sizeable portion of the risk himself and to withstand possible losses during the early stages of the new business.

Under these conditions, the SBA may guarantee up to 90 percent or $350,000, whichever is less, of a bank loan to a qualified small business. The loan may be for as long as 10 years, with working capital loans limited to six years. Interest rates are reasonable, varying according to the cost of money to the government. Security for an SBA-guaranteed loan may consist of mortgages and guarantees or personal endorsements. Inventories are not usually acceptable as loan security.

The steps in applying for a new business loan in which the SBA participates in any manner are

1. Describe in detail the type of business to be established.
2. Describe experience and management capabilities.
3. Prepare an estimate of how much the applicant and others will invest in the business and how much will be borrowed.
4. Prepare a current financial statement (balance sheet) listing all personal assets and liabilities.
5. Prepare a detailed projection of earnings for the first year of operation.
6. List the collateral to be offered as security for the loan, indicating the present market value of each item.
7. Request a direct bank loan based on this material; if refused, request that the bank make the loan under the SBA's Loan Guaranty Plan or participate with the SBA in a loan. If the loan is approved, the SBA deals directly with the bank.
8. If the preceding options are still refused by the bank, take the financial information directly to the nearest SBA office for consideration as a direct loan.

Another important source of outside financing available to some new businesses is in the form of credit from suppliers. Many manufacturers of store fixtures and equipment have financing plans available for new businesses, and suppliers and wholesalers may be willing to extend favorable credit terms on merchandise inventories, requiring no security other than the repossession rights of any unsold goods.

A principal cause of small business failure in general, and new business failure in particular, is inadequate financing. It is a primary responsibility of management to provide or acquire sufficient capital to supply a firm foundation for the business.

Business Organization

A business is a pursuit carried on for livelihood or profit. For a pursuit to be legally recognized as a business, a profit motive must be present and some type of economic activity must be involved. An activity is considered a business if it is entered into and carried on in good faith for the purpose of making a profit. In this way, a business is distinguished from an activity engaged in purely for personal satisfaction. An activity is only considered as being engaged in for profit if it produces a profit in any two out of five consecutive years, unless an Internal Revenue Service ruling can be obtained to the contrary.

Having decided to start a business, an early consideration should be what type of business entity to use. There are legal and tax matters to be considered in making this decision, and it is an area in which professional assistance should be obtained.

There are four different ways that the business can be organized: (1) a sole proprietorship, (2) a partnership, (3) a corporation, and (4) a "Subchapter S" corporation. In a sole proprietorship or a partnership, the business does not pay any federal income taxes, but the sole proprietor or the partners include the profits and losses from the business on their own income tax returns. Corporate profits, on the other hand, are taxed to both the corporation and the individual shareholders when the profits are distributed as dividends; losses sustained by the corporation usually are not available to its stockholders. If a corporation qualifies with the Internal Revenue Service as a Subchapter S corporation, the corporation is not subject to federal income taxes, and profits and losses can be distributed to the shareholders for inclusion on their individual tax returns.

Sole Proprietorships. Individuals engaged in business on their own account are sole proprietors, the simplest form of business organization. In this form, the business has no legal existence apart from the owner; its liabilities are the personal liabilities of the proprietor, and his proprietary interest ends when he dies. The proprietor undertakes all the risks of the business to the full extent of all his assets, whether or not the assets are used in the business. The income from a sole proprietorship is reported as a part of the owner's total gross income, and each asset in a sole proprietorship is treated separately for tax purposes.

Partnership. Even though a partnership is not a taxable entity, it must determine its income and file an income tax return in the same manner as an individual, except for certain items that must be stated separately. A partnership represents a relationship existing between two or more persons who join together to carry on a trade or business, with each partner contributing money, property, labor, or skill, and each expecting to share in the profits and losses of the business whether or not a formal partnership agreement has been drawn up. As with a sole proprietorship, each partner must report his share of the partnership's profits and losses on his own tax return (along with a copy of the partnership's tax return). Unless a partnership agreement specifically limits the liabilities of certain partners, each partner is fully liable for the firm's obligations.

Corporation. Corporate profits normally are taxed to the corporation. When the profits are distributed as dividends, the dividends are taxed to the individual shareholders. In computing its taxable income, a corporation generally can take the same deductions allowed to individuals, plus some special deductions available only to corporations. The formation of a corporation involves a transfer of money or property or both by the prospective shareholders in exchange for capital stock in the corporation. Every corporation must file an income tax return regardless of the amount of its income, even if it has ceased doing business and has disposed of virtually all its assets. Unlike a sole proprietorship or partnership, the personal liabilities of the individuals involved in the corporation are limited to their initial investment; the corporation is treated as an individual, and its obligations do not carry over to its shareholders.

Subchapter S Corporation. Subchapter S corporations are corporations that elect not to be taxed as corporations; instead, the shareholders of a Subchapter S corporation include in their individual gross incomes their proportionate shares of the corporate profits and losses. This type of business organization combines some of the advantages of proprietorships, partnerships, and regular corporations. To qualify under Subchapter S, the corporation must be a domestic corporation, must not be a member of an affiliated group, must have only one class of stock, must not have more than 10 shareholders, must have only individuals or estates as shareholders, and must not have a nonresident alien as a shareholder.

Locating Suppliers and Distributors

Deciding from whom to buy requires that suitable sources be found for the particular merchandise to be offered. Presumably the prospective business owner has sufficient familiarity with his chosen field to identify the leading manufacturers. This is one of the most important reasons for studying the publications and other sources of trade information in his business.

To locate the specific sources for the merchandise desired—whether it is to be obtained from manufacturers, manufacturers' representatives, wholesalers, distributors, or other suppliers—information can be obtained from

- Other shop owners
- Trade directories
- Trade associations
- Trade magazines
- Merchandise marts
- Trade shows
- Chambers of commerce
- Manufacturers' catalogs
- Wholesalers' catalogs

Salesmen representing either a single manufacturer or a number of different manufacturers are among the most helpful sources of product information. They generally know what is being bought by other similar businesses (both their own and competitors' lines) and can identify fast-moving items appropriate to a given market area. Catalogs can be obtained from these representatives or by contacting the manufacturers directly. An up-to-date catalog file should be maintained for reference, even if the merchandise is not of current interest.

Discount schedules and credit terms should also be obtained and retained for future reference. This information is useful in deciding whether to order directly or through distributors or wholesalers.

Merchandise Planning and Selection

If the new businessman does not have at least a general idea of the types of merchandise he expects to sell, he has either failed to do adequate planning or he is entering the wrong business.

If the new business has been purchased from a previous owner or if it is a franchise package, merchandise planning should present no major problem. There is at least a beginning inventory, even if it is not a good one; as the likes and dislikes of customers become known, the inventory can gradually be improved.

Planning a beginning inventory for a new business in a new location, however, is not easy. The owner must decide:

1. *What* to buy
2. *Who* to buy it from
3. *When* to buy it
4. *How much* of it to buy

The complexity of the problem is easy to visualize in almost any retail business. For a shoe store to carry only one pair of men's shoes in each size, color, and style currently available would require an inventory of more than 6000 pairs of shoes, most of which would never sell. For a book store to carry only one copy of each new book published during a single year would place over 30,000 books on its shelves, only a few of which would sell.

Deciding how to stock a shop with its beginning inventory, no matter what type of merchandise is handled, requires some familiarity with the types of customers within the shop's trade area. Some idea of customer preferences and attitudes can be found by visiting other shops in the immediate area. With this knowledge in hand, the merchandise can be classified into three groups:

1. Merchandise that you *know* will sell: Bibles, white paint, vanilla ice cream, tennis shoes, 12-gauge shotgun shells, white T shirts and candy for Valentine's Day.
2. Merchandise you *think* will sell: a new novel by a popular author, orange paint, the flavor of the month, wing-tip shoes, and neckties for Father's Day.
3. Merchandise you *hope* will sell, but are not very sure of: a new novel by a previously unpublished author, peanut butter ice cream, high-heeled men's shoes, a new style of women's skirts, funny T shirts, and roses for Mother-in-Law's Day.

The initial inventory is made up of items from all three categories. The real backbone of any retail business is the first category; as experience is accumulated and knowledge evolves into wisdom, the second and third categories become increasingly important and profitable.

The amount of merchandise to be stocked initially depends largely on the seasonal characteristics of the business. As a rough rule of thumb, unless better information is available for the specific business, consider stocking for the next three to four months' anticipated sales. If estimated sales for the next three months are $30,000 and the cost of goods sold is 60 percent of the selling price, plan to put approximately $18,000 into the beginning inventory. This total inventory investment can then be proportioned among the various items to be carried. Suggestions regarding basic inventory requirements for different businesses can usually be obtained from the appropriate trade associations serving their respective fields and from trade publications, suppliers, and distributors.

Finding, Hiring, and Training Employees

A large part of the success of any retail business is related to how well the employees and customers get along. A good employee creates goodwill and keeps customers coming back; a lazy, uninformed, or unpleasant employee drives customers away—many of them never come back. The careful choice of store personnel, therefore, is essential to protect the business' reputation. The extra personal service element is the small business' main advantage over big businesses; it is too important an advantage to risk forfeiting.

In general, the new business should delay as long as possible the hiring of any full-time employee, starting out on a small scale with only business partners or their families. This helps reduce the initial cash drain common to most beginning businesses and at the same time thoroughly familiarizes the owner or owners and their families with all the duties and responsibilities of the business. It also helps in defining exactly what is needed in and what will be expected of any employees who might be hired later, and will allow sufficient time to find the right individuals.

It should also be remembered that there is an inordinate amount of government paperwork associated with even one part-time employee. The difference between having no employees and having one part-time employee amounts to filling out some 26 government forms of one type or another each year.

Remember, too, that for an individually owned and operated business, having one good employee may mean the difference between working six or seven days a week with no vacations and being able to take time off. A capable employee who can be trusted to handle the routine functions of the business can mean the difference between the business being an enjoyable experience and its being a constant physical and emotional strain; it can mean the difference between being tied down or being free. A good employee can release the owner from routine duties so that he can perform his more important function as a manager.

Flexibility is one of the most desirable traits to look for in an employee of a small independent business. The more functions an employee can perform, the fewer are required of the owner. A good sales clerk is close to customers and aware of their preferences and is a great asset in merchandise planning and inventory control.

Finding good employees is not difficult if time is available to choose without the pressure of having to make an immediate decision. Sources of new employees include the suggestions of friends, associates, and sometimes competitors, government and private employment services, school placement offices, help-wanted advertisements in local newspapers, and walk-in job applicants.

It is important to work closely with a new employee until he or she is thoroughly familiar with the business routine and able to handle it capably and independently. Operating a cash register and making change can be a traumatic experience to one who has not done it before, as can writing sales slips, handling credit transactions, accepting returned merchandise, locating stock, and answering customers' requests for special help and product information. Sufficient time should be allowed for the new employee to become comfortable with the various duties, while performing the tasks under close supervision. The training period should then be followed up by an evaluation of the employee's performance, reexplaining key points and suggesting areas of possible improvement.

Getting rid of an employee who has proved unsatisfactory is an unpleasant task, especially since a great deal of time, effort, and expense has probably gone into his selection and training. Nevertheless, it must be done; a bad employee is far worse than no employee at all, and the greatest expense of all is customer dissatisfaction and a poor business reputation.

Advertising and Promotion for the New Business

Any new business is faced with the problem of drawing customers to an establishment they have done without in the past, away from the competing establishments with which they have done business and with which they have already established some kind of relationship.

The only persons who eagerly await the opening of a new small business are the owner and his immediate family and friends. Sad but common is the enthusiastically anticipated "grand opening" to which nobody comes or cares.

A certain amount of preopening publicity is necessary for any new business to help reduce the length of the expensive start-up period. A large window sign announcing the forthcoming arrival of the new business and the merchandise or services to be offered is a logical first step. Other advertising and promotional activities should commence as soon as a definite opening date can be established.

A listing in the classified section of the local telephone directory should be obtained at the earliest date possible. These directories may be published only once a year, and it will be worth the cost of several months' unused telephone service to be assured of listings under the appropriate categories in the next edition. Missing the cut-off date means missing a whole year's reference, and this cannot be afforded in a new business.

Preopening promotional activities should be aimed toward projecting the desired business image, character, or personality, generating store traffic as soon as the business opens, emphasizing the particular or unusual strengths, services, and consumer benefits of the business, and ultimately increasing its profits.

On opening, special promotions may be warranted to draw customers to the new business. These commonly include special drawings for prizes, special prices on promotional merchandise, gifts, refreshments, door prizes, and a variety of special offers. Advertising in local newspapers and magazines, handbills, posters, radio spots, news releases, and direct mail may all be employed at this time to lure customers away from established competitors.

Participation in local events, charities, clubs, and civic organizations also helps to get the name of the new business before the public; when people have heard the name often enough, it ceases to be thought of as "new." It then becomes an "established" business.

Promotional activities should be continued on a planned and continuing basis throughout the existence of the business; the owner's participation in a wide variety of activities is a key element of the overall program. Advertising should also be continued, but its emphasis must be changed and oriented toward the seasonal buying patterns that apply to the specific business.

Insurance

Adequate insurance protection is essential regardless of the precautions taken to prevent damage or loss of the physical property of the business.

Insurance covering physical loss includes

- Fire insurance
- Lightning insurance
- Windstorm insurance
- Flood insurance
- Use and occupancy insurance
- Robbery and burglary insurance
- Vandalism and malicious mischief insurance
- Riot insurance
- "Extended coverage" insurance (storm, explosion, smoke damage, etc.)
- Casualty insurance

Insurance to protect against claims for personal injury includes

- Public liability insurance
- Workmen's Compensation insurance

- Employer's liability insurance
- Product liability insurance

Other types of insurance that may be important, depending on the nature of the business and on the owner's personal and financial situation include

- Life insurance
- Health and accident insurance
- Automobile insurance
- Business interruption insurance
- Income continuation insurance
- Fidelity and surety bonds

The cost of insurance coverage ranges between 1.0 and 4.0 percent of the value of the property insured. Getting appropriate insurance coverage can be quite involved, and the recommendations of a reliable insurance agent, broker, or company representative are invaluable.

The new businessman will undoubtedly find that as soon as he opens his doors to the public, a large percentage of the people entering his shop are selling some type of insurance; these are *not* the ones whose advice should be sought. The business owner should *select* the insurance agent or agents with whom he wishes to work and whose advice he can confidently follow; he should *not* be selected *by* the insurance agents as one to whom insurance is to be sold.

Start-up Costs and Expenses

The checklist shown in Fig. 5 detailed some of the many costs and expenses involved in opening a new business. These items, however, cover only the expenditures incurred up to the time the business opens its doors to the public.

After that, there is a period of time necessary to build up the business to its normal operating level. The cost of supporting the business until it is able to support itself through sales must also be considered in estimating the total capital requirements of a new business.

Figure 6 illustrates two ways in which a new business might develop. Each consists of three stages of growth. Figure 6a shows a relatively slow start-up phase, followed by a period of rapid growth until the business reaches maturity and a more modest growth rate. Figure 6b

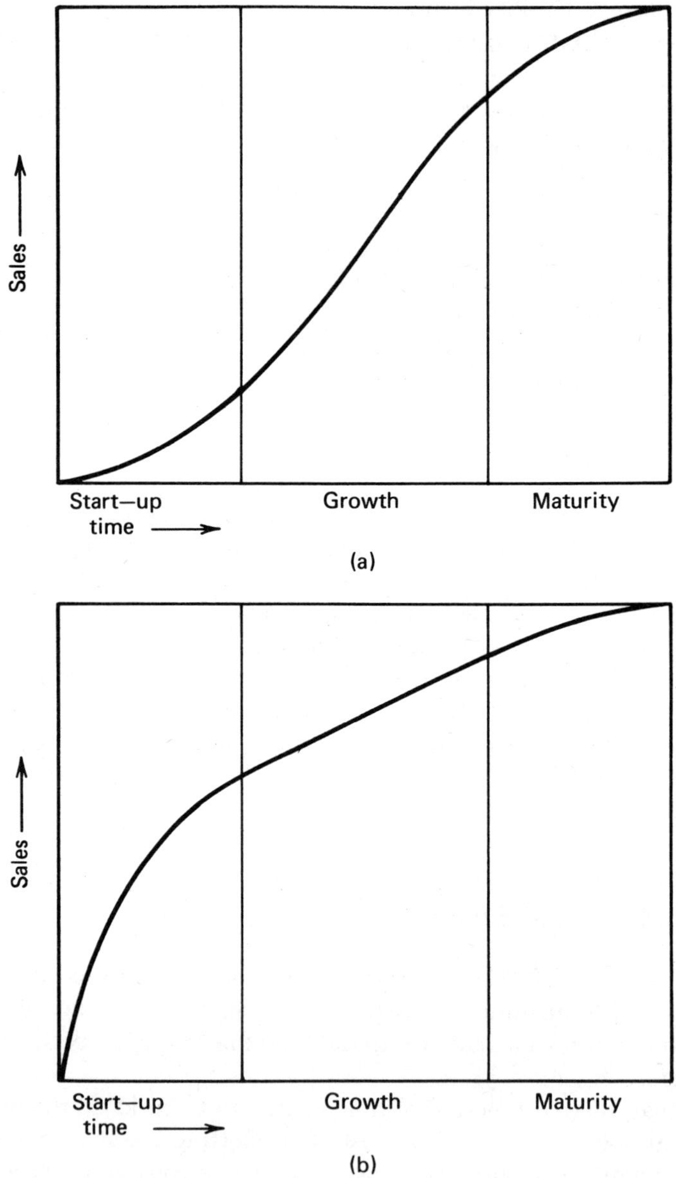

Figure 6. Growth stages in a new business. (a) Slow early growth. (b) Rapid early growth.

begins with a rapid growth period, which slows down in the second phase and levels off as the business matures. The pattern in Fig. 6a reflects the situation for a new business at a new location; Fig. 6b shows a pattern more indicative of a new business moving into a fully developed and operating shopping center.

On either pattern, the time scale can vary widely, from a month or two up to as much as several years. Some businesses have moved into new shopping centers as early tenants, only to find that years elapse before the center is completely leased. Being one of only a few tenants is both expensive (certain shopping center "common area" costs are shared by the existing tenants, regardless of how few) and lonely (few shoppers will bother to visit a center until it can offer a complete variety of shops).

Whether the start-up period takes months or years, it is essential that its costs be provided for in the operating budget. At least enough money should be on hand or readily obtainable to pay all cash expenses for a three-month period. The details of preparing a cash budget are discussed in Chapter 7.

Estimating Sales and Profits

Whether the primary purpose of a projected sales, cost, and profit statement is to obtain a bank loan, to estimate cash requirements, or to provide information for management planning, it should be done by *every* business *before* it begins operation. Later, as operating data become available, the projections can be continually updated and refined.

The steps involved in preparing the projected operating statement are straightforward and uncomplicated:

1. Start with the store size in square feet.
2. Estimate the annual sales per square foot for the business, based on sales per square foot for other businesses in the same trade area and similar businesses in other areas.
3. Calculate the total annual sales volume: dollars per square foot times square feet = total sales.
4. Estimate the seasonal sales patterns for the business, preferably on a monthly basis.
5. Allocate the total annual sales calculated in step 3 to months: annual sales times monthly percentage = monthly sales.
6. Adjust these "normal" monthly sales totals to reflect the start-up period; this is strictly a value judgment.
7. Deduct from the monthly sales totals the cost of goods sold; this

cost should be a fixed percentage of sales volume. The balance remaining is the gross operating profit.

8. Deduct estimated operating expenses from the gross operating profit. The resulting difference is the estimated net profit for the month.

For example, consider a 2000-square-foot retail store that moves into an established suburban shopping center. The overall average sales per square foot for the shopping center's tenants is $85 per square foot; other retail businesses of the type being opened average from $60 to $90 per square foot in annual sales. For this new operation, a "normal" sales volume of $80 per square foot appears reasonable. The estimated total annual sales for the business, once it becomes established, are

2000 sq. ft. @ $80/sq. ft. = $160,000.

If the business were not seasonal at all, monthly sales would be a steady 8.33 percent of the annual total, or $13,333. However, the sales in this business are known (either from experience or from information obtained from published data or knowledgeable individuals) to be strongly oriented toward the Christmas season. Sales during the January through September period are estimated at 6.0 percent of the annual total; October, 10.0 percent; November, 14.0 percent; and December, 22.0 percent. These percentages, applied to the estimated total annual sales of $160,000, give the normal monthly sales expectations.

Further, it is estimated that the first month of operation yields only half the "normal" amount; the second month climbs to 75 percent; the third month to 90 percent; and by the end of the fourth month, sales reach their normal monthly level. Table 4 shows the month-by-month sales projections for the new business, assuming it opens for business on June 1.

The effective margin on the merchandise lines handled by this store is estimated at 65.0 percent of sales, including allowances for freight and shrinkage. The gross operating profit for each month therefore amounts to 35.0 percent of the monthly sales receipts.

Fixed expenses—rent, utilities, minimum payroll, and other costs unrelated to the volume of business—are estimated at $2000 per month. Variable expenses—seasonal or overtime help and other items related to the volume of sales—are estimated at 15 percent of sales. Putting all this information together gives the results shown in Table 5 for the first year of operation of the business.

As indicated in Table 5, the store shows a net loss during its three-

TABLE 4
Example of Monthly Sales Projections for a New Retail Business

Month	Annual Sales (%)	Normal Monthly Sales	Adjustment for Start-Up	Adjusted Monthly Sales
June	6.0	9,600	0.50	4,800
July	6.0	9,600	0.75	7,200
August	6.0	9,600	0.90	8,640
September	6.0	9,600	1.00	9,600
October	10.0	16,000	1.00	16,000
November	14.0	22,400	1.00	22,400
December	22.0	35,200	1.00	35,200
January	6.0	9,600	1.00	9,600
February	6.0	9,600	1.00	9,600
March	6.0	9,600	1.00	9,600
April	6.0	9,600	1.00	9,600
May	6.0	9,600	1.00	9,600
Total	100.0	160,000		151,840

TABLE 5
Example of Projected Monthly Operations for a New Retail Business (in dollars)

Month	Estimated Sales	Cost of Sales	Gross Operating Profit	Fixed Expense	Variable Expense	Net Profit Before Taxes
June	4,800	3,120	1,680	2000	720	(1040)
July	7,200	4,680	2,520	2000	1080	(560)
August	8,640	5,616	3,024	2000	1296	(272)
September	9,600	6,240	3,360	2000	1440	(80)
October	16,000	10,400	5,600	2000	2400	1200
November	22,400	14,560	7,840	2000	3360	2480
December	35,200	22,880	12,320	2000	5280	5040
January	9,600	6,240	3,360	2000	1440	(80)
February	9,600	6,240	3,360	2000	1440	(80)
March	9,600	6,240	3,360	2000	1440	(80)
April	9,600	6,240	3,360	2000	1440	(80)
May	9,600	6,240	3,360	2000	1400	(80)
Total	151,840	98,696	53,144	24,000	22,775	6,368

month start-up period and almost breaks even during its normal January through September operations; all profits come during October, November, and December. This pattern is not unusual for businesses with strong seasonal orientations. It is unusual, however, for a new business to earn substantial profits during its first year or two of operation. A realistic sales, cost, and profit projection can reduce the uncertainty associated with a new venture and provide the owner with a sound basis for making management decisions.

4

Minding Your Own Business

You foolish man, you don't even know your own foolish business.

Chesterfield

Regardless of how thoroughly prepared he is, the new business owner encounters a multitude of unforseen and seemingly unsolvable problems during his first few months of operation—problems neither referred to nor envisioned in graduate schools of business administration. Some of the practical problems associated with operating the new business on a day-by-day basis are discussed in this chapter.

Purchasing Principles

Buying is the first of the important operations of any retail business, and skillful buying is essential for profitable operation. Merchandise planning, discussed in the preceding chapter, has to do with deciding what types of merchandise should be handled to satisfy customers; it is primarily market oriented. Buying or purchasing involves the details of deciding on the sources of supply, the optimum timing for these purchases, and the quantities to be ordered at any one time. Large companies sometimes separate the planning and the purchasing functions, with the merchandise planner geared toward the market and the purchasing agent aimed toward suppliers. This distinction, of course, is a luxury not available to the typical small business.

The same person who identifies the type, kind, quality, brand, size, color, and style of merchandise that will sell best to customers within the shop's trade area also places the orders with suppliers. He prices the merchandise when it arrives, sells it to customers, and pays for it.

The purchasing function requires close attention to salesmen, trade journals, catalogs, and, most important, the specific likes and dislikes of the business' own customers.

There are several alternatives in the acquisition of merchandise for resale. Merchandise can be bought directly from manufacturers, from wholesalers or distributors who have purchased from a number of different manufacturers, or through manufacturers' representatives, who may represent several different product lines and simply take the orders and forward them directly to the appropriate manufacturers for fulfillment. Each channel of supply has its advantages.

Large orders placed directly with the manufacturer usually provide the best discount. However, by ordering from a distributor or wholesaler, smaller quantities from a variety of different manufacturers can be combined to get a better overall discount than could be obtained if the smaller, separate orders were placed directly with the different manufacturers. For example, the "standard" discount offered by most large publishers on regular trade books is 40 percent, but to earn this 40 percent discount, five to ten books must be ordered at a time. As an alternative, major book wholesalers offer the same 40 percent discount on orders for 50 or more books, but the 50 books can consist of one book from each of 50 publishers. Similar situations exist in many other retail fields, and the general principle is simply: if you need many items from one manufacturer, buy from the manufacturer; if you need only a few items from many manufacturers, buy from a wholesale distributor.

If the business deals entirely in small quantities, it has little choice but to use whatever distribution channels are specified by the manufacturers. The selection is limited to the suppliers that carry the kind and quality of goods that are best suited to the desires of the customers.

Purchases can be spread among different suppliers to take advantage of the best prices and promotional offers available at any given time, or they may be concentrated with only a few suppliers; the small business is usually better off working on a more regular and larger-quantity basis with relatively few supply sources.

The question of timing purchases depends on the specific seasonal characteristics of the business. Merchandise inventories should anticipate future sales, building up for seasonal upturns in sales volume and being allowed to run down during slow sales periods. Having too much stock on hand is expensive and uses up valuable selling space or storage room. Having too little stock on hand results in lost sales at best and at worst in lost customers.

Good purchasing is a combination of science and art; careful analysis of sales data, close communication with customers, and most of all, good judgment ensure that the right merchandise is on hand at the right time.

Pricing Merchandise for Profit

Much of the success of a business depends on the way in which it prices its merchandise and service. There is virtually no limit to the quantities of goods and services that can be sold if they are sold cheaply enough and virtually no limit to the profits that can be made if goods and services are priced high enough. However, low prices offer little profit margin, and high prices generate little sales volume. In extreme cases, the options are to price low and make no profit or to price high and have no sales; in other words, a good chance of making nothing, or no chance of making a lot.

The pricing decision, therefore, is a strategic one. Products and services must be priced at levels that will assure the business of at least a fair chance of making a fair profit.

There are four ways to price a product:

1. The manufacturer's suggested list price
2. A percentage discount from this list price
3. A percentage markup based on cost
4. Whatever the market will bear

Pricing according to manufacturers' suggested list price is the easiest way, providing there is such a figure. Many items manufactured for retail sale are prepriced, with the price label already applied (as books) or listed in catalogs and advertisements. This eliminates the possibility of pricing the goods any higher, regardless of their cost or market demands for them.

Major discounters operate either way, marking down list prices or marking up costs. However, since manufacturers' discount schedules vary among different items, marking down a given percentage is a dangerous practice. Marking up from cost is a preferable approach.

As for charging whatever the market will bear, W. C. Fields once defined the three steps in business as:

1. Find out how much they got
2. Git it
3. Git out

Although this practice is not generally applicable in the retail and service field, there are certain types of businesses for which this method of pricing is the only realistic way to operate. An artist does not mark up the cost of his canvas, oils, and time by a fixed percentage, nor can an antique shop, selling a one-of-a-kind item that cannot be replaced after it has been sold.

The businessman must establish an overall price policy for his business before he opens. This policy depends on the expected customer base, as well as the shop's location, quality of goods handled, and services offered.

In pricing individual items, it is essential to know all the costs of doing business. Knowing the total expenses and revenue requirements of the business and the cost of the goods to be sold, it is not difficult to calculate the gross margins needed to cover the costs of doing business and return a profit. From this margin, the percentage markup can be determined easily.

For example, consider a new 2000-square-foot retail shop with estimated annual fixed costs and expenses of $50,000 and aiming for $12,000 in net profits before taxes, giving a total revenue requirement of $62,000. This $62,000 can be generated in any number of ways, such as:

selling merchandise costing $120,000 at a 51.7 percent markup on cost
selling merchandise costing $100,000 at a 62.0 percent markup on cost
selling merchandise costing $80,000 at a 77.5 percent markup on cost

or an infinite number of other combinations resulting in the same net revenue generation. The question is one of optimization: which combination of price and volume is most realistic in view of the prevailing market and competitive situation? Will it be easier to sell, for example, 12,000 units at $15.17 each, 10,000 units at $16.20 each, or 8000 units at $17.75 each? Or, looking at it another way, sales of $182,000 would be required for the first option, amounting to $91.00 per square foot per year; the second option requires sales of $162,000, or $81.00 per square foot per year; the third, sales of $142,000, or $71.00 per square foot per year. Which could best be attained? A strategic management decision is required.

In any case, a product's price falls somewhere in the range between the cost of the product and the price at which it can conveniently be obtained elsewhere.

Pricing Practices for Service Businesses

Many personal services, especially those operating from a fixed business location (such as barber and beauty shops, laundry and dry cleaning establishments, photo studios, repair services, etc.) are priced in much the same way as retail merchandise. The market has already established price levels for the various types of services offered, and unless some special additional features can be provided, it is difficult to compete in the marketplace at any higher price. The basic pricing principle for these businesses is to set prices at about the same level as the prices established by competitors and attempt to improve profitability by operating as efficiently as possible.

Business and professional services present a different situation. Here, the service provided is not a "standard" one; thus uniform pricing policies are not possible. Many of these services are priced on an hourly basis, with the hourly rate set to cover appropriate direct, indirect, and fixed costs. Sometimes the billing rate—the hourly rate at which a customer or client is charged for the service—is determined by applying a "multiplier" of 1.5 to 5.0 to an individual's base salary. Using a multiplier of 3.0 for a person with an annual salary of \$20,000, for example, gives an hourly billing rate of

$$\frac{\$20{,}000/\text{year}}{2000\ \text{hours}/\text{year}} \times 3.0 = \$30.00/\text{hour}$$

The major element of cost built into the multiplier is the cost of unbilled time; if only half of an individual's time can be charged directly to clients, his hourly base pay (plus all salary-related expenses such as sick pay, vacation pay, paid insurance, pension fund contributions, FICA, FUTA, etc.) must be multiplied by 2.0 to break even.

Figure 7 shows an example of a contract pricing proposal for professional services similar in format to that required by many government agencies. On government work, the overhead rates must be carefully documented; even on work for which the documentation is not required, all such figures should be accurately developed.

If the project illustrated in Fig. 7 involved only the \$8000 in direct labor, a multiplier could be worked out thus:

Estimated direct labor	\$ 8,000
Labor overhead	6,000
Total	14,000
General overhead @ 20 percent	2,800
Total	16,800
Profit @ 6 percent	1,008
Total contract price	\$17,808

The total contract price divided by the estimated direct labor cost gives the multiplier to be used when pricing the work on an hourly basis: \$17,808/8000 = 2.126. With this cost structure, then, a \$20,000 per year

Direct materials		
Detailed breakdown of purchased parts, subcontracted items, raw materials, standard commercial items, etc.	$6,000	
Materials overhead		
12 percent rate × $6000 base =	$ 720	
Total materials cost		$ 6,720
Direct labor		
Detailed breakdown of estimated man-hours at various hourly rates.	$8,000	
Labor overhead		
75 percent rate × $8000 base	6,000	
Total labor cost		$14,000
Other direct costs and expenses		
Detailed breakdown of any special testing or equipment required, travel, transporation and subsistence expenses, outside consultants and business services, telephone, surveys and miscellaneous supplies to be charged directly to the job.		$ 3,000
Total direct costs and project overheads		$23,720
General overheads and administrative expense		
20 percent rate × $23,720 base		$ 4,744
Total estimated cost		$28,464
Fee or profit		
6 percent rate × $28,464 base or fixed amount.		$ 1,708
Total contract price		$30,172

Figure 7. Example of contract pricing proposal for professional services.

employee would be billed at an hourly rate of $21.26. This rate pays for his total salary cost as well as a share of general overhead and administrative expenses and returns a profit to his employer. Exactly the same approach could be used by an individual working on his own, with the multiplier applied, for example, to the prevailing journeyman wages for his particular trade.

Selling

The objective of good salesmanship is not to make a sale, but to create a customer; not to force a sale, but to assist the customer in making a purchase.

Selling is accomplished directly and indirectly. The direct methods include personal sales efforts, advertising, and in-store displays. The indirect methods are of a promotional nature, establishing good relationships with customers and prospective customers through courtesy, special services, a good business reputation, and a pleasant shopping environment. The indirect methods of sales promotion should be carried on continually, both inside and outside the business.

Direct personal selling consists of four steps, called the AIDA approach: attention, interest, desire, action.

- Attract the customer's *attention* to the product.
- Arouse the customer's *interest* in it.
- Generate a *desire* in the customer to own it.
- Motivate the customer to *action*.

The attention phase is often neglected in retail sales. Most sales clerks are order takers rather than salespeople; they wait until the customer asks for a specific item or at best offer a "How may I help you?" This is an area in which the small retail business, with its superior product knowledge and familiarity with individual customer's interests, has a real advantage over large department stores and discount houses. Items of special interest can easily be pointed out conversationally to customers as they browse.

Interest is aroused by briefly describing and emphasizing the most important and salable points of the product, pointing out the specific benefits for that particular customer. A desire for the product should develop as the special benefits are visualized, resulting in the act of purchasing. A sale has not been made; a customer has been assisted in making a purchase, by establishing a good relationship between the customer, the salesperson, and the product.

However, good salesmanship does not end with the purchase. The backbone of any retail business is the repeat customer (remember the 20/80 rule—20 percent of the customers account for 80 percent of the sales). If the customer is genuinely pleased with his or her purchase, long-term benefits accrue to the business and its customer. If the right merchandise is bought by the right customer, the customer will keep coming back—but the merchandise will not.

Credit and Collection

The availability of credit for customers can greatly increase the sales of even the smallest independent retail businesses and is essential for some. The type and terms of credit depend on the kinds and value of the merchandise handled.

An automobile dealership offers an interesting example of two opposite extremes in handling credit sales. On new car sales, almost anyone with a modest down payment is granted credit, but when the car is brought in for service, the owner may be expected to pay in cash. The "sales on credit, service for cash" concept reflects the profitability of the two ends of the same business; the profit is in new car sales, whereas service is offered only as a necessity. The availability of credit encourages sales; the lack of credit availability discourages customers.

For any business, offering credit requires a great deal of faith in the buyer. The seller must be reasonably certain that the buyer is willing and able to make payment when it is due, and that nothing will happen to prevent the payment from being made. Credit terms are extended more liberally on large purchases than on small ones; the availability of credit terms on large-ticket items tends to overcome some of the price resistance. Also, these items can be repossessed if necessary.

There are several ways in which the small independent business might offer credit to its customers. These include

- Store charge accounts
- Bank credit cards
- Sales contracts

The store charge account offers several distinct advantages, even though it creates time-consuming paperwork and may result in collection problems. A charge customer is usually a good customer who makes frequent purchases. Having an account with a small business gives the feeling of an intimate relationship, encouraging more business to be done there. Maintaining in-house charge accounts also provides the business with names and addresses for its mailing list.

A separate file should be kept on each customer, showing the date, the merchandise purchased, the amount, and the date and amount of each payment, along with copies of sales tickets. Monthly statements should be mailed promptly; most people pay all their bills at one time, and if the statement does not arrive by that time, payment is unlikely until the following month. Collections are sometimes a problem with customers who are habitual late payers, but a certain amount of this can be tolerated; most customers are worth carrying for several months and will pay eventually if reminded regularly.

The major bank credit cards—Master Charge and VISA (formerly BankAmericard)—are almost necessary for the small retail business. The sales made through these credit cards, like cash, are deposited directly in the business' account at local banks. Possible credit losses are eliminated as long as the transaction is handled as specified by the credit card company. The disadvantages of the bank credit cards are the expense (ranging from one to five percent of the amount of the sale, depending on the number and size of credit sales) and the loss of identity with the charge customer (the cards do not list the cardholder's address).

Large-ticket items such as major appliances may be handled by some form of sales contract. Often the terms provide for no interest or carrying charges if the total amount is paid within 60 or 90 days; otherwise, interest is charged on the unpaid balance. Some firms sell these contracts to finance companies; if this is done, the customer should be told in advance to avoid badwill.

Every effort should be made to collect on delinquent accounts before turning them over to an agency or attorney for collection or repossession. Often a telephone reminder or a personal letter is all that is required.

Books and Recordkeeping

There are only two reasons to keep records of a business operation: they are required by law or they are useful to the businessman in his functions as a manager.

Records *must* be kept to determine the tax liabilities of the individual or business. Regardless of the type of bookkeeping system employed, the records must be permanent, accurate, and complete, and must clearly establish income, deductions, credits, employee information, and anything else specified by federal, state, and local regulations. The law does not require any particular kind of records, only that they be complete and separate for each business.

When starting in business, the type and arrangement of books and records most suitable for the particular business operation should be established, keeping in mind the taxes for which the business is liable and the times at which they are due. If this is not a subject in which the new businessman is competent, outside professional help is called for; it must be done only once, and setting up efficiently makes things much easier later on.

Double-entry bookkeeping is usually the preferred method for keeping business records, making use of journals and ledgers. Transactions are entered first in a journal, and then monthly totals of the transactions are posted to the appropriate ledger accounts. The ledger accounts include five categories: (1) income, (2) expense, (3) asset, (4) liability, and (5) net worth. Income and expense accounts are closed each year; asset, liability, and net worth accounts are maintained on a permanent and continuing basis.

At the end of each accounting period, an income statement and balance sheet can be derived from the accounts. The income statement reflects current operations for the year, and the balance sheet shows the financial position of the business in terms of its assets, liabilities, and net worth as of a specific date.

Single-entry bookkeeping, although not as complete as the double-entry method, may be used effectively in the small business, especially during its early years. The single-entry system can be relatively simple, recording the flow of income and expense through a daily summary of cash receipts, a monthly summary of receipts, and a monthly disbursements journal (such as a check book). This system is entirely adequate for the tax purposes of a small business.

All business receipts should be deposited in a separate bank account, with a petty cash fund established for small expenses. All business expenses paid by cash should be supported by documents that clearly show that the expenses were incurred for business purposes.

All disbursements should be made by check if possible so that business expenses can be well documented. If a cash payment is necessary, a receipt for the payment, or at least an explanation of it, should be included in the business records. All cancelled checks, paid bills, duplicate deposit slips, and other documents that substantiate the entries in the business records should be filed in an orderly manner and stored in a safe place. Accounts should be classified in groups relating to income, expense, assets, liabilities, and net worth. Asset accounts should be classified as current or fixed and should record in detail the dates of acquisition, cost, depreciation, and any other items affecting the accounts.

Employment records present another set of problems. The difference between having no employees and having one employee is as great as the difference between having no children and having one; the entire life style changes. Having one, two, three, or many (either employees or children) makes little difference in the amount of work required in their care; 24 hours a day is the absolute maximum amount of time that can be devoted to any problem, no matter how great.

An employer—regardless of the number of employees—must maintain all records pertaining to employment taxes (income tax withholding, social security, and Federal unemployment tax) for at least four years after the tax became due or was paid, whichever is later. There are 20 different kinds of employment records that must be maintained just to satisfy federal requirements; these are summarized in Table 6.

All books and records of the business must be available at all times for inspection by Internal Revenue Service officers. The records must be retained as long as they might become material in the administration of any Internal Revenue law.

TABLE 6

Employment Records Required by Federal Law

Income Tax Withholding Records

1. Name, address, and social security number of each employee.
2. Amount and date of each payment of compensation.
3. Amount of wages subject to withholding in each payment.
4. Amount of withholding tax collected from each payment.
5. Reason that the taxable amount is less than the total payment.
6. Statements relating to employees' nonresident alien status.
7. Market value and date of noncash compensation.
8. Information about payments made under sick pay plans.
9. Withholding exemption certificates.
10. Agreements regarding the voluntary withholding of extra tax.
11. Dates and payments to employees for nonbusiness services.
12. Statements of tips received by employees.
13. Requests for different computation of withholding taxes.

Social Security (FICA) Tax Records

1. Amount of each payment subject to FICA tax.
2. Amount and date of FICA tax collected from each payment.
3. Explanation for the difference, if any.

Federal Unemployment Tax (FUTA) Records

1. Total amount paid during calendar year.
2. Amount subject to unemployment tax.
3. Amount of contributions paid into the state unemployment fund.
4. Any other information requested on the unemployment tax return.

Records supporting the items on a federal tax return should be kept until the statute of limitations (ordinarily three years after the return is due) expires. Records relating to depreciable property should be retained for as long as they are useful in determining the cost basis of the original or replacement property. Copies of federal income tax returns should be kept forever; they may even be helpful to the executor of the businessman's estate.

Coping with Government Paperwork

The number of forms to be filled out, taxes to be paid, and reports to be filed by even the smallest of businesses is almost overwhelming—enough to make an ordinary person (who is nearly driven up the wall by his annual federal and state income tax returns) cry. Enough, in fact, to make the hardiest of businessmen cry.

Every government entity, bureau, or agency that has any legal jurisdiction whatsoever over the business requires that *something* be submitted in writing, usually accompanied by a payment on a monthly, quarterly, or annual basis.

If more could, they would. If a new football stadium is to be built, new taxes on business are proposed to build it; if a major convention is coming to town, assessments on businesses are proposed to help finance it; if there were any way for the local baseball team to levy a franchise tax on small businessmen, it would probably try.

Since the list of taxes, licenses, regulations, and reports is virtually endless, any such list cannot possibly be complete. For example, the authors of this book, who own and operate a small retail business with one full-time paid employee, are subject to the following:

Description	*Frequency*
Federal	
Income tax	Annually
Estimated income tax deposits	Quarterly
Self-employment tax	Annually
Income tax withholding	Annually
Income tax withholding deposits	Quarterly
FICA (social security) tax	Annually
FICA tax deposits	Quarterly
FUTA (unemployment) tax	Annually
FUTA tax deposits	Quarterly
State	
Income tax (state of residence)	Annually
Income tax (state in which business is located)	Annually
Estimated income tax (state of residence)	Quarterly
Estimated income tax (state in which business is located)	Quarterly
Withholding tax	Annually
Withholding tax deposits	Quarterly
Sales tax	Quarterly
Conservation tax	Quarterly
Retail sales license	Once, when business starts
Report on unemployment experience	Annually

Description	Frequency
County	
Personal property business tax	Annually
Merchants inventory tax	Annually
Merchants license	Annually
City	
Sales tax	Quarterly
Transportation tax	Quarterly
Earnings tax	Annually
Earnings tax withholding	Quarterly
Business earnings and profits tax	Annually
Business personal property tax	Annually
Occupational license	Annually
Other	
Sales report to landlord	Monthly

The 30 items require the completion of a total of 76 forms a year. For a larger business, most of the quarterly returns must be filed monthly, bringing the total to 172 forms annually.

These taxes are all directly attributable to owning a small business and are in addition to the real estate, personal property, intangibles, and other taxes required of the general public.

The title of this section is perhaps misleading, since there is no way to cope adequately with these time- and money-consuming chores. Some small businesses employ bookkeeping services to handle the paperwork of this type; however, most of the forms are not difficult to complete, and the problem is more emotional than real. The most important requirement is to make a list of all the forms to be filed and the dates on which they are due; then set aside whatever time is necessary to complete them. Considerable time and effort can be saved by completing them all at once, since many of them call for the same basic information.

Inventory Planning and Control

Inventory planning and control are concerned with having exactly the right amount of exactly the right merchandise on hand at exactly the right time. The right amount, in most cases, is only a little more than what can be sold. Having a little too much of an item only costs a little money;

having less than enough not only loses sales, it can lose customers. Inventory control is tied closely to the merchandise planning and purchasing functions.

The seasonal demands of the business dictate effective inventory planning. Most retail and many service businesses exhibit certain predictable seasonal patterns, and it is these patterns that must be taken into account to prevent excessive inventory buildups or shortages.

Retail trade in general is highly sensitive to certain gift-oriented holidays such as Valentine's Day, Easter, Mother's Day, Father's Day, graduation, and Christmas. With the possible exception of Christmas, over 90 percent of the sales specifically attributable to a particular occasion occur during the four weeks prior to the occasion. Merchants who depend on the sales of merchandise appropriate to the occasion (candy for Valentine's Day, flowers for Mother's Day, neckties for Father's Day, toys for Christmas, etc.) must therefore plan their inventories carefully. Figures 8, 9, and 10 show the percentage of total seasonal sales during the eight weeks prior to these major "holidays."

This type of information for the appropriate seasons and merchandise lines handled, plus a knowledge of the necessary time lapse between ordering and receiving the merchandise, enable the retailer to plan his inventory requirements.

Once the merchandise is in the shop, it is important to keep track of it. Stock control requires that some records be kept so that the stock can be kept in balance—neither too large nor too small—with a proper proportion and an adequate assortment of sizes, colors, styles, qualities, prices, and so on. Knowing the customers in the shop's trade area is, of course, the most important factor. If it is properly maintained, the inventory control system provides a useful guide to what, from whom, when, and how much to buy.

An inventory control system offers several important benefits to the business owner, whether it is a simple listing of what is in stock, when it was bought, and from whom it was bought, or consists of a complex computerized program. Either way, it

- Produces sales histories of individual items or merchandise lines
- Provides the information needed to generate general inventory reports
- Enables the owner to analyze sales areas by major categories to aid in purchasing
- Facilitates reordering of items running low in stock
- Helps in identifying slow-moving merchandise that should be marked down or returned to suppliers for credit

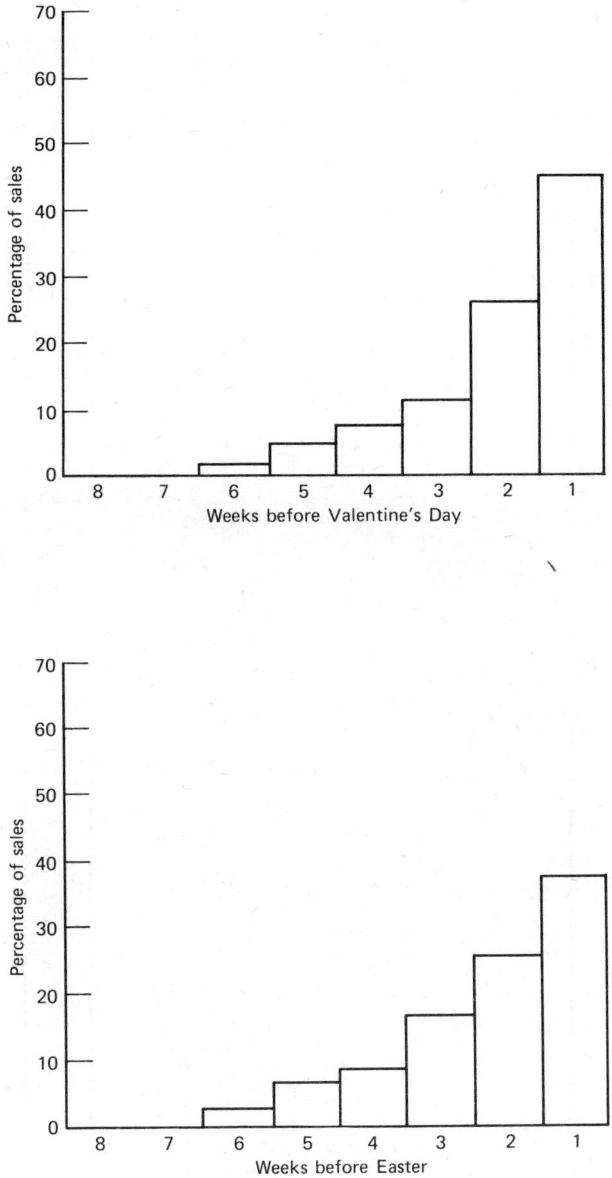

Figure 8. Percentage of seasonal sales taking place before Valentine's Day and Easter.

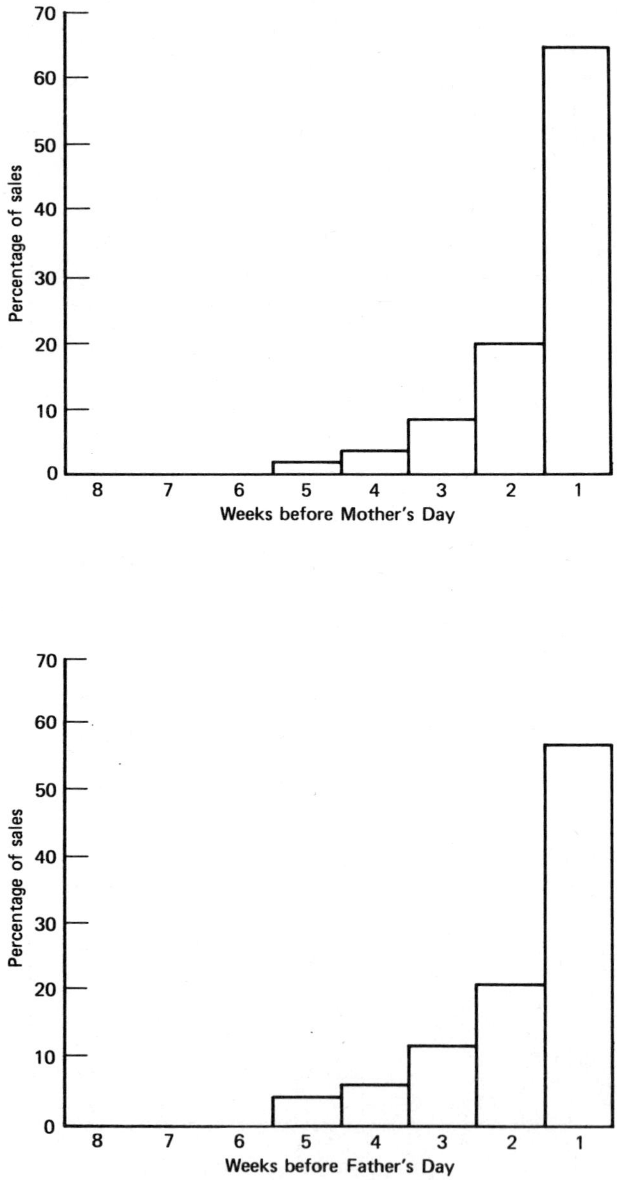

Figure 9. Percentage of seasonal sales taking place before Mother's Day and Father's Day.

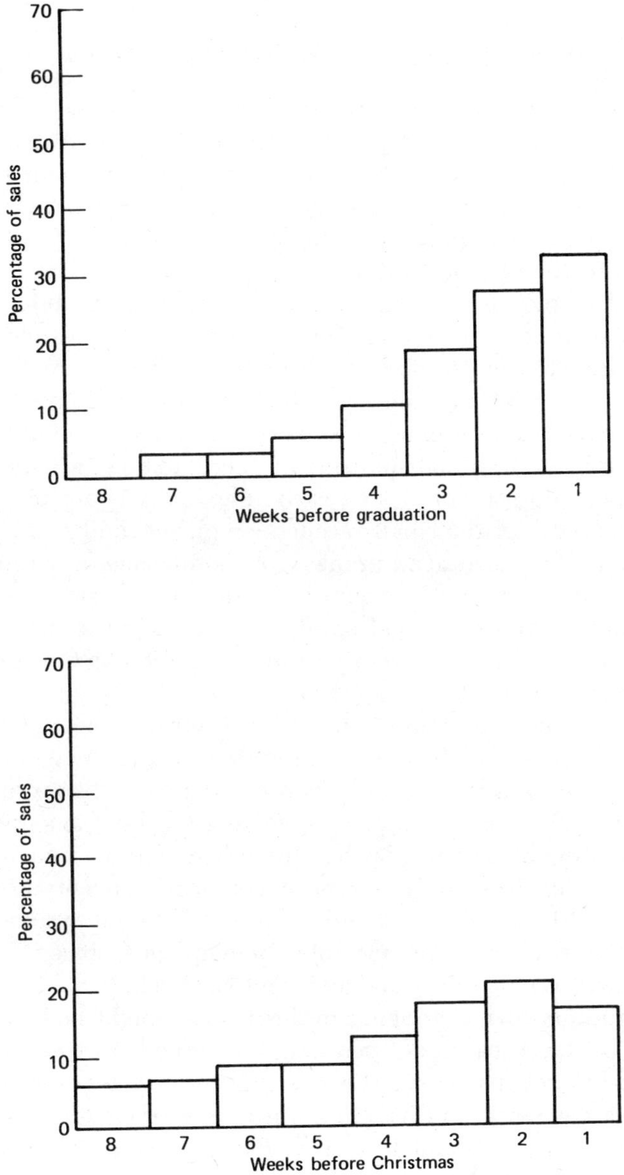

Figure 10. Percentage of seasonal sales taking place before graduation and Christmas.

Personnel Policies and Fringe Benefits

Employment in a small independent business often provides a second source of family income or a part-time occupation. In either case, it need not constitute a primary family-supporting income. For this reason, both pay scales and fringe benefits are generally low. What is lacking in direct benefits is somewhat offset by the opportunity for a flexible working schedule and the pleasant, intimate environment of the small shop. Even so, a good employee is a tremendous business asset, and the total job package should be made as attractive as economically possible.

The first step in establishing personnel policies is to define exactly what is expected of the employee in terms of job responsibilities and working hours. If the business is to be open from 9:00 am to 6:00 pm, for example, it is essential that someone be there; untold customer ill will results from opening late or closing early. Flexibility is one of the most important attributes of the small business employee, and employee participation should be encouraged in many of the management functions such as merchandise planning, inventory control, purchasing decisions, and promotional activities. A good employee gets to know the customers as well as or better than the owner and must function as the store manager in the owner's absence.

Employee compensation can take the form of a straight salary, a straight commission, with wages computed as a percentage of sales, or a combination of salary and commission or salary and bonus arrangement. The straight salary is the simplest, involving the least amount of clerical work. The straight commission has the advantage of reducing fixed expenses, but this form of payment encourages concentration on high-priced and fast-moving merchandise. A combination system frequently works well, especially if there is only one employee, since it provides the employee with a base salary and an incentive to sell.

The authors' own experience in this respect might be helpful. During the first Christmas season of operation, part-time help was added to handle the additional customers. However, the part-time employees had difficulty locating stock and assisting customers efficiently, and the additional expense was difficult to justify. For the second Christmas season, the one full-time employee was put on an incentive payment plan, with the regular straight-time base salary plus a small percentage of sales over a certain daily amount. This system worked so well that it has been continued, and no other paid help has been needed. The owners and the employee are equally pleased with a busy day.

Fringe benefits are usually minimal in the small independent business and may consist of nothing more than paid vacation and holiday time. Pension and retirement plans can be handled individually if desired through an Independent Retirement Account (IRA) or Keogh Plan. The IRA allows any wage earner who is not covered by a company pension plan to establish one for himself; up to $1500 per year or 15 percent of his wages, whichever is less, can be put into an IRS-approved account without current income tax liability.

Small group health, accident, and life insurance programs are available, but they are usually expensive, and comparable coverage is often available through trade associations and other organizations.

Business Security

Many individuals and organizations are determined to separate the small business owner from his money. Some of the major threats take the form of pilferage, embezzlement, shoplifting, burglary, robbery, bad checks, and fraudulent solicitations.

Pilferage refers to the petty theft of parts, supplies, or store furnishings by employees or customers. If an employee steals office supplies, it is pilferage; if he steals cash, it is embezzlement. If a customer steals your ashtray, it is pilferage; if he steals merchandise, it is shoplifting. Pilferage is very difficult to control. Internal controls may reduce employee pilferage, but the opportunities to control customer pilferage are limited. All that can be done is to estimate the losses due to pilferage and include them in the overall cost structure of the business.

Embezzlement refers to stealing anything entrusted to one's care; it can range from a cashier or salesperson who takes money from the cash register to a bookkeeper (or partner) who "juggles the books." Probably the most common form of embezzlement in the small independent business is the clerk who pockets the cash from a sale, without ringing it up on the cash register, or rings up only part of a sale and pockets the rest. Fake refund slips—in which the cashier picks up a discarded cash register receipt, puts it back into the register along with a refund slip, and takes the refund himself—may also be a problem.

"Book juggling" involves a number of more sophisticated techniques. Lapping refers to the practice of stealing cash from a customer's account, then covering the theft with another theft from another account, with the practice continually escalating in amount and number of accounts involved, until the embezzler is finally unable to cover one of the thefts and is caught. Check kiting involves a similar procedure, using checks and bank accounts. A check is cashed and covered by a check drawn on another bank, which in turn is covered by a check drawn on still another bank. Lapping can sometimes continue for years, but check kiting is usually detected fairly quickly unless the money taken initially can be returned before the banks' accounting systems catch up with the perpetrator.

Other embezzlement techniques include payroll padding (adding a fictitious name to the payroll and collecting his wages), the use of dummy suppliers, where fictitious supplies are paid for with real money, and conspiracies between purchasing agents and suppliers, where goods may be contracted for at inflated prices, with part of the purchase price "kicked back" to the purchasing agent. Above all, embezzlement control requires that the business owner know his employees. He should carefully audit all financial statements, bank statements, deposit slips, and checks; he should handle his own mail and bank deposits and watch merchandise returns and credits closely.

Shoplifting accounts for about 35 percent of all merchandise shrinkage (inventory shortages from all causes) and can amount to as much as five percent of a retail store's total sales. Women's clothing stores are especially hard hit by shoplifters. Shoplifters come in different types, ranging from professionals to juveniles. The main deterrent to shoplifting is eternal vigilance—keep all customers and all merchandise under constant surveillance. This can be accomplished by using strategically located convex surveillance mirrors, two-way mirrors, closed circuit television, and trained sales clerks. Small and expensive merchandise should be kept where it is visible but not accessible to customers except with employee assistance, and larger items might be tethered or otherwise secured. Protective devices such as electronic-coded sales tags (which trigger an alarm if the tagged merchandise leaves the area without removal of the tag) are often used on expensive clothing items.

Burglary poses a threat to almost any business, even those whose merchandise would be awkward to move and difficult to resell. Good locks, good lighting, and good visibility into the store provide the main deterrents to burglary. Cash should not be left in the store, nor should valuable merchandise be left in a display window. Burglaries can be discouraged or detected but not prevented; a display window can be smashed and a large part of a store's most valuable contents removed so rapidly that, even with an alarm system, the thieves can be gone before the police can react. However, alarm systems are useful in deterring burglars (especially if the windows and doors are marked with labels declaring that an alarm system is protecting the premises) and will, at the very least, unnerve a burglar who enters the building and sets off a siren. Burglar alarm systems range from very simple to very complex, and their selection depends on exactly what is hoped to be accomplished. The cost of protecting a small business with an alarm system can range from several hundred dollars for an ultrasonic motion detector (which sets off a siren when any motion occurs within its range) to several thousand dollars for total perimeter protection capable of detecting a prowler before he gains entrance to the premises.

Robbery is the greatest threat of all, since it involves the possibility of physical injury or death not only to the business' employees, but also to the customers present. Except in very unusual situations, police recommend that robbery victims follow orders; do not fight or argue with the robber, cooperate quickly and try to avoid any surprises that might startle him, and as soon as he leaves, stay in the store and call the police. Try to write down an accurate description of the robber, noting his height, weight, coloring, clothing, mannerisms, and any other characteristics that might help in identification. Liquor stores, drug stores, convenience food stores, and service stations are among the small businesses most susceptible to armed robberies because of their locational characteristics and operating schedules. Cash should be kept to a minimum, good visibility from the outside should be maintained, and, if possible, customer access to the merchandise should be kept high and access to the employee limited. For vulnerable businesses in high-risk locations, then, the self-service concept should be employed to the greatest extent possible. The employee should be isolated and protected and the store access limited (such as by electric push-button door locks). The guiding principle in any robbery situation is, do not risk a life to save money or merchandise.

Bad checks can be a problem in any retail business, with the type of merchandise and the type of neighborhood having a strong influence on the magnitude of the problem. Cashing a check is a function of banks; the small retail business should not get involved in this at all. Personal checks should be accepted only for the amount of the purchase, only when drawn on local banks, and only with proper identification (driver's license, auto registration, or credit cards). The customer's name, address, and telephone number should be on the check; this information is also useful in adding names to the business' mailing list. An upper limit should be set on check amounts, and all checks received should be deposited immediately. If a check is returned marked "insufficient funds," it can be redeposited over and over until it finally clears.

Fraudulent solicitations include requests for payments, contributions, and advertising. Most of these solicitations come by telephone; some may be legitimate, but many are not. Every organization seems to publish some type of yearbook or magazine, but some organizations publish only for the purpose of selling advertising space. Others sell tickets or subscriptions, with only a small part of the receipts used for any charitable purpose. There is no way a small business can subscribe or contribute to all such requests for donations. The businessman should decide for himself which causes he wishes to support, and he should not be intimidated into supporting unknown organizations. Before making any donation for a supposedly charitable purpose, always insist that the request be submitted in writing, with a description of the organization's use of the funds collected. If a donation is to be made, make sure it is provided for in the business' budget and made at the business' convenience. Do not fall for the approach, "we'll have a man in your neighborhood this afternoon to pick up your check and leave your membership card" (or decal, or badge, or anything else).

Making Your Advertising Pay

Effective advertising requires that the advertiser know three things:

1. The product, or *what* is to be advertised
2. The market, or *who* will buy it and *when* they will buy it
3. The media, or *how* the market can be reached with the product information

The problems that face the small business in its advertising are not the same as those of large businesses; thus a different advertising strategy is required. The main differences are in the size of the respective trade areas and the amount of money available for advertising.

Large mass merchandisers, with stores located in major regional shopping centers throughout a metropolitan area, can blanket the entire area with their advertising campaigns; the small business, with a single shop location, can draw customers only from a small geographic area. The large business may have $30,000 or more a month with which to promote its merchandise and corporate image; the small business may be hard pressed to raise a tenth of that amount for its total annual advertising activities, with one-fourth or more already commited to its listing in the classified telephone directory.

For the small business, the choice of advertising media is severely limited, making it especially important that every advertising dollar be spent wisely.

The media available for advertising include

- Television
- Radio

- Metropolitan daily newspapers
- Suburban weekly or biweekly newspapers
- Direct mail
- Magazines
- Classified telephone directory
- Local school and organization publications
- Specialties (calendars, matchbook covers, pens, etc.)
- Printed inserts (sack stuffers)
- Bags and boxes with store imprint
- Signs

Television offers wide exposure at high cost; its cost effectiveness for the small business is low. The same is true of metropolitan daily newspapers unless they include a special regional section that emphasizes the specific trade area of the business.

The effectiveness of radio advertising varies; if the station is oriented toward a particular type of listener or special interest (classical music, business news, sports, etc.), it may be worthwhile for businesses dealing in those markets to advertise, provided the advertising message is aired at the right time, preferably during "driving time."

Suburban newspapers offer good coverage of local trade areas, but many have questionable readership; they may also provide for printed inserts or delivery of handbills to homes and businesses in specified areas. Local magazines of special interest (society, hobbies, sports, etc.) sometimes have good readership and favorable rates, as do publications sponsored by schools, local clubs, and other organizations.

Although there may be considerable disagreement on this point, the authors' own experience has shown two media to be the most effective: the classified telephone directory (the "Yellow Pages") and direct mail.

The classified telephone directory is one of the few "buying" directories available to the general public. In it the small business can project whatever image it wishes; here it can compete equally with big businesses within its trade area. According to surveys, 81 percent of the adult population of the United States use the Yellow Pages each year, averaging 34 uses per person; 84 percent of these references are followed up by action in the form of a phone call or visit. Prospective customers generally look under a product or service heading in the directory and begin calling the advertisers located closest to them, buying from the first one with the desired merchandise or service. Since the directory is usually published only once a year, it is important to be sure that the listing is contracted for prior to the closing date for advertising.

Direct mail is a very cost effective means of reaching customers with an advertising message. Depending on the type of material sent out, the cost ranges from a few cents up (plus the postage cost). In direct mail, the objectives are to get the prospect to (1) open it, (2) read the message, and (3) take action. Standard-size envelopes should be used and weight kept to a minimum to avoid excessive postage costs. The message might concern a special promotion, merchandise of special seasonal interest, or imprinted catalogs and product information.

A good mailing list is the key to successful direct mail advertising. The best mailing list is generally made up of the business' own customers. By taking names and addresses from customer's checks or simply by asking them for their names and addresses, a mailing list can be built up quickly and efficiently. The names should be filed alphabetically to avoid duplication (3 by 5 inch index cards are useful for this purpose). The mailers can be addressed by hand directly from this file until the list size becomes unmanageable; then some type of automatic addressing system may be justified, especially if mailings are conducted with any frequency.

The importance of a sign cannot be overemphasized; this is the shop's only means of communication with outside traffic. The sign should clearly identify the business and describe the merchandise or services offered. This, coupled with the window display, is the only way that people who are not already aware of the business and its services can be brought inside the premises, where interior displays and promotional ideas can be used to make a sale and create a new customer.

Retailers normally spend between one and five percent of their total annual sales receipts on advertising, with the percentage varying widely according to the size and type of business. Small businesses spend a higher percentage, as do stores in less favorable locations, new or expanding stores, stores stressing price appeal, and stores that face especially stiff competition.

However, spending five percent of sales receipts on advertising does not necessarily mean that each dollar spent on advertising returns $20 in sales. In other words, you can spend $5 out of every $100 you earn, but that does not mean that you can earn $100 for every $5 you spend.

Advertising pays only if it nets the advertiser more money than it costs. For example, a business operating with a variable cost ratio of 0.80 (80 percent) needs sales of $5 for every dollar spent to break even on the expenditure (see Chapter 6 for the arithmetic). In this case, as long as each dollar spent on advertising brings in more than $5 in additional sales, it pays to continue the advertising.

Knowing when to advertise is as important as knowing what, where, and how to advertise. All businesses are seasonal; people buy according to clearly predictable patterns. All advertising should be planned to take advantage of this predictability, offering the customers what they want when they want it. Most retail businesses exhibit a strong orientation toward the Christmas season; thus the bulk of their advertising takes place during November and December. On the other hand, if a store specializes in air conditioners or swimming suits, its advertising should be concentrated in the May–July period.

Advertising expenditures should follow roughly the same seasonal patterns as sales. To check the effectiveness of the timing of advertising expenditures, it is necessary only to calculate the percentages of total sales and total advertising expenditures for each month during the preceding year and to compare these monthly percentages. Months that show a higher percentage of sales receipts than advertising expenditures justify a larger proportion of the total advertising budget; the increased expenditures during these months should be balanced by cutting back on advertising during periods in which the percentage of advertising expenditures exceeds the percentage of sales receipts.

How to write good advertising copy for direct mail or other media is beyond the scope of this book. Several good references on the subject are cited in the appendix. These general principles should be kept in mind:

1. Keep it simple.
2. Make it look worthwhile.
3. Use a positive approach.
4. Use short sentences and familiar words.
5. Emphasize benefits.
6. Provide enough information on which to make a buying decision.
7. Specify the brand, model, and price.
8. Include the business name, address, and telephone number.
9. Encourage prompt action.
10. Do not exaggerate or make unbelievable claims.

Store Displays

The three important on-site selling tools for a retail business are

1. An eye-catching sign to alert passersby, either drivers or pedestrians, to the presence and location of the business.
2. An attractive window display, informing potential customers of the store's contents and encouraging them to enter.
3. An effective interior store display, creating an environment that puts customers in a buying mood.

The sign is the shop's only contact with much of the outside world. Although garish signs should generally be avoided unless garish merchandise is being sold, the sign should be sufficiently bright and conspicuous to attract attention and sufficiently informative to let prospective customers know what is there.

An effective window display can bring many people into the store by arousing their interest. Window displays are sometimes described as taking either a "shotgun" approach—exhibiting a little of everything—or a "rifle" approach, in which only a few specially selected items, subjects, or styles are covered in depth. Many stores employ a combination of these two approaches, prominently displaying seasonal merchandise or merchandise of current topical interest along with some stable items of continuing appeal.

The sign attracts attention, and the window display arouses interest; the interior store display must create the desire to buy.

The interior display and layout planning can be used effectively to introduce a new product, stimulate impulse buying, draw customers into the store, or trigger an emotional appeal. The layout should be designed with several objectives in mind. Expensive items should be kept highly visible but physically inaccessible to minimize the possibility of shoplifting or damage. Merchandise displayed within the store can be located to take advantage of the store's natural traffic flow or to encourage high traffic flow in certain areas. Some low-margin or promotional merchandise can be used effectively for this purpose, as can popular high-turnover or low-priced items, requiring customers to walk through areas containing more profitable merchandise displays.

Special Business Problems

Many of the frustrating problems that confront the small businessman have to do with demands on his limited resources—either his time or his money. Scarcely a day will pass without some smooth-talking salesman or solicitor attempting to separate the small businessman from his money.

Conferences with salesmen require a considerable amount of the small businessman's time. Those who represent the merchandise lines carried by the business cannot be considered a burden, since they represent one of the best sources of trade and product information. The time spent in selecting merchandise with a good sales representative is almost always worthwhile, even though these salesmen frequently arrive without appointment at inconvenient times.

A second category of salesmen may be selling anything from advertising to signs to burglar alarms. Some are reluctant to leave if given the slightest encouragement; interest should be carefully concealed unless the product is something really needed. Even so, decisions should be avoided until the proposal can be considered objectively, in private, and at the businessman's convenience; any pressure for an on-the-spot financial commitment should be rejected.

A third category is made up of high-pressure door-to-door salesmen who are oblivious to the real needs of the business but concentrate on selling unwanted products or services to small businesses. They travel individually or in pairs and can be identified by their large briefcases, sample cases, or cardboard cartons. Again, no encouragement should even be hinted except encouragement to leave the premises.

Probably the most irritating salesmen of all are those who come in masquerading as customers, browsing, asking questions about the merchandise, and then launching a high-pressure sales pitch. The immediate impulse is to throw them out bodily, but making it obvious that their efforts will be completely futile is the only rational countertactic.

Unpleasant customers must be tolerated to a certain degree; complaints about merchandise or prices are normal to the business. Above all, the salesperson should not prolong the unpleasantness by arguing with the customer, although referral to a competitor's shop might be considered acceptable.

The small business is solicited by many charities and organizations seeking donations of cash or merchandise. All requests for cash donations should be submitted in writing, describing the use to be made of the collected funds; this policy discourages the less-than-legitimate operators, and the rest can be looked over and a decision made on whether or how much to donate.

Requests for merchandise donations are usually legitimate; they are often for a local charity auction or similar purpose. Some inexpensive but representative merchandise might be kept on hand for this purpose.

Paperwork—paying the bills, making out bank deposit slips, compiling customer mailing lists, filling out government forms, and so on—can best be accomplished when the business is closed. Much routine work of this kind can be accomplished by arriving an hour or so before opening time and ignoring the ringing telephone except during regular business hours.

Specially ordered merchandise can be a problem if the customer fails to pick it up; the merchant may find himself stuck with some weird size, color, or type of merchandise that is virtually unsellable. A small deposit on specially ordered merchandise usually ensures pickup by the customer.

Finding time for a vacation, or even for lunch or going to the bathroom, can be a real problem in a one-person business. The only way to get away for a vacation, even for just a day or two, is to close the business. A sign posted in the door or window well in advance of the closing period should warn customers, and the vacation should be planned during a slack business season. It must be remembered, however, that the vacation costs the small businessman double—in added expense and lost income.

For the small business with relatively few customers, taking a lunch or restroom break poses no problem, but for a small shop with customers on the premises all day, it can be physically agonizing. The cardinal rule is to "do it fast whenever you get a chance; don't wait until you have to!"

One advantage of the small independent business is that the owner can set his own operating schedule. If business activity drops to nothing late on Saturday afternoon, he can schedule his business to close early on Saturday afternoons, or if customers do not begin shopping in the area until late in the morning, he can schedule his opening for late morning. If other businesses in the immediate area stay open late, he can do it or not, as he chooses, after determining the business potential for the extended hours.

Once an operating schedule is established, it is essential to stay with the schedule. If a customer arrives five minutes before the scheduled closing time and finds that the owner has left early, the customer is justifiably angry and possibly lost forever as a customer.

Solving Business Problems

Problems are bound to arise in any new business. Some require immediate action; others can be delayed. If the businessman felt guilty about every bad decision he made or worried about whether he was going to make the right decisions in the future, he would quickly become ineffective at tending to today's business. Establishing general policies to handle routine problems associated with day-to-day operations relieves the businessman of much of the pressure. If the policies are made clear and in writing, an employee can handle them without difficulty or an immediate decision can be postponed "because of company policy" until it can be studied in greater depth.

Few important business decisions need be made in immediate response to a telephone request or the presence of a salesman or solicitor. Procrastination in doing stupid things is a virtue, and many stupid things that might be done on the spur of the moment can be avoided with just a little thought.

When something important does come up, it should be approached systematically. This approach works well:

1. Write it down.
2. Gather additional information on the subject.
3. Consider new or different ways to handle the problem.
4. Try out whatever looks good.
5. Adopt whatever works best.

This approach may not result in the best solution to every problem, but it is certain to avoid the worst. The difference between success and failure in business is the difference between being right 51 percent of the time instead of 49 percent of the time.

5
The Economics of Small Business

People don't plan to fail; they just fail to plan.

The economics of small businesses are essentially the same as the economics of big businesses, differing chiefly in terms of the scale of operations and the scope of individual responsibilities. This chapter explores some of the important economic characteristics of small businesses, especially those characteristics unique to small businesses, explaining why some businesses succeed and others fail.

What Happens to Most Small Businesses

Small businesses are more likely to fail than large ones, new businesses are more likely to fail than old ones, and independent businesses are more apt to fail than those affiliated with national chains or franchises. What chance, then, does a small new independent business have?

Very little; most fail.

Some fail for financial reasons, and others are closed for other reasons, but either way only about half of the independent businesses started manage to survive for more than two years. More than one-third of the new independent businesses never make it beyond a year.

Figure 11 shows the survival rate for new businesses, indicating the percentage of the businesses surviving at various stages during their critical first two years of operation.

These data do not correspond to published figures on business failures, but are based on surveys of new small independent businesses. According to published reports, about 10,000 businesses fail each year. However, many of the discontinued small businesses never become sta-

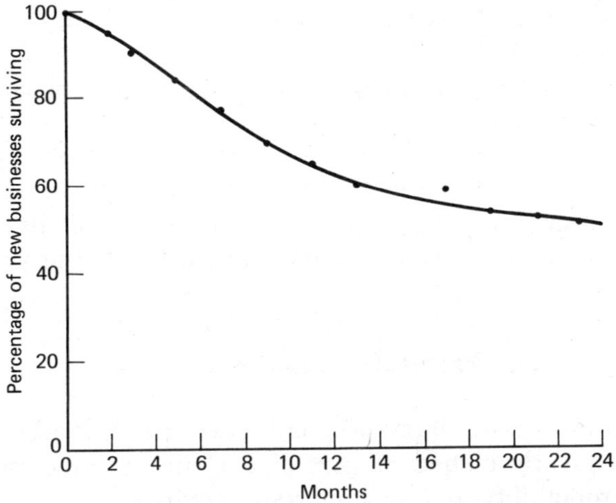

Figure 11. Survival rate for new independent businesses.

tistics; they come and go before they can even be counted. Others may give the impression of continuity even though they are failures in reality. Some are sold to another prospective but uninformed businessman who fails to realize that the business lacks sufficient economic justification to warrant its continued operation. In such cases the same business may continue for some time, periodically injected with fresh capital.

All new businesses can be classified into one of seven broad categories based on their early performance.

1. *Stillbirths* are those firms that close within their first two months of operation. Their demise is almost wholly attributable to bad management and poor preparation.

2. *Infant deaths* refer to businesses that struggle through their first year before giving up. A poor location or merchandise not suited to the trade area are typical reasons for failure.

3. A business that makes it through the first year but succumbs during the next year is classified as a *lost cause.* Overestimating sales potential or underestimating costs are among the contributing causes of failure.

4. The *marginal survivors* manage to cover their costs of operation and continue their existence, but fail to provide their owners with a reasonable living. The owners of these establishments often have an independent source of outside income.

5. *Limited successes* offer their owners about the same income that they could have earned by working as an employee in some other business. Their continued survival depends on the degree of personal satisfaction felt by the owners.

6. *Potentially profitable businesses* provide their owners with a respectable living and show promise of enabling them to earn a reasonable return on their invested capital. Good management can make this business successful.

7. *Profitable enterprises* allow their owners to draw management-level salaries and in addition generate an attractive return on investment. With continued good management, appropriate merchandise, and strong markets, the profitable enterprise should expand and prosper.

Characteristics of Successful Businesses

All successful businesses—large or small, new or old, local or national in scope, independently owned or part of a chain or franchise—owe their success and profitability to three important factors:

1. Good management
2. Appropriate merchandise, products, or services for their trade area
3. An adequate market demand within their trade area for whatever they are selling

A weakness in any one of these three categories may not necessarily mean failure, but it most certainly stands in the way of success. There are millions of marginal firms in the United States that owe their positions to mediocrity or worse in one or more of these three areas.

The strengths in these three areas are ultimately reflected in the growth and profitability of the business. Table 7 shows some of the characteristics of the most successful regional general merchandisers.

TABLE 7
Characteristics of the Most Successful Large Regional General Merchandisers

Characteristic	*Range*
Sales per employee	$30,000–45,000
Return on net worth	12–20%
Return on total assets	6–15%
Inventory/sales ratio	15–25%
Annual sales growth	12–40%
Annual growth in profits	15–35%

As shown in Table 7, successful retail firms are characterized by

- High sales per employee, indicating efficient employment of manpower.
- A high percentage return on net worth, making the business an attractive investment for its owners.
- A good return on total assets, showing that the firm's resources are being utilized effectively.
- A low inventory/sales ratio, reflecting good merchandise planning and control.
- Healthy growth in both sales and profits, showing that management is successful in bringing the merchandise and markets together.

Good management must span three eras: the past, the present, and the future. The effective manager must analyze the past so that he can understand the present and predict the future. From knowledge (of the past) comes understanding (of the present), and from understanding comes wisdom (to antipicate and plan for the future).

A new business obviously presents a much greater challenge than an existing one. In addition to the obstacles presented by offering an untried product or service to an undeveloped or untested market, management may lack the body of past experience-based knowledge on which to base a sound business plan.

Basic Economic Considerations

Getting down to the basic economic considerations of business enterprise, there are two items of utmost importance: income and expense. Overestimating income and/or underestimating expenses have probably caused the demise of more businesses, especially new ones, than any other management fault. It is essential to know not only how much, but also how, income is produced and expenses are incurred.

Many service businesses are characterized by high fixed costs and low variable costs, with one of the most important overhead items being the cost of unutilized employee (or owner) time. This is as true for a barber as it is for a consulting engineer. In contrast, most manufacturing, wholesaling, and retailing operations have high variable costs and low fixed costs.

The variable cost rate of a business—the ratio of total variable costs to total business receipts—is particularly important, since it determines the breakeven point and defines the amount of profit to be made at any sales volume above the breakeven point (or the amount of loss to be incurred at any sales volume below the breakeven point). The economics of business in general can be summed up in one short, simple formula:

$$\text{Breakeven point} = \frac{\text{Fixed costs}}{1.0 - \text{Variable cost rate}}$$

In this equation, the fixed costs and the variable cost rate are called, in technical terms, the independent variables; they vary according to the type of business, the kinds of merchandise carried, locational factors, and how well management is able to control costs.

The sales volume required to break even is called the dependent variable; it is a calculated amount, totally dependent on the values of the two independent variables.

If fixed costs are expressed in total, the breakeven point is also a total amount; if fixed costs are expressed in dollars per square foot, the breakeven point defines the sales per square foot required to break even.

If the actual sales per square foot (or total sales) of a business are higher than the amount calculated from its fixed expense and variable cost rate, the business is making a profit; if actual sales per square foot (or total sales) are lower than the calculated value, the business is losing money.

The three legs of the stool are again brought to mind here:

- Sales per square foot depend on the *market.*
- The variable cost rate is determined by the *merchandise.*
- Fixed costs are controlled by *management.*

Sales Intensity and Store Size

The characteristics of the market for the products, services, or merchandise offered by a business determine how much is sold within a given trade area. It is important that the total sales potential within the area be considered in choosing an appropriate store size. A store that occupies 10,000 square feet of floor space, for example, sells no more than one that occupies 2000 square feet if the market is not there for its merchandise; it only spreads the same total sales volume over a larger area.

Small retail businesses typically occupy less than 10,000 square feet. Table 8 shows the range of sizes.

As indicated in Table 8, 70 percent of the small independent retail and service businesses operate with 2500 square feet or less. In contrast,

TABLE 8
Typical Shop Size for Small Independent Retail and Service Businesses

Size (sq. ft.)	*Businesses (%)*
1000 and under	17.5
1000–1500	18.8
1500–2000	25.0
2000–2500	10.0
2500–3000	7.5
3000–3500	2.5
3500–4000	7.5
4000 and over	11.2
Total	100

major department stores in regional shopping centers often occupy 100,000 square feet or more. The average small business probably leases around 2000 square feet.

The store size, coupled with the intensity of sales (measured in dollars per square foot), determines the total sales of a business. Table 9 shows the average sales per square foot in major shopping centers throughout the United States.

TABLE 9
Average Sales per Square Foot in Major Regional Shopping Centers

Sales per Square Foot (in dollars)	*Major Shopping Centers (%)*
56–60	7.0
61–65	7.0
66–70	10.5
71–75	15.1
76–80	9.3
81–85	18.6
86–90	12.8
81–95	11.6
96 and over	8.1
Total	100

Significant variations in sales per square foot occur among different shopping centers in the same metropolitan area, as well as between different cities. The overall average is approximately $80 per square foot.

Before making any major commitment, the prospective small business owner should carefully review the sales intensity of any shopping center under consideration as a possible location. Even if the business is one that typically generates high sales per square foot, it is difficult to do so in a shopping center in which high sales per square foot are uncommon.

Fixed Costs

Fixes costs are related to the capacity or availability to do business. These costs are incurred with time, regardless of the amount of sales.

The main items that go into determining fixed expenses are space charges and fixed payroll costs. Space charges refer primarily to rent and utilities; they must be paid on a monthly basis even if the business has no customers.

Fixed payroll costs represent the minimum number of employees that must be there to be ready to do business. For a business to be open, regardless of its size, it must have at least one person in attendance. A store that occupies a large amount of floor space probably requires more than one person at least part of the time. Table 10 is presented as a rough guide for estimating the basic manpower requirements for retail stores.

The minimum number of employees required for stores of various sizes shown in Table 10 assumes only a 40 hour per week operating schedule. In practice, the owner or owners may represent the only employees; nevertheless, their time should be charged in the same manner and at the same hourly rate as if they were hired employees. In certain types of businesses, especially those with relatively few but large sales, such as furniture and major appliances, the fixed payroll can be lower than shown; others, with many small sales, require more.

The second important factor that influences fixed expenses—space charges—can be estimated accurately in advance. The rent is established in the lease agreement, and estimates of utility costs can be obtained directly from the utility companies, the landlord, or other tenants in the area.

Other fixed expenses include depreciation, insurance, some taxes, advertising, and a variety of other items that are incurred regularly regardless of the amount of business conducted.

The total fixed costs experienced by small independent retail and

TABLE 10
Minimum Employee Requirements for Various Retail Store Sizes

Store Size (sq. ft.)	*Minimum Number of Employees Required*
1,000 or less	1.0
1,500	1.3
2,000	1.6
2,500	1.9
3,000	2.1
3,500	2.4
4,000	2.7
4,500	2.9
5,000	3.1
6,000	3.5
7,000	3.9
8,000	4.3
9,000	4.7
10,000	5.0
11,000	5.3
12,000	5.7

service businesses, expressed in dollars per square foot, are shown in Table 11. Most small businesses have total fixed expenses between $10 and $25 per square foot, averaging about $17. Of this total, from $4 to $8 are for fixed payroll expense.

The Variable Cost Rate

In retail business, the most important variable cost is the cost of the merchandise sold; this is usually from 50 to 75 percent of the selling price of the merchandise.

Items other than the purchase price enter into the cost of goods sold. Transportation charges and losses due to breakage, spoilage, theft, markdowns, and other forms of shrinkage increase the direct cost of the merchandise and reduce profit margins.

The next most important element of variable cost is the variable payroll. This refers to the additional employees (beyond those required to keep the business open for a minimum number of hours per year) needed

TABLE 11
Typical Fixed Costs for Small Independent Retail and Service Businesses

Annual Fixed Costs per Square Foot (in dollars)	*Businesses (%)*
Under 10	2.5
10–15	31.2
15–20	40.0
20–25	12.5
25–30	6.3
Over 30	7.5
Total	100

to handle additional sales volume or to keep the business open for longer hours or additional days. Also included in the variable cost rate are certain discretionary expenses that can be controlled by management but are generally related to the amount of business volume. Advertising, for example, may be budgeted at some percentage of sales; store supplies such as sacks and wrapping paper vary directly with sales, and some rental agreements call for payments based on a percentage of sales.

Table 12 shows the variable cost rates for a variety of small retail and service businesses.

Most businesses have variable cost rates between 0.6 and 0.8, with the average for retail businesses falling in the 0.70 to 0.75 range.

TABLE 12
Typical Variable Cost Rates for Small Indepedent Retail and Service Businesses

Variable Cost Rate	*Businesses (%)*
0.400 and under	3.8
0.400–0.500	6.3
0.500–0.600	6.3
0.600–0.700	16.2
0.700–0.800	58.7
0.800–0.900	8.7
0.900 and over	0
Total	100

Breakeven Points for Small Businesses

Given the right combination of fixed expenses and variable cost rates, some small retail businesses can break even on sales of less than $40 per square foot; others may require more than $100 per square foot to reach their breakeven point. Table 13 shows how the breakeven requirements vary within this extreme range.

TABLE 13
Typical Breakeven Points for Small Independent Retail and Service Businesses

Breakeven Point of Annual Sales (in dollars/sq. ft.)	*Businesses (%)*
$40 and under	8.7
$40–50	16.3
$50–60	16.3
$60–70	18.7
$70–80	18.7
$80–90	8.7
$90–100	3.9
$100 and over	8.7
Total	100

About 70 percent of the small businesses included in this survey need sales of $40 to $80 per square foot to break even. Putting together a combination of typical store sizes and fixed expense and variable cost rates gives these results for a typical retail business:

Store size	2,000 sq. ft.
Sales intensity	$80/sq. ft.
Total sales	$160,000
Variable cost rate	0.75
Total variable cost	$120,000
Fixed cost rate	$17/sq. ft.
Total fixed expense	34,000
Total operating expense	$154,000
Net profit before taxes	$6,000

This "typical" operation's breakeven point can be calculated from the formula given earlier:

$$\text{Breakeven point} = \frac{\text{Fixed cost}}{1 - \text{Variable cost rate}}$$

$$= \frac{34{,}000}{1 - 0.75} = \$136{,}000$$

or

$$\frac{17.00}{1 - 0.75} = \$68/\text{sq. ft.}$$

The operating statement at the breakeven point would look like this:

Total sales	$136,000
Variable costs @ 75%	102,000
Fixed costs @ $17/sq. ft.	34,000
Total operating expense	$136,000
Net profit	0

On a per-square-foot basis, operations at the breakeven point would be

Sales per sq. ft.	$68.00
Variable costs per sq. ft.	51.00
Fixed costs per sq. ft.	17.00
Total expense per sq. ft.	$68.00
Net profit per sq. ft.	0

Table 14 is presented as an aid in determining the breakeven point, given different combinations of variable cost rates and fixed costs per square foot.

To use this table, it is necessary to determine the appropriate variable cost rate for the business under consideration and estimate the total fixed expense for the given location. From these two factors, Table 14 gives the total sales per square foot required to break even.

For example, suppose a person were considering opening a new retail store in a major regional shopping center. For the merchandise lines to be carried, manufacturers' discount schedules indicate that the base cost of goods sold would be 60 percent of the suggested selling price, with transportation costs and shrinkage adding another five percent. Other variable costs are estimated at five percent of sales, bringing the total variable cost rate to 70 percent, or 0.70. Rent is $8 per square foot,

TABLE 14
Total Sales per Square Foot Required to Break Even for Various Combinations of Fixed Expenses and Variable Cost Rates

Total Fixed Expense (dollars/ sq. ft.)	*Variable Cost Rate* 0.60	0.65	0.70	0.75	0.80	0.85	0.90
10	25	28.57	33.33	40	50	66.67	100
12	30	34.28	40.00	48	60	80.00	120
14	35	40.00	46.67	56	70	93.33	140
16	40	45.71	53.33	64	80	106.67	160
18	45	51.43	60.00	72	90	120.00	180
20	50	57.14	66.67	80	100	133.33	200
22	55	62.85	73.33	88	110	146.67	220
24	60	68.57	80.00	96	120	160.00	240
26	65	74.28	86.67	104	130	173.33	260
28	70	80.00	93.33	112	140	186.67	280
30	75	85.71	100.00	120	150	200.00	300

and utilities are estimated at $2 per square foot; two full-time employees keep the store open year-round at a cost of $8 per square foot; other fixed costs come to $4 per square foot. Total fixed costs, then, are $22 per square foot.

Referring to Table 14, reading across from the $22 fixed expense line to the 0.70 variable cost rate column gives a breakeven point of $73.33 per square foot.

The problem is considerably simplified now. The question is simply whether net sales of $73.33 can be achieved at the particular location. If tenants in the shopping center as a whole average, say, $90 per square foot and adjacent shops are doing well, the proposed venture shows merit, but if the average sales for the shopping center are only $65 per square foot, or if nearby shops are operating at below the calculated breakeven amount, a great deal of caution should be exercised before making any commitment.

Economics of Store Size and Sales Intensity

Businessmen sometimes think in strange ways. One of the strangest is the owner of an unprofitable or marginally profitable operation who feels that his business should be expanded by adding space. If the business is not profitable in its existing space, the reason for its not being profitable can seldom be attributed to the lack of space. If space is added, costs certainly go up, but sales do not necessarily increase.

Table 15 illustrates the effects of store size and sales intensity on profits. Three store sizes—1000, 2000, and 4000 square feet—are considered at sales intensities of $50, $100, and $200 per square foot. In each case, fixed costs of $12.50 per square foot are assumed, accompanied by a variable cost rate of 0.75.

TABLE 15
Economics of Store Size and Sales Intensity

		Sales per Square Foot	
	$50 ($1000)	$100 ($1000)	$200 ($1000)
1000 square foot store			
Total sales	50.0	100.0	200.0
Variable expense	37.5	75.0	150.0
Fixed expense	12.5	12.5	12.5
Total expense	50.0	87.5	162.5
Net profit	–0–	12.5	37.5
2000 square foot store			
Total sales	100.0	200.0	400.0
Variable expense	75.0	150.0	300.0
Fixed expense	25.0	25.0	25.0
Total expense	100.0	175.0	325.0
Net profit	–0–	25.0	75.0
4000 square foot store			
Total sales	200.0	400.0	800.0
Variable expense	150.0	300.0	600.0
Fixed expense	50.0	50.0	50.0
Total expense	200.0	350.0	650.0
Net profit	–0–	50.0	150.0

Here, under these assumptions, several important points become clear:

- Doubling the store size while maintaining the same intensity of sales will double profits.

- Doubling the sales intensity while maintaining the same store size will triple profits.
- Expanding the area occupied by a profitable business without increasing its total sales will greatly decrease the net profit.
- Most important, expanding the area occupied by an unprofitable small store will only result in an unprofitable large store.

The Chances of Success for New Businesses

As pointed out earlier, only about half of new independent businesses are able to survive for more than two years, and many of those that survive are only marginally successful. Unless a new business has some distinct competitive advantages with respect to its merchandise, management, or markets, its chances for success are slim.

By objectively evaluating the new business in terms of how favorably its merchandise, management, and market factors compare with competitive businesses, it is possible to predict with fair reliability the probability of the success of the business. Table 16 presents a rating scale for the three factors, showing the relative probability of business success associated with different performance levels for the merchandise, management, and market.

In using Table 16, each of the three factors must be assigned a rating, indicating whether the new business will be better than competition, equal to competition, or inferior to competition. The combination of these ratings determines the chance of success of the business.

If, for example, a new business is to offer the same merchandise (or service) as its competition and has no particular advantages in terms of management capabilities or market strength, it gets an "equal" in all three factors; its probability of success is found to be 25 percent, or one chance in four. If it has a definite advantage in one factor and equality in the other two, its chances for success increase to 40 percent. A competitive advantage in two factors and equality in the other gives a 60 percent chance of success. Only if the new business has an advantage over its competition in all three respects is it virtually assured of success.

The Business Plan

The business plan (or business strategy) goes back to the concept of the three-legged stool, in which the three legs represent the foundations on which the success of any business is built:

TABLE 16
The Chances of Success for a New Retail or Service Business

Rating Factors[a]			
The Product, Service, or Merchandise	The Management	The Market	*Relative Probability of Business Success*
+	+	+	100
+	+	=	60
+	+	−	25
+	=	+	60
+	=	=	40
+	=	−	15
+	−	+	25
+	−	=	15
+	−	−	5
=	+	+	60
=	+	=	40
=	+	−	15
=	=	+	40
=	=	=	25
=	=	−	10
=	−	+	15
=	−	=	10
=	−	−	3
−	+	+	25
−	+	=	15
−	+	−	5
−	=	+	15
−	=	=	10
−	=	−	3
−	−	+	5
−	−	=	3
−	−	−	1

[a] + represents good, or better than competition;
= represents average, or equal to competition;
− represents poor, or inferior to competition.

1. The product, service, or merchandise offered
2. The market for that product, service, or merchandise
3. The management that matches the merchandise to the market or the market to the merchandise

Although a business plan can be designed to accommodate different goals depending on management's value judgments, the basic objectives of a good business plan should always include at least these two elements:

1. Stability, making sure that the three legs are all the same length; only when there is good balance in all three areas can efforts be directed effectively toward
2. Growth or entrenchment, or both, by proportionately lengthening and strengthening the three legs.

The merchandise, product, or service leg is lengthened by identifying additional products or services that can be offered to existing customers or clients in existing markets. The market leg's strength comes from bringing in new customers or clients for the firm's existing products or services, and the management leg is strengthened by improving management's ability to plan, organize, lead, and control, thus utilizing its available and potential resources to bring together the market and the product or service.

Formulating a business strategy simply involves setting realistic objectives and deciding exactly how to accomplish them, remembering that logic and reality do not always go together. This approach requires that the manager focus on the future as well as the present.

Obviously, before one can decide how to get wherever it is one wants to go, he must be fairly certain of where he is. This business planning affair, then, resolves into a three-step process, requiring that the following questions be given some serious consideration:

1. What is the present status of the business?
2. Where should its focus lie in the future?
3. How can it best get from here to there?

What is the business? The existing business should be defined in functional as well as physical terms: not only what it sells, but also what it does for its customers or clients. Every successful business must sell something more than a product or service, since the same product or service can almost certainly be obtained from several different competitors at comparable prices. In service businesses, the superiority of performance is a salable commodity, and geographic location and personal relationships can also contribute to a firm's success in specific fields. The competitive strengths and weaknesses of the business in each functional area should be realistically evaluated, since good strategy (defined as "skillful management in getting the better of an adversary") dictates employing one's major strengths against competitors' major weaknesses.

Where should the business go? A business can set different types of goals for itself that are not necessarily consistent, and management must decide which to pursue. Some strategic options available to management in its goal-setting include

- Achieving maximum short-term or long-term profits (in total dollars) or profitability (measured as a percentage return on invested capital).
- Developing maximum penetration of existing markets or expanding into new or different markets.
- Reinvesting profits from the business back into the business in an attempt to produce maximum growth, or distributing the excess profits to partners or shareholders as current income.

How can the business get there? Once the present situation is analyzed and the desired future is projected, the human, financial, and physical resources necessary to progress toward the firm's goals can be identified. This involves personnel—whether there are enough of the right kind of people available to capably manage the anticipated type and amount of work, money—how much is needed, and where it can be obtained, and facilities—whether new or additional space, equipment, or supply sources are required. With these items realistically identified, quantified, and priced, appropriate plans can be laid for strengthening the available resources in weak areas and developing whatever other capabilities may be needed in new areas. All this must be done in view of the prospective risks and within the relevant time and budget restraints.

One of the major reasons that many small business managers fail to plan adequately for the future is their preoccupation with day-to-day operating problems; this amounts to putting out brush fires while the forest is burning to the ground. Certainly, an overemphasis on current performance can be made only with a corresponding sacrifice of the long-term needs and prospects of the business.

As with life in general, those who fail to plan for the future cannot expect to have much of one!

6

Techniques of Financial Analysis

The art is not in making money, but in keeping it.

The failure to keep adequate financial records is often cited as a major cause of business failure; it means that the businessman operates in the dark, lacking a sound basis for evaluation and decision making. Only by keeping adequate records and analyzing a firm's financial performance on a regular basis can its functions and competitive position be clearly understood and placed in a proper perspective. This chapter presents the techniques of financial analysis that are especially useful to the small businessman.

Recordkeeping for Financial Analysis

Excessive recordkeeping should be avoided. Records should be kept only if they are required by law or if they are expected to serve some useful purpose in financial analysis or business planning.

The two major financial reporting documents are the balance sheet and the operating (or profit-and-loss) statement. The balance sheet shows the company's financial resources as of a specific date; the profit-and-loss statement describes in dollars the business' operations over a period of time. The operating statement is required by law; this is the information that goes into federal and state income tax returns. A balance sheet is required only of corporations on the federal level, but it is nevertheless necessary for purposes of establishing credit with suppliers and obtaining outside financing from banks and other lending institutions. Both the balance sheet and operating statement are extremely useful management tools.

Table 17 shows an example of a balance sheet for a small independent retail business, and Table 18 illustrates the accompanying profit-and-loss statement for the same business. Neither statement is intended to reflect a "typical" business operation, although the accounts are probably representative of many small retail businesses.

In looking at any financial statement, it is important to realize that it is not only the amounts that are significant, but also the relationships among the various figures, the changes that occur over time, and the comparisons of the amounts and ratios with other businesses.

On the balance sheet, current assets refer to the portion of the resources that can be converted to cash within a relatively short time. Fixed assets are of a more permanent nature; they are necessary in making the firm's merchandise or services available to its customers, but not offered for sale. Most fixed assets can be depreciated for income tax purposes,

TABLE 17

Balance Sheet for Small Independent Retail Business

Assets	
Current assets	
Cash	$ 1,010
Accounts receivable	8,300
Inventory	25,225
Other current assets	800
Total current assets	$35,335
Fixed assets	
Store fixtures	$ 5,717
Equipment	2,600
Other fixed assets	500
Total fixed assets	8,817
Total assets	$44,152
Liabilities	
Current liabilities	
Accounts payable	$10,562
Short-term notes payable	4,000
Total current liabilities	$14,562
Long-term loans payable	14,900
Total liabilities	29,462
Capital	14,690
Total liabilities and capital	$44,152

TABLE 18
Operating Statement for Small Independent Retail Business

Gross sales	$109,920
Less returns and allowances	3,365
Net sales	106,555
Cost of goods sold	
Inventory at beginning of year	$ 24,125
Purchases during year	+72,741
Inventory at end of year	−25,225
Cost of goods sold	71,641
Gross profit	34,914
Operating expenses	
Salaries and wages	$ 14,350
Rent	3,500
Interest	871
Taxes and licenses	1,988
Bad debts	250
Repairs	235
Depreciation	2,083
Supplies and materials	860
Advertising	3,500
Utilities	2,100
Other operating expenses	891
Total operating expenses	30,628
Net profit before income taxes	$ 4,286

with their original cost written off annually over their estimated useful service life.

Current liabilities represent the business' short-term financial obligations, either money owed to creditors for purchased assets or due to lenders within a year. Long-term liabilities refer to obligations due over a period of years, such as mortgages, long-term notes payable, and installment loans.

The difference between total assets and total liabilities defines the capital account, or the net worth of the business. The net worth, then, represents the owner's equity (his share of the ownership) in the business.

The operating statement summarizes the income and expenses of the business, breaking down the expenses into categories acceptable to the Internal Revenue Service and useful to management in developing the information required in planning and budgeting.

Allocating Costs and Expenses

The balance sheet and profit-and-loss statement provide most of the basic data needed for financial analysis and planning. However, the operating data must be broken down further to define the exact nature of the costs and expenses incurred. It is particularly important to distinguish between fixed and variable costs. Table 19 shows how the cost and expense accounts listed in the operating statement (Table 18) might be allocated between their fixed and variable elements.

TABLE 19
Allocation of Costs and Expenses

		Amount Allocated to	
Account	*Total*	Fixed Expense	Variable Expense
Net sales	$106,555		
Cost of goods sold	71,641		$71,641
Salaries and wages	14,350	$ 8,200	6,150
Rent	3,500	3,000	500
Interest	871	871	0
Taxes and licenses	1,988	1,450	538
Bad debts	250	0	250
Repairs	235	185	50
Depreciation	2,083	2,083	0
Supplies and materials	860	60	800
Advertising	3,500	1,750	1,750
Utilities	2,100	2,100	0
Other operating expenses	891	591	300
Total expenses and costs	$102,269	$20,290	$81,979

The operating statement alone does not provide sufficient information to make the breakdown between fixed and variable costs. Each account must be analyzed in detail to determine in which category it belongs, and management judgment must be applied in putting things in the right place. Also, many of the accounts include both fixed and variable expense items.

In the example, salaries and wages are split between fixed and variable categories; the fixed portion represents the part applying to keeping the business open, whereas the variable portion represents the extra help needed to handle the added sales volume, perhaps on a part-time, overtime, or seasonal basis.

Rent is usually a fixed cost; if the lease calls for a percentage payment based on net sales, any amount above the minimum monthly payment should be considered a variable expense.

Interest and depreciation are both accrued with time rather than sales activity and are therefore classified as fixed expenses, as are utility costs.

Bad debts are solely related to sales and are entirely variable in nature. The other accounts might be classified either way or both ways, depending on the specific cost items included.

The total costs and expenses in this example are broken down thus:

Total variable costs	$ 81,979
Total fixed expenses	20,290
Total costs and expenses	$102,269

In the example, the variable cost rate works out to be 76.9 percent or 0.769. The breakeven point is therefore

$$\frac{\$20{,}290}{1 - 0.769} = \$87{,}835$$

If the business occupies 1200 square feet of leased space, its breakeven point is $73.20 per square foot, with fixed expenses of $16.91 per square foot.

Financial Ratios for Business Analysis

One of the best ways to judge the effectiveness of the performance of a business is to analyze its financial statements. This analysis should enable the business owner to spot weaknesses and potential trouble spots before they become so serious that the financial condition is damaged beyond repair.

The current financial standing and past financial performance of a business can be interpreted most conveniently when the relationships among various balance sheet and profit-and-loss statement items are expressed as ratios. The calculated ratios for a particular business can then be used to compare its performance to those of similar businesses or to its own operations over a period of time.

There are three basic types of financial ratios:

1. Balance sheet ratios, showing the relationships among various balance sheet items
2. Operating ratios, relating expense accounts to income accounts on the profit-and-loss statement
3. Combined ratios, involving items on both the balance sheet and profit-and-loss statement.

Some ratios are important only in certain businesses, whereas others are more generally applicable. The following 12 ratios are especially significant to small businesses:

1. Current assets to current liabilities
2. Net profit to net sales
3. Net profit to net worth
4. Net profit to total assets
5. Net sales to net worth
6. Net sales to working capital
7. Net sales to inventory
8. Net sales to total assets
9. Fixed assets to net worth
10. Current liabilities to net worth
11. Total liabilities to net worth
12. Net worth to total assets

Table 20 shows the typical range of values for each of these 12 ratios for small retail businesses.

Current Assets to Current Liabilities. This ratio—also known as the "current ratio"—is one of the most commonly used ratios in balance sheet analysis. It gives an indication of the margin of protection for short-term creditors, a 2 : 1 ratio being considered standard. In general, the more liquid the current assets (cash, for example), the less margin is needed to cover current liabilities.

Net Profit to Net Sales. The net profit on sales, or profit margin, is an important financial yardstick. It indicates to some extent a company's competitive strength or its vulnerability to a decrease in either its sales volume or its profits. Usually, an increase in sales widens the profit margin, since fixed costs do not rise in direct proportion to sales. For the same reason, profit margins also decrease at a more rapid rate than sales, with fixed expenses spread over a smaller base. The profit margin also reflects the competitive situation within a business, with certain types of businesses characterized by low profit margins and high asset turnover.

TABLE 20
Financial Ratios for Business Analysis

Ratio	*Typical Range for Retail Businesses*	*Typical Value*
Current assets/current liabilities	2.0–4.0X	2.5X
Net profit/net sales	1.5–6.0%	4.0%
Net profit/net worth	8.0–30.0%	12.0%
Net profit/total assets	4.0–15.0%	5.5%
Net sales/net worth	3.0–8.0X	4.5X
Net sales/working capital	3.5–7.5X	5.0X
Net sales/inventory	3.0–6.0X	4.0X
Net sales/total assets	2.0–4.0X	3.0X
Fixed assets/net worth	12.0–35.0%	20.0%
Current liabilities/net worth	40.0–80.0%	50.0%
Total liabilities/net worth	80.0–140.0%	90.0%
Net worth/total assets	30.0–90.0%	65.0%

Net Profit to Net Worth. The net profit/net worth ratio is one of the most important financial ratios, since it measures the efficiency with which invested capital has been employed. The percentage return on net worth should always be higher than the cost of borrowed money, with 12 percent a bare minimum. A well-managed and successful business should earn better than 25 percent on its capital.

Net Profit to Total Assets. This ratio provides a measurement similar to the net profit/net worth ratio, except that here the theory is that the return on investment should be related to all capital employed in the business, whether supplied by the owners or from borrowing. As such, it is probably the most realistic measure of the efficiency of money management in a business.

Net Sales to Net Worth. This ratio measures the rate of capital turnover, showing how actively the capital of the business is being put to work. If capital is turned over too rapidly, liabilities may build up at an excessive rate; if capital is turned over too slowly, profitability suffers.

Net Sales to Working Capital. The rate of working capital turnover can highlight a financial problem if it is very low or very high. A high sales/working capital ratio is an indication that the business may be relying too much on credit as a substitute for an adequate margin of current operating funds.

Net Sales to Inventory. The sales/inventory ratio measures the number of times inventory turns over during a year, or the average shelf life of the merchandise stocked. Rapid inventory turnover is one of the main keys to success in retail trade; a high rate is indicative of good merchandise planning and inventory control.

Net Sales to Total Assets. The rate of total asset turnover has the same significance as the sales/net worth ratio, except that the measure is applied to all assets instead of only the owner's equity. A high ratio shows the efficient use of total resources.

Fixed Assets to Net Worth. A tendency to overinvest in fixed assets can often be identified by this ratio. A high ratio of fixed assets to net worth results in heavy depreciation and interest expenses, which can lead to serious profit problems if any sales difficulties are encountered. This ratio should generally be below 75 percent.

Current Liabilities to Net Worth. The ratio of current liabilities to net worth provides a means of evaluating a business' financial condition by comparing what is owed with what is owned. A high ratio—anything over 80 percent—indicates that the business is overly dependent on its creditors.

Total Liabilities to Net Worth. Whenever the total liabilities/net worth ratio exceeds 100 percent, it indicates that creditors have a greater equity in the firm's assets than the owners. Such top-heavy liabilities make the business vulnerable to unexpected contingencies and severely restrict its financial flexibility.

Net Worth to Total Assets. This ratio provides another means of measuring the owner's equity in the total assets and reflects the extent of outside financing. A low ratio limits the opportunity to raise additional capital from outside sources.

Breakeven Analysis

One of the greatest problems confronting the new independent businessman is his inability or failure to recognize fully the cost structure of his business. It is particularly important that fixed costs, or overheads, be considered along with direct costs before making decisions regarding major expenditures and pricing policies.

For the small business especially, overhead expenses constitute a significant portion of the firm's overall cost of doing business. The smallest retail or service business generally incurs annual out-of-pocket fixed expenses of $8000 or more, even without a paid employee. Adding employees easily doubles this amount and increases the amount of record-keeping required. A small shop of almost any kind, occupying, say, 1000 square feet of space, can quickly run up a $20,000 per year overhead.

Since retail sales are generally between $50 and $150 per square foot of selling space, this type of operation would be expected to generate revenues as low as $50,000 or as high as $150,000 annually. Higher sales might be achieved by extending business hours (thereby increasing variable salary expenses), or by occupying an especially good location (with a higher fixed rent expense).

An ordinary, sound, going retail business, however, might be expected to have sales of around $100,000 annually, with overhead expenses of $20,000 made up of roughly the following elements:

Salaries and wages	$ 7,000
Rent	4,000
Depreciation, insurance, taxes	4,000
Utilities	2,000
Advertising	2,000
Miscellaneous	1,000
Total annual fixed expenses	$20,000

These are the costs that the business faces just to be open and ready for its customers.

The total direct cost of merchandise purchased for resale averages between 70 and 75 percent of total sales for all retail businesses (ranging from less than 50 percent to more than 80 percent, depending on the type of business). This means that the average retailer operates on a 25 to 30 percent profit margin; for every hundred dollars he rings up on his cash register, between $70 and $75 must pay for the merchandise he just sold and the other $25 to $30 goes toward covering his overheads and, hopefully, returning a profit.

Until the overhead is covered, there can be no profit. This is where breakeven analysis can provide a valuable planning tool for the businessman.

The breakeven point of a business represents the sales volume at which the margin on goods or services sold is sufficient to cover the annual overhead. At the breakeven point, there is neither profit nor loss. Figure 12 shows a breakeven chart for a business with fixed costs of $20,000 and variable costs totaling 75 percent of sales.

The breakeven point is a direct function of the markup (or variable cost rate) and the overhead (or fixed expenses). The term markup, however, is interpreted differently in different businesses. To the contractor or manufacturer, markup is the percentage added to his costs to arrive at a selling price. To the retailer, markup represents his profit margin, the difference between price and cost. If a retailer buys something for $50 and sells it for $100, he considers his markup to be 50 percent, even though it actually represents a 100 percent markup above his cost.

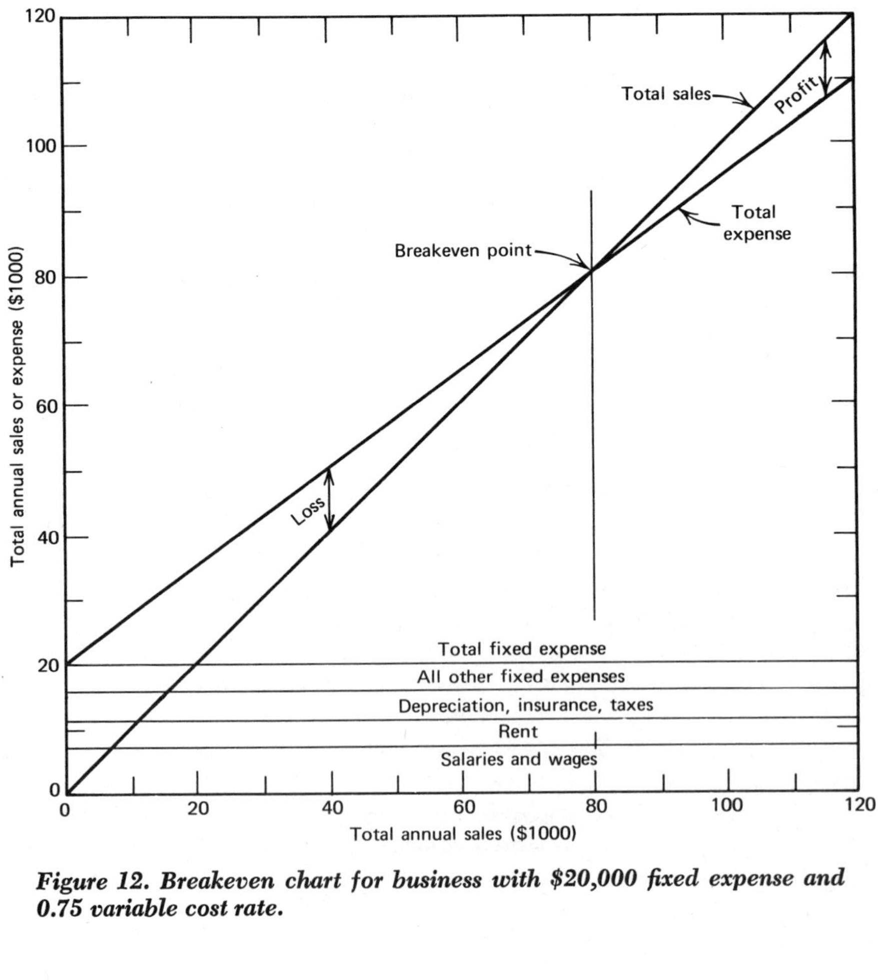

Figure 12. Breakeven chart for business with $20,000 fixed expense and 0.75 variable cost rate.

The retailer whose merchandise cost is 75 percent of his sales is in reality working on a 25/75 = 33.3 percent markup on cost. With this markup, to break even, his annual sales must amount to four times his overhead expense. If merchandise costs were 65 percent of their selling price, he would have to generate sales of about 2.5 times his overhead; at a 55 percent product cost, he would have to do 2.8 times his overhead to break even.

This situation is illustrated in Figure 13 using the example of a $20,000 annual overhead with direct costs incurred at rates ranging from 60 to 80 percent of total sales. Here the breakeven point can be seen to decline rapidly as the profit margin (or markup) increases. With the direct cost of goods sold at 75 percent, the breakeven point is $80,000; at 65 percent (representing a 35 percent margin or 53.8 percent markup on

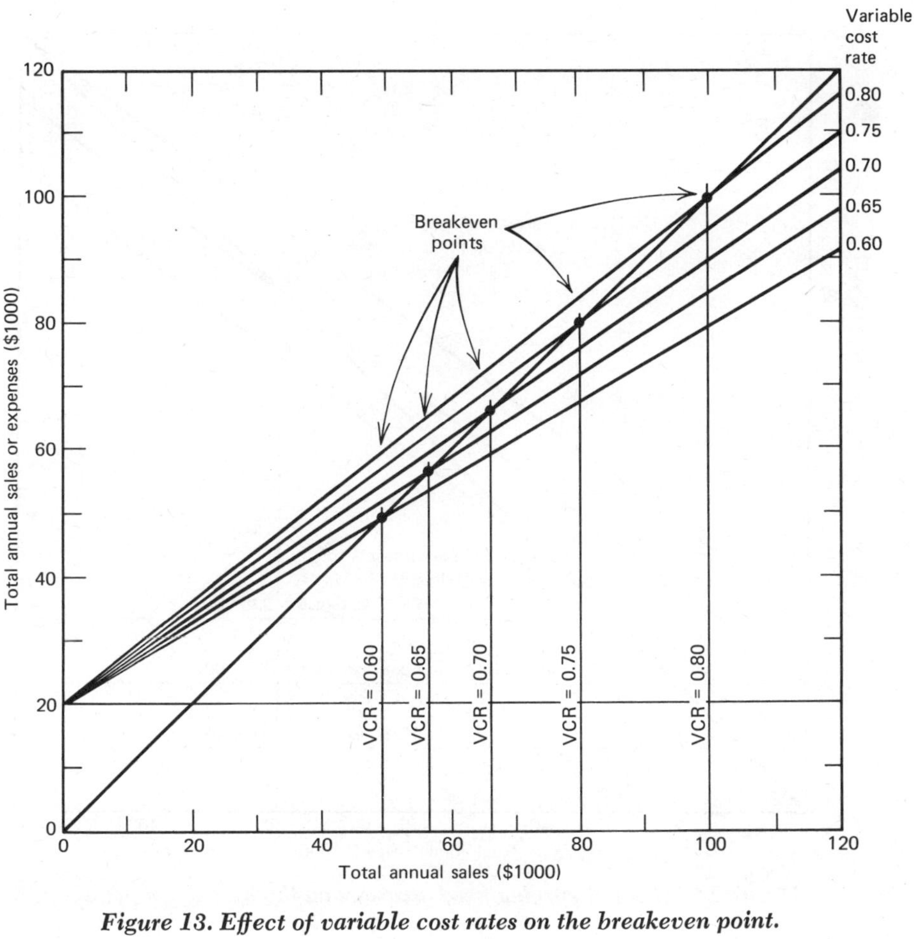

Figure 13. Effect of variable cost rates on the breakeven point.

cost), the business breaks even with sales of $57,200; a 60 percent cost of sales (40 percent margin) results in a breakeven point of $50,000.

The impact of the markup on the required sales volume should be carefully considered before adding any new merchandise or product lines carrying markups different from those that apply to the regular lines of the business. Most retail businesses simply cannot afford to stock items that carry substandard discounts.

Fixed costs, too, have an important impact on the breakeven point. Figure 14 shows how changing fixed costs move the breakeven point up for higher fixed costs or down for lower fixed costs.

As shown in Fig. 14, the breakeven point for the business with $20,000 in fixed costs and a 75 percent variable cost rate is $80,000. If fixed costs are increased by $10,000 (to a total of $30,000), the breakeven

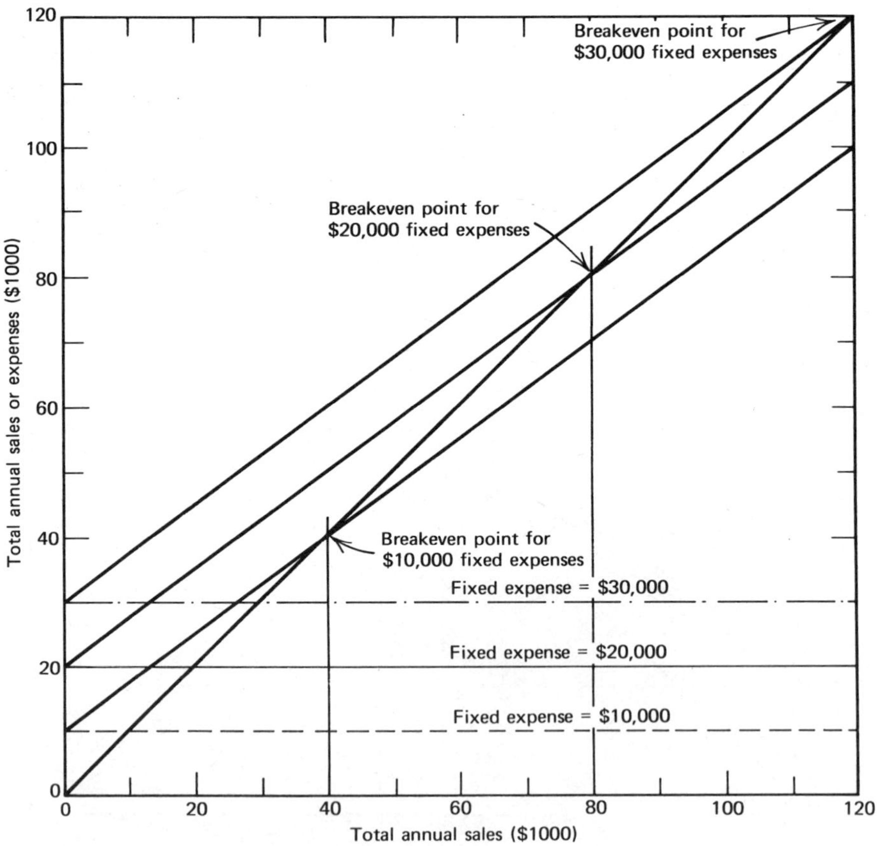

Figure 14. Effect of varying fixed expenses on the breakeven point.

point moves up to $120,000; if fixed costs are decreased by $10,000 (dropping them to $10,000 total), the breakeven point is only $40,000. In other words, a 50 percent increase in fixed costs increases the breakeven point by 50 percent, whereas the same percentage decrease in fixed costs lowers the breakeven point by 50 percent.

This is an extremely important effect to consider when any major outlay of money is proposed. The expenditure can be treated as an overhead cost, and it must return a certain number of dollars for each dollar spent simply to pay for itself. The required return per dollar spent depends on the variable cost rate of the business. Tables 21 and 22 show the breakeven factors for different variable cost rates between 0.40 and 0.90 and for different percentage markups on direct cost ranging from 5 to 300 percent. These breakeven factors are presented graphically in Fig. 15.

If, for example, an intensive advertising campaign proposed for a particular media costs $200 per week, the businessman should be confident that the campaign will generate sufficient additional sales to make

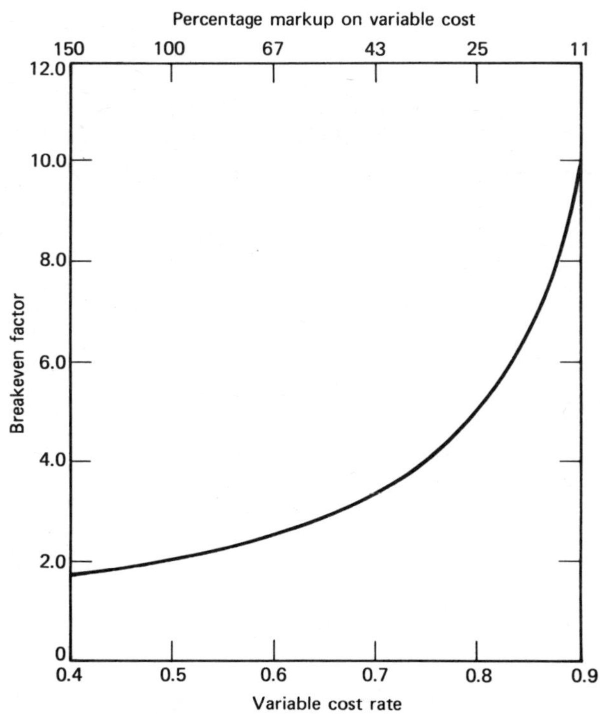

Figure 15. Effect of variable cost rates and markups on the breakeven factor.

TABLE 21
Relationship Between Variable Cost Rates and Breakeven Factors

Variable Cost Rate	*Breakeven Factor*
0.40	1.67
0.45	1.82
0.50	2.00
0.55	2.22
0.60	2.50
0.65	2.86
0.70	3.33
0.75	4.00
0.80	5.00
0.85	6.67
0.90	10.00

TABLE 22
Relationship Between Percentage Markups and Breakeven Factors

Percentage Markup Added to Total Variable Cost	*Breakeven Factor*	*Percentage Markup Added to Total Variable Cost*	*Breakeven Factor*
5	21.00	110	1.91
10	11.00	120	1.83
20	6.00	130	1.77
30	4.33	140	1.71
40	3.50	150	1.67
50	3.00	160	1.63
60	2.67	170	1.59
70	2.43	180	1.56
80	2.25	190	1.53
90	2.11	200	1.50
100	2.00	300	1.33

it worthwhile. Table 21 or Fig. 15 show that if the business operates with a 75 percent variable cost rate, $4 in sales are required to break even on each dollar spent. If there is sufficient reason to believe that the proposed advertising will bring in an extra $800 in sales each week, the program is worth considering. If it brings in more than $800 weekly, the investment in advertising will show a profit. If weekly sales do not increase by $800, the investment is supporting the advertising media rather than the business.

Profit/Volume Analysis

Breakeven analysis is actually a special case of profit analysis in which there is zero profit. In profit/volume analysis, the same techniques are employed to identify the profit resulting from any given sales volume.

The same data used in constructing a breakeven chart are used for developing the profit/volume relationship. Again, all that is needed is a breakdown of costs into their variable and fixed components, total sales, and the profits resulting from that sales volume. Take, for example, the same data used in developing the breakeven chart in Fig. 12.

Total sales	$100,000
Operating cost	
Variable	$ 75,000
Fixed	20,000
Total costs	95,000
Net profit before taxes	$ 5,000

Figure 16 shows a profit/volume (P/V) chart constructed from this information. In the P/V chart the vertical axis is divided into two parts, the top part representing net profit and the lower segment representing net loss.

The horizontal axis is drawn through the zero profit point on the vertical axis, representing the breakeven point. The units along the horizontal axis measure the total sales volume of the business.

At zero sales, the net loss is equal to the amount of the overhead or fixed costs. The P/V line then intersects the vertical axis at a net loss of $20,000.

Since, according to the operating statement, the business showed a net profit of $5000 at a sales volume of $100,000, the $5000 figure can be plotted above the $100,000 point on the horizontal axis.

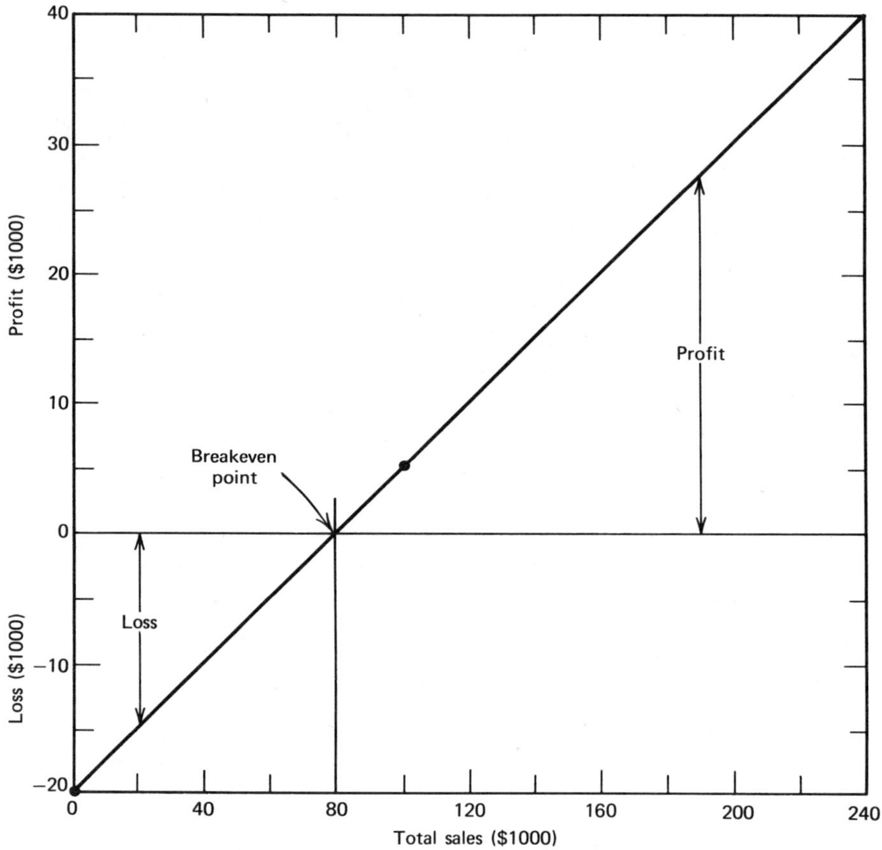

Figure 16. Profit/volume chart for business with $20,000 fixed expense and 0.75 variable cost rate.

A straight line connecting these two points defines the profit/volume relationship, giving the amount of profit or loss corresponding to any given level of sales, assuming that all other factors—the total amount of overhead expense and the variable cost rate—remain the same. The point at which the P/V line intersects the horizontal axis—$80,000 in this case—is the breakeven point.

The profits or losses associated with any desired or expected sales volume can be easily interpolated or extrapolated. It is apparent from this P/V chart that, when a straight-line relationship between profit and volume exists, any uniform change in volume results in a uniform change in profits. In this case each $10,000 change in volume causes a corresponding $1500 change in profits.

The Laws of Profits

The relationships between profits, sales volumes, fixed expenses, variable costs, and profit margins lead to some general observations and conclusions. Briefly, these "laws of profits" are

- All costs—not only out-of-pocket direct costs—must be included when analyzing the economic situation of a business.
- Any change in fixed costs changes the net profit by the same amount in the opposite direction.
- A given percentage change in fixed costs changes the breakeven point of the business by the same percentage and in the same direction, provided that other cost relationships hold steady.
- A change in the rate at which variable costs are incurred changes both the breakeven point and the net profit earned at a specified sales volume, if fixed costs remain constant.
- Increasing the variable cost rate raises the breakeven point and lowers profits; decreasing the variable cost rate lowers the breakeven point and increases profits.
- An increase in the percentage markup applied to direct costs lowers the breakeven point and increases the profits associated with any sales volume. Decreasing the markup has the opposite effect.
- A change in both fixed costs and the variable cost rate has a significant effect on profits if both change in the same direction; if they move in opposite directions, the changes tend to offset each other.

7
Principles of Money Management

A man can have more money than brains, but not for long.

Whereas financial analysis entails an interpretive function conducted over a period of time, money management is directed toward the effective use of the cash on hand. It is possible to get in deep financial trouble, even when financial analysis shows a fundamentally profitable operation, if cash inflows and cash outflows are not budgeted properly. This chapter emphasizes the necessity for maintaining adequate working capital and cash reserves by controlling the flows of money in and out of the business.

Capital and Operating Budgets

The fact that the operations of a small business are difficult to forecast because of its vulnerability to a variety of external factors beyond its control is no excuse for not operating the business under close budgetary control. These difficulties, in fact, emphasize the need for and potential benefits of a thoughtfully prepared budget analysis.

A budget, by definition, is a "statement of expected revenues and expenditures." Budgetary control refers to an overall plan for analyzing and monitoring these expected revenues and expenditures by setting standards against which the actual performance of the business can be measured. A good budget program can detect inefficiencies, point out trouble spots before they occur, and help the owner get the most out of his limited financial resources.

The basic purpose of any budget is to provide information for making the best possible decisions under existing conditions; the effectiveness of the budget can be measured only in terms of the usefulness of the information it provides. The budget serves as an economic "model" of the whole business, giving a broad overview of the entire operation. It fits in closely with short and long range plans, serving as a comprehensive blueprint of the firm's future.

Financial budgets can be classified as cash (or operating) budgets or capital budgets. They may be either short range (a year or less) or long range (covering from one to five years). The capital budget is primarily a planning tool, showing where the business hopes to find itself on a given date in the future in terms of a projected balance sheet. The operating or cash budget is an operational tool, indicating expectations rather than plans.

In both cash and capital budgets, the amounts should be as accurate as possible with the information available at the time of preparation. Short-term accuracy is greater than that for long-term projections, but in either case there should be at least enough detail to recognize any important variations from the expected values.

Capital Budgets. The capital budget refers to estimated expenditures on balance sheet items—the business' plans for expanding inventories, remodeling existing facilities, expanding into new facilities, acquiring new equipment, or replacing old equipment. It is concerned with how much, on what, and when the business' money is invested. Projected balance sheets make up an important part of the capital budgeting process, reflecting anticipated changes in the firm's financial position and providing a basis for measuring its financial effectiveness.

Cash Budgets. The cash or operating budget shows the projected flow of money into and out of the business. Cash budgeting entails both estimating and controlling these cash flows, summarizing the expected receipts and disbursements on a monthly or yearly basis. The figures included in the cash budget should reflect reasonably efficient operations and realistic operating conditions.

There are five major steps involved in developing an effective budget program:

1. Accumulate background data pertaining to the activities and operations of the business over at least the past year, breaking down sales, costs, and profits by major departments or merchandise categories. Even in a small shop, sales per square foot vary substantially for different items, as do the monthly demands for different types of merchandise.

2. Develop basic marketing assumptions regarding the nature of the demand for the main types of merchandise handled; this market forecast refers to total demand, not only for the business firm itself. Leading trade journals, for example, usually publish annual forecasts of business activity in their fields. This overall economic outlook is especially important to small businesses.
3. Put together a business plan, defining the particular product lines to be emphasized, the amount of time and money to be devoted to sales promotion, new merchandise to be added, the availability of money, and the adequacy of existing facilities.
4. Make projections of cash and capital flows for the future based on a careful analysis of historical data regarding past performance, estimates of future performance, changing competitive conditions within the trade area of the business, and the outlook for business in general.
5. After the budget has been prepared and implemented, each decision—whether for a new product line, a new equipment item, a new media advertising program, or anything else—must be weighed to see if it fits in with the budgeted amounts. If not, other accounts in the budget must be adjusted to provide the necessary funds. By continually reviewing all figures and assumptions incorporated in the budget and making appropriate revisions and adjustments in light of changing conditions, the budget is a practical and valuable management tool.

Sales Forecasting for the Small Business

Forecasting is said to be "sometimes a science, sometimes an art, and most often a little of both." In business, everything depends on future sales, and an accurate forecast can mean the difference between success and failure, or at least between profit and loss. A small business, especially, can operate profitably on a small sales volume—but not if its operations are scaled in anticipation of a large sales volume.

Before the future can be projected, the present must be known; this requires some analysis of the past.

Figure 17 shows one of the best and most useful ways of keeping track of annual sales. This graph plots the cumulative 12-month sales totals for a small business, with each point representing the preceding year's operation up through that month.

Apparently some small businessmen feel that annual sales totals can be computed only on a calendar year basis; when they fill out a credit report, for example, the figure they know and report as annual sales ac-

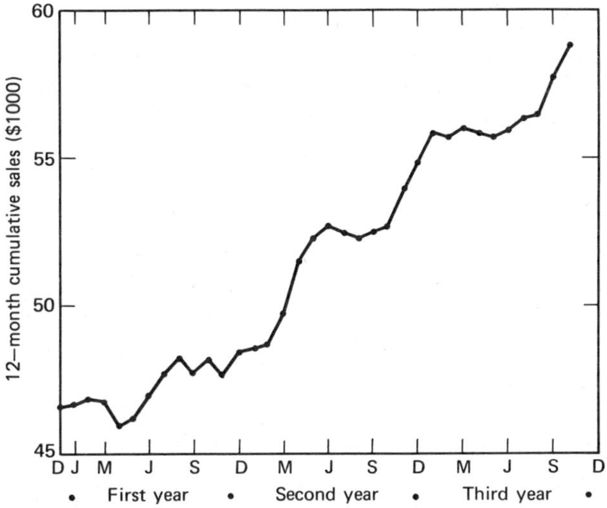

Figure 17. Twelve-month cumulative sales chart.

tually represents their sales for the 12 months ended last December 31, not their most recent 12 months' sales performance. Even during November and December, they think of their annual sales as what they achieved during the period that ended almost a year ago.

Annual sales totals should be kept up to date on at least a monthly basis and revised as soon as each month's sales totals become available. The procedure for doing this takes no more than a minute. For example, on July 1 the following arithmetic calculation can be made:

Sales for 12 months ended May 31	$64,562
Plus sales for this June	+ 5,330
Total	$69,892
Less sales for last June	− 4,831
Sales for 12 months ended this June 30	$65,061

This simple calculation tells the businessman exactly where he stands in terms of annual sales. Plotted on a monthly basis as in Fig. 17, sales trends and cycles are clearly evident.

The 12-month cumulative sales chart can then be used as a basis for making projections into the future, employing the "lost horse" forecasting technique. The "lost horse" approach states that the best way to find a lost horse is to go where it was last seen and start looking in whatever direction it was heading.

In fact, patterns and trends established in the past often continue long enough to warrant using them as a basis for predicting the future. Extending the already established trend into the future is far more reliable for a small business than attempting to employ more sophisticated statistical techniques.

When the 12-month total goes up, it indicates that the preceding month was better than the same month a year ago; if it goes down, last month's sales were less than those of a year ago.

Monthly sales can be projected by using this same "principle of historical continuity"; unless there is some valid reason to believe otherwise, whatever trends have taken place in the past can generally be expected to continue into the future. Figure 18 shows an example of trend projections for two different months, based on the sales results of those two months during the past few years.

By projecting individual months or cumulative totals in this manner, the effects of seasonal variations are eliminated. Once sufficient operating data are accumulated from past experience, the resulting estimates should provide a reliable guide to what the business can expect in the future. When it comes to business, "the best surprise is no surprise."

Seasonality of Sales

An ideal business is one with a uniform and predictable growth rate, in which sales from month to month and year to year grow steadily and predictably. There is, of course, no such thing as this ideal business. Clients or customers often come in bunches or not at all, and seldom at the seller's convenience.

Every business has its seasons, and this seasonality must be an important part of the firm's business planning. Retail businesses, for example, probably experience the widest fluctuations in month-to-month sales, but are probably among the least affected by these fluctuations because they are best able to anticipate them.

There is little the businessman can do about the seasonality of his business; it is generally created by the buyer, not the seller. The businessman must identify and anticipate the season for doing business and then react with whatever measures are necessary to get his share when the business is there.

One of the first steps in setting up any effective kind of business plan, promotional program, or financial forecast is to identify the seasonal characteristics of the particular business.

Figures 19 and 20 illustrate the seasonal characteristics of eight dif-

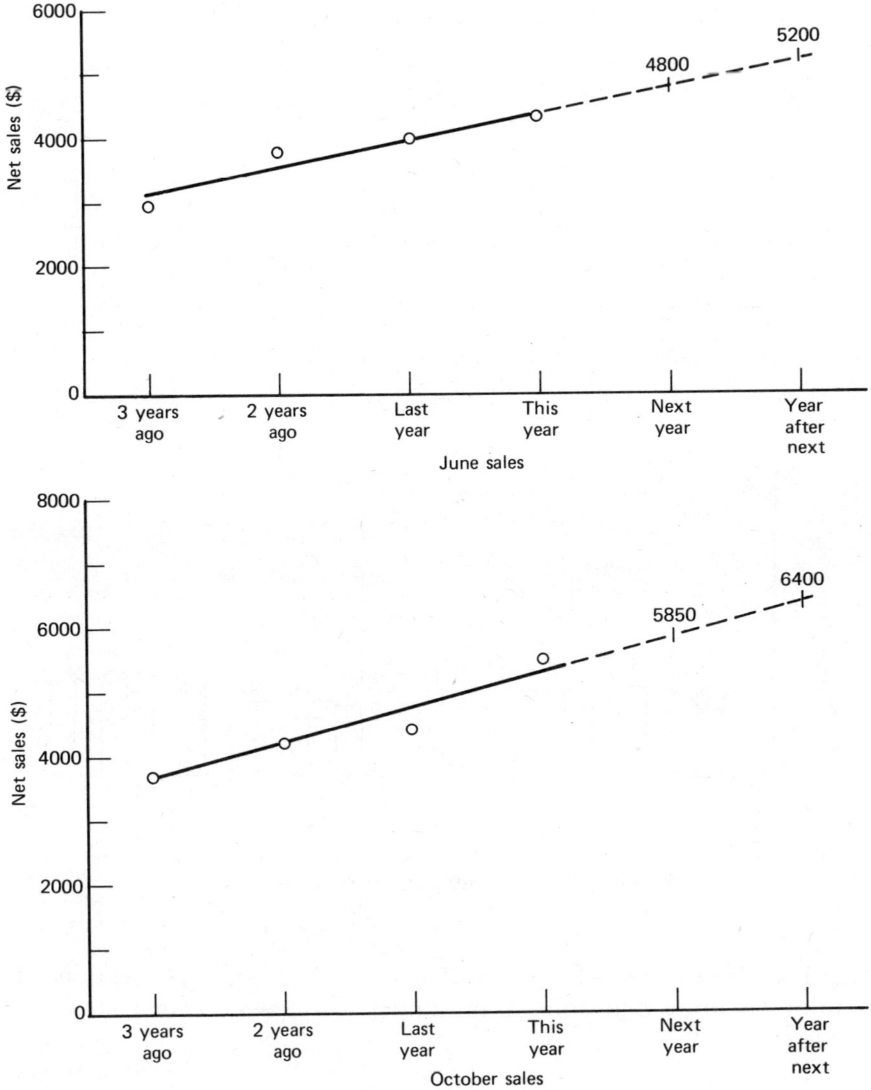

Figure 18. Projecting monthly sales.

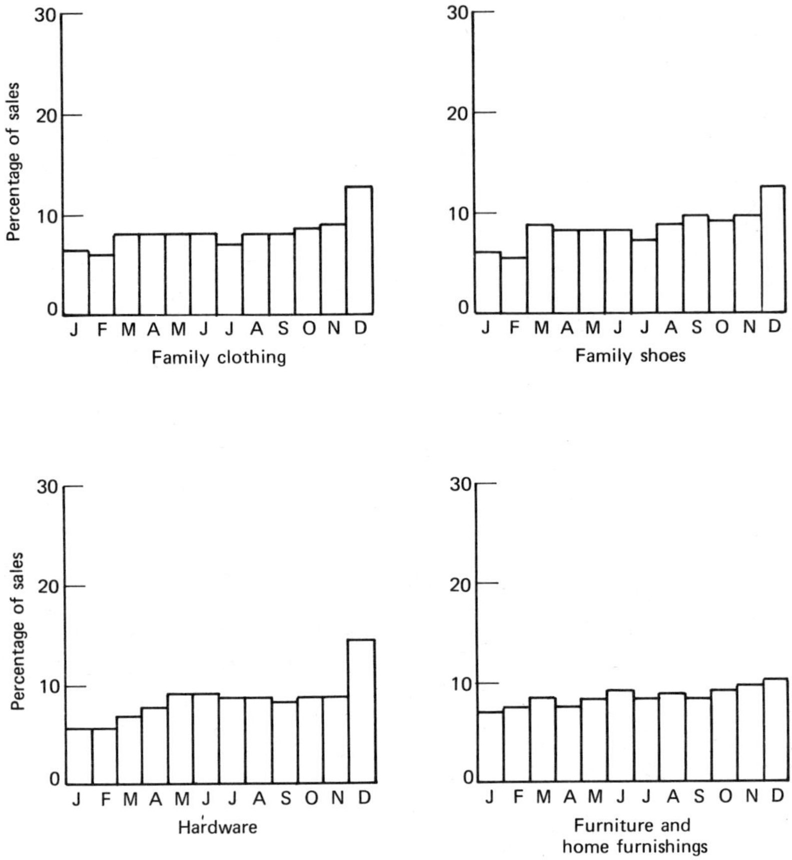

Figure 19. Seasonality of retail sales.

ferent kinds of retail businesses, ranging from relatively unseasonal in nature (furniture and home furnishings) to highly seasonal (toys and games).

The more seasonal operations are obviously confronted with real problems in purchasing, inventory, and overhead cost control. Many highly seasonal types of businesses are delighted to barely break even during their slack season, knowing that their one or two good months will make a good year for them.

Service firms are faced with some similar problems, although not to the same extent or predictability. Service businesses, however, are often able to build up a sufficient backlog during their good season to carry them through the slow months. The season for getting business is still there, but the business obtained can be spread out. There are few

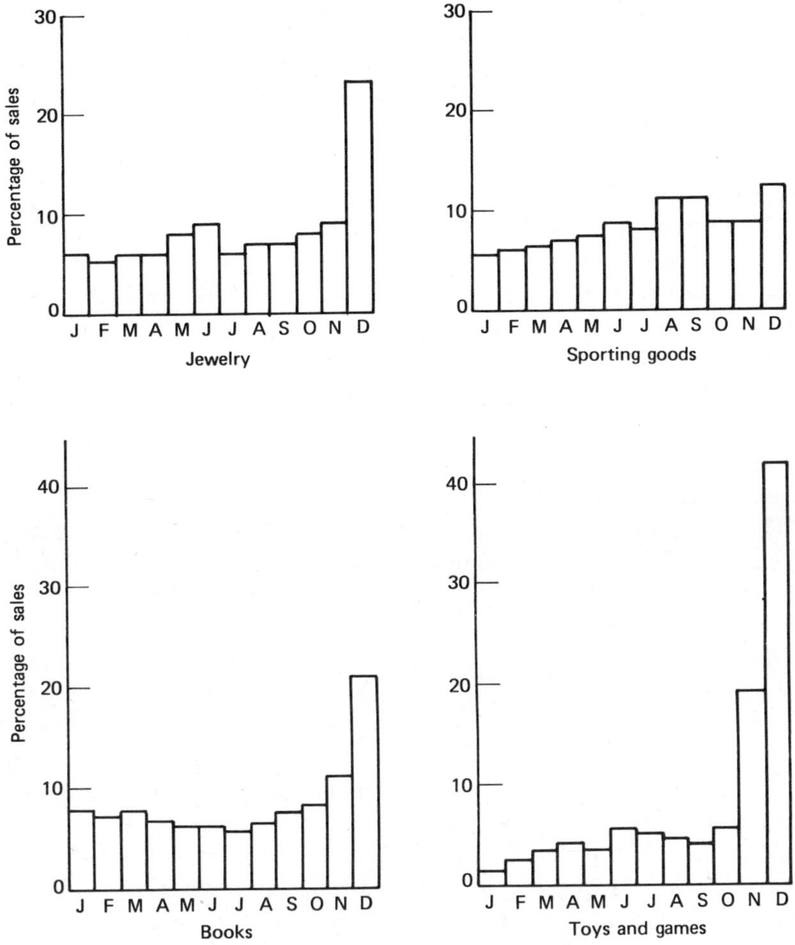

Figure 20. Seasonality of retail sales.

things more satisfying to the service business than a large backlog of projects that can be called on to carry their high fixed overheads when new projects are not coming in. For budget planning purposes, it is vital to distinguish between the times the projects are sold and when they are actually billed.

A steady, year-round promotional program is the only effective answer to the problem of seasonal business patterns, with the promotional efforts concentrated at the times at which the most business is available. Monthly sales goals should be set on this basis, with sufficient resources made available for the promotional activities required to meet those goals.

The firm's present level of business should never interfere with its future business development program, or it will end up scratching for sales when there is no market demand. Just as the large chemical companies cannot sell their agricultural chemicals when the farmers are not ready to use them, the small businessman cannot sell his merchandise or services when his prospective clients or customers do not need them. The buyer, not the seller, establishes seasonal business patterns.

The best way to identify the seasonal aspects of any business is to analyze the firm's own experience. Do not wait until more business is needed to start looking for it; find out when the market is there, then do whatever is necessary to get your share.

Depreciation and Cash Flow

Depreciation is the accounting technique by which a capital asset's original cost can be written off as an annual expense during the period it is in use. The objective of this depreciation allowance is to enable the asset's owner to set aside enough money to replace the asset when it will no longer serve its intended purpose because of functional obsolescence or physical deterioration.

In preparing cash flow analyses and operating budgets, the amounts paid for depreciable assets represent actual cash outflows. The annual depreciation charges, even though they constitute an important fixed expense item on the profit-and-loss statement, are not cash outflows. Depreciation is a "paper" expense, a purely artificial legal and accounting device permitted for income tax purposes.

Even though the depreciation expense reported on the income tax statement does not represent an actual cash outlay, it does have an important impact on the amount of income tax paid—which does involve a cash outlay.

For example, consider the following condensed operating statement:

Net sales	$100,000
Operating expenses	
Variable costs	$ 70,000
Fixed costs (excluding depreciation)	15,000
Depreciation	3,000
Total expenses	88,000
Net profit before income tax	$ 12,000
Income taxes at 30 percent	3,600
Net profit after taxes	$ 8,400

In this situation, the business owner nets $8400 after payment of income taxes. However, his real cash inflow from the business consists not only of the $8400 profit, but also includes the $3000 in depreciation charges that were deducted from gross income in computing the tax. This $3000 was not actually paid out; the net cash flow, the total amount of money available to spend, is $11,400.

Now, if the same situation were to exist without the provision for depreciation, the operating statement would look like this:

Net sales	$100,000
Operating expenses	
Variable costs	$ 70,000
Fixed costs	15,000
Total expenses	85,000
Net profit before income tax	$ 15,000
Income taxes at 30 percent	4,500
Net profit after taxes	$ 10,500

In this case, the $10,500 after-tax profit also represents the cash flow of the business. Even with a higher pretax profit, cash flow is actually $900 less than before—reduced by the amount of the effective tax rate times the total depreciation allowance in the first example.

The amount of annual depreciation expense allowed depends on the type of asset being depreciated, its estimated useful life, and the method employed in the depreciation calculation.

The first step in computing depreciation is to determine the estimated useful life of the asset. No average useful life for an item is applicable in all businesses; the depreciable life depends on such things as its frequency of use, its age at the time of acquisition, the care and maintenance it receives, and a number of other factors peculiar to the trade or business in which it is used. The useful life of the depreciable asset should be determined on the basis of the operating conditions and past experience of the business, or general experience in the industry can be used if personal experience is lacking. The depreciable assets used in wholesale and retail trade and in personal and professional services are commonly depreciated over a period of about 10 years.

After the useful service life of the depreciable property has been estimated, a depreciation method must be chosen. Any reasonable method that is consistently applied over the asset's life can be used, but the three most common approaches are

1. The straight-line method
2. The declining-balance method
3. The sum of the years digits method

In the straight-line method, the base cost of the asset is divided by its useful service life to arrive at the annual depreciation expense allowance.

In the declining-balance method, the depreciation taken each year is subtracted from the cost of the property before computing the next year's depreciation. The percentage allowed can range from 1.25 to 2 times the annual rate taken under the straight-line method.

With the sum of the years digits method, a different fraction is applied each year to the asset's original cost. The fraction's denominator (lower part) is the total of the digits representing the years of estimated useful life of the property; for a five-year depreciation period, it would be $1 + 2 + 3 + 4 + 5 = 15$. The numerator (the top number in the fraction) represents the years of useful life remaining at the beginning of each year. For the first year, 5/15 of the original cost would be allowed; the second year, 4/15, and so on, down to the fifth year, when the last 1/15 of the original cost would be taken.

Table 23 shows the annual depreciation expense allowed for depreciable assets with a 10-year useful service life, using the three different depreciation methods. The declining balance percentage is taken at twice the straight-line rate, or 20 percent.

As shown in Table 23, the annual depreciation deductions allowed under the declining balance method never total 100 percent. Many companies switch from the declining-balance method to a straight-line method beginning in the sixth year (at half the asset's life), a practice generally permitted by the Internal Revenue Service. This gives a uniform deduction of 6.55 percent for the final five years of the asset's life, thereby recovering the entire amount.

Either of the accelerated depreciation methods—the sum of the years digits or the declining-balance—probably provides greater economic advantages to a business than the straight-line method, since the firm's cash flow position is improved by the larger deductions earned during the early years of the asset's life. However, the straight-line method has the virtue of simplicity. The best depreciation method for a particular business depends largely on the individual owner's personal tax situation.

Cash Flow in the Small Business

Many businesses that appear to be operating profitably and successfully according to their annual financial statements have gotten in a lot of

TABLE 23
Percentage of Asset Cost to Be Depreciated Each Year Under Different Depreciation Methods

			Declining Balance	
Year	*Straight Line*	*Sum of Years Digits*	Undepreciated Balance	Annual Amount
1	10	18.18	100.00	20.00
2	10	16.36	80.00	16.00
3	10	14.55	64.00	12.80
4	10	12.73	51.20	10.24
5	10	10.91	40.96	8.19
6	10	9.09	32.77	6.55
7	10	7.27	26.22	5.24
8	10	5.45	20.98	4.20
9	10	3.64	16.78	3.36
10	10	1.82	13.42	2.68
Total	100	100		89.26

trouble when they suddenly and unexpectedly ran out of cash to pay their bills. This has happened to large well-known corporations, and it is one of the major causes of failure of small firms.

The cash flow statement, consequently, is probably the single most important document to the manager of a small business. It is the one document that tells him exactly how much money he will have available to meet his immediate obligations at any given point in time.

Accounting terms such as "profit" and "income" can be quite misleading to the person actually operating a business. Cash is the fuel that runs the business, and it is seldom the same as income. Income or profit cannot be used to pay the bills; creditors insist on cash, as do the firm's employees.

Cash flow is generally defined for accounting purposes as a firm's net profit after taxes, plus depreciation, depletion, and other "paper" expenses. As such, it tells how much money is left on hand after all the cash expenses have been paid, but it does not allow for the replacement of fixed assets as they expire.

The timing of cash flows is especially important in determining a firm's working capital requirements. In retail businesses, merchandise inventory requirements must be anticipated and ordered several months in advance, and usually they must be paid for before they generate any substantial cash sales. Any business that buys by the hundreds but sells one at a time is bound to have occasional cash flow problems.

Service businesses are faced with an equally awkward, but different, situation. Payrolls, rent, and many other expenses must be paid as they come due, exerting a constant drain on cash reserves, even though work may be billed to the client on a monthly basis. Thus cash is not received to cover the cash spent for a period of perhaps 30 to 60 days. Last month's expenses may be billed this month, but payment may not be received until next month.

As an example, consider a consulting business whose annual cash flow statement looks like this:

Total billings	$500,000
Cash expenses	
Rent and utilities	$ 36,000
Payroll	324,000
General expenses	48,000
Other cash expenses	76,000
Total cash expenses	$484,000
Net cash inflow for year	$ 16,000

This statement implies that the firm will, at the end of a year, have generated $16,000 more in cash than it spent.

However, this does not necessarily mean that there will be enough cash on hand throughout the year to meet the monthly payroll unless the firm has an unusually fortunate timing of its cash flows.

Table 24 shows a monthly cash flow projection for the service business in question, summarizing the monthly cash receipts and disbursements.

Table 24 shows that the business is expected to run out of pocket as much as $29,000 by March, before the cash receipts from client billings begin to reduce the cash deficit. A cash surplus does not appear until July.

This statement tells the management that $29,000 must be financed in some manner, from the firm's previously accumulated earnings or by borrowing, to meet current obligations early in the year. If this were a new business venture without a previous earnings history, the situation could be much different and far more difficult.

Regardless of the type of business—retail, service, or any other—the computation of the monthly cash flow position entails only the arithmetic involved in balancing a personal checkbook:

Cash on hand at beginning of month
+ Cash receipts during month
− Cash paid out during month
= Cash on hand at end of month

TABLE 24

Cash Flow Projection for Consulting Service Business[a]

	January	February	March	April	May	June	July	August	September	October	November	December
Cash inflow												
Amount billed	30	35	45	50	55	55	50	50	45	35	25	25
Total cash in	25	30	35	45	50	55	55	50	50	45	35	25
Cash outflow												
Rent and utilities	3	3	3	3	3	3	3	3	3	3	3	3
Payroll	26	26	26	26	26	28	30	30	28	26	26	26
General expense	4	4	4	4	4	4	4	4	4	4	4	4
Other cash expense	5	7	8	9	9	8	8	7	5	3	3	4
Total cash out	38	40	41	42	42	43	45	44	40	36	36	37
Net cash flow	(13)	(10)	(6)	3	8	12	10	6	10	9	(1)	(12)
Cumulative balance	(13)	(23)	(29)	(26)	(18)	(6)	4	10	20	29	28	16

[a] Figures in thousands of dollars.

TABLE 25
Cash Flow Pattern For Moderately Seasonal Retail Business

Month	Cash Inflow	Cash Outflow	Cumulative Cash Inflow	Cumulative Cash Outflow	Cumulative Difference
January	6,500	6,700	6,500	6,700	(200)
February	6,000	6,300	12,500	13,000	(500)
March	7,500	7,400	20,000	20,400	(400)
April	7,500	7,400	27,500	27,800	(300)
May	8,000	7,800	35,500	35,600	(100)
June	7,500	7,400	43,000	43,000	0
July	6,500	6,700	49,500	49,700	(200)
August	7,500	7,400	57,000	57,100	(100)
September	8,000	7,800	65,000	64,900	100
October	9,000	8,400	74,000	73,300	700
November	10,000	9,200	84,000	82,500	1500
December	16,000	13,500	100,000	96,000	4000
	100,000	96,000			

Tables 25 and 26 show typical cash flow patterns for two different small retail businesses. Table 25 represents a moderately seasonal sales pattern; Table 26 illustrates a highly seasonal business.

Both these businesses have the same total cash inflows, outflows, and profits for the year, yet the differences in their cash requirements during the year are substantial. The moderately seasonal business (Table 25) nearly breaks even in terms of cash flows throughout the first eight months of the year; in September, it begins to show a small cash surplus. In contrast, the highly seasonal business (Table 26) accumulates a negative cash balance of $8900 by the end of October and does not show a positive cash balance until year-end. Obviously, either substantial working capital must be provided for in this business or outside financing must be obtained; otherwise, it cannot exist.

The cash flow statement is probably the first document a banker or other lender would request before considering the approval of a business loan.

For most small businesses, a cash flow projection should be kept current on a monthly basis for the next 12-month period, with annual cash flow projections for the next one to five years.

One of the saddest happenings in business is the potentially success-

TABLE 26
Cash Flow Pattern for Highly Seasonal Retail Business

Month	*Cash Inflow*	*Cash Outflow*	*Cumulative Cash Inflow*	*Cumulative Cash Outflow*	*Cumulative Difference*
January	1,500	3,100	1,500	3,100	(1600)
February	2,500	3,800	4,000	6,900	(2900)
March	3,500	4,500	7,500	11,400	(3900)
April	3,500	4,500	11,000	15,900	(4900)
May	3,500	4,500	14,500	20,400	(5900)
June	5,500	6,000	20,000	26,400	(6400)
July	5,000	5,600	25,000	32,000	(7000)
August	4,500	5,200	29,500	37,200	(7700)
September	4,000	4,900	33,500	42,100	(8600)
October	6,000	6,300	39,500	48,400	(8900)
November	19,000	15,700	58,500	64,100	(5600)
December	41,500	31,900	100,000	96,000	4000
	100,000	96,000			

ful firm that goes broke while operating at a profit because of its failure to anticipate its cash requirements. The cash flow statement should be prepared with Robert Ringer's thought in mind:

> To those in the know,
> the game is cash flow.

Effect of Outside Financing on Profitability

No amount of outside financing can turn a basically unprofitable business into a profitable business. However, if a substantial portion of the capital required to finance a new business or a business expansion program can be obtained from outside sources at an interest rate considerably less than what the business can earn on its total assets, the percentage return on the owner's equity (or the net worth of the business) can be amplified considerably.

This "leverage" afforded by using other people's money is one of the most important financial tools available to the businessman.

For example, if a $100,000 total investment in the business is expected to yield a 15 percent annual net return, and if the owner were able to borrow $75,000 of that amount at a nine percent interest rate, the return on his out-of-pocket $25,000 investment would be 33 percent, calculated as follows:

Owner's investment	$ 25,000
Outside capital	75,000
Total investment	$100,000
Gross return at 15 percent	$ 15,000
Interest on $75,000 @ 9 percent	−6,750
Net return	$ 8,250
Return on owner's equity	33.0%

However, leverage also works in the other direction if the business fails to earn at the expected rate. When losses are incurred in a highly leveraged situation, the impact can be devastating. Earning just a little less than the cost of the borrowed money can have a damaging effect on the financial strength of a business.

Using the same example, if the businessman who borrowed 75 percent of his capital at a nine percent interest rate managed to earn only six percent on the total amount invested in the business, he would end up with an out-of-pocket loss of $750; his business would earn $6000 while paying out $6750 in interest charges. If the position were more highly leveraged—say in the 80 to 90 percent range—or if the return on total capital were down in the three to five percent range, the impact would be far greater.

Appendix 1
Characteristics of Selected Small Businesses

> ***Experience is a hard teacher. She gives the test first, and the lesson afterwards.***

Many small businesses are started by uninformed individuals with a strong desire for independence, but with little or no idea of what to expect in the way of sales, costs, profits, or investment requirements for their new business. Useful data are hard to find and are not generally available from any single source.

This section presents a variety of useful operating and financial data for 80 different types of small retail and service businesses, based on a "model" or "typical" size for each. Using these data, along with whatever else can be learned about the specific business and location under consideration, the prospective entrepreneur should be able to put together a reasonably complete and accurate pro forma balance sheet and profit-and-loss statement for the new business.

The "Typical" Small Business

Every small business presents its owners with different opportunities, and problems. Even the same kinds of business show widely varying characteristics and performances, depending not only on the products or services offered, but also on a number of important managerial and locational factors.

Financial and operating data are presented here for 80 different small retail and service business opportunities. Sufficient data are included to allow at least a preliminary economic analysis and feasibility study of a proposed or existing business venture in those or related similar lines. It must be emphasized, however, that these data represent only a "typical" operation or range of operations, unlikely to resemble any specific operation, and they should not be interpreted otherwise.

Do not use the data presented here as a basis for making a decision regarding the attractiveness of a proposed business venture; use it as a basis for making an analysis of the specific business and location under consideration, on which a rational and informed decision can then be based.

In many, probably most, proposed new business ventures, specific cost information should be available prior to the time at which a heavy financial commitment is required. It should therefore be possible to pin down many of the major items during the early stages of an analysis; rent, payroll expenses, and merchandise discount schedules, for example, can be closely estimated at an early stage. For this reason, space is provided on each of the 80 "economic characteristics" forms for filling in specific data, when known, for a proposed operation. Estimated figures pertaining to the proposed operation should be filled in the blank space provided. If there is no basis whatsoever for making an informed estimate, the figures shown for the "typical" operation can be employed until something more specific can be found.

What is most difficult—even impossible—to estimate with any real certainty until some operating experience has been gained is the sales volume for a new business operation. Consequently, a range is given for each type of business. Although it is common and desirable for prospective business owners to hope for the best, it is common sense and essential to prepare for the worst. Then, when the worst happens—which is far too often—it can be handled, thus averting a total financial disaster.

Included with the operating data is a brief description of each business, covering the types of merchandise or services generally offered, locational factors, space requirements, and other pertinent considerations. Finally, for each business a breakeven chart is shown, based on a business of typical size with typical operating characteristics.

Economic Characteristics of Small Businesses

Tables A1 and A2 show the format used for the presentation of operating data on the various businesses; Table A1 represents a retail business; Table A2 is more typical of a service firm. The format illustrated here is highly simplified, with most of the items actually encompassing several different elements of cost.

Typical Size. For the purpose of the economic analyses shown here, a typical size of operation was selected for each business, recognizing that few businesses can be called typical. Different businesses require

TABLE A1
Example of Economic Characteristics of Small Retail Businesses

	Low	Typical Operation	High	Proposed Operation
Typical size (sq. ft.)		2,000		
Typical investment				
Inventory		40,000		
Depreciable assets		20,000		
All other		20,000		
Total investment		80,000		
Operating Economics				
Sales per square foot	50	100	200	
Net annual sales	100,000	200,000	400,000	
Cost of goods sold	64,000	128,000	256,000	
Gross operating margin	36,000	72,000	144,000	
Fixed operating expenses				
Rent and utilities	20,000	20,000	20,000	
Fixed payroll	12,000	12,000	12,000	
Other fixed expenses	4,000	4,000	4,000	
Total fixed expenses	36,000	36,000	36,000	
Variable operating expenses				
Variable payroll	9,000	18,000	36,000	
Other variable expenses	5,000	10,000	20,000	
Total variable expenses	14,000	28,000	56,000	
Total operating expenses	50,000	64,000	92,000	
Net profit (loss) before taxes	(14,000)	8,000	52,000	
Typical operating ratios				
Net profit/net sales	—	4.0%	13%	
Net sales/total investment	1.3x	2.5x	5x	
Net profit/total investment	—	10.0%	65%	
Net sales/inventory	2.5x	5.0x	10x	

different amounts of space, and what might be considered small for one type of business (a variety store or family clothing store, for example) would be far more space than another kind of operation (such as a photo studio or pipe and tobacco shop) could ever use. The size indicated as typical is intended to depict approximately a median size for the particular business: about half the existing businesses in that field would be

TABLE A2
Example of Economic Characteristics of Small Service Businesses

Typical size (sq. ft.)		2,000		
Typical investment				
Inventory		10,000		
Depreciable assets		40,000		
All other		30,000		
Total investment		80,000		

	Low	*Typical Operation*	*High*	*Proposed Operation*
Operating Economics				
Sales per square foot	50	100	200	
Net annual sales	100,000	200,000	400,000	
Cost of goods sold	39,000	78,000	156,000	
Gross operating margin	61,000	122,000	244,000	
Fixed operating expenses				
Rent and utilities	20,000	20,000	20,000	
Fixed payroll	50,000	50,000	50,000	
Other fixed expenses	4,000	4,000	4,000	
Total fixed expenses	74,000	74,000	74,000	
Variable operating expenses				
Variable payroll	15,000	30,000	60,000	
Other variable expenses	5,000	10,000	20,000	
Total variable expenses	2,000	40,000	80,000	
Total operating expenses	94,000	114,000	154,000	
Net profit (loss) before taxes	(33,000)	8,000	90,000	
Typical operating ratios				
Net profit/net sales	—	4.0%	22.5%	
Net sales/total investment	1.3x	2.5x	5.0x	
Net profit/total investment	—	10.0%	112.5%	
Net sales/inventory	10.0x	20.0x	40.0x	

larger, and about half would be smaller. A range of sizes is also given so that the prospective businessman can look at a proposed location and determine whether it falls generally within the normal size range for the purpose for which its use is intended.

Typical Investment. A lot of money can be tied up in a small business, often more than the owners have anticipated, yet less than they ultimately discover is needed. Three categories of investment are covered here: (1) inventory, (2) depreciable assets, and (3) everything else.

The income-producing part of the investment in a retail business is inventory, the merchandise purchased and stocked for resale. For most service businesses, inventory requirements are minimal, and most of the total investment is tied up in less tangible assets. The inventory investment is generally from 40 to 60 percent of the total investment of a retail business; it accounts for a much lower percentage of the total investment requirements of a service business.

Depreciable assets include the furniture, fixtures, and equipment needed to operate the business. Usually, but not always, service businesses must invest heavily in the specialized equipment used in performing their services. A retail business, on the other hand, might get by on an investment of $5 to $10 per square foot for carpeting, display fixtures, and lighting.

In the "everything else" category, working capital is undoubtedly the most important, yet most overlooked, item; the lack of adequate working capital has caused the premature failure of many small businesses. Working capital is the money needed to finance day-to-day operations, paying the bills and covering the payroll expenses, while waiting for cash to come in from credit customers and daily sales. In general, working capital should be adequate to cover at least three months' expenses; it seldom is.

Altogether, the total investment in a business—the total of inventory, depreciable assets, and all other capital requirements—is usually between 25 and 50 percent of the annual sales volume of the business. As used here, the total investment represents all funds invested in the business regardless of source, whether borrowed or put up entirely by the owner or owners. The amounts shown are presented simply as typical, not necessarily adequate.

Operating Economics. Three sets of operating data are shown for each of the 80 businesses; all assume the physical size of the business as defined earlier. Again, the typical operation is roughly a median operation, with half expected to do better and half worse. The "low" set of data assumes about the worst sales per square foot that would be encountered, and the "high" assumes about the best sales per square foot that could be hoped for. Thus the three sets of data depict an extreme range of economic possibilities for the typical size of business. A new business should do better than the low and is unlikely to do as well as the high; still, it is important to define the overall range of conditions within which the business might reasonably be expected to operate.

Sales per square foot is one of the most important but less predictable factors in small retail and service businesses, because it is so strongly affected by the type of business and the location. Shops that operate in a high-traffic shopping center can easily show sales per square foot of several times that achievable by the same types of shops located in less desirable neighborhoods. Rental costs are, naturally, closely related to sales per square foot, with the more desirable locations demanding correspondingly higher charges. The high and low sales-per-square-foot figures shown for the various businesses were selected only to bracket the typical operation; as such they represent the economic extremes. Few establishments will be found to have either lower or higher sales per square foot than the lows and highs shown here. The typical sales per square foot is representative of the types of shopping centers or other locations in which the businesses are generally found.

Net annual sales are a direct function of shop size and sales per square foot. There are only two ways to increase the annual sales volume: (1) expand the store area or (2) increase the sales per square foot. More effective utilization of available space is obviously the superior way, and physical space should be increased only when the upper limit has been reached in terms of sales per square foot.

The cost of goods sold varies widely among the different businesses, depending on the sources of supply and the policies and discount schedules of suppliers. This category makes up the major part of a retailer's total cost of doing business (from 50 to 75 percent, averaging around 65 percent), but a relatively small portion (less than half in most cases) of the cost of running a service business. The cost of goods sold for retailers may seem high in view of the 40 to 50 percent discounts common for many types of retail merchandise. However, the buyer generally pays shipping costs, and the merchandise is further subject to theft, breakage, spoilage, damage, markdowns, and returns. If a going business can achieve a lower cost of goods sold than that shown here, its success can be attributed to efficient buying, effective inventory planning and control, and generally good management.

The gross operating margin represents the amount of money left over from sales receipts, after the goods or services sold are paid for, to pay the other costs of running the business.

Fixed Operating Expenses. Fixed operating expenses are those costs of doing business that must be paid regardless of the volume of business. They are related to the capacity to do business or simply to the fact of its being open. Fixed expenses are accrued with time, even if nothing is sold. Rent, utilities, and fixed payroll are the main items.

Rent and utilities are charged on a monthly contractual basis regardless of the amount of business conducted; even percentage rentals usually have some fixed base minimum. Retail or office space rents for anywhere from $2 to $20 per square foot per year, depending on its location and the size of the operation.

The fixed payroll represents the annual cost of having sufficient staff to keep the business open. Even the smallest retail shop requires at least one person, and more are required if the shop is kept open for extended hours. Larger areas require more people to cover them adequately.

Other fixed expenses take in a wide range of costs and expenses that will be incurred regardless of the level of sales. These other expenses might include depreciation of fixed assets, interest on business indebtedness, insurance, maintenance and repairs, general housecleaning and upkeep, inventory charges, business licenses, professional services (legal, accounting, etc.) and some basic advertising costs.

Variable Operating Expenses. Variable operating expenses are those expenses which increase with increasing sales or can be cut back if sales go down. As such, they are largely discretionary.

The variable payroll refers to whatever additional people are needed to handle the sales volume actually achieved, beyond the minimum level (the fixed payroll) needed simply to be open for business. Extra help hired to handle peak business hours during the day, to extend the times for being open, or to assist during a holiday rush period fall into this category.

Other variable expenses cover the assorted costs that are related directly to the amount of business conducted, whether they cause or are caused by the additional volume. For a retail store, this category might include expendable supplies (such as sacks), advertising expenditures, some taxes, percentage rent, sales commissions, and losses from bad debts.

Total operating expenses, then, consist of the sum of the fixed operating expenses and the variable operating expenses. This total, deducted from the gross operating margin, leaves the net profit or loss before taxes.

The net profit represents the return to the business's owners. In many small businesses, the owners are actively involved in running the business, functioning as the sales staff in addition to their other responsibilities. In such cases, the owners themselves probably make up the fixed payroll, and their cash drawings would include both the fixed payroll amount and the net profit; what they take from the fixed payroll represents wages, while the net profit constitutes their return on invested capital.

Operating Ratios. Four operating ratios are shown for each of the three levels of operation for each of the 80 businesses: (1) net profit to net sales, (2) net sales to total investment, (3) net profit to total investment, and (4) net sales to inventory. The first three ratios are important to all the businesses covered; the fourth (net sales to inventory) is important only in the retail field.

The net profit/net sales ratio, also called the profit margin, is a universal and important financial yardstick. It indicates a business firm's competitive strength or its vulnerability to a decrease in sales volume or profits. Usually an increase in sales widens the profit margin, since the fixed operating expenses do not rise in proportion to sales. For the same reason, profits increase and decrease more rapidly percentagewise than do sales.

The net sales/investment ratio measures the rate of capital turnover, one of the keys to success in any business. A high rate of capital turnover indicates the efficient utilization of invested capital and can yield a high return on investment from even a low profit margin.

The net profit/total investment ratio is probably the most important financial ratio in any business, since it represents the only true measure of profitability: the percentage return on the total capital invested in the business, regardless of the source of the capital. If the return on capital is higher than the cost of capital, the business likely warrants additional investment and expansion. Otherwise, profits from the business would be expected to earn greater returns by investing them outside the business.

The net sales/inventory ratio is extremely important in retail businesses, in which inventory makes up a large part of the total investment, but it lacks any real significance in service businesses in which the investment in inventory is relatively minor. Rapid inventory turnover (a high sales/inventory ratio) is the key to achieving high sales efficiency and good space utilization in a retail store. Slow-moving merchandise reduces the turnover rate and takes away space needed for faster-moving items that can yield higher sales per square foot. A better than average inventory turnover rate for a business indicates that management has been doing a good job with merchandise planning, buying, and inventory control.

Economic Analyses of Selected Businesses

The information presented in each "economic characteristics" table can be used to calculate the breakeven point for that particular business.

First, the variable cost rate must be established; this is done by adding the cost of goods sold to the total variable expenses and dividing by the net annual sales for the typical operation. This variable cost rate simply defines the portion of a firm's total sales that go toward paying its variable or volume-related costs and expenses. For the 80 businesses included here, the variable cost rates range from 0.25 to 0.85. Service businesses generally have variable cost rates of 0.40 to 0.60, whereas the variable costs of most retail firms range from 50 to 90 percent of their total sales.

The breakeven point—the sales volume at which receipts equal costs and expenses, with neither a profit nor a loss—is found from the formula:

$$\text{BEP} = \frac{\text{FC}}{1 - \text{VCR}}$$

where BEP is the breakeven point, FC, the total fixed costs, and VCR, the variable cost rate expressed as a decimal. For the retail business illustrated in Table A1, the variable cost rate is

$$\frac{28{,}000 + 128{,}000}{200{,}000} = 0.78$$

and, with fixed costs of $36,000, the breakeven point is

$$\frac{36{,}000}{1 - 0.78} = \$163{,}600$$

which, for a 2000-square-foot area, comes to

$$\frac{163{,}600}{2{,}000} = \$81.82 \text{ per square foot.}$$

A breakeven chart is shown for this operation in Fig. A1.

Similarly, the breakeven point for the service business described in Table A2 can be easily determined:

$$\text{VCR} = \frac{78{,}000 + 40{,}000}{200{,}000} = 0.59$$

$$\text{BEP} = \frac{74{,}000}{1 - 0.59} = \$180{,}500$$

$$\frac{80{,}500}{2{,}000} = \$90.24 \text{ per square foot.}$$

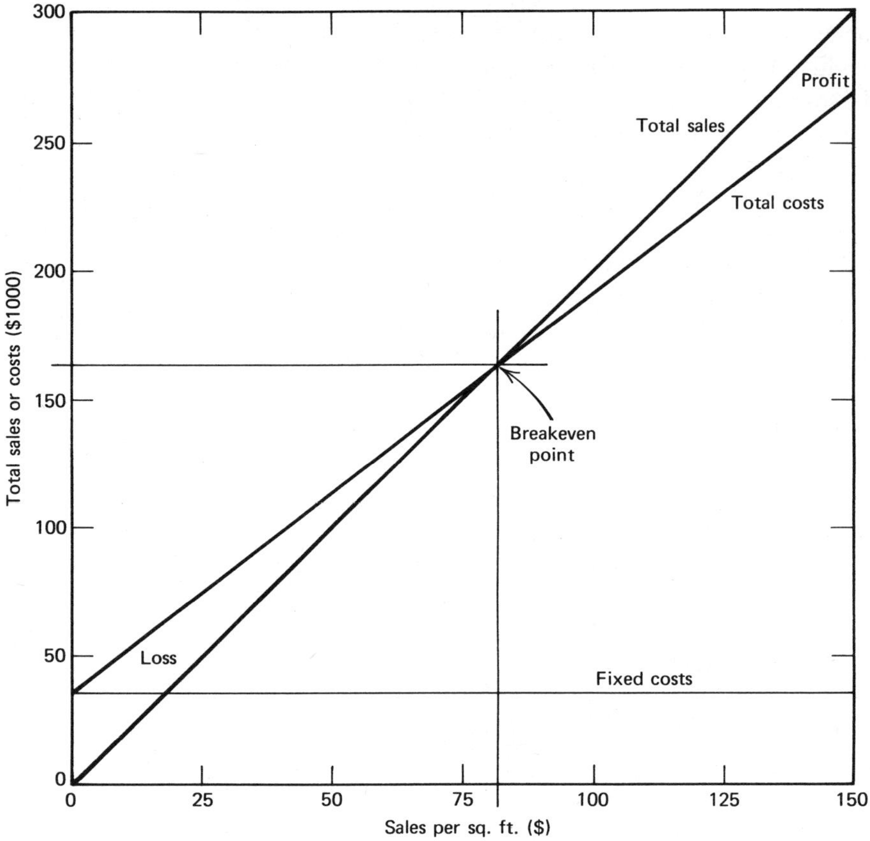

Figure A1. Breakeven chart for 2000 sq. ft. retail business.

The breakeven chart for this illustrative service business is shown in Fig. A2.

It is important to note here one of the basic differences between a service and a retail business. The service business usually has a relatively low variable cost rate and high fixed costs, whereas the retail business is usually characterized by high variable costs and relatively low fixed costs.

The service firm shows a far greater loss than the retail business at any given volume below its breakeven point, because of its high fixed costs; however, it shows far greater profits above the breakeven point, since those fixed costs are spread over a greater sales volume. Since a large part of each dollar's worth of merchandise sold by a retailer goes to pay for the merchandise itself, incremental profits (profits accrued for each dollar's sales above the breakeven point) come at a much lower rate.

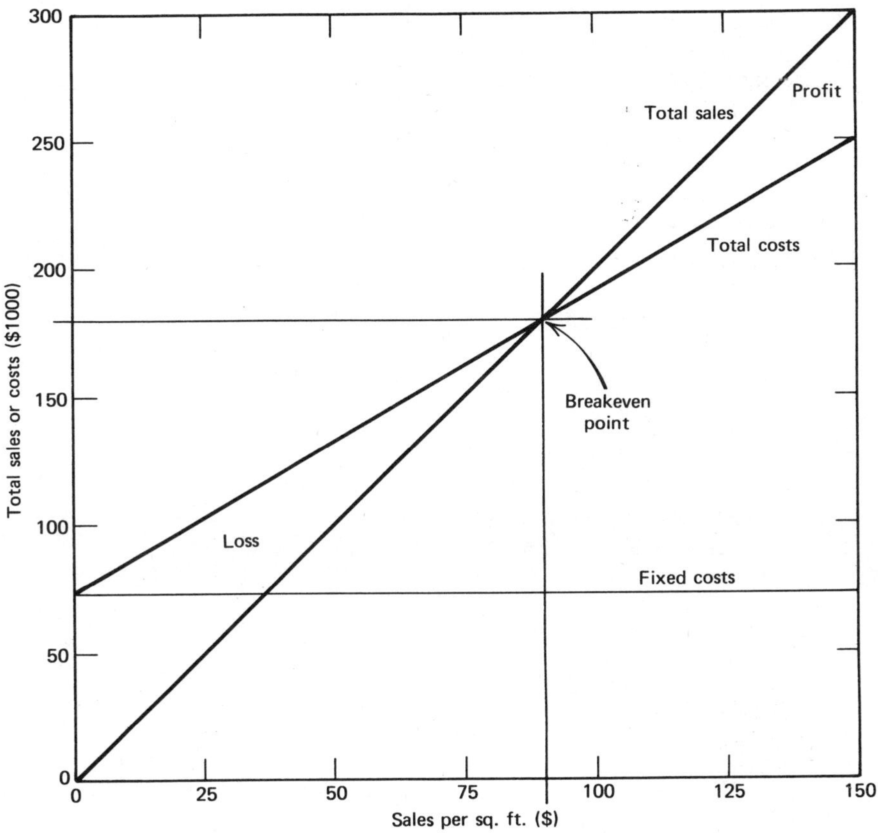

Figure A2. Breakeven chart for 2000 sq. ft. service business.

It should also be noted that some types of business combine the characteristics of retail and service businesses. Restaurants, for example, are usually classified as retail businesses even though most of their expenses are related to their services rather than products.

The Eighty Businesses

The 80 small retail and service business opportunities for which data are presented are grouped into ten broad categories:

1. *Building Materials and Hardware*
   Floor Coverings
   Hardware
   Paint and Wallpaper

2. *Food Products*
   Retail Bakery
   Candy and Nuts
   Candy Making
   Convenience Foods
   Retail Dairy Products
   Delicatessen
   Donut Shop
   Health Foods
   Liquor
   Retail Meat Market
   Specialty Foods
   Wine and Cheese

3. *Eating and Drinking Places*
   Fast-Food Restaurant
   Ice Cream Parlor
   Restaurant with Liquor
   Restaurant without Liquor
   Pizzeria

4. *Retail Clothing and Accessories*
   Bridal Shop
   Children's Clothing
   Children's Shoes
   Family Clothing
   Family Shoes
   Furs
   Ladies' Ready-to-Wear
   Ladies' Shoes
   Ladies' Specialties
   Lingerie and Hosiery
   Maternity Wear
   Men's and Boys' Clothing
   Unisex/Jeans

5. *Retail Furniture, Home Furnishings, and Equipment*
   Major Appliances
   Curtains and Draperies
   Furniture
   Lamps and Lighting Fixtures
   Radio, TV, and Electronics

6. *Miscellaneous Retail Stores*
   Art Gallery
   Arts and Crafts
   Books and Stationary

Cameras
Candles
Cards and Gifts
China and Glassware
Cosmetics
Drugs
Florist
Hobbies
Jewelry
Lawn and Garden Supplies
Luggage and Leather Goods
Musical Instruments
Office Supplies and Equipment
Pets
Pipes and Tobacco
Records and Tapes
Sewing Machines
Sporting Goods
Toys
Variety Store
Yard Goods and Fabrics

7. *Amusements*
   Arcades and Amusement Centers
   Bowling
   Movies

8. *Personal Services*
   Barber Shop
   Beauty Shop
   Coin-Operated Laundry
   Dry Cleaning
   Keys
   Photo Studio
   Travel Agency

9. *Automotive Products and Services*
   Gasoline Service Station
   Auto Exhaust System Service
   Auto Painting
   Auto Transmission Repair
   Tires, Batteries, and Accessories

10. *Miscellaneous Services*
    Small Gasoline Engine Repair
    Motel
    Fast Printing

Many of the businesses presented here are usually franchised, although most are independently owned and operated. In either case, the overall operating economics should be comparable. If the investment requirements for a particular franchise are substantially higher than those shown here, the prospective franchisee should be fairly certain that he is not paying more for the franchise name than the business warrants on an economic basis. Obviously, some franchise names are worth a great deal (especially in certain fast foods), but in many areas there is little or no customer loyalty or recognition factor to make the franchise name a particular asset in terms of its ability to generate additional sales beyond what an individually owned and independently operated business could achieve.

BUILDING MATERIALS AND HARDWARE

Floor Coverings

The floor coverings offered in a retail store primarily include carpets and carpet paddings, rugs, linoleum, and various types of tile. Installation services should be provided, usually through outside contractors. Retail stores may specialize in different floor coverings, and related product lines may be incorporated (such as kitchen and bathroom fixtures, along with floor, wall, and countertop materials).

The business is tied closely to the residential construction and home remodeling businesses, and commercial accounts may constitute a large part of sales; this necessitates carrying accounts receivable in substantial amounts, requiring considerable working capital.

Store locations are mostly (three-fourths) in community and neighborhood shopping centers. The ownership is 88 percent local, with 60

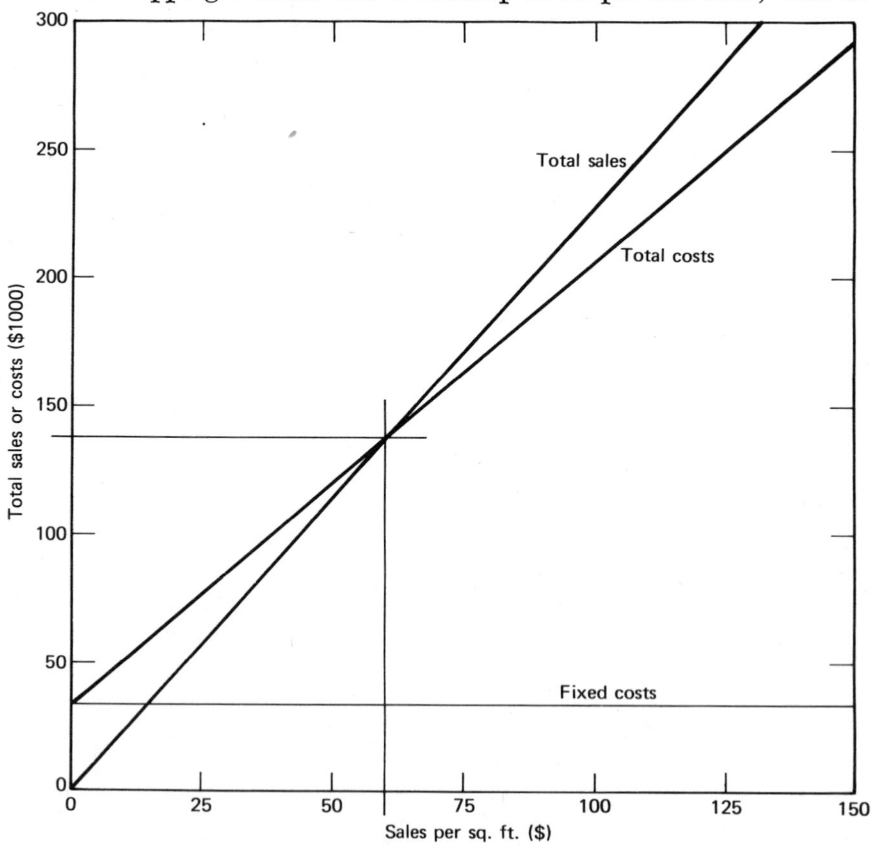

Breakeven chart for 2300 sq. ft. floor coverings store.

percent of the stores being single-store operations. Sizes range from 600 square feet to 5500 square feet, mostly between 2000 and 3700 square feet.

A typical 2300-square-foot floor coverings store needs just under $140,000 in annual sales, or $60.72 per square foot, to break even.

Economic Characteristics of Retail Floor Coverings Stores

Typical size (sq. ft.)		2,300		
Typical investment				
Inventory		25,000		
Depreciable assets		8,000		
All other		26,000		
Total investment		59,000		

	Low	*Typical Operation*	*High*	*Proposed Operation*
Operating Economics				
Sales per square foot	45	70	160	
Net annual sales	103,500	161,000	368,000	
Cost of goods sold	68,900	107,200	245,000	
Gross operating margin	34,600	53,800	123,000	
Fixed operating expenses				
Rent and utilities	13,800	13,800	13,800	
Fixed payroll	13,200	13,200	13,200	
Other fixed expenses	4,700	4,700	4,700	
Total fixed expenses	31,700	31,700	31,700	
Variable operating expenses				
Variable payroll	6,000	9,300	21,300	
Other variable expenses	5,100	8,000	18,300	
Total variable expenses	11,100	17,300	39,600	
Total operating expenses	42,800	49,000	71,300	
Net profit (loss) before taxes	(8,200)	4,800	51,700	
Typical operating ratios				
Net profit/net sales	—	3.0%	14.0%	
Net sales/total investment	1.8x	2.8x	6.2x	
Net profit/total investment	—	8.1%	87.6%	
Net sales/inventory	4.1x	6.4x	14.7x	

Hardware

Hardware stores handle a diverse variety of different basic lines and frequently branch out into essentially unrelated product areas that are of interest to their hardware customers. A bare minimum selection of merchandise would include hand and small power tools, paint and builders' supplies; most stores offer a fairly extensive inventory of housewares, household appliances, and cutlery, and many get into hunting, fishing, and other sporting goods. If a substantial business is conducted with commercial accounts, the working capital must reflect the credit terms extended to builders.

Most retail hardware stores carry the lower-quality, lower-priced lines of hand and power tools, aimed at the home handyman rather than the professional. The chief competition in these lines comes from the large discount houses and mass merchandisers.

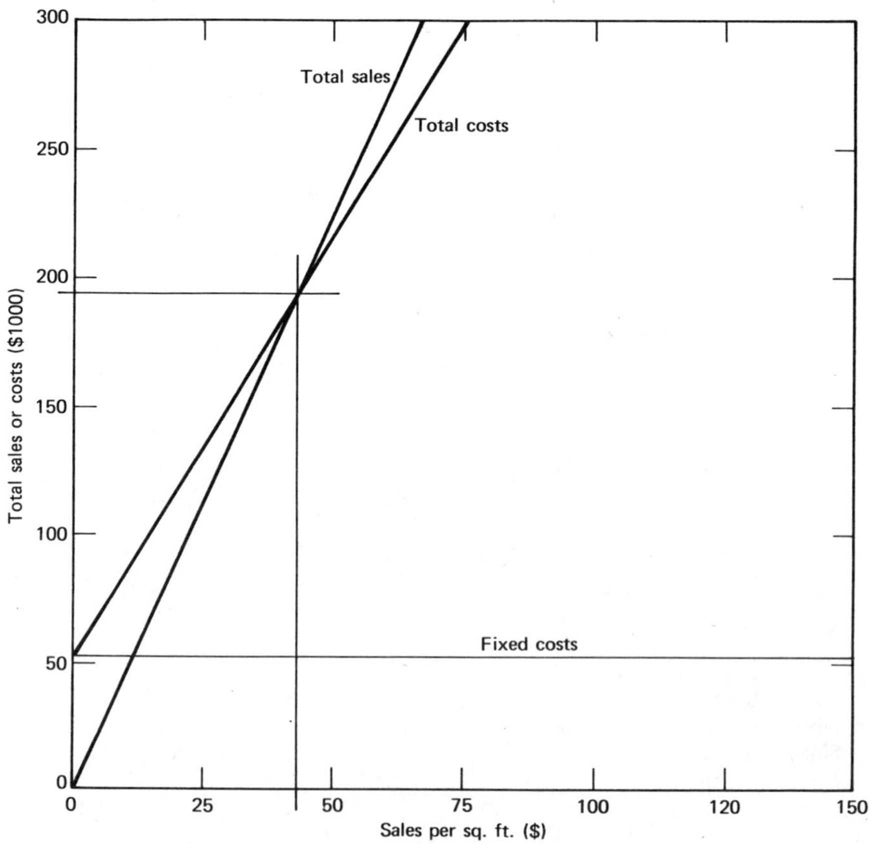

Breakeven chart for 4500 sq. ft. hardware store.

Hardware stores are usually found in smaller shopping areas, away from their largest competitors. Store sizes may be as high as 34,000 square feet for the complete, full-line building supply dealer; most are between 3800 and 9400 square feet. Franchised complete-package stores are not uncommon, but most hardware dealers find it advantageous to have only a loose national affiliation to improve their purchasing position.

A typical 4500-square-foot hardware store can break even with annual sales of $43.43 per square foot, totalling $195,000 per year.

Economic Characteristics of Retail Hardware Stores

Typical size (sq. ft.)		4,500		
Typical investment				
Inventory		49,000		
Depreciable assets		21,000		
All other		25,000		
Total investment		95,000		
	Low	*Typical Operation*	*High*	*Proposed Operation*
Operating Economics				
Sales per square foot	30	50	90	
Net annual sales	135,000	225,000	405,000	
Cost of goods sold	87,800	146,400	263,500	
Gross operating margin	47,200	78,600	141,500	
Fixed operating expenses				
Rent and utilities	22,500	22,500	22,500	
Fixed payroll	21,500	21,500	21,500	
Other fixed expenses	7,600	7,600	7,600	
Total fixed expenses	51,600	51,600	51,600	
Variable operating expenses				
Variable payroll	4,900	8,200	14,800	
Other variable expenses	6,600	11,000	19,800	
Total variable expenses	11,500	19,200	34,600	
Total operating expenses	63,100	70,800	86,200	
Net profit (loss) before taxes	(15,900)	7,800	55,300	
Typical operating ratios				
Net profit/net sales	—	3.5%	13.7%	
Net sales/total investment	1.4x	2.4x	4.3x	
Net profit/total investment	—	8.2%	58.2%	
Net sales/inventory	2.8x	4.6x	8.3x	

Paint and Wallpaper

Paint and wallpaper stores sell primarily to the general public but may also do a large business with painting and decorating contractors. They also handle a complete line of tools and accessories for performing these tasks. A good wallpaper business is the key to success; paint can be bought almost anywhere, but wallpaper buyers are far fussier, and a good selection attracts customers from a considerable distance.

Close working relationships should be developed with painting contractors, who are in a position to buy and recommend the store's products. As with other stores with commercial customers, working capital requirements are relatively high.

The peak business months for a paint and wallpaper business extend

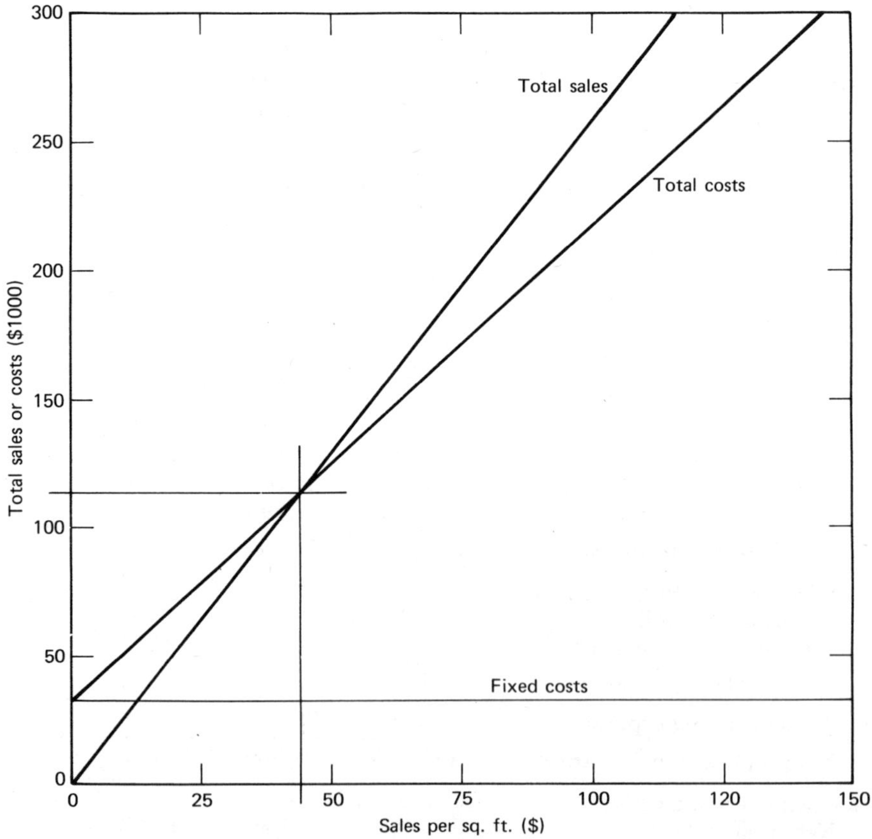

Breakeven chart for 2600 sq. ft. paint and wallpaper store.

from April through October. Almost half the stores are connected with a specific paint company, either as company-owned stores or as franchised businesses.

Store sizes range between 600 and 5600 square feet; most are between 1300 and 3100 square feet. A typical 2600-square-foot paint and wallpaper store needs $114,300 in annual sales, or $43.97 per square foot, to break even.

Economic Characteristics of Retail Paint and Wallpaper Stores

Typical size (sq. ft.)		2,600		
Typical investment				
Inventory		21,000		
Depreciable assets		15,000		
All other		24,000		
Total investment		60,000		

	Low	*Typical Operation*	*High*	*Proposed Operation*
Operating Economics				
Sales per square foot	35	50	90	
Net annual sales	91,000	130,000	234,000	
Cost of goods sold	55,600	79,400	142,900	
Gross operating margin	35,400	50,600	91,100	
Fixed operating expenses				
Rent and utilities	14,300	14,300	14,300	
Fixed payroll	14,400	14,400	14,400	
Other fixed expenses	4,800	4,800	4,800	
Total fixed expenses	33,500	33,500	33,500	
Variable operating expenses				
Variable payroll	4,200	6,000	10,800	
Other variable expenses	4,600	6,500	11,700	
Total variable expenses	8,800	12,500	22,500	
Total operating expenses	42,300	46,000	56,000	
Net profit (loss) before taxes	(6,900)	4,600	35,100	
Typical operating ratios				
Net profit/net sales	—	3.5%	15.0%	
Net sales/total investment	1.5x	2.2x	3.9x	
Net profit/total investment	—	7.7%	58.5%	
Net sales/inventory	4.3x	6.2x	11.1x	

FOOD PRODUCTS

Retail Bakery
Candy and Nuts
Candy Making
Convenience Foods
Retail Dairy Products
Delicatessen
Donut Shop
Health Foods
Liquor
Retail Meat Market
Specialty Foods
Wine and Cheese

Retail Bakery

Retail bakeries sell breads, rolls, cakes, cookies, pies, and other baked goods; most of the goods are baked on the premises. Some bakeries sell primarily over the counter to individual customers, whereas others also do a good business with commercial accounts such as restaurants. Specially decorated cakes for weddings, birthdays, anniversaries, and other special occasions may be an important part of the business.

The freshness of the baked goods is one of the most important considerations, and it is important to plan each day's production carefully. Baking must be an early morning activity, beginning perhaps around 2:00 am and continuing until the day's anticipated demands have been met.

Retail bakeries are located most often in community and smaller

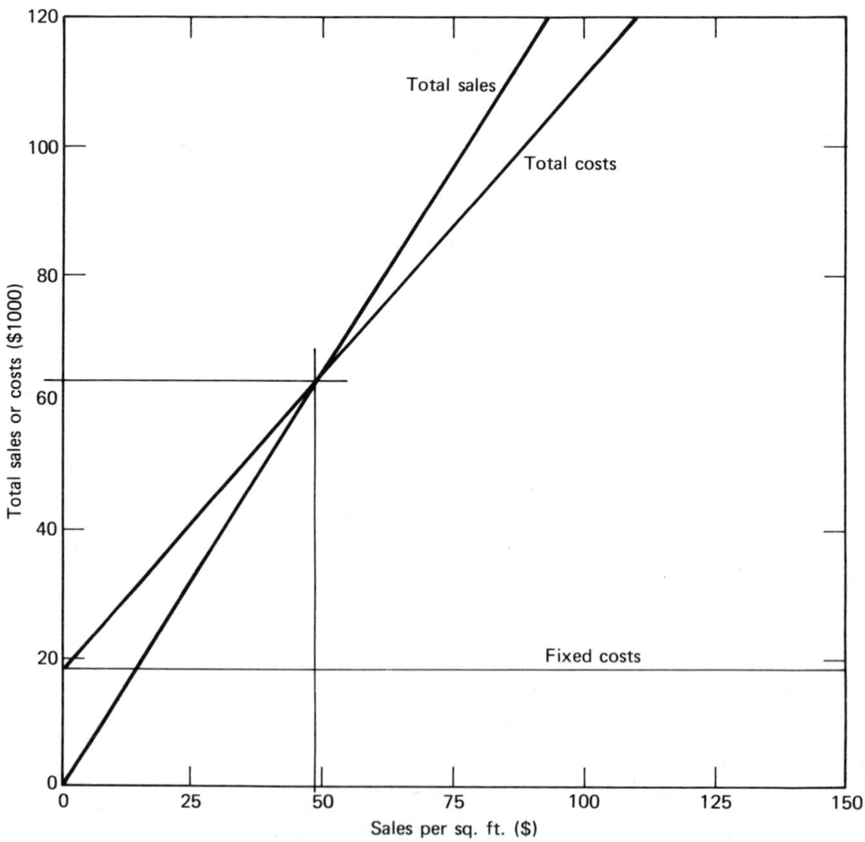

Breakeven chart for 1300 sq. ft. retail bakery.

regional shopping centers, although the neighborhood bakery is still an important factor. National interests have not penetrated this field; more than 95 percent of the retail bakeries are locally owned.

The size of a bakery can be anywhere from 300 to 4100 square feet, usually 1000 to 1600 square feet. The business is relatively nonseasonal.

A typical 1300-square-foot retail bakery breaks even on annual sales of $63,000; this represents sales of $48.47 per square foot per year.

Economic Characteristics of Retail Bakeries

Typical size (sq. ft.)		1,300		
Typical investment				
Inventory		3,400		
Depreciable assets		10,000		
All other		7,600		
Total investment		21,000		

	Low	*Typical Operation*	*High*	*Proposed Operation*
Operating Economics				
Sales per square foot	35	55	100	
Net annual sales	45,500	71,500	130,000	
Cost of goods sold	24,900	39,100	71,100	
Gross operating margin	20,600	32,400	58,900	
Fixed operating expenses				
Rent and utilities	7,800	7,800	7,800	
Fixed payroll	8,900	8,900	8,900	
Other fixed expenses	1,700	1,700	1,700	
Total fixed expenses	18,400	18,400	18,400	
Variable operating expenses				
Variable payroll	5,000	7,900	14,400	
Other variable expenses	2,300	3,600	6,500	
Total variable expenses	7,300	11,500	20,900	
Total operating expenses	25,700	29,900	39,300	
Net profit (loss) before taxes	(5,100)	2,500	19,600	
Typical operating ratios				
Net profit/net sales	—	3.5%	15.1%	
Net sales/total investment	2.2x	3.4x	6.2x	
Net profit/total investment	—	11.9%	93.3%	
Net sales/inventory	13.4x	21.0x	38.2x	

Candy and Nuts

Retail candy shops usually sell candy and nuts in prepackaged and bulk quantities, handle other confections (like popcorn and ice cream), and may operate a soda fountain or snack bar.

A high-traffic major shopping center location is almost essential, with the business heavily dependent on incidental walk-in trade. The business is highly seasonal, centered around traditional candy-giving holidays such as Valentine's day, Mothers' Day, and Christmas.

National chains and franchises are an important factor in the candy business, accounting for some 58 percent of the shops. Shop sizes may be

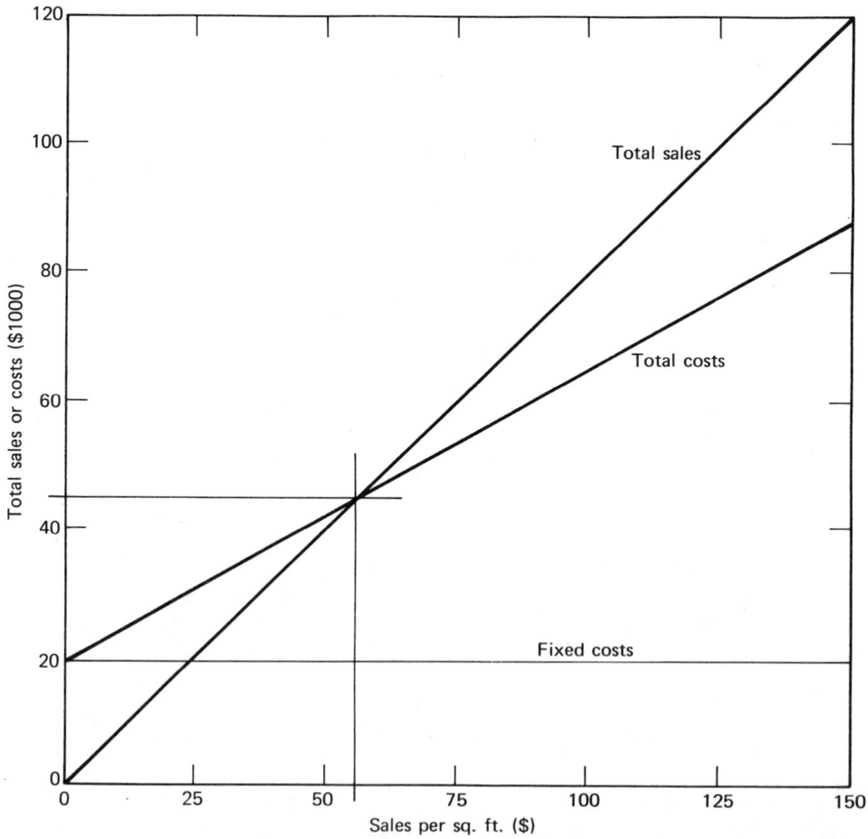

Breakeven chart for 800 sq. ft. candy and nut shop.

from as little as 200 square feet on up to 2300 square feet; most are small, between 750 and 850 square feet.

A typical 800-square-foot shop specializing in candy and nuts needs $44,300 in annual sales, or $55.43 per square foot, to break even.

Economic Characteristics of Retail Candy and Nut Shops

Typical size (sq. ft.)		800		
Typical investment				
Inventory		8,700		
Depreciable assets		8,200		
All other		4,800		
Total investment		21,700		

	Low	*Typical Operation*	*High*	*Proposed Operation*
Operating Economics				
Sales per square foot	40	90	175	
Net annual sales	32,000	72,000	140,000	
Cost of goods sold	19,300	43,400	84,400	
Gross operating margin	12,700	28,600	55,600	
Fixed operating expenses				
Rent and utilities	10,400	10,400	10,400	
Fixed payroll	7,500	7,500	7,500	
Other fixed expenses	1,700	1,700	1,700	
Total fixed expenses	19,600	19,600	19,600	
Variable operating expenses				
Variable payroll	1,400	3,200	6,200	
Other variable expenses	1,600	3,600	7,000	
Total variable expenses	3,000	6,800	13,200	
Total operating expenses	22,600	26,400	32,800	
Net profit (loss) before taxes	(9,900)	2,200	22,800	
Typical operating ratios				
Net profit/net sales	—	3.0%	16.3%	
Net sales/total investment	1.5x	3.3x	6.5x	
Net profit/total investment	—	10.1%	105.1%	
Net sales/inventory	3.7x	8.3x	16.1x	

Candy Making

A candy-making specialty shop produces its candy on the premises for direct over-the-counter sale. The operation is usually conducted in the open so that customers can watch the candy being made. It is sold by the pound or piece, packaged as it is purchased, and often mailed as requested by the customer.

These operations are usually found in "tourist area" shopping centers and follow the same seasonal patterns as other shops in the vicinity. Those located in metropolitan areas would have the same seasonal characteristics as regular candy stores, peaking just before Valentine's Day, Mothers' Day, and Christmas. If the candy-making venture proves suc-

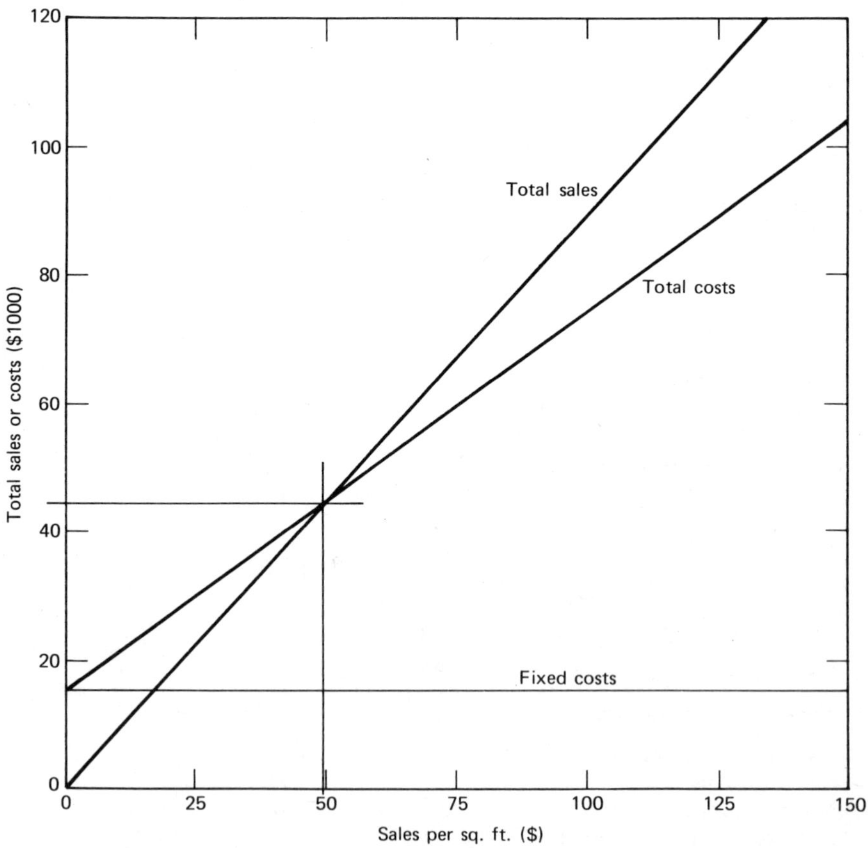

Breakeven chart for 900 sq. ft. candy-making shop.

cessful, the business can easily be extended to include several retail candy shops as outlets.

The size depends on location and market emphasis. A typical 900-square-foot candy-making shop can break even with annual sales of $44,300 or $49.24 per square foot per year.

Economic Characteristics of Candy-Making for Retail Sale

Typical size (sq. ft.)		900		
Typical investment				
Inventory		9,300		
Depreciable assets		7,100		
All other		6,100		
Total investment		22,500		

	Low	*Typical Operation*	*High*	*Proposed Operation*
Operating Economics				
Sales per square foot	35	55	100	
Net annual sales	31,500	49,500	90,000	
Cost of goods sold	17,500	27,500	50,000	
Gross operating margin	14,000	22,000	40,000	
Fixed operating expenses				
Rent and utilities	6,300	6,300	6,300	
Fixed payroll	7,500	7,500	7,500	
Other fixed expenses	1,800	1,800	1,800	
Total fixed expenses	15,600	15,600	15,600	
Variable operating expenses				
Variable payroll	1,300	2,100	3,800	
Other variable expenses	1,600	2,500	4,500	
Total variable expenses	2,900	4,600	8,300	
Total operating expenses	18,500	20,200	23,900	
Net profit (loss) before taxes	(4,500)	1,800	16,100	
Typical operating ratios				
Net profit/net sales	—	3.6%	17.9%	
Net sales/total investment	1.4x	2.2x	4.0x	
Net profit/total investment	—	8.0%	71.6%	
Net sales/inventory	3.4x	5.3x	9.7x	

Convenience Foods

A convenience food store offers its customers convenience in location and operating schedule. It is generally located in residential neighborhoods and is open for business from 15 to 24 hours daily every day.

The typical convenience food store offers little or no produce, no red meat, and not much in the way of dry groceries. It stocks only the top-selling brands in fast-moving lines, at premium prices. The average sale is less than $2.

Cigarettes and beer account for about 30 percent of the convenience store's sales; soft drinks, bakery products, and snack foods make up another 30 percent. These stores are not in direct competition with supermarkets for grocery customers; most of the products sold are probably consumed within an hour after they leave the store.

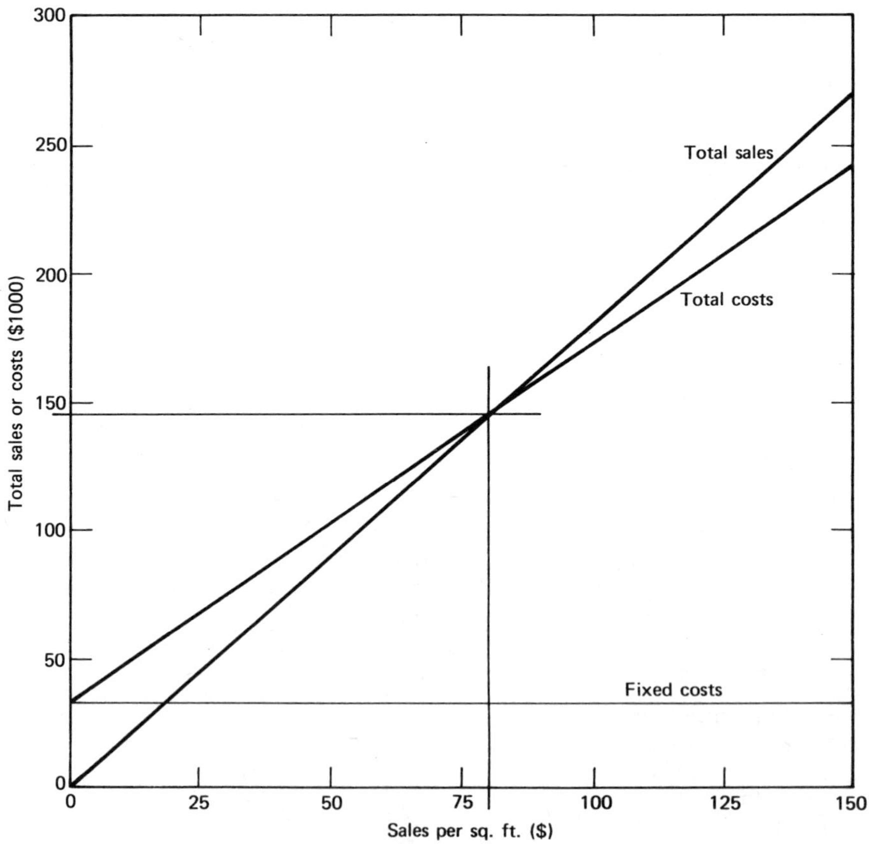

Breakeven chart for 1800 sq. ft. convenience food store.

Because of the extended operating hours, these stores have suffered frequently from armed robberies. Cash should be kept to a minimum, and security should be kept as tight as possible.

The sizes of such a store varies from 1000 square feet to more than 3000 square feet. A typical 1800-square-foot operation grosses $146,300 to break even, averaging $81.29 per square foot. National chains and franchises dominate the convenience food store business; these average about $250,000 in annual sales.

Economic Characteristics of Convenience Food Stores

Typical size (sq. ft.)		1,800		
Typical investment				
Inventory		11,000		
Depreciable assets		9,600		
All other		6,900		
Total investment		27,500		
	Low	*Typical Operation*	*High*	*Proposed Operation*
Operating Economics				
Sales per square foot	55	90	160	
Net annual sales	99,000	162,000	288,000	
Cost of goods sold	67,900	111,100	197,500	
Gross operating margin	31,100	50,900	90,500	
Fixed operating expenses				
Rent and utilities	12,600	12,600	12,600	
Fixed payroll	18,800	18,800	18,800	
Other fixed expenses	2,200	2,200	2,200	
Total fixed expenses	33,600	33,600	33,600	
Variable operating expenses				
Variable payroll	3,400	5,600	10,000	
Other variable expenses	5,000	8,100	14,400	
Total variable expenses	8,400	13,700	24,400	
Total operating expenses	42,000	47,300	58,000	
Net profit (loss) before taxes	(10,900)	3,600	32,500	
Typical operating ratios				
Net profit/net sales	—	2.2%	11.3%	
Net sales/total investment	3.6x	5.9x	10.5x	
Net profit/total investment	—	13.1%	118.2%	
Net sales/inventory	9.0x	14.7x	26.2x	

Retail Dairy Products

The basic business of a dairy products store consists of over-the-counter sales of milk, butter, cheese, eggs, ice cream, and related products. Many operate a soda fountain, and some carry a variety of picnic and convenience foods and supplies.

More than 60 percent of the dairy products stores are affiliated with national firms, and another 30 percent are operated by large local dairies, leaving less than 10 percent for the small independent operator. They can be found in all types of shopping centers.

The size of a dairy store ranges from 600 to 3200 square feet, and most are between 1100 and 2100 square feet. Except for ice cream and

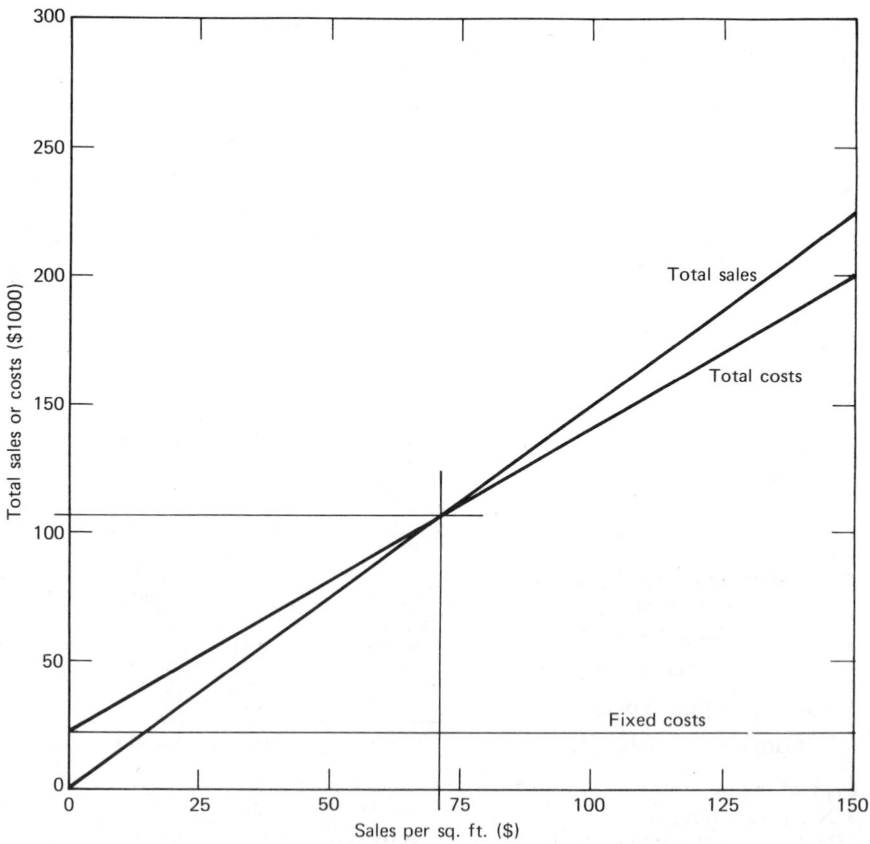

Breakeven chart for 1500 sq. ft. dairy products store.

soda fountain sales, the store's volume is fairly steady on a monthly basis.

A typical dairy products store occupies 1500 square feet and requires sales of $71.45 per square foot ($107,200 per year) to break even.

Economic Characteristics of Retail Dairy Products Stores

Typical size (sq. ft.)		1,500		
Typical investment				
Inventory		5,200		
Depreciable assets		27,500		
All other		12,000		
Total investment		44,700		

	Low	*Typical Operation*	*High*	*Proposed Operation*
Operating Economics				
Sales per square foot	35	80	160	
Net annual sales	52,500	120,000	240,000	
Cost of goods sold	34,600	79,000	158,000	
Gross operating margin	17,900	41,000	82,000	
Fixed operating expenses				
Rent and utilities	10,500	10,500	10,500	
Fixed payroll	9,800	9,800	9,800	
Other fixed expenses	3,600	3,600	3,600	
Total fixed expenses	23,900	23,900	23,900	
Variable operating expenses				
Variable payroll	3,600	8,200	16,400	
Other variable expenses	2,600	6,000	12,000	
Total variable expenses	6,200	14,200	28,400	
Total operating expenses	30,100	38,100	52,300	
Net profit (loss) before taxes	(12,200)	2,900	29,700	
Typical operating ratios				
Net profit/net sales	—	2.4%	12.4%	
Net sales/total investment	1.2x	2.7x	5.4x	
Net profit/total investment	—	6.5%	66.4%	
Net sales/inventory	10.1x	23.1x	46.2x	

Delicatessen

Most delicatessens specialize in specially processed meats, cheeses, breads, canned foods, teas, coffees, spices, and other items not ordinarily stocked in regular food markets or grocery stores. Some delicatessens prepare sandwiches for carry-out customers, and others provide tables and cold drinks for eat-in customers.

Most delicatessens are located in community and smaller regional shopping centers, although they are also found in most large regional and many small neighborhood centers. About 70 percent are locally owned, and 30 percent are either nationally franchised or parts of national chains. Sales are not especially seasonal, but the preparation of gift packages and

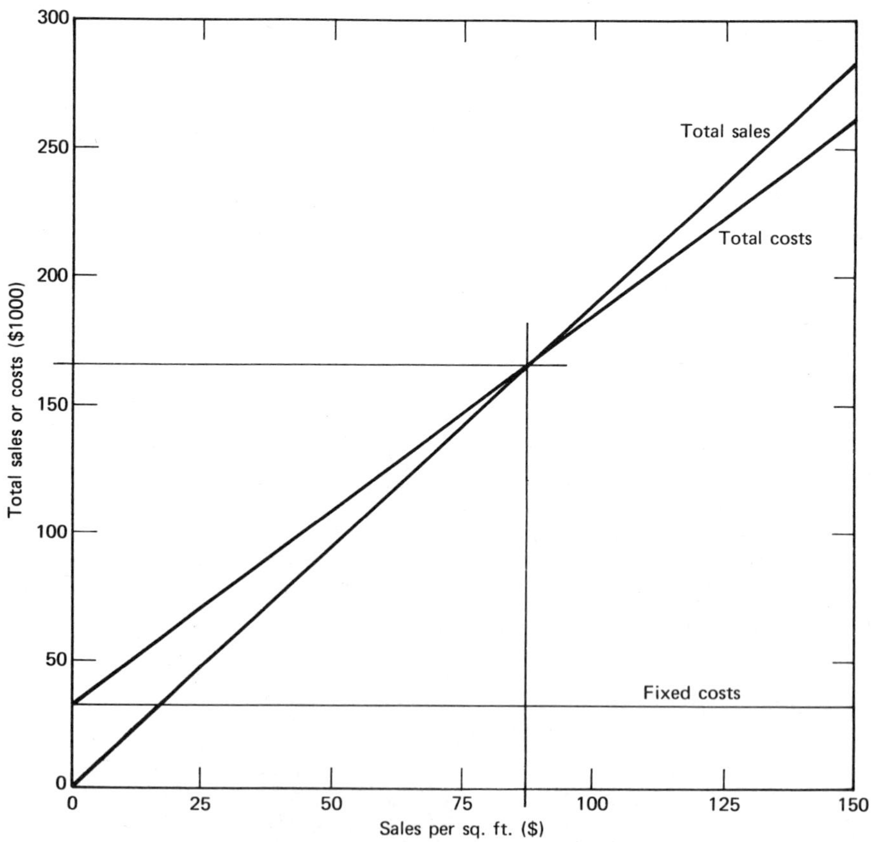

Breakeven chart for 1900 sq. ft. delicatessen.

assortments can help gain an increased share of the Christmas retail business.

Delicatessens range in size from 500 to more than 5000 square feet; 1100 to 2400 square feet is common.

The typical 1900-square-foot delicatessen needs sales of $87.28 per square foot, totaling $165,800 per year, to break even.

Economic Characteristics of Retail Delicatessens

Typical size (sq. ft.)	1,900	
Typical investment		
Inventory	12,100	
Depreciable assets	11,500	
All other	7,000	
Total investment	30,600	

	Low	*Typical Operation*	*High*	*Proposed Operation*
Operating Economics				
Sales per square foot	40	95	160	
Net annual sales	76,000	180,500	304,000	
Cost of goods sold	56.000	132,900	223,800	
Gross operating margin	20,000	47,600	80,200	
Fixed operating expenses				
Rent and utilities	19,000	19,000	19,000	
Fixed payroll	11,600	11,600	11,600	
Other fixed expenses	2,400	2,400	2,400	
Total fixed expenses	33,000	33,000	33,000	
Variable operating expenses				
Variable payroll	1,100	2,700	4.500	
Other variable expenses	3,800	9,000	15,200	
Total variable expenses	4,900	11,700	19,700	
Total operating expenses	37,900	44,700	52,700	
Net profit (loss) before taxes	(17,900)	2,900	27,500	
Typical operating ratios				
Net profit/net sales	—	1.6%	9.0%	
Net sales/total investment	2.5x	5.9x	9.9x	
Net profit/total investment	—	9.5%	89.9%	
Net sales/inventory	6.3x	14.9x	25.7x	

Donut Shop

For the businessman who has trouble sleeping in the morning, the donut shop may offer a solution. Most donut shops begin preparations by about 2:00 am and are open for business by 6:00 am. Product freshness is essential, and donut buyers start early. Some donut shops offer only over-the-counter, carry-out sales; others sell coffee and milk and provide tables or counter space for the eat-in trade.

Retail purchases are small; thus commercial accounts such as restaurants and other food service businesses are encouraged. The location is extremely important, with quick and easy access to automobile traffic essential.

About one-fourth of the donut shops are national franchises, with the rest locally owned and operated. A well-recognized national franchise can generate substantial additional sales, but other things being equal, the

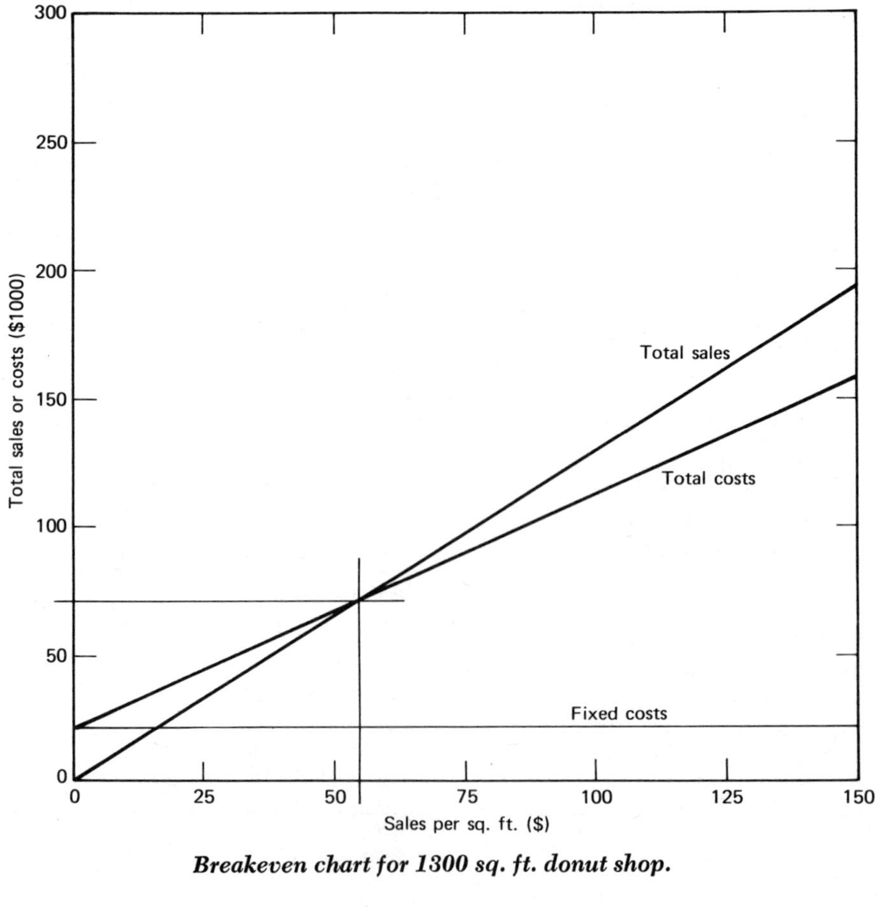

Breakeven chart for 1300 sq. ft. donut shop.

location is more important than the name for a donut shop. Customers do not usually travel out of their way for "brand-name" donuts unless the quality is obviously superior to shops with more convenient locations.

The size of a donut shop is usually between 900 and 1500 square feet (mostly working space rather than retail sales space), but sizes from 100 to 3800 square feet can be found. A typical 1300-square-foot operation breaks even with annual sales of $70,900 (or $54.52 per square foot); some national chains average close to $130,000 per location.

Economic Characteristics of Retail Donut Shops

Typical size (sq. ft.)		1,300		
Typical investment				
Inventory		3,800		
Depreciable assets		10,900		
All other		8,200		
Total investment		22,900		

	Low	*Typical Operation*	*High*	*Proposed Operation*
Operating Economics				
Sales per square foot	40	60	100	
Net annual sales	52,000	78,000	130,000	
Cost of goods sold	27,200	40,800	68,000	
Gross operating margin	24,800	37,200	62,000	
Fixed operating expenses				
Rent and utilities	11,700	11,700	11,700	
Fixed payroll	8,400	8,400	8,400	
Other fixed expenses	1,800	1,800	1,800	
Total fixed expenses	21,900	21,900	21,900	
Variable operating expenses				
Variable payroll	6,100	9,200	15,300	
Other variable expenses	2,600	3,900	6,500	
Total variable expenses	8,700	13,100	21,800	
Total operating expenses	30,600	35,000	43,700	
Net profit (loss) before taxes	(5,800)	2,200	18,300	
Typical operating ratios				
Net profit/net sales	—	2.8%	14.1%	
Net sales/total investment	2.3x	3.4x	5.7x	
Net profit/total investment	—	9.6%	79.9%	
Net sales/inventory	13.7x	20.5x	34.2x	

Health Foods

Health food stores usually carry a large assortment of nutritive supplements along with foods such as brewers yeast, unrefined vegetable oils, unsalted nuts, yogurt, kelp, canned vegetarian meat analogs, sea salt, canned and bottled juices, and, occasionally, organically produced meat. Brand names dominate the health food market, but health foods are sold primarily through the influence of health food writers.

About 70 percent of the health food stores are located in regional shopping centers, with 20 percent in community centers and 10 percent in neighborhood centers. Some 40 percent are franchised or parts of

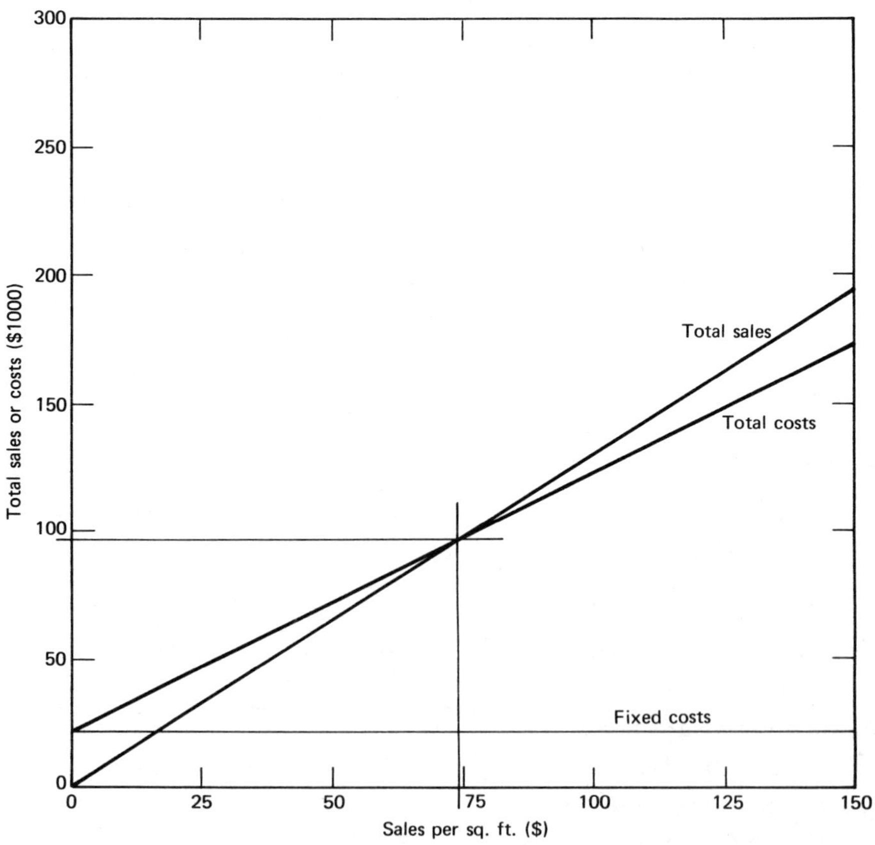

Breakeven chart for 1300 sq. ft. health food store.

national chains, whereas the rest are locally owned, independent businesses.

The size of a health food store varies between 300 and 3200 square feet, with 900 to 1600 square feet the typical range. A typical 1300-square-foot health food store breaks even with annual sales of $96,900 or $74.51 per square foot.

Economic Characteristics of Retail Health Food Stores

Typical size (sq. ft.)	1,300	
Typical investment		
Inventory	22,500	
Depreciable assets	7,600	
All other	5,500	
Total investment	35,600	

	Low	*Typical Operation*	*High*	*Proposed Operation*
Operating Economics				
Sales per square foot	50	85	180	
Net annual sales	65,000	110,500	234,000	
Cost of goods sold	45,700	77,700	164,500	
Gross operating margin	19,300	32,800	69,500	
Fixed operating expenses				
Rent and utilities	10,400	10,400	10,400	
Fixed payroll	8,400	8,400	8,400	
Other fixed expenses	2,800	2,800	2,800	
Total fixed expenses	21,600	21,600	21,600	
Variable operating expenses				
Variable payroll	1,600	2,700	5,700	
Other variable expenses	3,200	5,500	11,600	
Total variable expenses	4,800	8,200	17,300	
Total operating expenses	26,400	29,800	38,900	
Net profit (loss) before taxes	(7,100)	3,000	30,600	
Typical operating ratios				
Net profit/net sales	—	2.7%	13.1%	
Net sales/total investment	1.8x	3.1x	6.6x	
Net profit/total investment	—	8.4%	86.0%	
Net sales/inventory	2.9x	4.9x	10.4x	

Liquor

Liquor stores sell packaged alcoholic beverages and nonalcoholic mixes for consumption outside the business premises. They sometimes carry drink-related merchandise such as glasses, ice, snack foods, and party goods.

Liquor stores are subject to heavy federal and state regulation. Depending on the location and hours of operation, these stores may be particularly vulnerable to armed robberies, and this possibility should be carefully weighed by anyone considering a new business.

Liquor stores are distributed more or less uniformly among the various types of shopping centers at a rate of about one store for every 5000

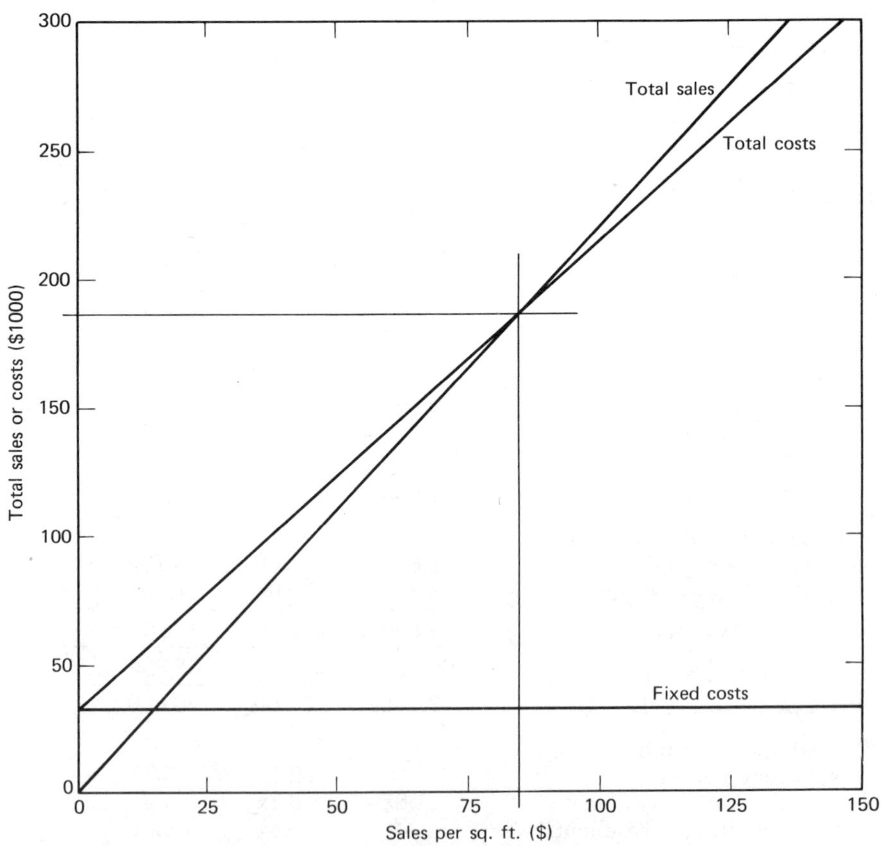

Breakeven chart for 2200 sq. ft. liquor store.

population. Some 40 percent of the stores are parts of locally owned chains; the rest are independent operations.

The sale of liquor is only moderately seasonal, with about 12 percent of the total annual sales occurring in December. Store sizes range from 750 to 12,500 square feet, but are usually between 2000 and 5600 square feet. A typical 2200-square-foot liquor store breaks even with annual sales of $184,500, or $83.87 per square foot per year.

Economic Characteristics of Retail Liquor and Wine Stores

Typical size (sq. ft.)		2,200		
Typical investment				
Inventory		21,000		
Depreciable assets		27,000		
All other		15,000		
Total investment		63,000		

	Low	*Typical Operation*	*High*	*Proposed Operation*
Operating Economics				
Sales per square foot	60	100	300	
Net annual sales	132,000	220,000	660,000	
Cost of goods sold	102,100	170,100	510,300	
Gross operating margin	29,900	49,900	149,700	
Fixed operating expenses				
Rent and utilities	13,200	13,200	13,200	
Fixed payroll	12,800	12,800	12,800	
Other fixed expenses	5,000	5,000	5,000	
Total fixed expenses	31,000	31,000	31,000	
Variable operating expenses				
Variable payroll	1,100	1,900	5,700	
Other variable expenses	6,600	11,000	33,000	
Total variable expenses	7,700	12,900	38,700	
Total operating expenses	38,700	43,900	69,700	
Net profit (loss) before taxes	(8,800)	6,000	80,000	
Typical operating ratios				
Net profit/net sales	—	2.7%	12.1%	
Net sales/total investment	2.1x	3.5x	15.5x	
Net profit/total investment	—	9.5%	127.0%	
Net sales/inventory	6.3x	10.5x	31.4x	

Retail Meat Market

A retail meat market specializes in selling fresh, frozen, and cured meats, fish, shellfish, and other seafoods, as well as poultry and perhaps some dairy products, eggs, and other fast-moving commodities. Some meat markets may butcher animals on their own, buy from others for resale, or do custom butchering for individual customers.

There is very little national involvement in this field on the retail level; 97 percent of the shops are locally owned. Locational preferences are for smaller regional, community, and neighborhood shopping centers.

The size of a meat market varies between 500 and 3500 square feet,

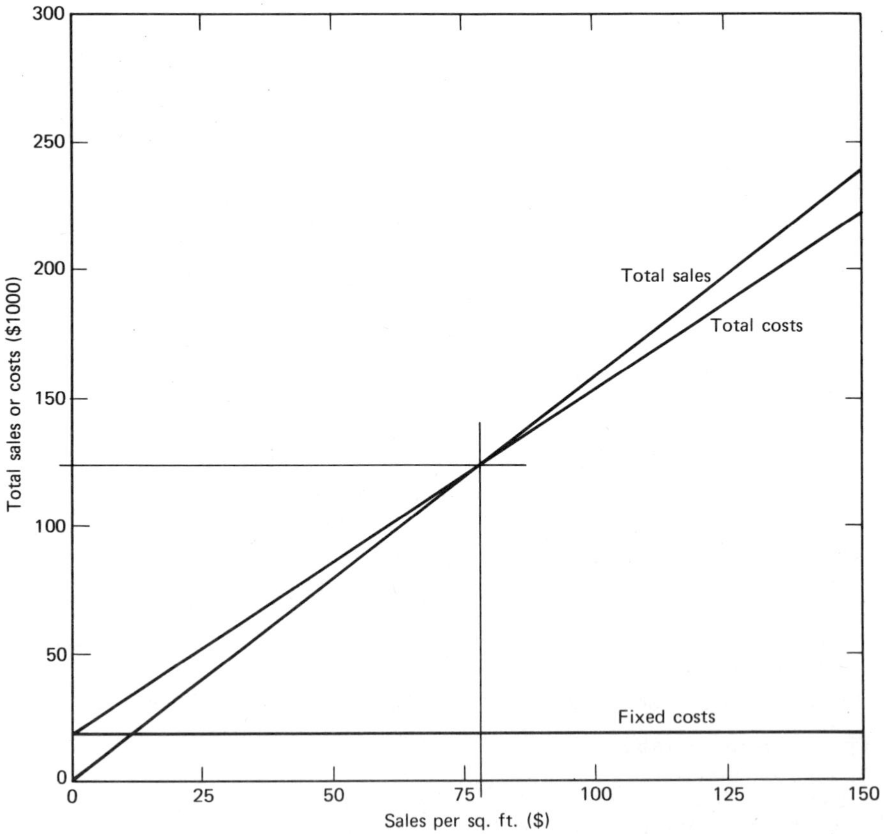

Breakeven chart for 1600 sq. ft. meat market.

with most in the 1200 to 2500 square foot range. Sales are not especially seasonal, although the last half of the year is above average.

A typical 1600-square-foot meat market requires sales of about $78 per square foot (or $124,800 per year) to reach its breakeven point.

Economic Characteristics of Retail Meat Markets

Typical size (sq. ft.)		1,600		
Typical investment				
Inventory		3,900		
Depreciable assets		4,500		
All other		8,800		
Total investment		17,200		

	Low	*Typical Operation*	*High*	*Proposed Operation*
Operating Economics				
Sales per square foot	60	85	240	
Net annual sales	96,000	136,000	384,000	
Cost of goods sold	73,400	104,000	293,600	
Gross operating margin	22,600	32,000	90,400	
Fixed operating expenses				
Rent and utilities	8,000	8,000	8,000	
Fixed payroll	10,200	10,200	10,200	
Other fixed expenses	1,400	1,400	1,400	
Total fixed expenses	19,600	19,600	19,600	
Variable operating expenses				
Variable payroll	2,700	3,800	10,700	
Other variable expenses	4,800	6,800	19,200	
Total variable expenses	7,500	10,600	29,900	
Total operating expenses	27,100	30,200	49,500	
Net profit (loss) before taxes	(4,500)	1,800	40,900	
Typical operating ratios				
Net profit/net sales	—	1.3%	10.7%	
Net sales/total investment	5.6x	7.9x	22.3x	
Net profit/total investment	—	5.8%	237.8%	
Net sales/inventory	24.6x	34.9x	98.5x	

Specialty Foods

The specialty foods business includes many of the meats, cheeses, and other products found in regular delicatessens, plus a variety of other domestic and imported food items not found elsewhere. The chief difference is often in the packaging and merchandising; the specialty foods shop might be considered a "gift shop" for food. Some specialty shops limit their lines to only a few items such as coffees, spices, or gourmet foods, and they may carry related lines of hardware and cooking aids, cookbooks, and utensils.

About one-half the specialty food shops are located in smaller regional shopping centers, with another one-fourth found in the largest

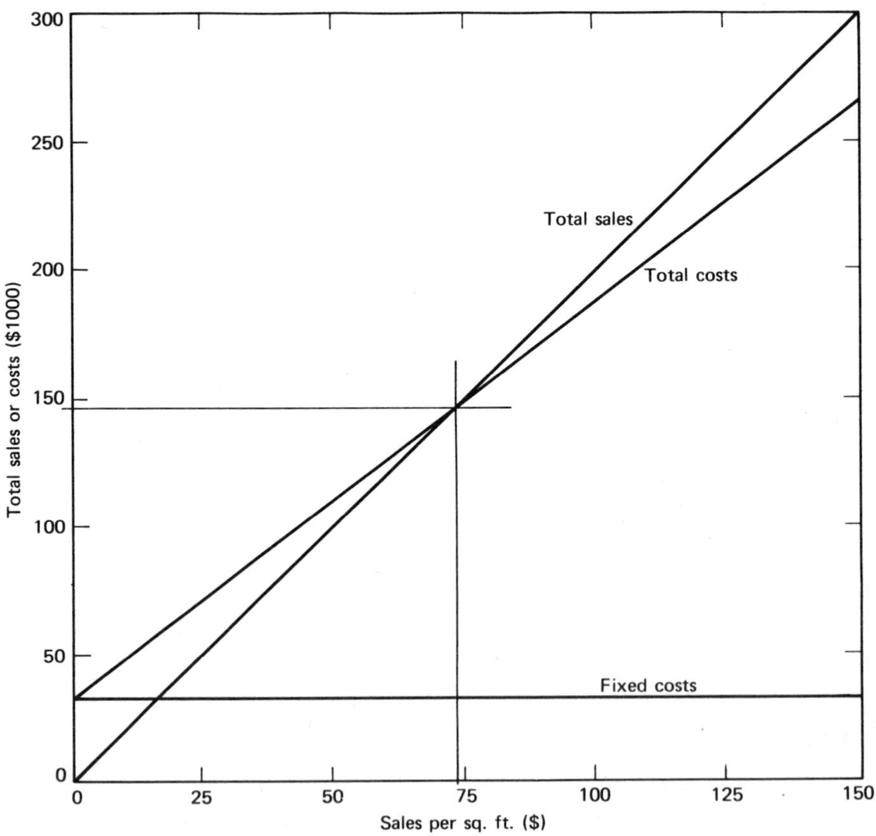

Breakeven chart for 2000 sq. ft. specialty foods store.

centers. Some 56 percent have a national connection of some type; the rest are locally owned.

The sizes of specialty food shops range from 300 square feet to 4000 square feet; they are typically between 500 and 2600 square feet.

A typical 2000-square-foot specialty food shop needs sales of $148,700 or $74.35 per square foot annually, to break even.

Economic Characteristics of Retail Specialty Foods Shops

Typical size (sq. ft.)		2,000		
Typical investment				
Inventory		10,600		
Depreciable assets		10,200		
All other		6,300		
Total investment		27,100		

	Low	*Typical Operation*	*High*	*Proposed Operation*
Operating Economics				
Sales per square foot	50	80	150	
Net annual sales	100,000	160,000	300,000	
Cost of goods sold	64,600	103,400	193,900	
Gross operating margin	35,400	56,600	106,100	
Fixed operating expenses				
Rent and utilities	20,000	20,000	20,000	
Fixed payroll	12,000	12,000	12,000	
Other fixed expenses	2,200	2,200	2,200	
Total fixed expenses	34,200	34,200	34,200	
Variable operating expenses				
Variable payroll	7,400	11,800	21,900	
Other variable expenses	5,000	8,000	15,000	
Total variable expenses	12,400	19,800	36,900	
Total operating expenses	46,600	54,000	71,100	
Net profit (loss) before taxes	(11,200)	2,600	35,000	
Typical operating ratios				
Net profit/net sales	—	1.6%	11.7%	
Net sales/total investment	3.7x	5.9x	11.1x	
Net profit/total investment	—	9.6%	129.2%	
Net sales/inventory	9.4x	15.1x	28.3x	

Wine and Cheese

A wine and cheese shop must carry a large inventory of domestic and imported wines and cheeses; several hundred different labels are not uncommon for wines. Buying must be carefully done; some technical expertise is required in assuring a well-balanced and salable selection, and considerable restraint must be exercised to keep from overspending.

Although traffic flow is important, the type of customer is far more critical. Most wine buyers take their buying quite seriously, and many are extremely knowledgeable.

Essentially all wine specialty shops are located in major regional shopping centers, with about 40 percent of the shops affiliated with na-

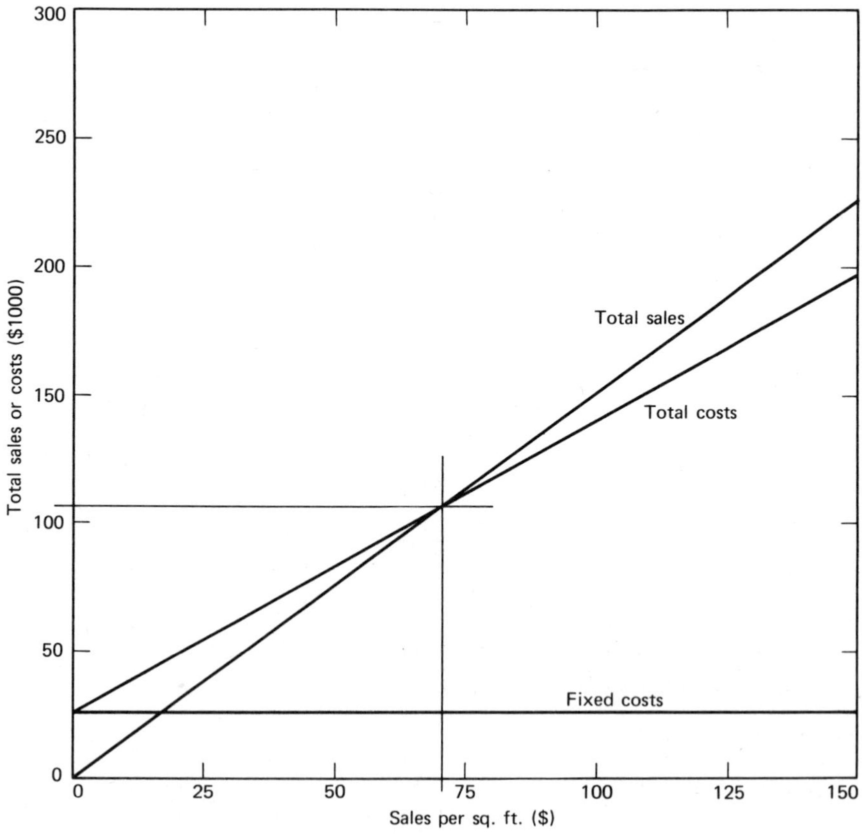

Breakeven chart for 1500 sq. ft. wine and cheese shop.

tional chains. The balance are primarily single-shop, independent operations.

Sizes range from 500 to 3400 square feet, with most wine shops in the 1500 to 2300 square foot bracket. A typical 1500-square-foot shop breaks even with sales of $106,700 annually, or $71.11 per square foot.

Economic Characteristics of Retail Wine and Cheese Shops

Typical size (sq. ft.)		1,500		
Typical investment				
Inventory		11,300		
Depreciable assets		10,600		
All other		6,700		
Total investment		28,600		

	Low	*Typical Operation*	*High*	*Proposed Operation*
Operating Economics				
Sales per square foot	60	80	110	
Net annual sales	90,000	120,000	165,000	
Cost of goods sold	61,700	82,300	113,200	
Gross operating margin	28,300	37,700	51,800	
Fixed operating expenses				
Rent and utilities	13,500	13,500	13,500	
Fixed payroll	9,800	9,800	9,800	
Other fixed expenses	2,300	2,300	2,300	
Total fixed expenses	25,600	25,600	25,600	
Variable operating expenses				
Variable payroll	2,200	2,900	4,000	
Other variable expenses	4,500	6,000	8,300	
Total variable expenses	6,700	8,900	12,300	
Total operating expenses	32,300	34,500	37,900	
Net profit (loss) before taxes	(4,000)	3,200	13,900	
Typical operating ratios				
Net profit/net sales	—	2.7%	8.4%	
Net sales/total investment	3.1x	4.2x	5.8x	
Net profit/total investment	—	11.2%	48.6%	
Net sales/inventory	8.0x	10.6x	14.6x	

EATING AND DRINKING PLACES

Fast-Food Restaurant
Ice Cream Parlor
Restaurant with Liquor
Restaurant without Liquor
Pizzeria

Fast-Food Restaurant

The fast foods field is overwhelmingly dominated by nationally franchised operations. Their menu emphasis is on hamburgers, fried chicken, fish, and ethnic foods, primarily Mexican and Italian.

A good franchise name in a good location can almost guarantee success, but good franchises are difficult to obtain, and many desirable locations have been almost fully saturated. Local chains and independent operations still account for about one-half of the fast-food businesses, but for nowhere near one-half of the dollar volume.

The most conspicuous locations for fast-food businesses are along busy streets, although all types of shopping centers are popular; about

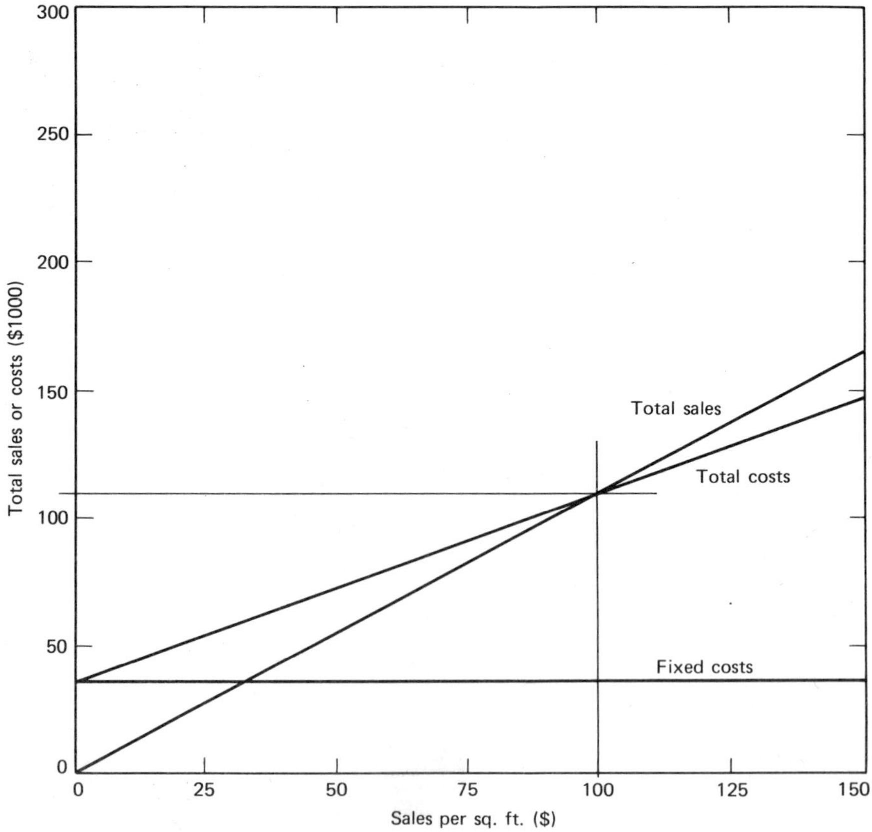

Breakeven chart for 1100 sq. ft. fast-food restaurant.

one-half of the major fast-food restaurants are located in or near regional centers.

Sizes can range from less than 500 square feet to more than 4000 square feet, with the typical range between 900 and 1900 square feet (exclusive of parking area). A typical independent fast-food business needs $110,200 in annual volume, or $100.18 per square foot for a 1100-square-foot operation, to break even.

Economic Characteristics of Fast-Food Restaurants

Typical size (sq. ft.)		1,100		
Typical investment				
Inventory		3,000		
Depreciable assets		25,000		
All other		15,000		
Total investment		43,000		

	Low	*Typical Operation*	*High*	*Proposed Operation*
Operating Economics				
Sales per square foot	80	115	225	
Net annual sales	88,000	126,500	247,500	
Cost of goods sold	41,100	59,100	115,600	
Gross operating margin	46,900	67,400	131,900	
Fixed operating expenses				
Rent and utilities	14,300	14,300	14,300	
Fixed payroll	18,800	18,800	18,800	
Other fixed expenses	3,400	3,400	3,400	
Total fixed expenses	36,500	36,500	36,500	
Variable operating expenses				
Variable payroll	13,400	19,200	37,600	
Other variable expenses	4,400	6,300	12,300	
Total variable expenses	17,800	25,500	49,900	
Total operating expenses	54,300	62,000	86,400	
Net profit (loss) before taxes	(7,400)	5,400	45,500	
Typical operating ratios				
Net profit/net sales	—	4.3%	18.4%	
Net sales/total investment	2.0x	2.9x	5.8x	
Net profit/total investment	—	12.6%	105.8%	
Net sales/inventory	29.3x	42.2x	82.5x	

Ice Cream Parlor

Ice cream parlors sell soft drinks and ice cream in single servings for consumption on the premises and hand-packed ice cream for carry-out customers. The business is highly seasonal throughout the year and highly erratic throughout the day. Either customers are impatiently awaiting service, or the management is impatiently awaiting customers. Even a small ice cream parlor must scoop out a quarter of a million servings a year, one scoop at a time: labor costs can easily run one-fourth or more of the total sales dollar.

Ice cream parlors, some 60 percent of which are either nationally owned or franchised, are widely distributed throughout all types of shopping centers, from neighborhood to large regional in scope. They are sometimes unwelcome tenants, since other shopowners discourage browsers with ice cream cones.

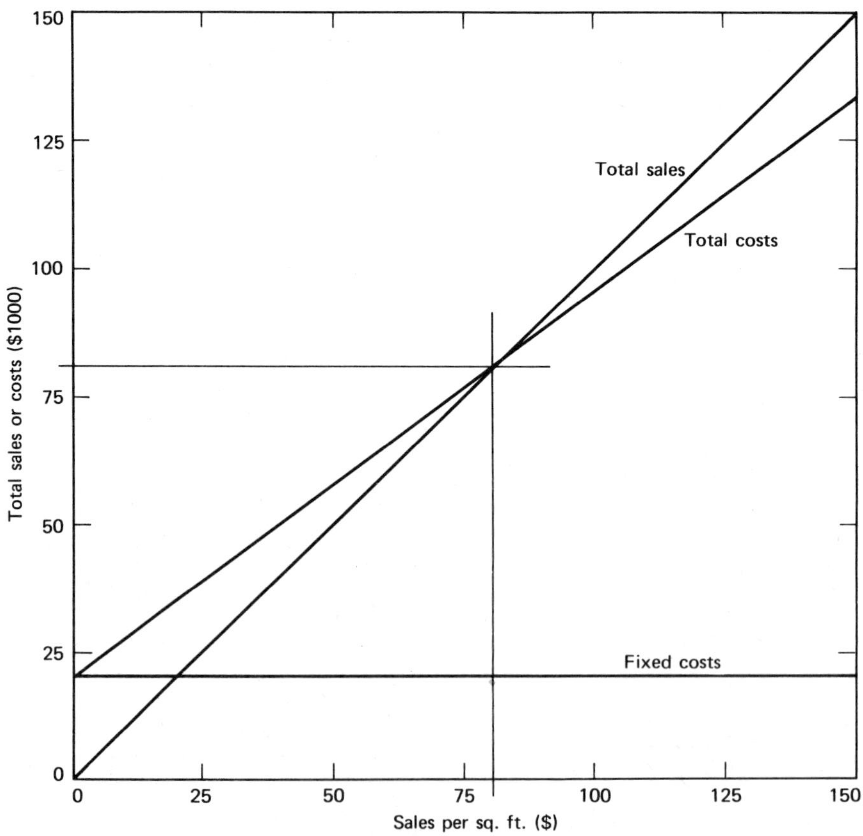

Breakeven chart for 1000 sq. ft. ice cream parlor.

Sizes for ice cream parlors range between 200 and 5000 square feet, with 900 to 2400 square feet most common. A typical 1000-square-foot ice cream parlor needs sales of $81.12 per square foot per year ($81,100 total) to break even; this means that a sales rate of well over $100 per square foot is required during the warm-weather months to compensate for slow winter sales.

Economic Characteristics of Retail Ice Cream Parlors

Typical size (sq. ft.)		1,000		
Typical investment				
Inventory		3,900		
Depreciable assets		20,500		
All other		8,900		
Total investment		33,300		

	Low	*Typical Operation*	*High*	*Proposed Operation*
Operating Economics				
Sales per square foot	40	90	150	
Net annual sales	40,000	90,000	150,000	
Cost of goods sold	21,200	47,700	79,500	
Gross operating margin	18,800	42,300	70,500	
Fixed operating expenses				
Rent and utilities	10,000	10,000	10,000	
Fixed payroll	7,500	7,500	7,500	
Other fixed expenses	2,700	2,700	2,700	
Total fixed expenses	20,200	20,200	2,200	
Variable operating expenses				
Variable payroll	6,800	15,400	25,700	
Other variable expenses	2,000	4,500	7,500	
Total variable expenses	8,800	19,900	33,200	
Total operating expenses	29,000	40,100	53,400	
Net profit (loss) before taxes	(10,200)	2,200	17,100	
Typical operating ratios				
Net profit/net sales	—	2.4%	11.4%	
Net sales/total investment	1.2x	2.7x	4.5x	
Net profit/total investment	—	6.6%	51.4%	
Net sales/inventory	10.3x	23.1x	38.5x	

Restaurant With Liquor

Adding liquor to a restaurant's menu changes the entire character of the establishment. It may also change the type of menu offered, operating schedules, and locational requirements, as well as requiring a totally different emphasis to reach a totally different market. The restaurant with liquor, then, does not necessarily compete for the same trade as the family restaurant.

Restaurants that serve liquor tend to locate in less-trafficed shopping areas, since they are less concerned with the family shopping group than with those whose primary reason for going out is to eat and drink; theirs is more a direct trade than an incidental one. Ownership is 80 percent local; more than one-half are single-establishment businesses.

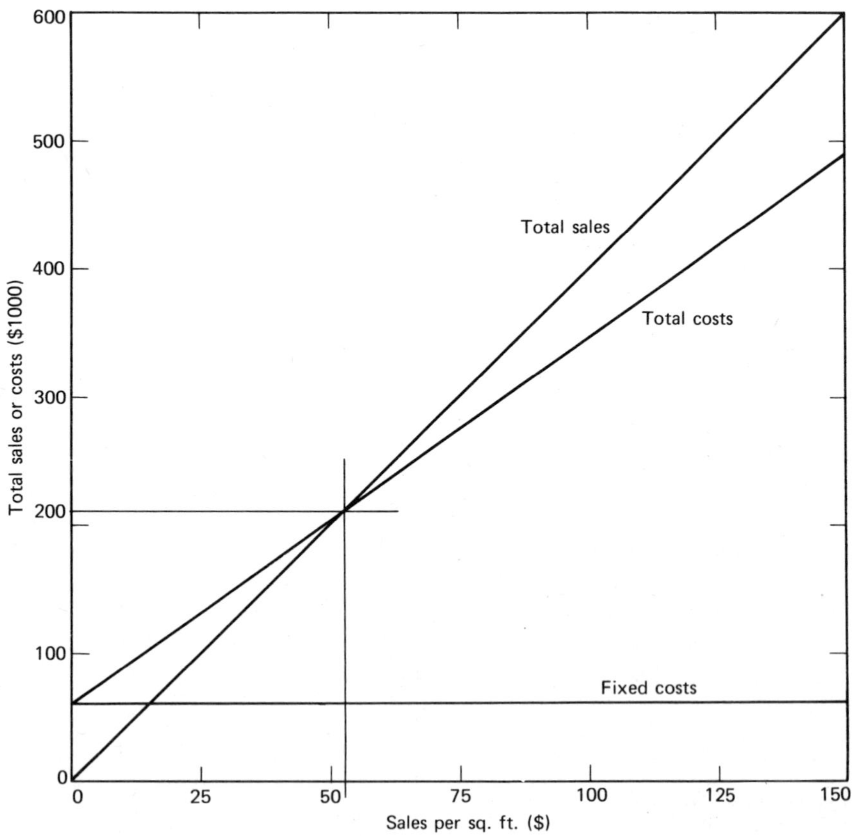

Breakeven chart for 4000 sq. ft. restaurant with liquor.

Sizes range from 1200 square feet to 14,000 square feet, with most in the 2800 to 7300 square foot bracket.

A typical 4000-square-foot eating and drinking place needs sales of $210,300 to break even, amounting to $52.59 per square foot.

Economic Characteristics of Restaurants with Liquor

Typical size (sq. ft.)		4,000		
Typical investment				
Inventory		8,000		
Depreciable assets		76,000		
All other		32,000		
Total investment		116,000		

	Low	*Typical Operation*	*High*	*Proposed Operation*
Operating Economics				
Sales per square foot	40	62	140	
Net annual sales	160,000	248,000	560,000	
Cost of goods sold	78,100	121,000	273,200	
Gross operating margin	81,900	127,000	286,800	
Fixed operating expenses				
Rent and utilities	32,000	32,000	32,000	
Fixed payroll	20,000	20,000	20,000	
Other fixed expenses	9,000	9,000	9,000	
Total fixed expenses	61,000	61,000	61,000	
Variable operating expenses				
Variable payroll	27,700	43,000	97.100	
Other variable expenses	7,700	12,000	27,100	
Total variable expenses	35,400	55,000	124,200	
Total operating expenses	96,400	116,000	185,200	
Net profit (loss) before taxes	(14,500)	11,000	101,600	
Typical operating ratios				
Net profit/net sales	—	4.4%	18.1%	
Net sales/total investment	1.4x	1.1x	4.8x	
Net profit/total investment	—	9.5%	87.6%	
Net sales/inventory	20.0x	31.0x	70.0x	

Restaurant Without Liquor

Although restaurants are generally classified as retail businesses, their economic characteristics more closely resemble those of a service business; their costs are related more to the services offered than to the cost of food served.

"Family" type restaurants are found in all types of shopping areas—from the largest regional centers to the smaller neighborhood centers. Most regional shopping centers have one or more restaurants; about one-half the community centers have one, and about one-third of the neighborhood centers.

The independent restaurant's competition for the family trade comes from two main directions, both of national origin: the fast-food franchise and the large national chain restaurants, either franchised or company owned. However, ease of access, diversity of menus, quality of food,

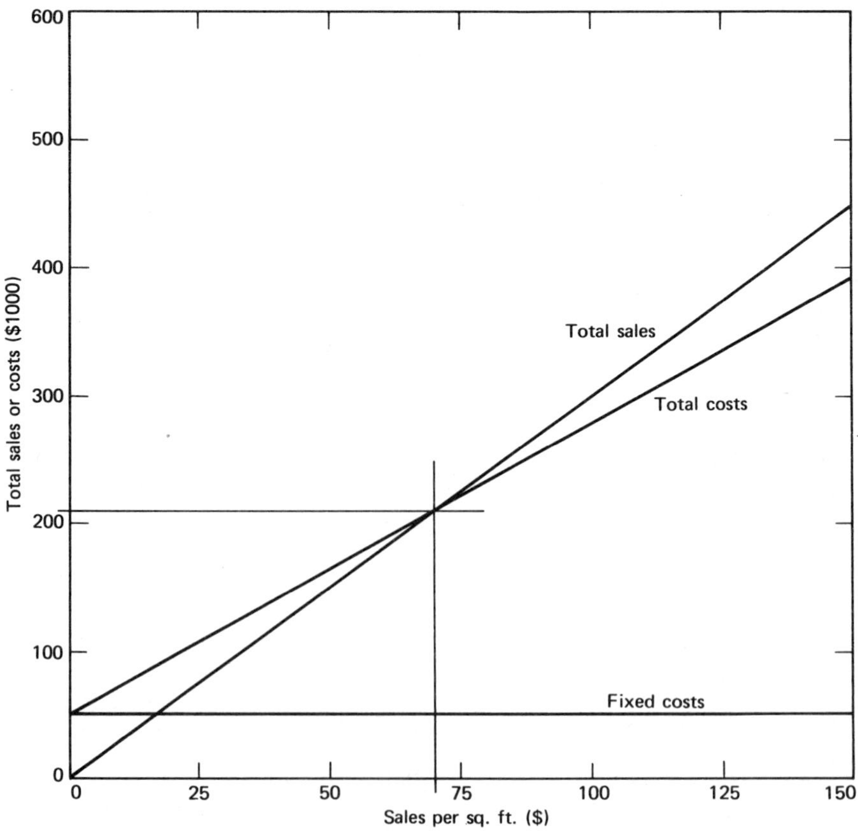

Breakeven chart for 3000 sq. ft. restaurant without liquor.

pleasantness of surroundings, and other factors important to a restaurant's success are not the proprietary domain of the chain restaurant, and a well-run independent operation in a good location can more than adequately survive the competition. Three-fourths of all restaurants are still locally owned and independent.

Sizes can range from 250 square feet up to 14,000 square feet, with the 1600 to 4800 square foot range encompassing most restaurant operations. A typical 3000 square-foot family restaurant can break even on sales of $69.56 per square foot, or $208,700 annually.

Economic Characteristics of Restaurants Without Liquor

Typical size (sq. ft.)		3,000		
Typical investment				
Inventory		8,000		
Depreciable assets		74,000		
All other		31,000		
Total investment		113,000		

	Low	*Typical Operation*	*High*	*Proposed Operation*
Operating Economics				
Sales per square foot	40	80	150	
Net annual sales	120,000	240,000	450,000	
Cost of goods sold	62,500	125,000	234,400	
Gross operating margin	57,500	115,000	215,600	
Fixed operating expenses				
Rent and utilities	25,500	25,500	25,500	
Fixed payroll	16,000	16,000	16,000	
Other fixed expenses	9,000	9,000	9,000	
Total fixed expenses	50,500	50,500	50,500	
Variable operating expenses				
Variable payroll	22,500	45,000	84,400	
Other variable expenses	6,000	12,000	22,500	
Total variable expenses	28,500	57,000	106,900	
Total operating expenses	79,000	107,500	157,400	
Net profit (loss) before taxes	(21,500)	7,500	58,200	
Typical operating ratios				
Net profit/net sales	—	3.1%	12.9%	
Net sales/total investment	1.1x	2.1x	4.0x	
Net profit/total investment	—	6.6%	51.5%	
Net sales/inventory	15.0x	30.0x	56.3x	

Pizzeria

Pizzerias have either a young adult or family-type orientation; few appeal to both groups at the same time. A large part of the business consists of carry-out orders, beer, and soft drinks. Many offer free home delivery.

Most pizzerias are actually a cross between a regular restaurant and a fast-food operation. Their limited menus and general informality are coupled with food prepared to the customer's order.

Pizzerias are found virtually everywhere, from large regional shopping malls to local neighborhood convenience centers. National chains and franchises are an important factor in this business, but local chains

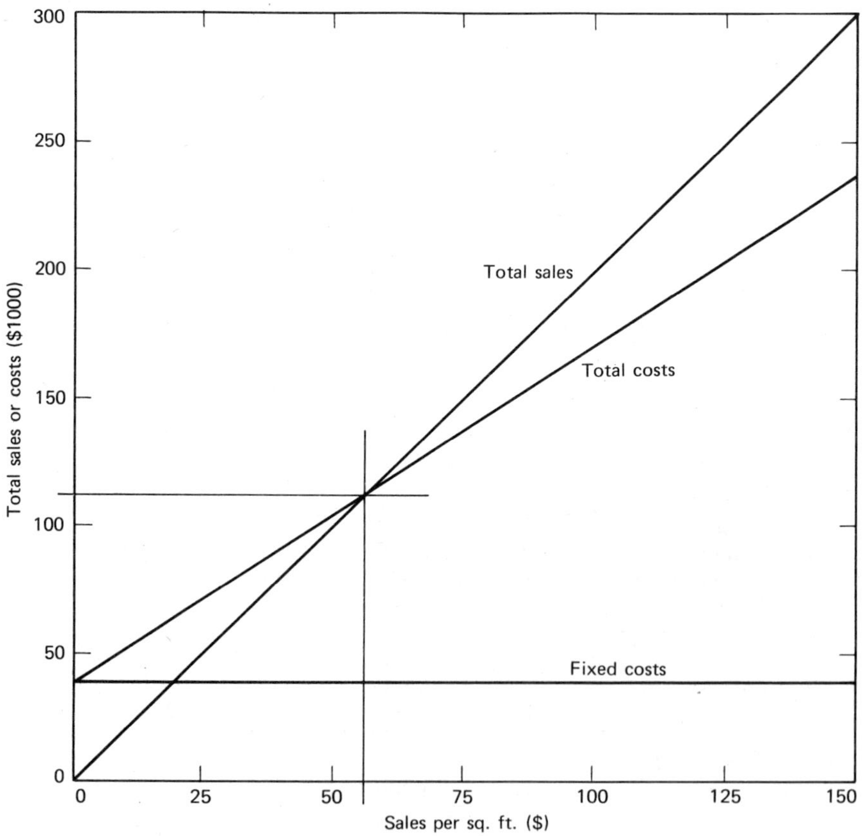

Breakeven chart for 2000 sq. ft. pizzeria.

and independent pizzerias can be equally successful as long as their locations and market emphasis are carefully planned.

Pizzerias can occupy as little as 800 square feet or as much as 6000 square feet. A typical 2000-square-foot pizzeria needs $61.01 per square foot in annual sales (a total of $122,000) to break even.

Economic Characteristics of Pizzerias

Typical size (sq. ft.)		2,000		
Typical investment				
Inventory		3,000		
Depreciable assets		24,000		
All other		13,000		
Total investment		40,000		

	Low	*Typical Operation*	*High*	*Proposed Operation*
Operating Economics				
Sales per square foot	45	70	150	
Net annual sales	90,000	140,000	300,000	
Cost of goods sold	49,600	77,100	165,200	
Gross operating margin	40,400	62,900	134,800	
Fixed operating expenses				
Rent and utilities	13,000	13,000	13,000	
Fixed payroll	22,500	22,500	22,500	
Other fixed expenses	3,200	3,200	3,200	
Total fixed expenses	38,700	38,700	38,700	
Variable operating expenses				
Variable payroll	7,400	11,500	24,600	
Other variable expenses	4,500	7,000	15,000	
Total variable expenses	11,900	18,500	39,600	
Total operating expenses	50,600	57,200	78,300	
Net profit (loss) before taxes	(10,200)	5,700	56,500	
Typical operating ratios				
Net profit/net sales	—	4.1%	18.8%	
Net sales/total investment	2.3x	3.5x	7.5x	
Net profit/total investment	—	14.3%	141.3%	
Net sales/inventory	30.0x	46.7x	100.0x	

RETAIL CLOTHING AND ACCESSORIES

Bridal Shop
Children's Clothing
Children's Shoes
Family Clothing
Family Shoes
Furs
Ladies' Ready-to-Wear
Ladies' Shoes
Ladies' Specialties
Lingerie and Hosiery
Maternity Wear
Men's and Boys' Clothing
Unisex/Jeans

Bridal Shop

The bridal shop is a highly specialized operation dealing in bridal gowns, bridesmaids' gowns, and accessories for other members of the wedding party. Profitable sidelines may include catering and photography, and most bridal shops are equipped to handle their own tailoring and alterations.

The bridal shop need not depend on incidental, walk-in pedestrian traffic; thus nearly all shops are located in smaller regional and larger community shopping centers. Ownership is overwhelmingly local (90 percent), with more than 70 percent of all bridal shops being single-shop operations.

The business is as seasonal as weddings. Prospective customer lists

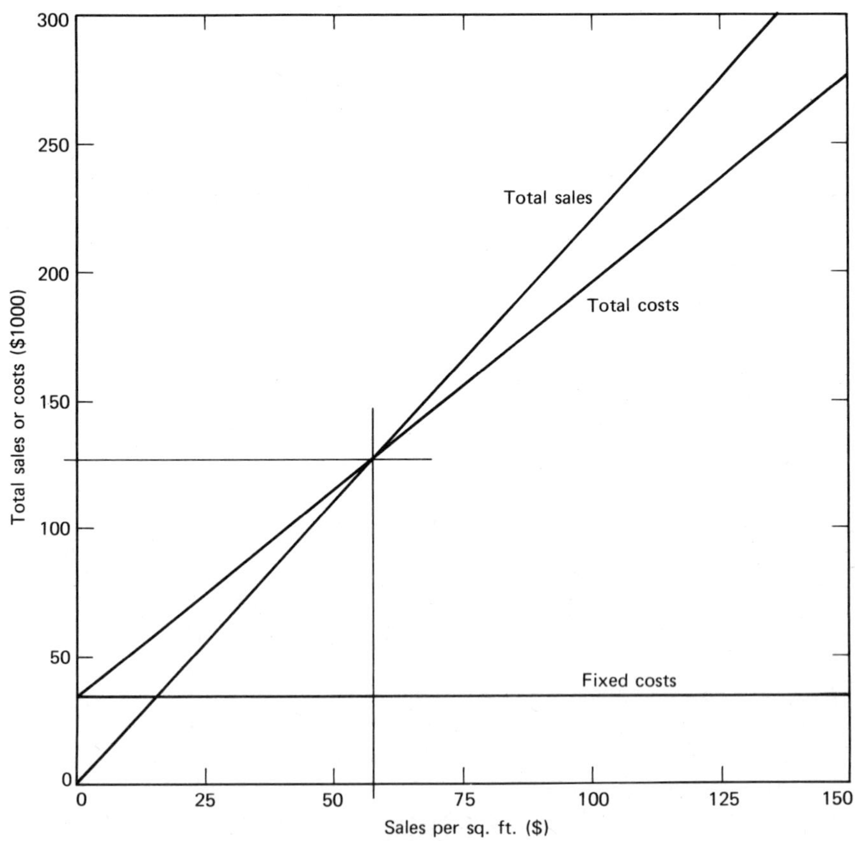

Breakeven chart for 2200 sq. ft. bridal shop.

can easily be drawn up from engagement announcements in local newspapers and society journals, and prospective customers can be approached with special promotions.

Bridal shops range in size from 600 to 3400 square feet and typically fall in the 1400 to 2300 square foot range. The typical 2200-square-foot business breaks even with annual sales of $127,200, or $57.81 per square foot.

Economic Characteristics of Retail Bridal Shops

Typical size (sq. ft.)		2,200		
Typical investment				
Inventory		11,300		
Depreciable assets		3,300		
All other		17,100		
Total investment		31,700		

	Low	*Typical Operation*	*High*	*Proposed Operation*
Operating Economics				
Sales per square foot	50	65	125	
Net annual sales	110,000	143,000	275,000	
Cost of goods sold	66,400	86,300	166,000	
Gross operating margin	43,600	56,700	109,000	
Fixed operating expenses				
Rent and utilities	19,800	19,800	19,800	
Fixed payroll	12,800	12,800	12,800	
Other fixed expenses	2,500	2,500	2,500	
Total fixed expenses	35,100	35,100	35,100	
Variable operating expenses				
Variable payroll	7,800	10,100	19,400	
Other variable expenses	5,500	7,200	13,800	
Total variable expenses	13,300	17,300	33,200	
Total operating expenses	48,400	52,400	68,300	
Net profit (loss) before taxes	(4,800)	4,300	40,700	
Typical operating ratios				
Net profit/net sales	—	3.0%	14.8%	
Net sales/total investment	1.4x	4.5x	8.7x	
Net profit/total investment	—	13.6%	128.4%	
Net sales/inventory	9.7x	12.7x	24.3x	

Children's Clothing

Specialists in children's clothing carry a complete and diversified assortment of clothing and accessories for children from infancy up to about early teen age.

Most children's clothing specialty shops are located in smaller regional and community shopping centers (72 percent), with the remaining 28 percent divided equally between large regional and small neighborhood centers.

Only 12 percent are nationally owned stores, with local ownership accounting for the rest. About 60 percent of all children's clothing stores are single-shop, independent operations.

Store sizes run from 700 square feet to 11,000 square feet; most

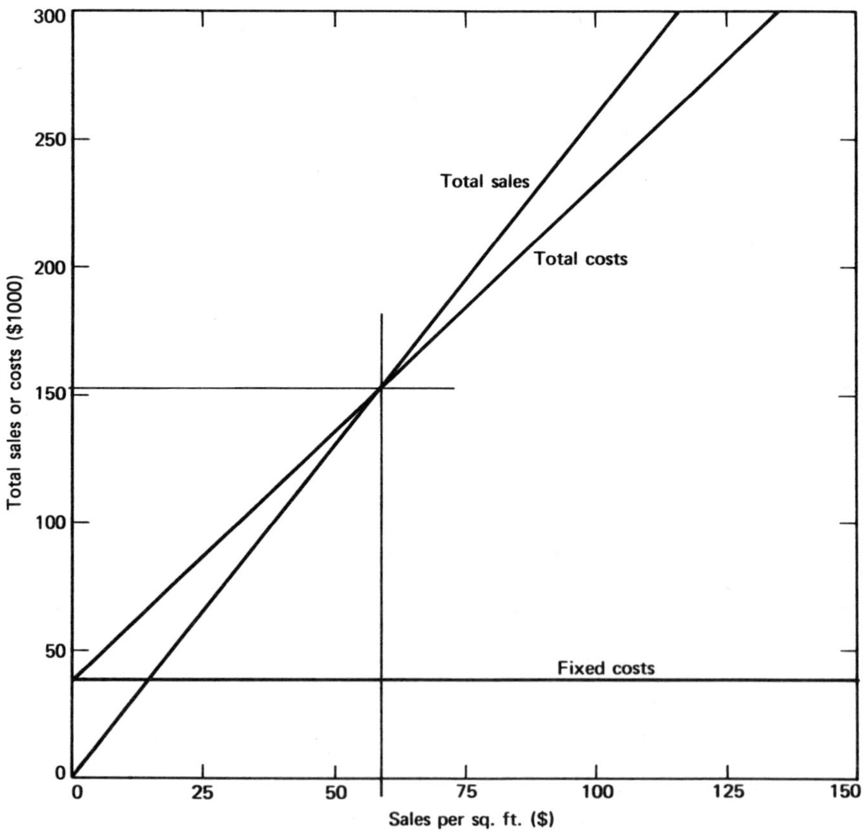

Breakdown chart for 2600 sq. ft. children's clothing store.

are between 2000 and 3800 square feet. From 15 to 20 percent of the annual sales come in December, but the August-to-November period is also strong. January is usually the worst month unless special promotions are emphasized.

A typical 2600-square-foot children's clothing store can break even on sales of $152,200 annually, amounting to $58.54 per square foot.

Economic Characteristics of Retail Children's Clothing Stores

Typical size (sq. ft.)		2,600		
Typical investment				
Inventory		36,700		
Depreciable assets		17,200		
All other		15,900		
Total investment		69,800		
	Low	*Typical Operation*	*High*	*Proposed Operation*
Operating Economics				
Sales per square foot				
Net annual sales	104,000	182,000	338,000	
Cost of goods sold	59,400	114,300	212,300	
Gross operating margin	44,600	67,700	125,700	
Fixed operating expenses				
Rent and utilities	18,200	18,200	18,200	
Fixed payroll	14,400	14,400	14,400	
Other fixed expenses	5,600	5,600	5,600	
Total fixed expenses	38,200	38,200	38,200	
Variable operating expenses				
Variable payroll	7,400	12,900	24,000	
Other variable expenses	5,200	9,100	16,900	
Total variable expenses	12,600	22,000	40,900	
Total operating expenses	50,800	60,200	79,100	
Net profit (loss) before taxes	(6,200)	7,500	46,600	
Typical operating ratios				
Net profit/net sales	—	4.1%	13.8%	
Net sales/total investment	1.5x	2.6x	4.8x	
Net profit/total investment	—	10.7%	66.8%	
Net sales/inventory	2.8x	5.0x	9.2x	

Children's Shoes

Children's shoe stores specialize in shoe sizes and styles for infants up to early teenagers. Most of these shoes are outgrown rather than worn out, and careful fitting is a prime requirement. Repeat business is a must, and since growth is predictable, a good mailing list of customers is a real asset. Steady reminders that it is time for a refitting can bring back customers regularly for a dozen years once the parents' confidence has been gained.

These specialty stores are found in most large regional shopping centers and in about one-third of the smaller regional centers; only one-fifth of the children's shoe stores are located in smaller shopping centers.

Ownership is divided between national chains (34 percent), local chains (28 percent), and single-store independents (38 percent). Sizes

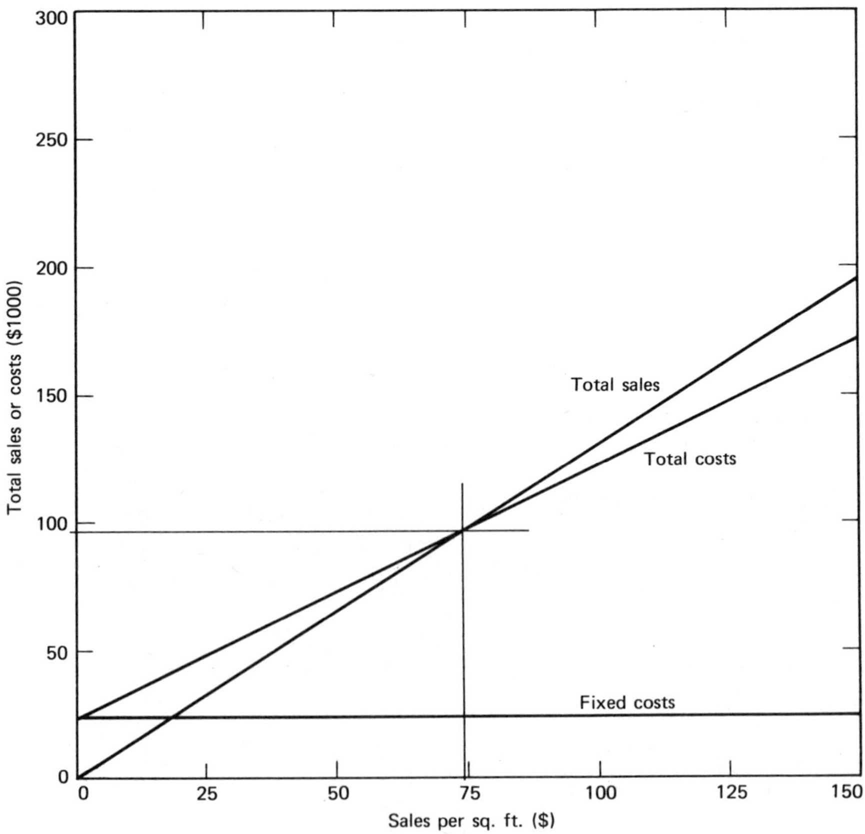

Breakeven chart for 1300 sq. ft. children's shoe store.

range between 600 and 2900 square feet, with 1200 to 1400 square feet typical.

Sales are fairly steady throughout the year, although they slack off somewhat during the winter months. Easter and back-to-school times were once the peak periods, but this is no longer true in most stores, although April is still the best single month.

A typical 1300-square-foot children's shoe store breaks even with sales of $97,200 annually, or $74.77 per square foot per year.

Economic Characteristics of Retail Children's Shoe Stores

Typical size (sq. ft.)		1,300		
Typical investment				
Inventory		32,100		
Depreciable assets		10,000		
All other		9,800		
Total investment		51,900		

	Low	*Typical Operation*	*High*	*Proposed Operation*
Operating Economics				
Sales per square foot	50	85	100	
Net annual sales	65,000	110,500	130,000	
Cost of goods sold	41,500	70,600	83,100	
Gross operating margin	23,500	39,900	46,900	
Fixed operating expenses				
Rent and utilities	11,700	11,700	11,700	
Fixed payroll	8,400	8,400	8,400	
Other fixed expenses	4,200	4,200	4,200	
Total fixed expenses	24,300	24,300	24,300	
Variable operating expenses				
Variable payroll	4,000	6,800	8,000	
Other variable expenses	3,200	5,500	6,500	
Total variable expenses	7,200	12,300	14,500	
Total operating expenses	31,500	36,600	38,800	
Net profit (loss) before taxes	(8,000)	3,300	8,100	
Typical operating ratios				
Net profit/net sales	—	3.0%	6.2%	
Net sales/total investment	1.3x	2.1x	2.5x	
Net profit/total investment	—	6.4%	15.6%	
Net sales/inventory	2.0x	3.4x	4.0x	

Family Clothing

Family clothing stores or small-town department stores sell all types of clothing, furnishings and accessories for men, women, and children, without specializing in any particular line. In major metropolitan areas, these stores are usually found in smaller regional shopping centers, with large centers generally having at least one. About one in five community shopping centers has a family clothing store.

Ownership is divided about equally between national and local; most local owners have two or more stores. The business is seasonal, but because of the wide variety of merchandise lines, sales tend to level out. Overall, about 16 percent of the total sales are in December, with October

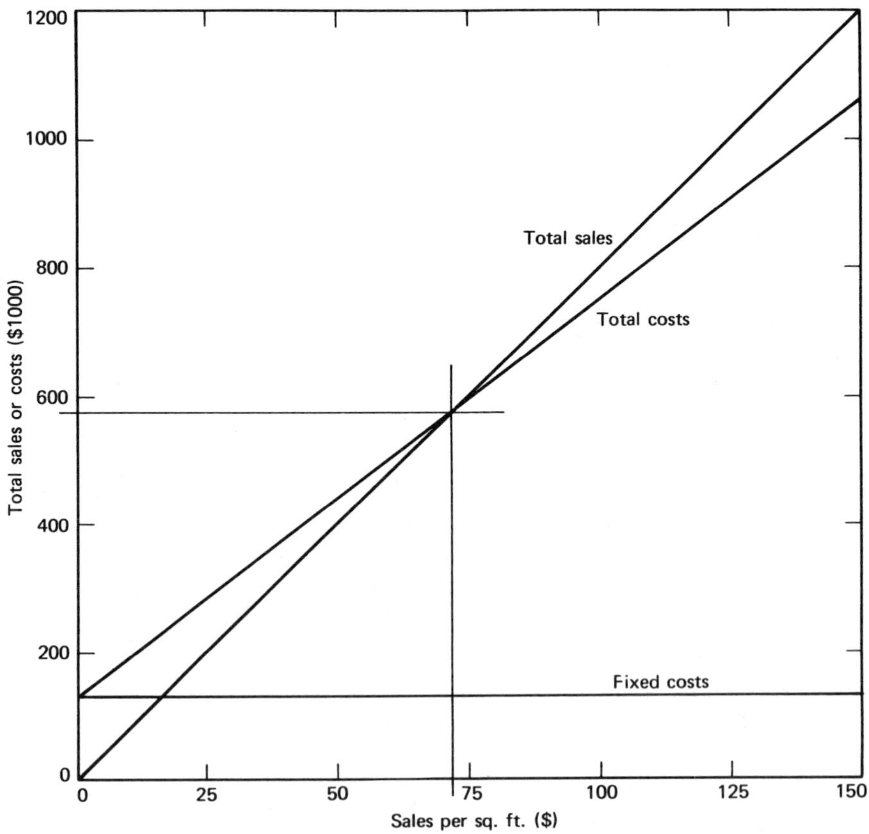

Breakeven chart for 8000 sq. ft. family clothing store.

and November together accounting for about 18 percent. Individual products may, of course, peak during other months.

Considerable space is required to accommodate the large and varied inventory. Sizes range up to 28,000 square feet, although most are under 10,000 square feet. A typical 8000-square-foot family clothing store breaks even with sales of $579,000, or $72.39 per square foot, yearly.

Economic Characteristics of Retail Family Clothing Stores

Typical size (sq. ft.)		8,000		
Typical investment				
Inventory		136,000		
Depreciable assets		102,400		
All other		26,600		
Total investment		265,000		

	Low	*Typical Operation*	*High*	*Proposed Operation*
Operating Economics				
Sales per square foot	45	80	130	
Net annual sales	360,000	640,000	1,040,000	
Cost of goods sold	223,100	396,700	644,600	
Gross operating margin	136,900	243,300	395,400	
Fixed operating expenses				
Rent and utilities	80,000	80,000	80,000	
Fixed payroll	32,000	32,000	32,000	
Other fixed expenses	21,200	21,200	21,200	
Total fixed expenses	133,200	133,200	133,200	
Variable operating expenses				
Variable payroll	36,000	64,000	104,000	
Other variable expenses	18,000	32,000	52,000	
Total variable expenses	54,000	96,000	156,000	
Total operating expenses	187,200	229,200	289,200	
Net profit (loss) before taxes	(50,300)	14,100	106,200	
Typical operating ratios				
Net profit/net sales	—	2.2%	10.2%	
Net sales/total investment	1.4x	2.4x	3.9x	
Net profit/total investment	—	5.3%	40.1%	
Net sales/inventory	2.6x	4.7x	7.6x	

Family Shoes

Family shoe stores offer a complete selection of men's, women's, and children's shoes and accessories. They frequently carry related lines such as hosiery, gloves, handbags, and other leather goods, and may offer repair and dyeing services.

They rank among the most frequent tenants of all types of shopping centers; there are usually several family shoe stores in regional shopping centers, at least one in every community center, and about one in every six neighborhood centers.

Two-thirds of the family shoe stores are branches of national chains; 17 percent are operated by local chains; and 16 percent are single-store

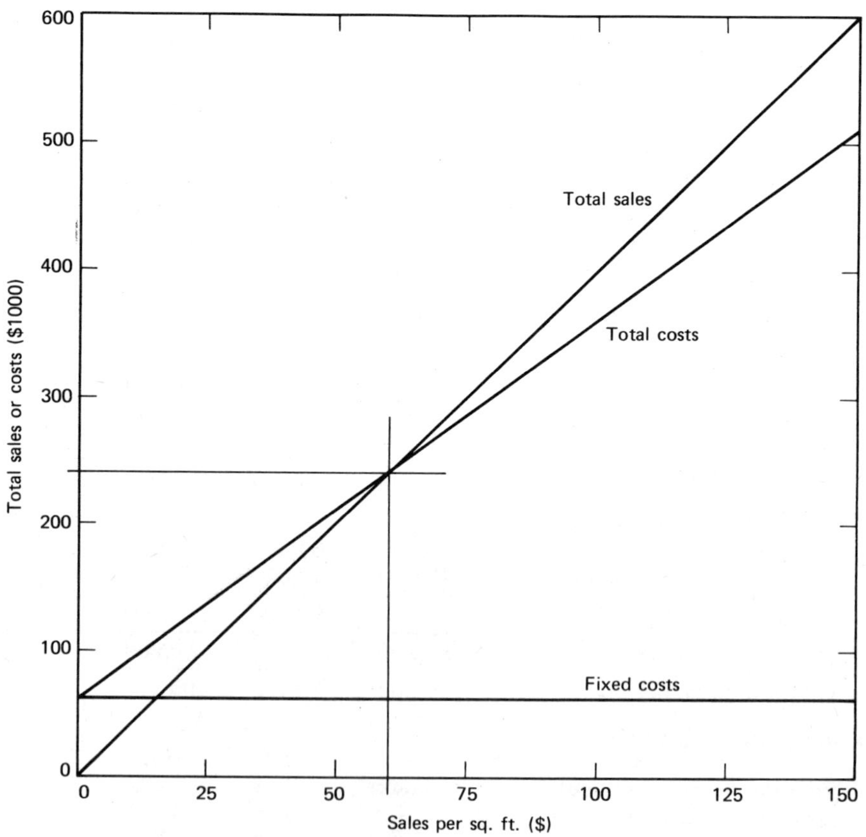

Breakeven chart for 4000 sq. ft. family shoe store.

independents. Sizes vary from 1000 to 9000 square feet, with most in the 2400 to 4400 square foot range.

December is the best month for shoe sales, with about 13 percent of the year's total. Other above-average months include the spring (March through May) and fall (September to November) months.

A typical 4000-square-foot family shoe store needs annual sales of $240,000 or $60 per square foot per year to break even.

Economic Characteristics of Retail Family Shoe Stores

Typical size (sq. ft.)	4,000	
Typical investment		
Inventory	78,900	
Depreciable assets	24,600	
All other	24,100	
Total investment	127,600	

	Low	*Typical Operation*	*High*	*Proposed Operation*
Operating Economics				
Sales per square foot	30	68	130	
Net annual sales	120,000	272,000	520,000	
Cost of goods sold	75,200	170,500	326,000	
Gross operating margin	44,800	101,500	194,000	
Fixed operating expenses				
Rent and utilities	32,000	32,000	32,000	
Fixed payroll	20,000	20,000	20,000	
Other fixed expenses	10,200	10,200	10,200	
Total fixed expenses	62,200	62,200	62,200	
Variable operating expenses				
Variable payroll	7,700	17,500	33,500	
Other variable expenses	6,000	13,600	26,000	
Total variable expenses	13,700	31,100	59,500	
Total operating expenses	75,900	93,300	121,700	
Net profit (loss) before taxes	(31,100)	8,200	72,300	
Typical operating ratios				
Net profit/net sales	—	3.0%	13.9%	
Net sales/total investment	0.9x	2.1x	4.1x	
Net profit/total investment	—	6.4%	56.7%	
Net sales/inventory	1.5x	3.4x	6.6x	

Furs

Most retail furriers, in addition to selling fur coats and other fur apparel, also handle custom-made items. Facilities are also usually provided for fur storage.

This business does not depend on the number of customers; it is, instead, characterized by relatively few, but large, sales. It need not therefore incur the high rent associated with a high-traffic major regional shopping center; ideally it is located in a less-trafficked portion of an affluent (preferably elegant) community or smaller regional center.

Essentially all retail furriers are independently operated, and most are single-shop operations. As would be expected, the sale of furs is highly seasonal, with December accounting for 20 percent of the year's sales and the October through January months representing some 55 per-

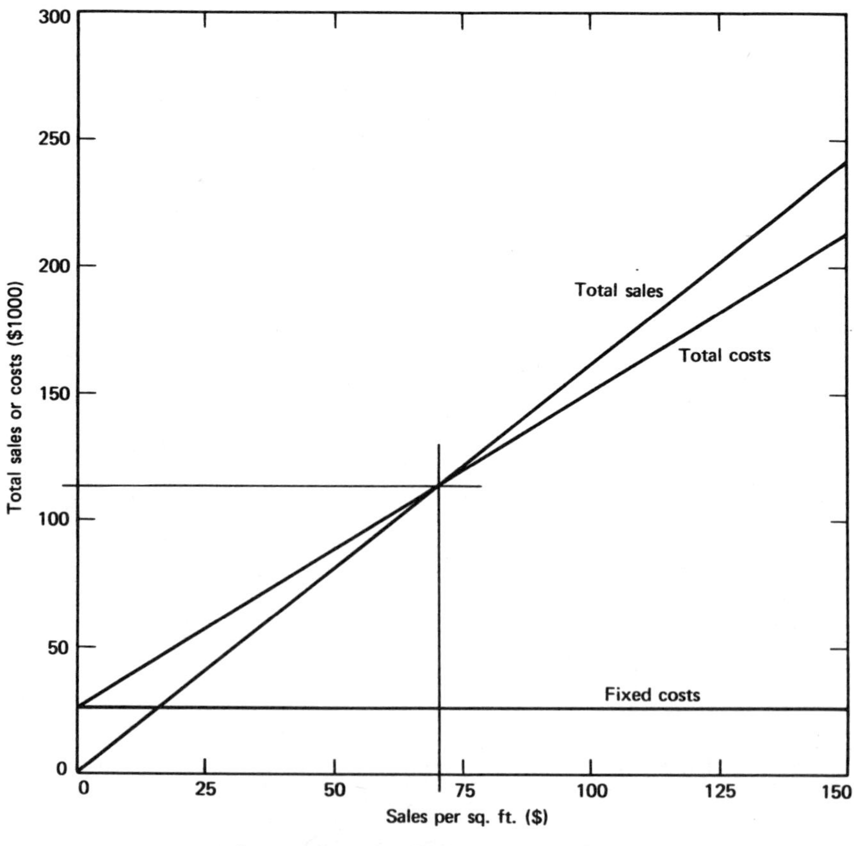

Breakeven chart for 1600 sq. ft. retail furrier.

cent of the annual total. In April, May, and June, however, more than 60 percent of the related fur services (storage, cleaning, etc.) are performed.

Fur shops range from 600 to 7000 square feet in area, usually between 1500 and 1800 square feet. If a large part of the sales consists of custom work, inventory investment need not be especially high, but customer credit requirements may result in high accounts receivable.

The typical 1600-square-foot fur shop should break even with sales of $114,300, or $71.43 per square foot, annually.

Economic Characteristics of Retail Furriers

Typical size (sq. ft.)		1,600		
Typical investment				
Inventory		11,000		
Depreciable assets		3,000		
All other		18,000		
Total investment		32,000		

	Low	*Typical Operation*	*High*	*Proposed Operation*
Operating Economics				
Sales per square foot	60	90	200	
Net annual sales	96,000	144,000	320,000	
Cost of goods sold	60,100	90,200	200,400	
Gross operating margin	35,900	53,800	119,600	
Fixed operating expenses				
Rent and utilities	12,800	12,800	12,800	
Fixed payroll	10,200	10,200	10,200	
Other fixed expenses	2,600	2,600	2,600	
Total fixed expenses	25,600	25,600	25,600	
Variable operating expenses				
Variable payroll	9,600	14,400	32,000	
Other variable expenses	4,800	7,200	16,000	
Total variable expenses	14,400	21,600	48,000	
Total operating expenses	40,000	47,200	73,600	
Net profit (loss) before taxes	(4,100)	6,600	46,000	
Typical operating ratios				
Net profit/net sales	—	4.6%	14.4%	
Net sales/total investment	3.0x	4.5x	10.0x	
Net profit/total investment	—	20.6%	143.8%	
Net sales/inventory	8.7x	13.1x	29.1x	

Ladies' Ready-to-Wear

Ladies' ready-to-wear merchandise encompasses primarily coats, suits, dresses, blouses, and teen-age apparel. The operation often includes an in-house alterations department, although this work may be contracted outside by smaller stores.

Regional shopping centers have an average of at least a half-dozen ladies' ready-to-wear shops each, and most smaller shopping centers have at least one. Ownership is divided among national chains (37 percent), local chains (33 percent), and independents (30 percent). Store sizes vary from 800 to 14,000 square feet, but are usually between 1800 and 5300 square feet.

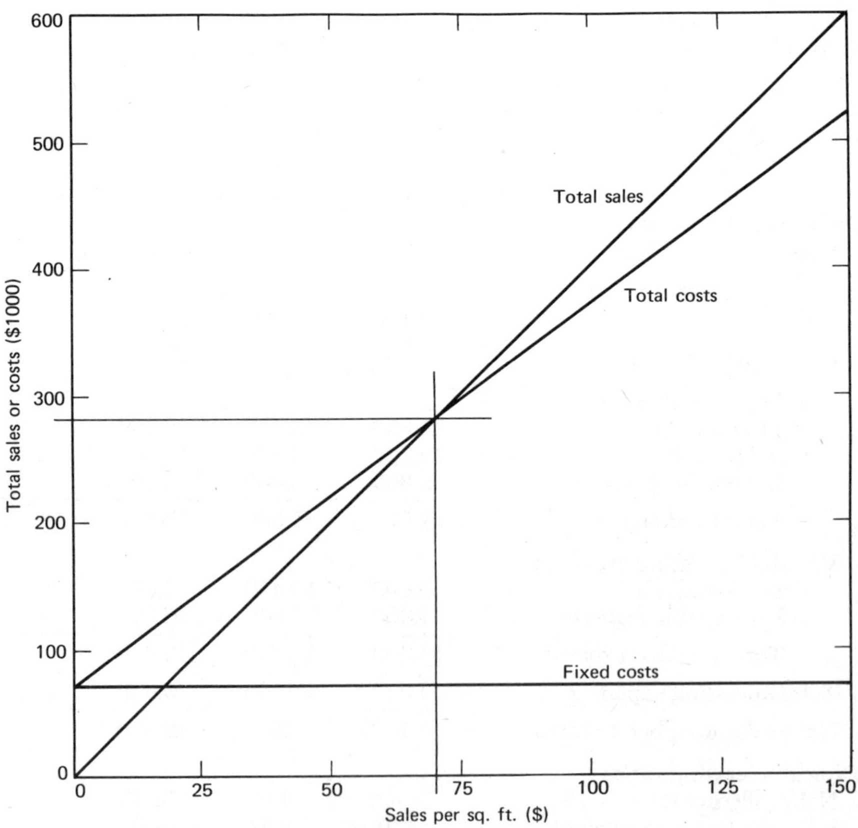

Breakeven chart for 4000 sq. ft. ladies' ready-to-wear shop.

Overall, December accounts for about 15 percent of the annual ladies' ready-to-wear sales, although seasonal style changes help to level out sales during the other months.

A typical 4000-square-foot ladies' ready-to-wear shop breaks even with sales of $282,500 ($70.62 per square foot) annually.

Economic Characteristics of Retail Ladies' Ready-To-Wear Shops				
Typical size (sq. ft.)		4,000		
Typical investment				
Inventory		49,600		
Depreciable assets		25,300		
All other		61,700		
Total investment		136,600		
	Low	*Typical Operation*	*High*	*Proposed Operation*
Operating Economics				
Sales per square foot	45	86	110	
Net annual sales	180,000	344,000	440,000	
Cost of goods sold	109,400	209,000	267,300	
Gross operating margin	70,600	135,000	172,700	
Fixed operating expenses				
Rent and utilities	40,000	40,000	40,000	
Fixed payroll	20,000	20,000	20,000	
Other fixed expenses	10,900	10,900	10,900	
Total fixed expenses	70,900	70,900	70,900	
Variable operating expenses				
Variable payroll	16,500	31,600	40,400	
Other variable expenses	9,000	17,200	22,000	
Total variable expenses	25,500	48,800	62,400	
Total operating expenses	96,400	119,700	133,300	
Net profit (loss) before taxes	(25,800)	15,300	39,400	
Typical operating ratios				
Net profit/net sales	—	4.4%	9.0%	
Net sales/total investment	1.3x	2.5x	3.2x	
Net profit/total investment	—	11.2%	28.8%	
Net sales/inventory	3.6x	6.9x	8.9x	

Ladies' Shoes

Ladies' handbags constitute the one absolutely essential item to be carried along with ladies' shoes, and related services such as stretching and dyeing may complement the merchandise lines.

The location is important, with about 90 percent of the ladies' shoe specialty shops to be found in regional shopping centers. About two-thirds of the shops are parts of national chains, with the remaining one-third representing locally owned independents. Store size is usually in the 2100 to 4600 square foot range, but some stores are as small as 1100 square feet or as large as 7500 square feet.

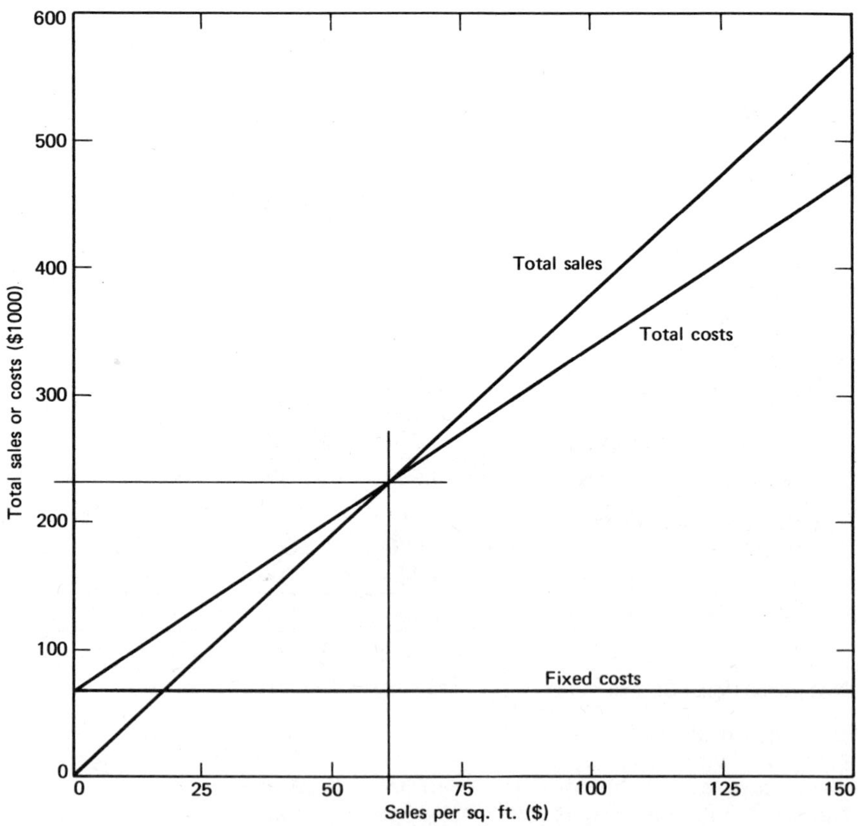

Breakeven chart for 3800 sq. ft. ladies' shoe store.

March is the leading month for ladies' shoe sales, with 12 percent of the year's total. April, September, and October are also good months.

A typical 3800-square-foot ladies' shoe store breaks even when sales total $232,300 for the year, requiring $61.13 per square foot.

Economic Characteristics of Retail Ladies' Shoe Stores

Typical size (sq. ft.)		3,800		
Typical investment				
Inventory		75,000		
Depreciable assets		23,400		
All other		22,900		
Total investment		121,300		

	Low	*Typical Operation*	*High*	*Proposed Operation*
Operating Economics				
Sales per square foot	35	68	100	
Net annual sales	133,000	258,400	380,000	
Cost of goods sold	79,500	154,500	227,200	
Gross operating margin	53,500	103,900	152,800	
Fixed operating expenses				
Rent and utilities	38,000	38,000	38,000	
Fixed payroll	19,200	19,200	19,200	
Other fixed expenses	9,700	9,700	9,700	
Total fixed expenses	66,900	66,900	66,900	
Variable operating expenses				
Variable payroll	8,500	16,500	24,300	
Other variable expenses	6,600	12,900	19,000	
Total variable expenses	15,100	29,400	43,300	
Total operating expenses	82,000	96,300	110,200	
Net profit (loss) before taxes	(28,500)	7,600	42,600	
Typical operating ratios				
Net profit/net sales	—	2.9%	11.2%	
Net sales/total investment	1.1x	2.1x	3.1x	
Net profit/total investment	—	6.3%	35.1%	
Net sales/inventory	1.8x	3.4x	5.1x	

Ladies' Specialties

Ladies' specialties include a combination of merchandise lines found individually in other types of shops, such as ready-to-wear and custom-made clothing, blouses, knitwear, foundation garments, lingerie, hosiery, costume jewelry, gloves, handbags, and other accessories.

These shops are located in all types of shopping centers, but mostly in regional centers, which usually number several as tenants. About 30 percent are located in the smaller community and neighborhood centers.

More than 70 percent are locally owned, with two-thirds of the locally owned operations consisting of a single shop. Sizes vary widely, from less than 100 square feet up to 10,000 square feet. Most stores are between 1300 and 5800 square feet.

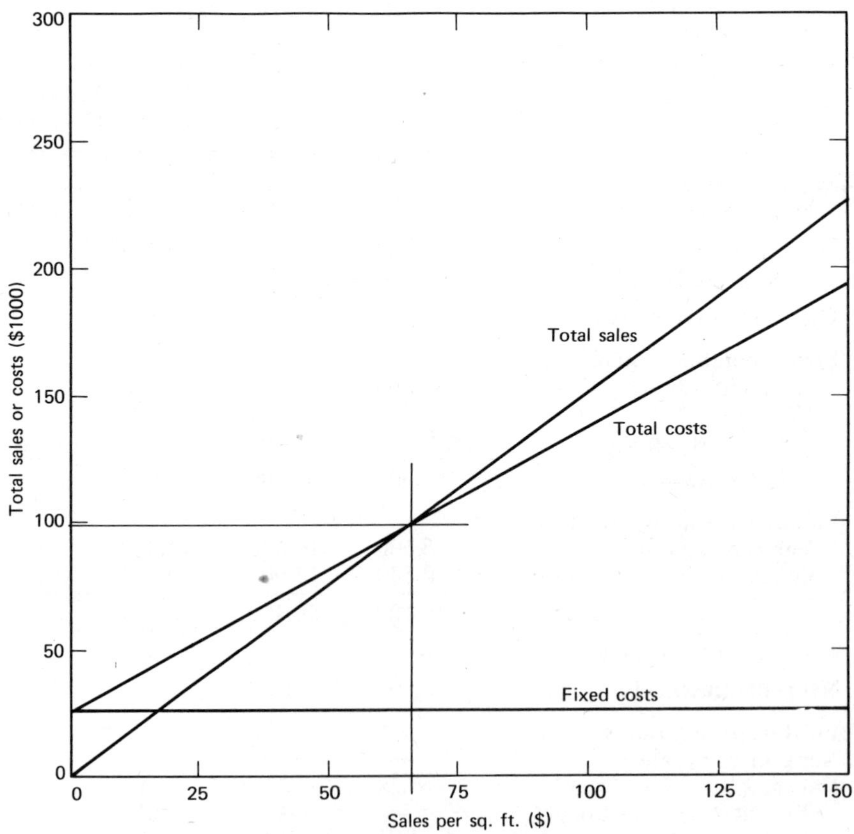

Breakeven chart for 1500 sq. ft. ladies' specialty shop.

Sales are seasonal, but careful merchandise selection and inventory control can level out sales fairly well. Still, some 15 percent of the year's business is likely to come during December.

A typical 1500-square-foot ladies' specialties shop requires just under $100,000 annual sales volume to break even, averaging $66.42 per square foot.

Economic Characteristics of Retail Ladies' Specialty Shops

Typical size (sq. ft.)		1,500		
Typical investment				
Inventory		17,300		
Depreciable assets		8,800		
All other		21,600		
Total investment		47,700		

	Low	*Typical Operation*	*High*	*Proposed Operation*
Operating Economics				
Sales per square foot	45	80	110	
Net annual sales	67,500	120,000	165,000	
Cost of goods sold	42,000	74,600	102,600	
Gross operating margin	25,500	45,400	62,400	
Fixed operating expenses				
Rent and utilities	13,500	13,500	13,500	
Fixed payroll	9,800	9,800	9,800	
Other fixed expenses	3,800	3,800	3,800	
Total fixed expenses	27,100	27,100	27,100	
Variable operating expenses				
Variable payroll	3,800	6,800	9,400	
Other variable expenses	3,400	6,000	8,300	
Total variable expenses	7,200	12,800	17,700	
Total operating expenses	34,300	39,900	44,800	
Net profit (loss) before taxes	(8,800)	5,500	17,600	
Typical operating ratios				
Net profit/net sales	—	4.6%	10.7%	
Net sales/total investment	1.4x	2.5x	3.5x	
Net profit/total investment	—	11.5%	36.9%	
Net sales/inventory	3.9x	6.9x	9.5x	

Lingerie and Hosiery

These ladies' specialty shops sell fashion hosiery, pajamas, gowns, robes, slips, slippers, undergarments, foundation garments, and related clothing items.

Well over 90 percent of the shops are located in regional shopping centers. About 80 percent are affiliated with national chains.

The business is highly seasonal, with May (Mother's Day) and November and December (Christmas) the biggest months. May accounts for about nine percent of the annual sales, November for 11 percent, and December for 24 percent.

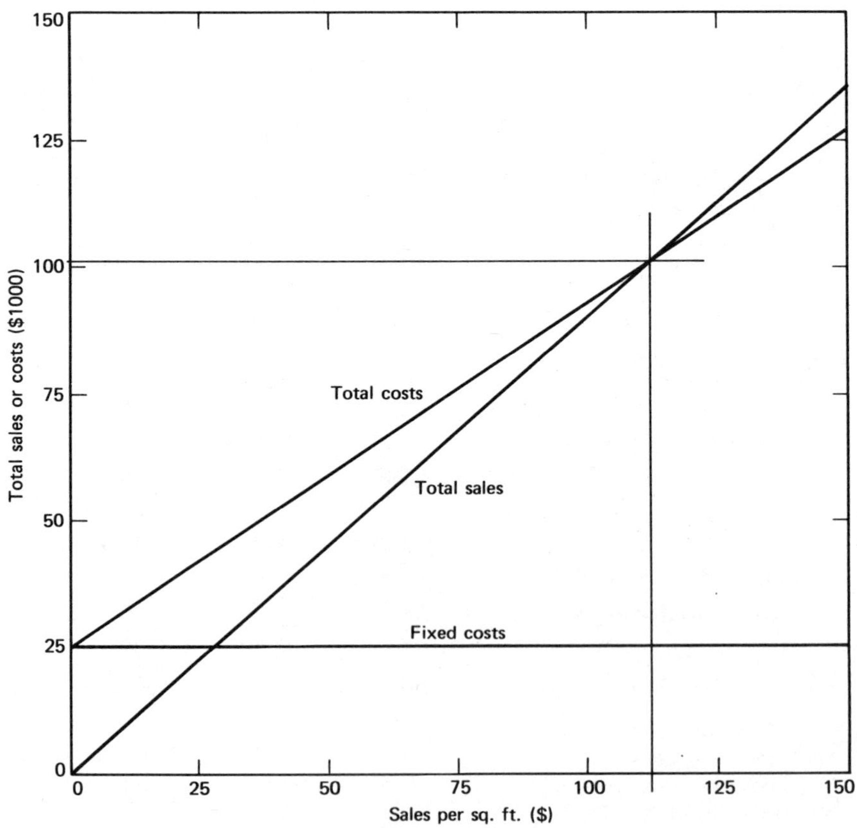

Breakeven chart for 900 sq. ft. lingerie and hosiery shop.

Shop sizes vary from 200 to 2000 square feet, with most in the 600 to 1100 square foot range. A typical 900-square-foot operation requires just under $101,000, or $112.13 per square foot, in sales per year to break even.

Economic Characteristics of Retail Lingerie and Hosiery Shops

Typical size (sq. ft.)		900		
Typical investment				
Inventory		26,700		
Depreciable assets		9,200		
All other		15,400		
Total investment		51,300		
	Low	*Typical Operation*	*High*	*Proposed Operation*
Operating Economics				
Sales per square foot	75	130	185	
Net annual sales	67,500	117,000	166,500	
Cost of goods sold	42,300	73,400	104,500	
Gross operating margin	25,200	43,600	62,000	
Fixed operating expenses				
Rent and utilities	13,500	13,500	13,500	
Fixed payroll	7,500	7,500	7,500	
Other fixed expenses	4,100	4,100	4,100	
Total fixed expenses	25,100	25,100	25,100	
Variable operating expenses				
Variable payroll	5,000	8,600	12,200	
Other variable expenses	3,400	5,900	8,300	
Total variable expenses	8,400	14,500	20,500	
Total operating expenses	33,500	39,600	45,600	
Net profit (loss) before taxes	(8,300)	4,000	16,400	
Typical operating ratios				
Net profit/net sales	—	3.4%	9.8%	
Net sales/total investment	1.3x	2.3x	3.2x	
Net profit/total investment	—	7.8%	32.0%	
Net sales/inventory	2.5x	4.4x	6.2x	

Maternity Wear

Although the birth rate has declined considerably, fashion maternity clothing has increased in variety, style, and price. In addition to outerwear, the maternity shop handles related accessories such as maternity and nursing bras, support hosiery, slips, gowns, robes, and many other items.

Here, location is extremely important, with most shops (88 percent) located in regional shopping centers; about one-half of these large centers have a shop specializing in maternity wear.

About one-half of all maternity shops are affiliated with national chains, with the rest divided between local chains and independent op-

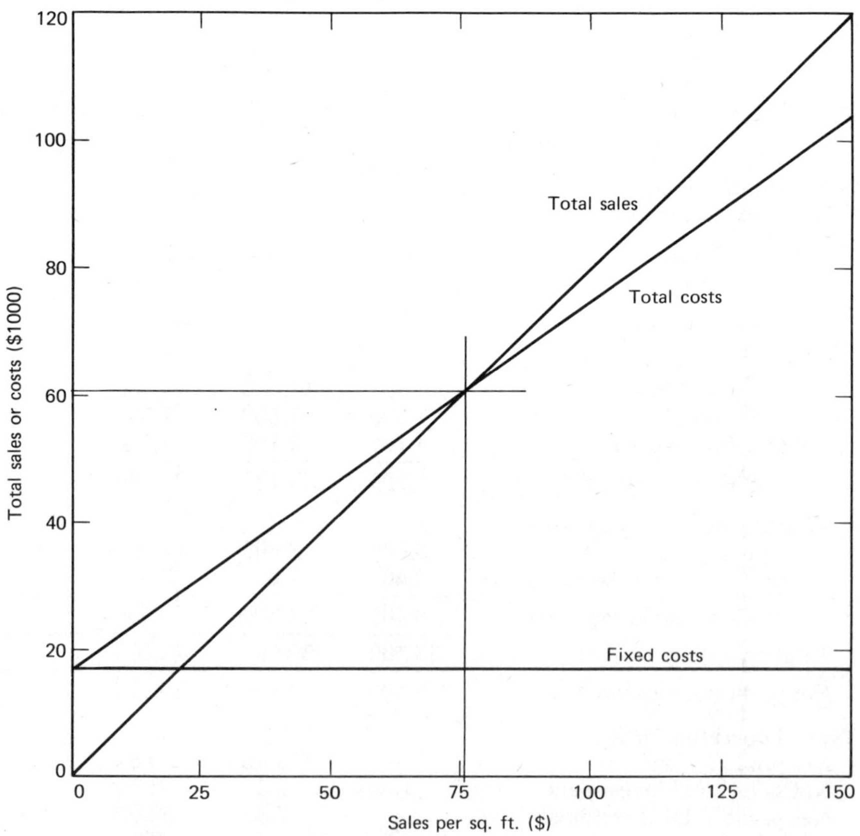

Breakeven chart for 800 sq. ft. maternity wear shop.

erators. Store sizes may be anywhere from 300 square feet to 4100 square feet, with most falling between 800 and 1600 square feet. The business is only as seasonal as pregnancies.

A typical 800-square-foot maternity shop can break even with a sales volume of $60,500, or $75.62 per square foot, annually.

Economic Characteristics of Retail Maternity Wear Shops

Typical size (sq. ft.)		800		
Typical investment				
Inventory		12,600		
Depreciable assets		5,700		
All other		10,000		
Total investment		28,300		

	Low	*Typical Operation*	*High*	*Proposed Operation*
Operating Economics				
Sales per square foot	50	85	140	
Net annual sales	40,000	68,000	112,000	
Cost of goods sold	25,500	43,300	71,300	
Gross operating margin	14,500	24,700	40,700	
Fixed operating expenses				
Rent and utilities	7,200	7,200	7,200	
Fixed payroll	7,500	7,500	7,500	
Other fixed expenses	2,300	2,300	2,300	
Total fixed expenses	17,000	17,000	17,000	
Variable operating expenses				
Variable payroll	1,300	2,200	3,600	
Other variable expenses	2,000	3,400	5,600	
Total variable expenses	3,300	5,600	9,200	
Total operating expenses	20,300	22,600	26,200	
Net profit (loss) before taxes	(5,800)	2,100	14,500	
Typical operating ratios				
Net profit/net sales	—	3.1%	12.9%	
Net sales/total investment	1.4x	2.4x	4.0x	
Net profit/total investment	—	7.4%	51.2%	
Net sales/inventory	3.2x	5.4x	8.9x	

Men's and Boys' Clothing

Men's and boys' clothing stores, handling a complete line of ready-to-wear and sometimes custom-tailored clothing and accessories such as hats, ties, belts, and related items, are among the most common tenants of regional shopping centers. Large regional centers may have a half-dozen or so of these shops, and most smaller regional centers have several. Many are also located in community centers. There is about one shop of this type for every 10,000 population.

Ownership is divided equally between national chains, local chains, and independent single-store operations. Sales are highly seasonal, with

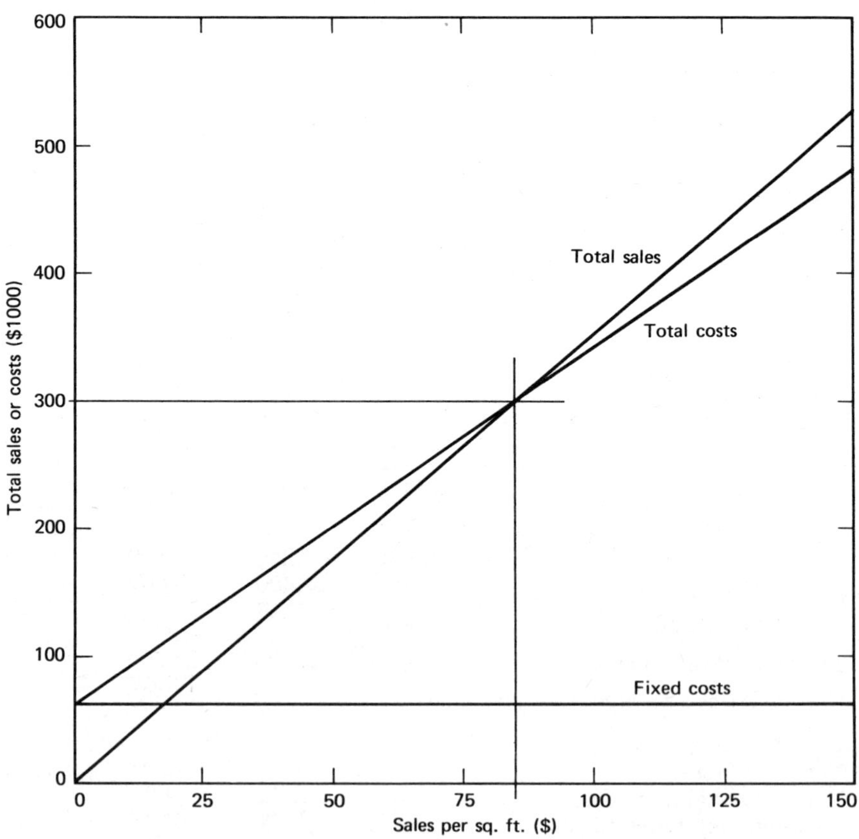

Breakeven chart for 3500 sq. ft. men's and boy's wear store.

one-third of the year's total in November and December. June (with Father's Day) is also a strong sales month.

Store sizes can range between 600 and 12,000 square feet, but are usually between 2000 and 7300 square feet. A typical 3500-square-foot operation breaks even with sales of $300,000, or $85.85 per square foot, annually.

Economic Characteristics of Retail Men's and Boys' Wear Shops

Typical size (sq. ft.)		3,500		
Typical investment				
Inventory		81,000		
Depreciable assets		30,000		
All other		59,000		
Total investment		170,000		

	Low	*Typical Operation*	*High*	*Proposed Operation*
Operating Economics				
Sales per square foot	60	95	225	
Net annual sales	210,000	332,500	787,500	
Cost of goods sold	134,500	212,900	504,200	
Gross operating margin	75,500	119,600	283,300	
Fixed operating expenses				
Rent and utilities	31,500	31,500	31,500	
Fixed payroll	18,000	18,000	18,000	
Other fixed expenses	13,600	13,600	13,600	
Total fixed expenses	63,100	63,100	63,100	
Variable operating expenses				
Variable payroll	21,000	33,200	78,600	
Other variable expenses	10,500	16,600	39,300	
Total variable expenses	31,500	49,800	117,900	
Total operating expenses	94,600	112,900	181,000	
Net profit (loss) before taxes	(19,100)	6,700	102,300	
Typical operating ratios				
Net profit/net sales	—	2.0%	13.0%	
Net sales/total investment	1.2x	2.0x	4.6x	
Net profit/total investment	—	3.9%	60.2%	
Net sales/inventory	2.6x	4.1x	9.7x	

Unisex/Jeans

The unisex/jeans shop specializes in clothing that can be worn by either sex such as jeans, belts, shirts, overalls, jumpsuits, and accessories. Many carry only a few name brands, meaning that the same merchandise can be obtained easily elsewhere, often at the same price and in the same area. A high-traffic location is therefore necessary, as is a wide selection of colors and sizes.

Some 80 percent of the unisex/jean shops are therefore located in regional shopping centers in which most young shoppers congregate. About one-third of the shops are affiliated with national chains; the rest are independent and locally owned. About 45 percent of the shop's annual sales

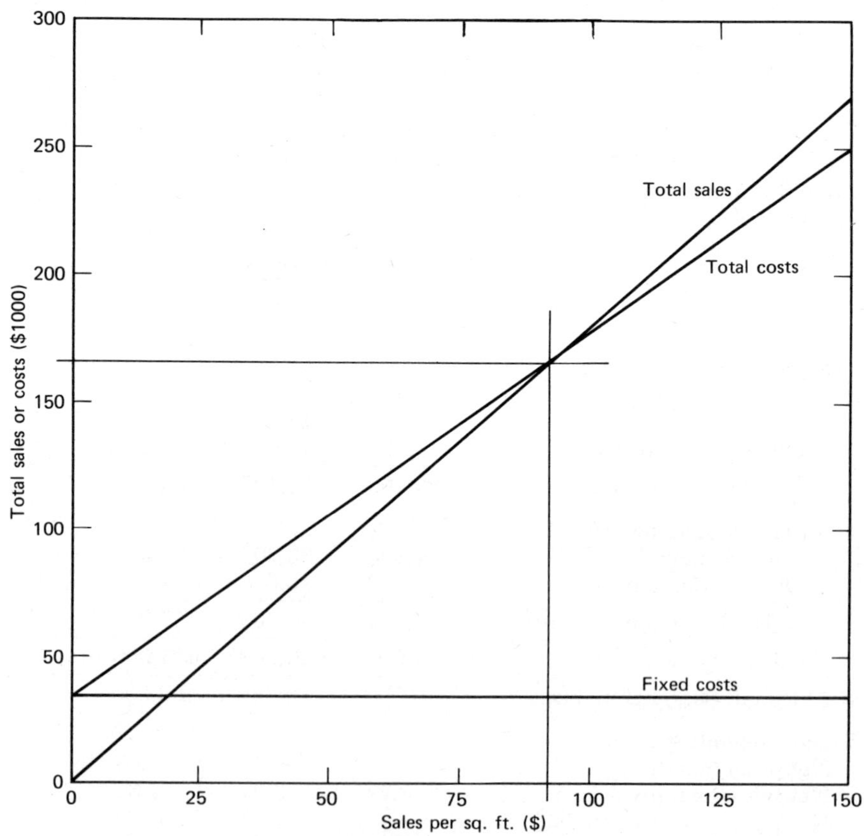

Breakeven chart for 1800 sq. ft. unisex/jeans shop.

come during the October to December period, and June is also a good sales month.

Store sizes range from 400 to 4800 square feet, depending on the variety of merchandise carried. From 1000 to 2000 square feet is a typical size.

A typical 1800-square-foot unisex/jeans shop breaks even with sales of $166,300, or $92.41 per square foot, yearly.

Economic Characteristics of Retail Unisex/Jeans Shops

Typical size (sq. ft.)		1,800		
Typical investment				
Inventory		49,500		
Depreciable assets		14,400		
All other		26,100		
Total investment		90,000		

	Low	*Typical Operation*	*High*	*Proposed Operation*
Operating Economics				
Sales per square foot	50	110	150	
Net annual sales	90,000	198,000	270,000	
Cost of goods sold	62,000	136,500	186,100	
Gross operating margin	28,000	61,500	83,900	
Fixed operating expenses				
Rent and utilities	18,000	18,000	18,000	
Fixed payroll	11,100	11,100	11,100	
Other fixed expenses	4,500	4,500	4,500	
Total fixed expenses	33,600	33,600	33,600	
Variable operating expenses				
Variable payroll	5,300	11,700	16,000	
Other variable expenses	4,500	9,900	13,500	
Total variable expenses	9,800	21,600	29,500	
Total operating expenses	43,400	55,200	63,100	
Net profit (loss) before taxes	(15,400)	6,300	20,800	
Typical operating ratios				
Net profit/net sales	—	3.2%	7.7%	
Net sales/total investment	1.0x	2.2x	3.0x	
Net profit/total investment	—	7.0%	23.1%	
Net sales/inventory	1.8x	4.0x	5.5x	

RETAIL FURNITURE, HOME FURNISHINGS, AND EQUIPMENT

Major Appliances

Major appliances include refrigerators, ranges, freezers, microwave ovens, air conditioning units, washing machines, clothes dryers, and other types of large and usually heavy equipment. Some stores also carry radio/TV sets, vacuum cleaners, garbage disposers, trash compactors, and other smaller appliances. Provision must be made for the delivery, installation, and service of the appliances sold. Also, since most of the merchandise is expensive, credit terms must be arranged; this means either a large investment in accounts receivable or selling the sales contracts at a discount to finance companies.

Even though only 19 percent of the major appliance stores are nationally owned, price competition from private-label appliances handled by large mass merchandisers is severe; the best defense is to offer reputable brand-name merchandise and good customer service policies.

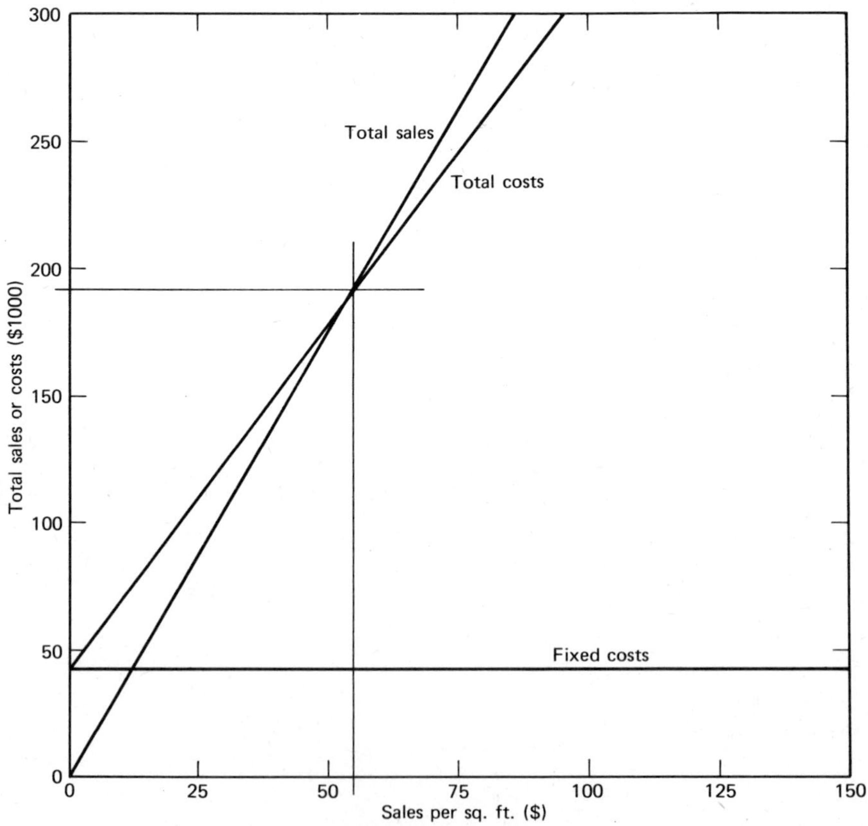

Breakeven chart for 3500 sq. ft. major appliances store.

Because of the size requirements to house a variety of major appliances, the preferred locations for appliance stores are in community and neighborhood shopping centers; they need not depend on walk-in trade, but must advertise heavily to attract appliance buyers.

Store sizes are usually in the 2700 to 7000 square foot range, with some stores occupying as much as 19,000 square feet. A typical 3500-square-foot operation needs sales of $54.49 per square foot ($190,700 per year) to break even.

Economic Characteristics of Retail Major Appliances Stores

Typical size (sq. ft.)		3,500		
Typical investment				
Inventory		45,000		
Depreciable assets		14,000		
All other		36,000		
Total investment		95,000		

	Low	*Typical Operation*	*High*	*Proposed Operation*
Operating Economics				
Sales per square foot	50	62	150	
Net annual sales	175,000	221,000	525,000	
Cost of goods sold	118,500	147,000	355,600	
Gross operating margin	56,500	74,000	169,400	
Fixed operating expenses				
Rent and utilities	17,500	17,500	17,500	
Fixed payroll	18,000	18,000	18,000	
Other fixed expenses	7,600	7,600	7,600	
Total fixed expenses	43,100	43,100	43,100	
Variable operating expenses				
Variable payroll	10,400	12,900	31,200	
Other variable expenses	9,000	11,100	26,900	
Total variable expenses	19,400	24,000	58,100	
Total operating expenses	62,500	67,100	101,200	
Net profit (loss) before taxes	(6,000)	6,900	68,200	
Typical operating ratios				
Net profit/net sales	—	3.1%	13.0%	
Net sales/total investment	1.8x	2.3x	5.5x	
Net profit/total investment	—	7.3%	71.8%	
Net sales/inventory	3.9x	4.9x	11.7x	

Curtains and Draperies

The shop specializing in curtains and draperies (and usually upholstery) must carry a wide variety of natural and synthetic fabrics for custom-made jobs, as well as a broad selection of sizes and styles of ready-made products. Custom work may be contracted out or done in-house; either way, it is important to the independent shop that the service be provided.

About one-third of the curtain and drapery shops are located in smaller regional shopping centers and another one-third in community centers. Some 12 percent are still in small neighborhood centers, with the rest in large regional centers. Since many customers who buy draperies may also be in the market for carpeting and wallpaper and perhaps interior decorating services, these related fields should at least be kept in mind when selecting a location.

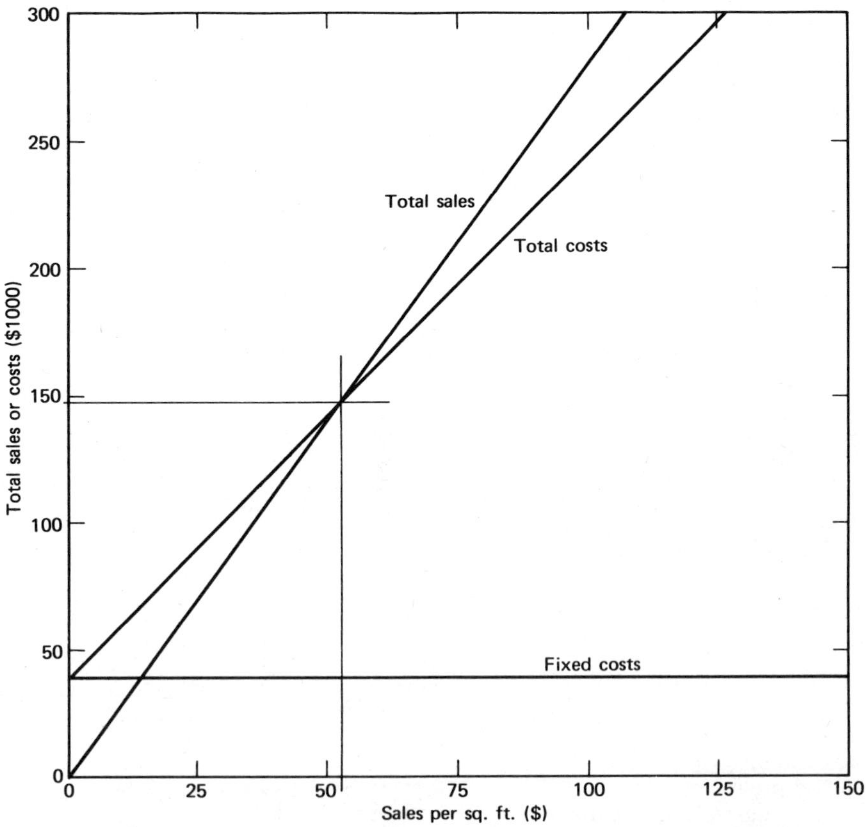

Breakeven chart for 2800 sq. ft. curtain and drapery store.

Ownership is almost all local, with only 10 percent of the shops having any national affiliation. The business is not especially seasonal, although October, November, and December are generally the best sales months.

Store sizes range from 400 to 7900 square feet, depending on the scope of merchandise and services offered. Most fall between 1900 and 3700 square feet, with 2800 square feet typical. The typical operation breaks even with sales of $52.84 per square foot ($148,000 total) annually.

Economic Characteristics of Retail Curtain and Drapery Shops

Typical size (sq. ft.)		2,800		
Typical investment				
Inventory		29,200		
Depreciable assets		8,600		
All other		25,300		
Total investment		63,100		

	Low	*Typical Operation*	*High*	*Proposed Operation*
Operating Economics				
Sales per square foot	35	60	125	
Net annual sales	98,000	168,000	350,000	
Cost of goods sold	54,100	92,800	193,300	
Gross operating margin	43,900	75,200	156,700	
Fixed operating expenses				
Rent and utilities	19,600	19,600	19,600	
Fixed payroll	15,200	15,200	15,200	
Other fixed expenses	5,000	5,000	5,000	
Total fixed expenses	39,800	39,800	39,800	
Variable operating expenses				
Variable payroll	12,600	21,600	45,000	
Other variable expenses	4,900	8,400	17,500	
Total variable expenses	17,500	30,000	62,500	
Total operating expenses	57,300	69,800	102,300	
Net profit (loss) before taxes	(13,400)	5,400	54,400	
Typical operating ratios				
Net profit/net sales	—	3.2%	15.5%	
Net sales/total investment	1.6x	2.7x	5.5x	
Net profit/total investment	—	8.6%	86.2%	
Net sales/inventory	3.4x	5.8x	12.0x	

Furniture

Household furniture is perhaps unique among retail businesses in that most customers have little brand recognition or knowledge. The range in quality and price is enormous, as is the range in retail operations.

For example, a small decorator shop offering close personal service in selecting high-quality pieces of furniture may work from a few sample pieces and custom order from catalogs for individual customers; this type of operation may require as little as 400 square feet. In contrast, there are huge discount furniture warehouses occupying as much as 47,000 square feet where "you could fire a cannon through it and never hit a solid piece of wood." There is, obviously, a market for both, and both must offer credit arrangements of some type.

High traffic is desirable for a furniture store location, but high space requirements may make a busy shopping center location economically

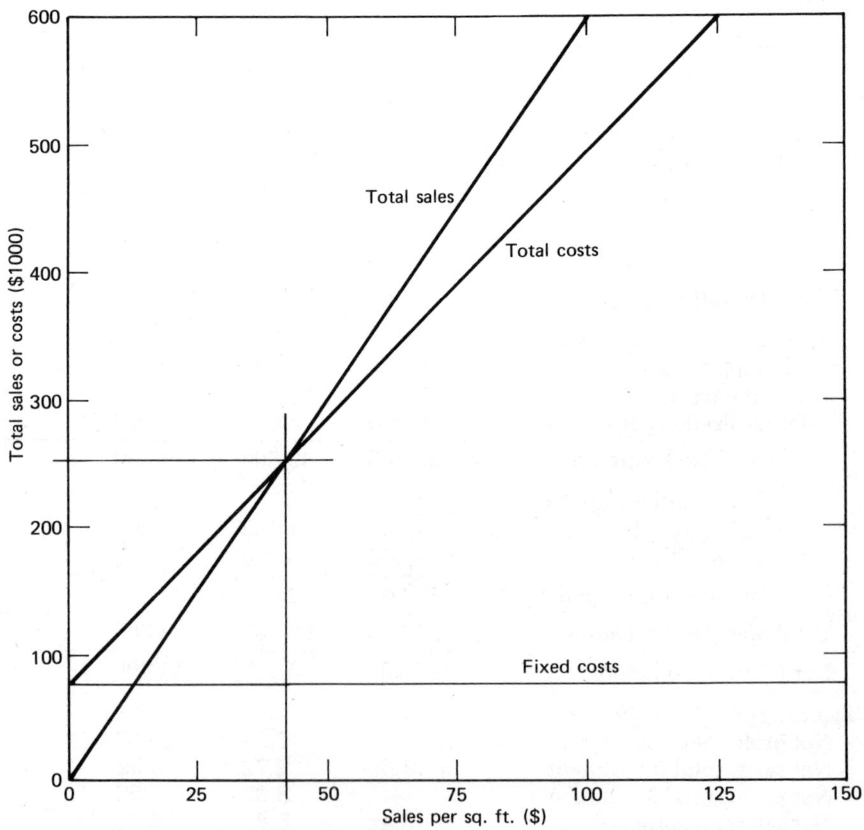

Breakeven chart for 6000 sq. ft. furniture store.

impractical. Most furniture stores are located in smaller regional and community shopping centers. Furniture "warehouses" may be off to themselves somewhere, and the department store tenants in large shopping centers usually have a furniture department. More than 80 percent of the stores specializing in furniture are locally owned. Sales are not particularly seasonal.

Most furniture stores have from 2000 to 16000 square feet of selling space. A typical 6000-square-foot furniture store breaks even on sales of $252,800 (or $42.13 per square foot) per year.

Economic Characteristics of Retail Furniture Stores

Typical size (sq. ft.)		6,000		
Typical investment				
Inventory		70,000		
Depreciable assets		27,000		
All other		98,000		
Total investment		195,000		
	Low	*Typical Operation*	*High*	*Proposed Operation*
Operating Economics				
Sales per square foot	30	48	140	
Net annual sales	180,000	288,000	840,000	
Cost of goods sold	103,800	166,000	484,200	
Gross operating margin	76,200	122,000	355,800	
Fixed operating expenses				
Rent and utilities	36,000	36,000	36,000	
Fixed payroll	26,000	26,000	26,000	
Other fixed expenses	15,600	15,600	15,600	
Total fixed expenses	77,600	77,600	77,600	
Variable operating expenses				
Variable payroll	12,000	19,200	56,000	
Other variable expenses	9,000	14,400	42,000	
Total variable expenses	21,000	33,600	98,000	
Total operating expenses	98,600	111,200	175,600	
Net profit (loss) before taxes	(22,400)	10,800	180,200	
Typical operating ratios				
Net profit/net sales	—	3.8%	21.5%	
Net sales/total investment	0.9x	1.5x	4.3x	
Net profit/total investment	—	5.5%	92.4%	
Net sales/inventory	2.6x	4.1x	12.0x	

Lamps and Lighting Fixtures

The lamps and lighting fixtures business actually has two different markets. Sales of lamps are directed primarily toward the retail customer, whereas fixtures constitute a builder-oriented market. It is not usually necessary to carry a large backstock of lighting fixtures, but a wide variety of fixtures must be on display at all times. Installation services should be available for retail customers; builders' accounts must be carried by the store, requiring a large working capital account.

Locational requirements depend on the store's emphasis. A regional shopping center location is desirable for retail sales, but the store can be located in less-trafficked areas if the bulk of sales are for the new home and remodeling markets.

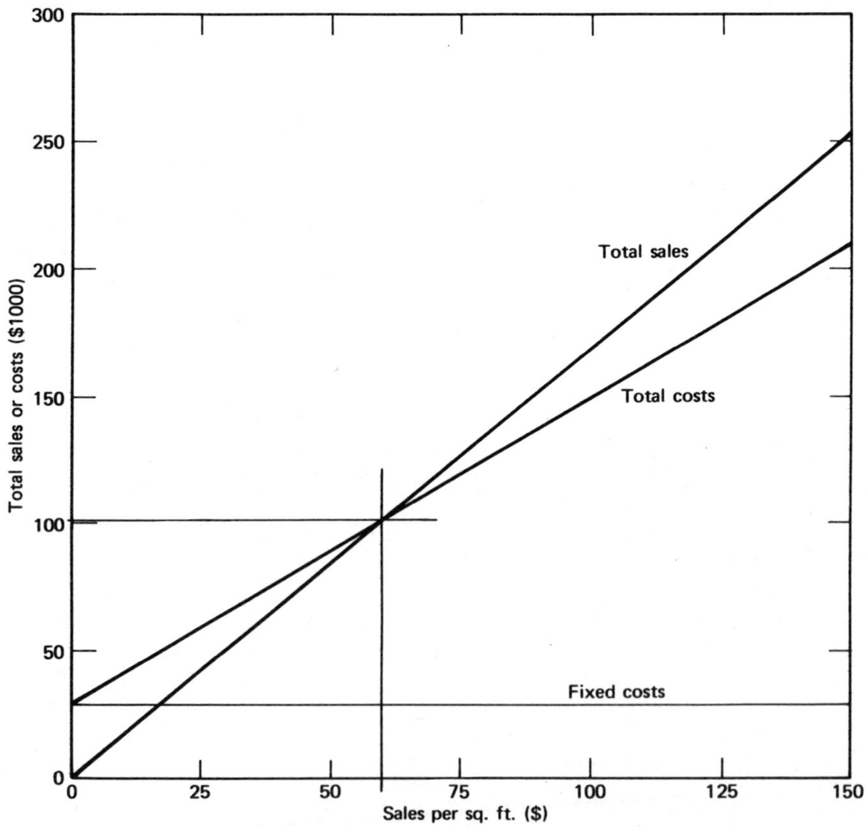

Breakeven chart for 1700 sq. ft. lamps and lighting fixtures store.

Store sizes range between 1000 and 3600 square feet, with 1700 square feet typical. This typical operation breaks even with sales of $101,100, or $59.44 per square foot, annually.

Economic Characteristics of Retail Lamps and Lighting Fixtures Shops

Typical size (sq. ft.)		1,700		
Typical investment				
Inventory		27,700		
Depreciable assets		10,600		
All other		38,700		
Total investment		77,000		
	Low	*Typical Operation*	*High*	*Proposed Operation*
Operating Economics				
Sales per square foot	40	68	110	
Net annual sales	68,000	115,600	187,000	
Cost of goods sold	41,400	70,400	113,900	
Gross operating margin	26,600	45,200	73,100	
Fixed operating expenses				
Rent and utilities	11,900	11,900	11,900	
Fixed payroll	10,700	10,700	10,700	
Other fixed expenses	6,200	6,200	6,200	
Total fixed expenses	28,800	28,800	28,800	
Variable operating expenses				
Variable payroll	3,800	6,400	10,400	
Other variable expenses	3,400	5,800	9,400	
Total variable expenses	7,200	12,200	19,800	
Total operating expenses	36,000	41,000	48,600	
Net profit (loss) before taxes	(9,400)	4,200	24,500	
Typical operating ratios				
Net profit/net sales	—	3.6%	13.1%	
Net sales/total investment	0.9x	1.5x	2.4x	
Net profit/total investment	—	5.5%	31.8%	
Net sales/inventory	2.5x	4.2x	6.8x	

Radio, TV, and Electronics

The home electronics market encompasses an ever-increasing variety of sophisticated and expensive equipment. For this reason, most retail stores have chosen to specialize in certain segments of the market. Some stores, for example, deal only in radio and television sets, usually representing only a few manufacturers; others may stress sound reproduction equipment, carrying a complete line of stereo components and tape equipment. Still others aim at a more technically oriented clientele, offering communications equipment, electronics kits, parts, and supplies. These diverse items may also be combined with household appliances and musical instruments.

The market for home electronics equipment is broad, and store locations reflect this fact. About 70 percent of the stores are located in smaller regional and larger community shopping centers, with the rest equally

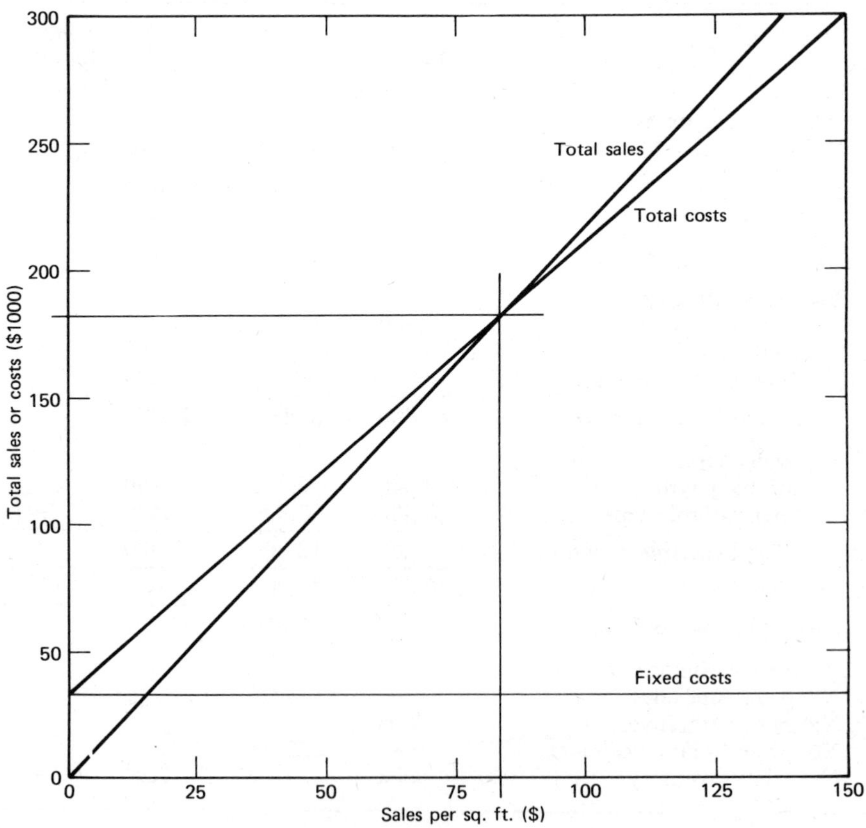

Breakeven chart for 2200 sq. ft. radio, TV, and electronics store.

divided between large regional and small neighborhood centers. Ownership is equally diverse; one-half of the stores are either parts of national chains or franchises, whereas the other one-half are locally owned chains or individual shops. Sizes are from 400 to 5500 square feet, mostly between 1600 and 3100 square feet. The September through January period accounts for about 60 percent of the year's total sales.

A typical 2200 square foot radio, TV, and electronics store breaks even with sales of $182,800 ($83.09 per square foot) annually.

Economic Characteristics of Retail Radio, TV, and Electronics Stores

Typical size (sq. ft.)		2,200		
Typical investment				
Inventory		58,000		
Depreciable assets		12,000		
All other		30,000		
Total investment		100,000		

	Low	*Typical Operation*	*High*	*Proposed Operation*
Operating Economics				
Sales per square foot	50	100	160	
Net annual sales	110,000	220,000	352,000	
Cost of goods sold	77,000	154,000	246,000	
Gross operating margin	33,000	66,000	106,000	
Fixed operating expenses				
Rent and utilities	13,200	13,200	13,200	
Fixed payroll	12,800	12,800	12,800	
Other fixed expenses	8,000	8,000	8,000	
Total fixed expenses	34,000	34,000	34,000	
Variable operating expenses				
Variable payroll	7,000	14,000	22,400	
Other variable expenses	5,500	11,000	17,600	
Total variable expenses	12,500	25,000	40,000	
Total operating expenses	46,500	59,000	74,000	
Net profit (loss) before taxes	(13,500)	7,000	32,000	
Typical operating ratios				
Net profit/net sales	—	3.2%	9.1%	
Net sales/total investment	1.1x	2.2x	3.5x	
Net profit/total investment	—	7.0%	32.0%	
Net sales/inventory	1.9x	3.8x	6.1x	

MISCELLANEOUS RETAIL STORES

Art Gallery
Arts and Crafts
Books and Stationery
Cameras
Candles
Cards and Gifts
China and Glassware
Cosmetics
Drugs
Florist
Hobbies
Jewelry
Lawn and Garden Supplies
Luggage and Leather Goods
Musical Instruments
Office Supplies and Equipment
Pets
Pipes and Tobacco
Records and Tapes
Sewing Machines
Sporting Goods
Toys
Variety Store
Yard Goods and Fabrics

Art Gallery

Art galleries sell original works of art, sometimes by known but usually by unknown local artists. These works of art include paintings, sculptures, lithographs, castings, metalworks, and other items. Quality reproductions are also generally available, and framing may constitute an important part of the business. Some of the original work may be bought outright by the gallery, but much of it is more likely to be handled on a consignment basis.

Almost all art galleries are locally owned independent operations, located in large community and regional shopping centers.

Variable costs are fairly high (0.59) considering the nature of the

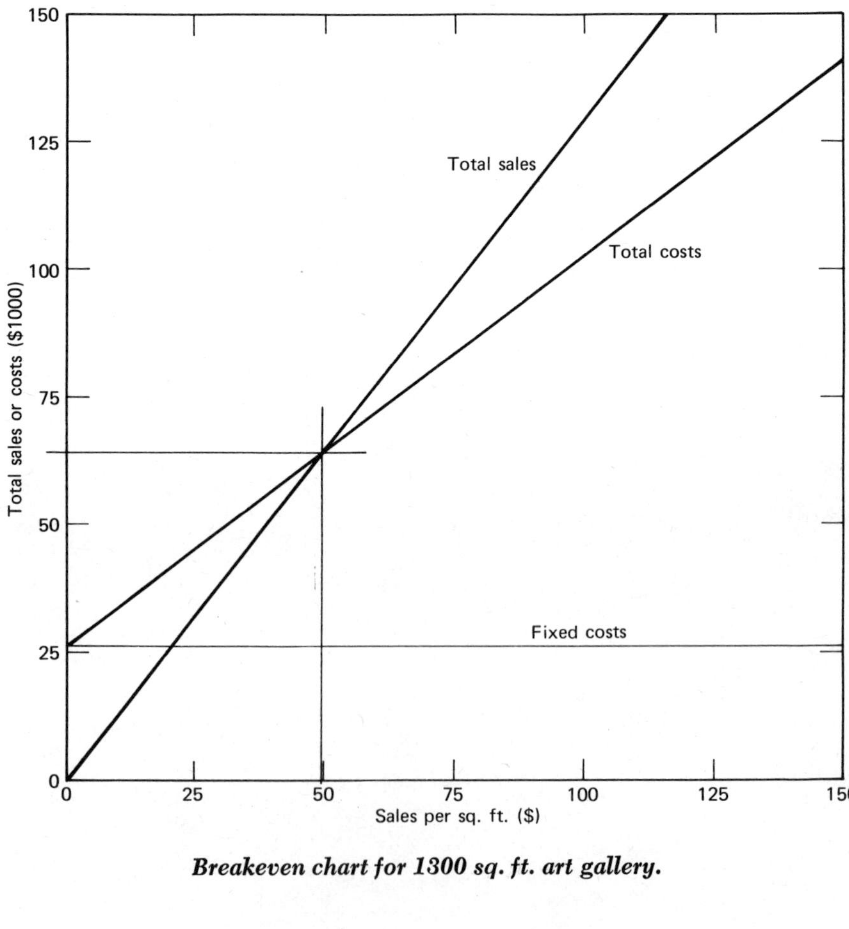

Breakeven chart for 1300 sq. ft. art gallery.

business, but most of the merchandise costs are paid only after the art work has been sold.

Gallery sizes range from 300 to 10,000 square feet; most fall between 1000 and 2100 square feet. The typical 1300-square-foot art gallery breaks even at an annual volume of $64,000, or $49.22 per square foot.

Economic Characteristics of Retail Art Galleries

Typical size (sq. ft.)		1,300		
Typical investment				
Inventory		28,600		
Depreciable assets		7,100		
All other		12,000		
Total investment		47,700		

	Low	*Typical Operation*	*High*	*Proposed Operation*
Operating Economics				
Sales per square foot	30	55	100	
Net annual sales	39,000	71,500	130,000	
Cost of goods sold	20,200	37,100	67,500	
Gross operating margin	18,800	34,400	62,500	
Fixed operating expenses				
Rent and utilities	11,700	11,700	11,700	
Fixed payroll	8,900	8,900	8,900	
Other fixed expenses	5,700	5,700	5,700	
Total fixed expenses	26,300	26,300	26,300	
Variable operating expenses				
Variable payroll	800	1,400	2,600	
Other variable expenses	2,000	3,600	6,500	
Total variable expenses	2,800	5,000	9,100	
Total operating expenses	29,100	31,300	35,400	
Net profit (loss) before taxes	(10,300)	3,100	27,100	
Typical operating ratios				
Net profit/net sales	—	4.3%	20.8%	
Net sales/total investment	0.8x	1.5x	2.7x	
Net profit/total investment	—	6.5%	56.8%	
Net sales/inventory	1.4x	2.5x	4.5x	

Arts and Crafts

Arts and crafts shops deal not in finished products, but in supplies, materials, kits, and equipment associated with locally popular craft activities. In addition, instructional books and classes are usually offered.

National chains and franchises are active in this field, accounting for 28 percent of the establishments, but the nature of the materials involved gives them little advantage over independently owned shops.

Large regional shopping centers usually have an arts and crafts shop, but most are found in the smaller regional and community centers. Sizes range from 300 to 5400 square feet; most are from 700 to 2700 square feet in size.

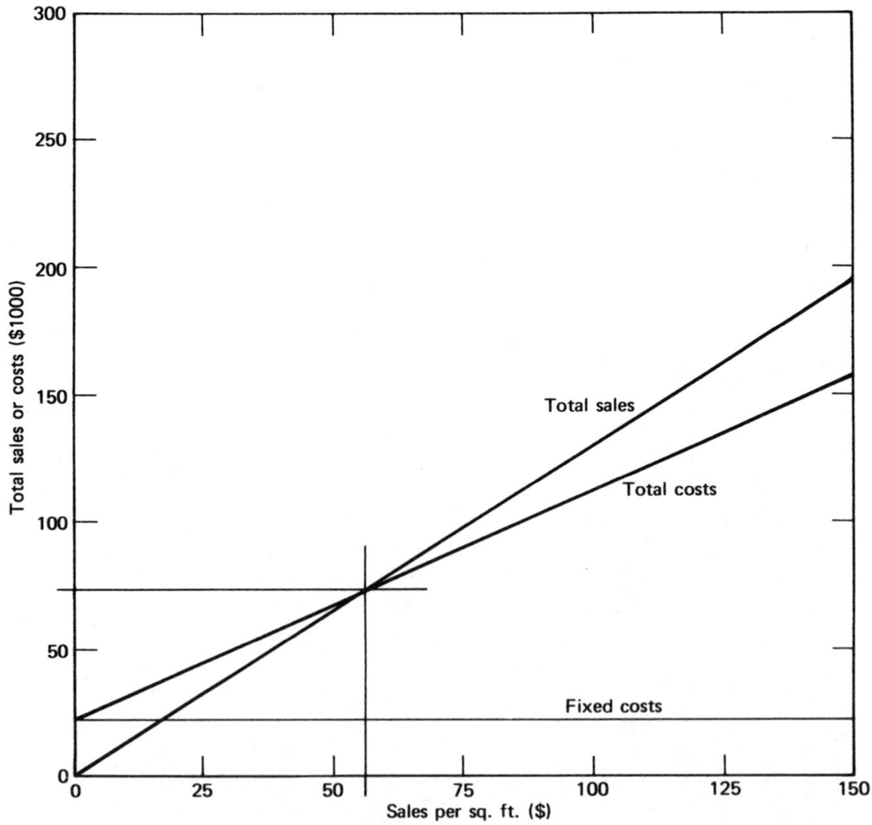

Breakeven chart for 1300 sq. ft. arts and crafts shop.

The typical 1300-square-foot arts and crafts shop needs $73,500, or $56.55 per square foot, in annual sales to break even.

Economic Characteristics of Retail Arts and Crafts Shops

Typical size (sq. ft.)		1,300		
Typical investment				
Inventory		12,000		
Depreciable assets		3,900		
All other		5,900		
Total investment		21,800		

	Low	*Typical Operation*	*High*	*Proposed Operation*
Operating Economics				
Sales per square foot	30	62	90	
Net annual sales	39,000	80,600	117,000	
Cost of goods sold	24,100	49,800	72,300	
Gross operating margin	14,900	30,800	44,700	
Fixed operating expenses				
Rent and utilities	11,700	11,700	11,700	
Fixed payroll	8,400	8,400	8,400	
Other fixed expenses	1,700	1,700	1,700	
Total fixed expenses	21,800	21,800	21,800	
Variable operating expenses				
Variable payroll	1,400	2,900	4,200	
Other variable expenses	1,900	4,000	5,800	
Total variable expenses	3,300	6,900	10,000	
Total operating expenses	25,100	28,700	31,800	
Net profit (loss) before taxes	(10,200)	2,100	12,900	
Typical operating ratios				
Net profit/net sales	—	2.6%	11.0%	
Net sales/total investment	1.8x	3.7x	5.4x	
Net profit/total investment	—	9.6%	59.2%	
Net sales/inventory	3.3x	6.7x	9.8x	

Books and Stationery

The complexities of operating an independent retail bookstore can scarcely be visualized by anyone outside the business. A 2000-square-foot store can stock perhaps 20,000 different titles, but some 30,000 new titles are published each year. Probably 25,000 of these new books would not sell a single copy in a small store; if they were stocked, they would simply take space away from the few titles that turn out to be salable.

When, occasionally, a book becomes popular, the few copies on hand are quickly sold, and a delay of from one to four weeks is encountered before it can be restocked. By then, it may have lost its popularity. Unsold books can be returned to the publisher for credit within specified time limits, but shipping costs (both ways) must be absorbed by the retailer. Book sales are highly seasonal, with one-third of the year's sales coming in November and December.

In most areas, discount stores have not affected the independent

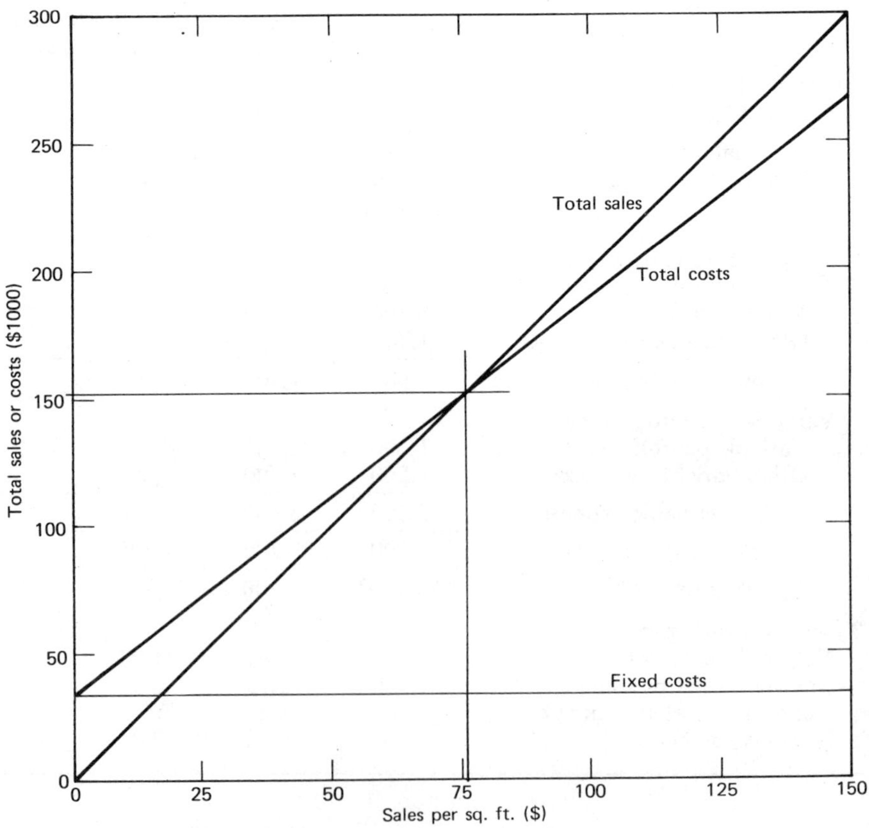

Breakeven chart for 2000 sq. ft. book shop.

bookseller. About one-third of all bookstores are now operated by national chains, whose primary emphasis is on current best-sellers. The independent store can compete quite effectively by offering personal service, quick response to customers' special orders for books not stocked, and careful selection of backlist titles for inventory.

About 75 percent of the retail bookstores are located in regional and community shopping centers, ranging generally from 1400 to 3900 square feet in size. A typical 2000-square-foot bookstore can break even on sales of $152,000, or $75.80 per square foot, annually.

Economic Characteristics of Retail Book and Stationery Shops

	Low	*Typical Operation*	High	*Proposed Operation*
Typical size (sq. ft.)		2,000		
Typical investment				
Inventory		33,000		
Depreciable assets		26,100		
All other		31,300		
Total investment		90,400		
Operating Economics				
Sales per square foot	50	88	175	
Net annual sales	100,000	176,000	350,000	
Cost of goods sold	65,000	114,400	227,500	
Gross operating margin	35,000	61,600	122,500	
Fixed operating expenses				
Rent and utilities	14,000	14,000	14,000	
Fixed payroll	12,000	12,000	12,000	
Other fixed expenses	7,200	7,200	7,200	
Total fixed expenses	33,200	33,200	33,200	
Variable operating expenses				
Variable payroll	8,100	14,200	28,200	
Other variable expenses	5,000	8,800	17,500	
Total variable expenses	13,100	23,000	45,700	
Total operating expenses	46,300	56,200	78,900	
Net profit (loss) before taxes	(11,300)	5,400	43,600	
Typical operating ratios				
Net profit/net sales	—	3.1%	12.5%	
Net sales/total investment	1.1x	1.9x	3.9x	
Net profit/total investment	—	6.0%	48.2%	
Net sales/inventory	3.0x	5.3x	10.6x	

Cameras

For a retail camera shop to succeed, it must offer its customers some valuable services that a discount store cannot provide; in other words, it must do much more than just sell cameras, film, and accessories. These items are available at discounted prices from the camera departments of large stores and heavily advertised mail-order houses.

A technical knowledge of photographic equipment and processes is essential for all salespeople in a retail camera store. Other services that distinguish a quality camera shop from a volume camera department include, in addition to reliable advice, custom film processing (requiring a good laboratory), acceptance of trade-ins on new equipment, repair services, and the presence of certain top-of-the-line cameras and equipment that are seldom discounted and never found in discount houses. The camera shop's best customers are those who take their photography seriously and are more conscious of quality than concerned about price.

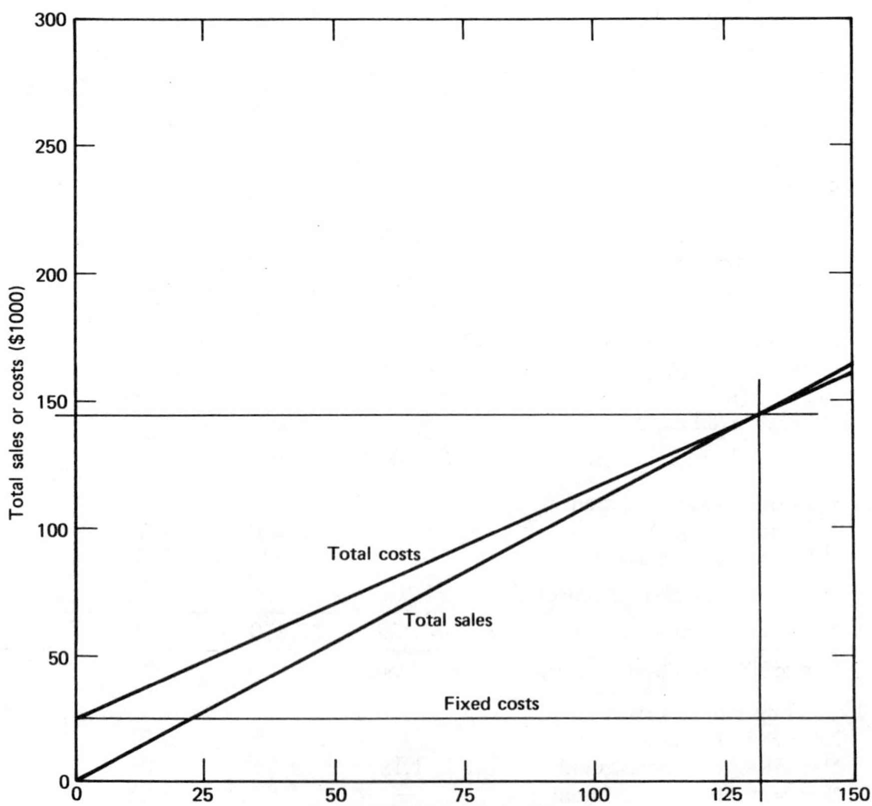

Breakeven chart for 1100 sq. ft. camera store.

The investment requirements are high if quality merchandise is to be carried, but the supply of quality cameras in certain lines may be limited, making inventory maintenance a greater problem than inventory turnover. December sales account for 18 percent of a typical store's annual volume.

A typical 1100-square-foot independently owned camera shop located in a large regional shopping center needs $145,400 in sales ($132.18 per square foot) annually to break even.

Economic Characteristics of Retail Camera Shops

Typical size (sq. ft.)		1,100		
Typical investment				
Inventory		30,500		
Depreciable assets		7,500		
All other		27,100		
Total investment		65,100		

	Low	*Typical Operation*	*High*	*Proposed Operation*
Operating Economics				
Sales per square foot	70	150	400	
Net annual sales	77,000	165,000	440,000	
Cost of goods sold	53,800	115,200	307,200	
Gross operating margin	23,200	49,800	132,800	
Fixed operating expenses				
Rent and utilities	12,100	12,100	12,100	
Fixed payroll	8,000	8,000	8,000	
Other fixed expenses	5,200	5,200	5,200	
Total fixed expenses	25,300	25,300	25,300	
Variable operating expenses				
Variable payroll	6,000	12,800	34,100	
Other variable expenses	3,900	8,300	22,100	
Total variable expenses	9,900	21,100	56,200	
Total operating expenses	35,200	46,400	81,500	
Net profit (loss) before taxes	(12,000)	3,400	51,300	
Typical operating ratios				
Net profit/net sales	—	2.1%	11.7%	
Net sales/total investment	1.2x	2.5x	6.8x	
Net profit/total investment	—	5.2%	78.8%	
Net sales/inventory	2.5x	5.4x	14.4x	

Candles

Candle shops are involved in making and selling decorated candles and candle holders, which are usually sold as art objects. The inventory may be handled on consignment, bought from wholesale dealers or manufacturers, made by the store owners, or purchased from local individuals. Candle-making supplies may also be carried for resale, including molds, waxes, wicks, scents, and colorings.

Almost 90 percent of candle shops are located in large regional shopping centers in which a high-traffic volume encourages walk-in impulse shoppers. Most shops are locally owned, although nationally franchised shops are becoming fairly common.

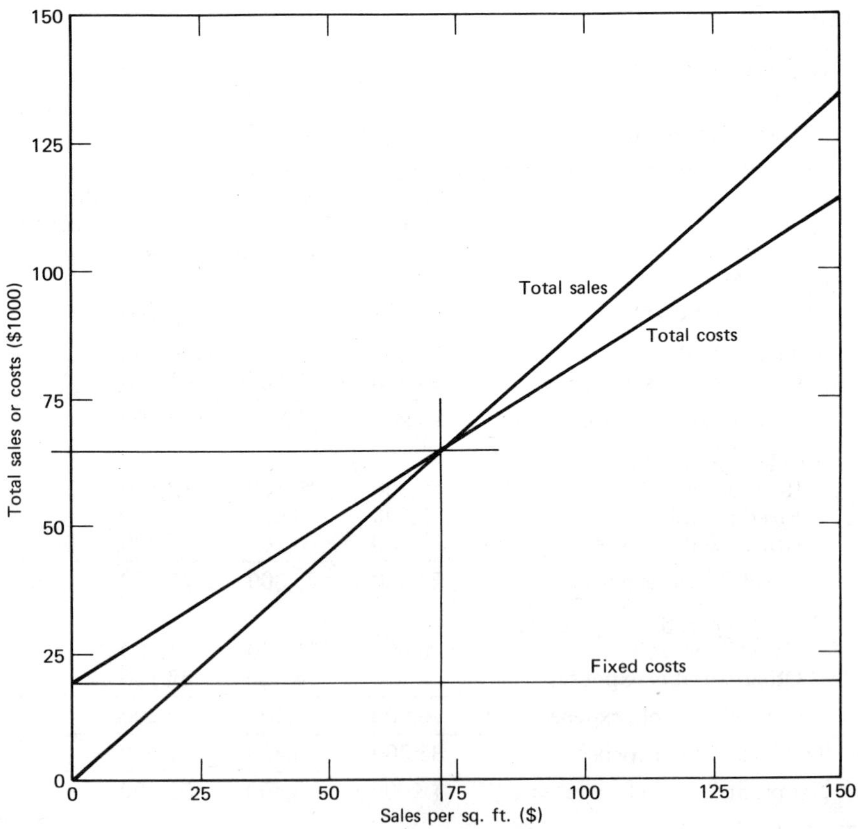

Breakeven chart for 900 sq. ft. candle shop.

The size requirements are minimal, with shops employing from 150 to 2200 square feet and most using from 700 to 1000 square feet. A typical 900-square-foot candle shop sells $65,100 or $72.30 per square foot, annually to break even.

Economic Characteristics of Retail Candle Shops

Typical size (sq. ft.)		900		
Typical investment				
Inventory		11,000		
Depreciable assets		3,700		
All other		5,500		
Total investment		20,200		

	Low	*Typical Operation*	*High*	*Proposed Operation*
Operating Economics				
Sales per square foot	45	83	115	
Net annual sales	40,500	74,700	103,500	
Cost of goods sold	26,100	48,200	66,800	
Gross operating margin	14,400	26,500	36,700	
Fixed operating expenses				
Rent and utilities	9,900	9,900	9,900	
Fixed payroll	7,500	7,500	7,500	
Other fixed expenses	1,600	1,600	1,600	
Total fixed expenses	19,000	19,000	19,000	
Variable operating expenses				
Variable payroll	500	1,000	1,400	
Other variable expenses	2,000	3,700	5,100	
Total variable expenses	2,500	4,700	6,500	
Total operating expenses	21,500	23,700	25,500	
Net profit (loss) before taxes	(7,100)	2,800	11,200	
Typical operating ratios				
Net profit/net sales	—	3.7%	10.8%	
Net sales/total investment	2.0x	3.7x	5.1x	
Net profit/total investment	—	13.9%	55.4%	
Net sales/inventory	3.7x	6.8x	9.4x	

Cards and Gifts

Several card and gift shops are found in almost every major shopping area, and greeting card departments abound in other types of larger stores. In addition to everyday greeting cards (birthdays, anniversaries, births, congratulations, weddings, convalescences, sympathy, and general friendship), seasonal cards (chiefly Valentine's Day, Mothers' Day, and Christmas) are important. Related merchandise such as note cards, stationery, writing instruments, and gift wraps also enjoy strong sales, and plaques, posters and party supplies are frequently carried in stock. Some craft and art gift items may be handled also.

Markups of 50 percent are standard, but most individual sales are small, and high pedestrian traffic is essential for success. Shops with

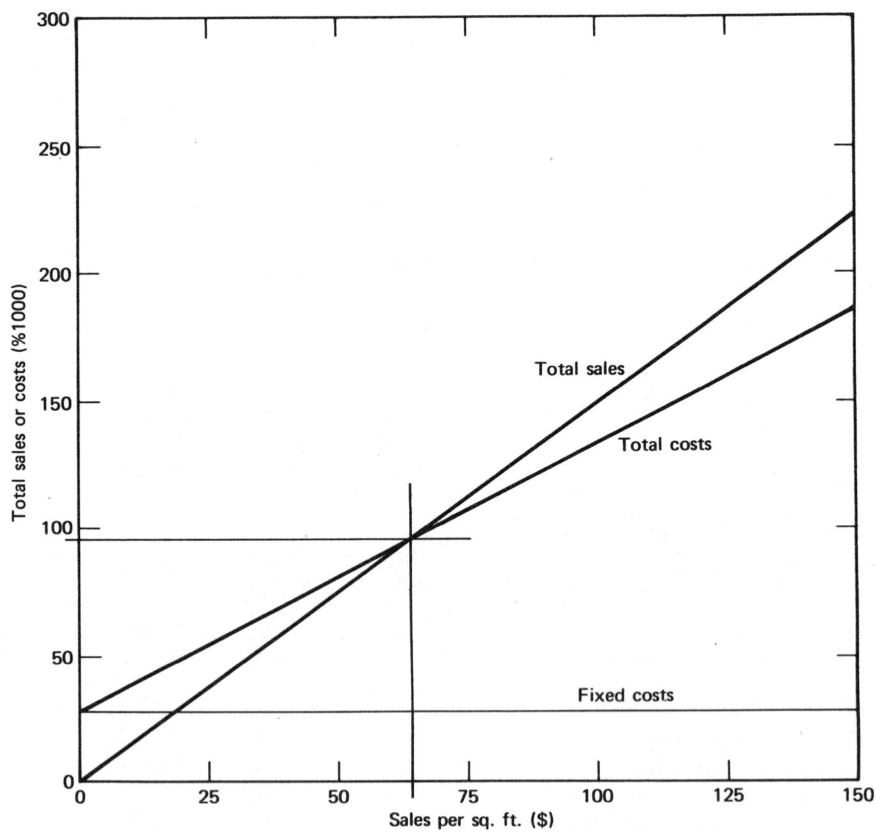

Breakeven chart for 1500 sq. ft. card and gift shop.

national-company affiliations may carry a complete line of one company's products, but independently owned stores (about 75 percent of the total) buy from a dozen or more different sources.

Sizes range between 400 and 4200 square feet; most stores are between 1400 and 2500 square feet. A typical 1500-square-foot shop breaks even at $96,200, or $64.11 per square foot, in annual sales.

Economic Characteristics of Retail Card and Gift Shops

Typical size (sq. ft.)		1,500		
Typical investment				
Inventory		26,300		
Depreciable assets		7,900		
All other		9,600		
Total investment		43,800		

	Low	*Typical Operation*	*High*	*Proposed Operation*
Operating Economics				
Sales per square foot	30	70	110	
Net annual sales	45,000	105,000	165,000	
Cost of goods sold	26,900	62,800	98,700	
Gross operating margin	18,100	42,200	66,300	
Fixed operating expenses				
Rent and utilities	15,000	15,000	15,000	
Fixed payroll	9,800	9,800	9,800	
Other fixed expenses	3,500	3,500	3,500	
Total fixed expenses	28,300	28,300	28,300	
Variable operating expenses				
Variable payroll	2,600	6,000	9,400	
Other variable expenses	2,300	5,300	8,300	
Total variable expenses	4,900	11,300	17,700	
Total operating expenses	33,200	39,600	46,000	
Net profit (loss) before taxes	(15,100)	2,600	20,300	
Typical operating ratios				
Net profit/net sales	—	2.5%	12.3%	
Net sales/total investment	1.0x	2.4x	3.8x	
Net profit/total investment	—	5.9%	46.3%	
Net sales/inventory	1.7x	2.4x	6.3x	

China and Glassware

The china and glassware business has a "gifty" nature, and, in addition to its basic china, glassware, and metalware lines for kitchen and table use, it probably carries related gift-type merchandise. It is expected to provide extensive gift wrapping and mailing services, with breakage on both incoming and outgoing shipments a constant and serious threat.

Two-thirds of the china and glassware specialty shops are single-store, independent operations. Location in a large, busy shopping center is almost a necessity.

The business is Christmas seasonal (11 percent of sales are in November, 18 percent in December), but less so than many other retail businesses.

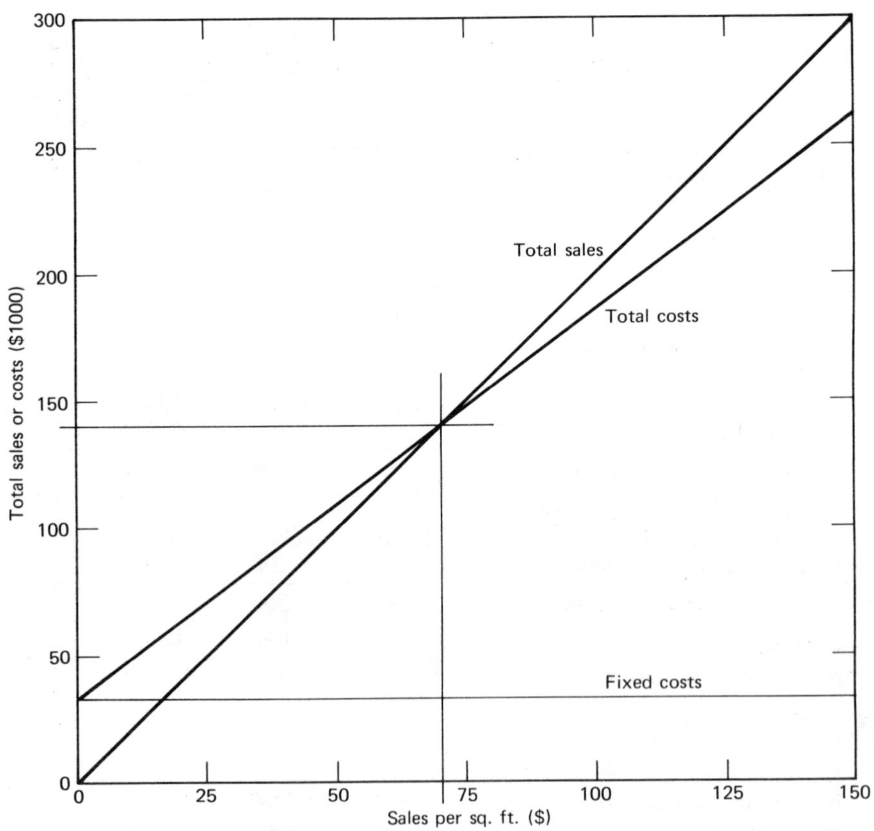

Breakeven chart for 2000 sq. ft. china and glassware shop.

Shop sizes range from 200 to 8300 square feet, with most shops occupying between 1500 and 2600 square feet.

A typical 2000-square-foot china and glassware shop breaks even with annual sales of $141,400, or $70.68 per square foot.

Economic Characteristics of Retail China and Glassware Shops

Typical size (sq. ft.)		2,000		
Typical investment				
Inventory		41,700		
Depreciable assets		10,400		
All other		17,500		
Total investment		69,600		

	Low	*Typical Operation*	*High*	*Proposed Operation*
Operating Economics				
Sales per square foot	40	80	140	
Net annual sales	80,000	160,000	280,000	
Cost of goods sold	50,600	101,200	177,100	
Gross operating margin	29,400	58,800	102,900	
Fixed operating expenses				
Rent and utilities	18,000	18,000	18,000	
Fixed payroll	12,000	12,000	12,000	
Other fixed expenses	3,500	3,500	3,500	
Total fixed expenses	33,500	33,500	33,500	
Variable operating expenses				
Variable payroll	6,400	12,800	22,400	
Other variable expenses	4,000	8,000	14,000	
Total variable expenses	10,400	20,800	36,400	
Total operating expenses	43,900	54,300	69,900	
Net profit (loss) before taxes	(14,500)	4,500	33,000	
Typical operating ratios				
Net profit/net sales	—	2.8%	11.8%	
Net sales/total investment	1.1x	2.3x	4.0x	
Net profit/total investment	—	6.5%	47.4%	
Net sales/inventory	1.9x	3.8x	6.7x	

Cosmetics

Cosmetics shops are highly specialized businesses dealing in body- and skin-care products. Most shops also provide consultations for customers' special needs, and some offer facial treatments and personal make-up services. These shops may be retail outlets for "house brands," or they may handle a variety of name-brand cosmetics.

Location in high-traffic areas is a must; 64 percent of the cosmetic specialty shops are located in regional shopping centers, with most of the rest in community centers. Very few are neighborhood businesses.

Just over one-half are franchises or local branches of national chains, although 30 percent are single-shop, independent businesses.

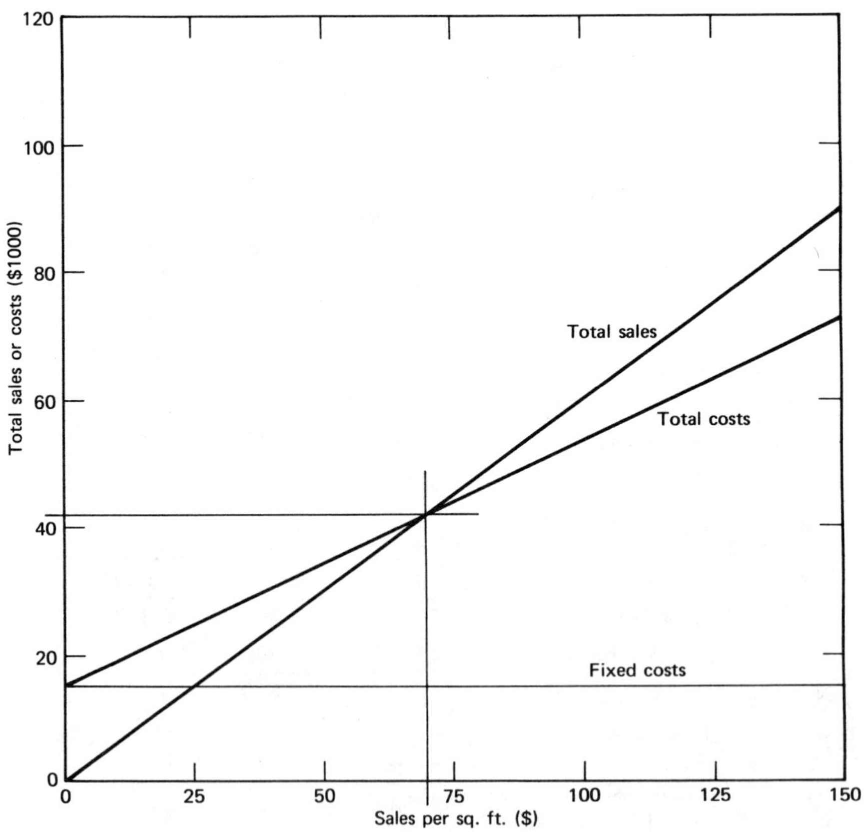

Breakeven chart for 600 sq. ft. cosmetics shop.

The size of a cosmetics shop can be as small as 200 square feet, seldom exceeding 2700 square feet. The typical shop occupies from 500 to 900 square feet in a smaller regional shopping center.

The typical operation requires sales of $41,800 ($69.71 per square foot) annually to break even.

Economic Characteristics of Retail Cosmetics Shops

Typical size (sq. ft.)		600		
Typical investment				
Inventory		12,200		
Depreciable assets		3,000		
All other		5,100		
Total investment		20,300		

	Low	*Typical Operation*	*High*	*Proposed Operation*
Operating Economics				
Sales per square foot	30	77	110	
Net annual sales	18,000	46,200	66,000	
Cost of goods sold	9,900	25,500	36,400	
Gross operating margin	8,100	20,700	29,600	
Fixed operating expenses				
Rent and utilities	6,000	6,000	6,000	
Fixed payroll	7,500	7,500	7,500	
Other fixed expenses	1,600	1,600	1,600	
Total fixed expenses	15,100	15,100	15,100	
Variable operating expenses				
Variable payroll	700	1,700	2,400	
Other variable expenses	900	2,300	5,500	
Total variable expenses	1,600	4,000	7,900	
Total operating expenses	16,700	19,100	23,000	
Net profit (loss) before taxes	(8,600)	1,600	6,600	
Typical operating ratios				
Net profit/net sales	—	3.5%	10.0%	
Net sales/total investment	0.9x	2.3x	3.3x	
Net profit/total investment	—	7.9%	32.5%	
Net sales/inventory	1.5x	3.8x	5.4x	

Drugs

Most large drug stores are, more realistically, variety stores that also handle prescription drugs and patent medicines. Cosmetics, toiletries, tobacco, and novelty merchandise make up a large part of the business, along with magazines, greeting cards, paperback books, and small personal and household appliances. Some drug stores operate a soda fountain or lunch counter, but the trend seems to be away from this type of service.

Drug stores are located virtually everywhere, from the largest regional shopping centers to the smallest neighborhood centers. There is a drug store for every 4000 people in the United States.

The drug stores located in regional shopping centers are usually af-

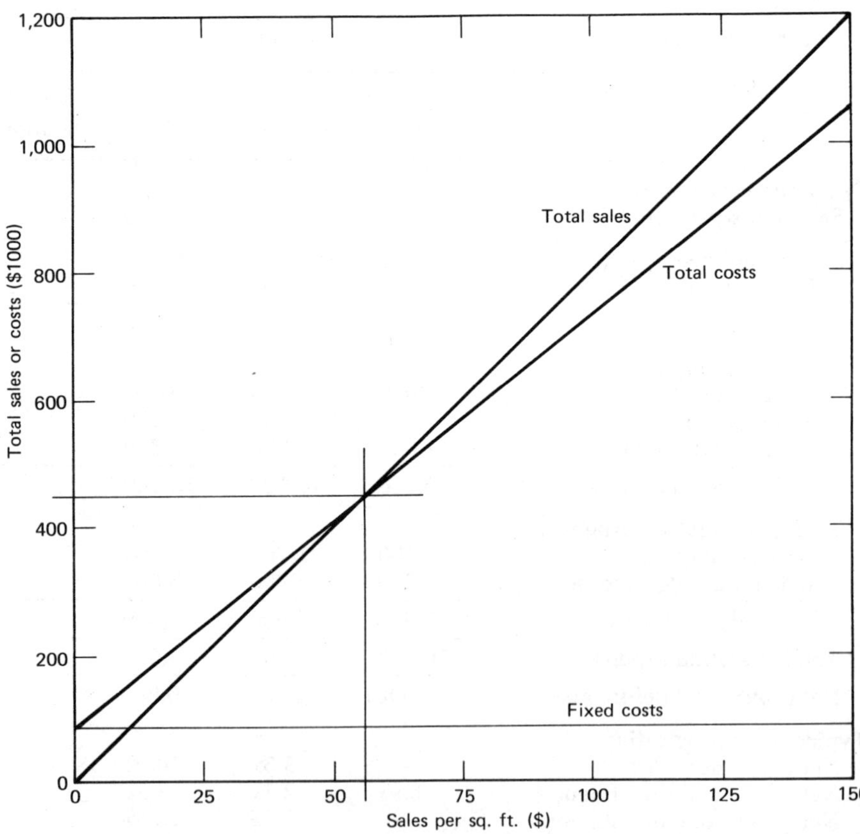

Breakeven chart for 8000 sq. ft. drug store.

filiated with national chains, whereas neighborhood drug stores are independently owned and operated. Sizes range from 800 to 22,000 square feet, with the neighborhood shops about 4000 square feet and the major shopping center stores averaging around 12,000 square feet.

A typical 8000-square-foot store located in a community shopping center can break even with annual sales of $453,000, or $56.61 per square foot.

Economic Characteristics of Retail Drug Stores

Typical size (sq. ft.)		8,000		
Typical investment				
Inventory		115,000		
Depreciable assets		38,700		
All other		28,000		
Total investment		181,700		

	Low	*Typical Operation*	*High*	*Proposed Operation*
Operating Economics				
Sales per square foot	50	70	150	
Net annual sales	400,000	560,000	1,200,000	
Cost of goods sold	269,200	376,900	807,600	
Gross operating margin	130,800	183,100	392,400	
Fixed operating expenses				
Rent and utilities	40,000	40,000	40,000	
Fixed payroll	32,000	32,000	32,000	
Other fixed expenses	14,500	14,500	14,500	
Total fixed expenses	86,500	86,500	86,500	
Variable operating expenses				
Variable payroll	34,300	48,000	102,900	
Other variable expenses	20,000	28,000	60,000	
Total variable expenses	54,300	76,000	162,900	
Total operating expenses	140,800	162,500	249,400	
Net profit (loss) before taxes	(10,000)	20,600	143,000	
Typical operating ratios				
Net profit/net sales	—	3.7%	11.9%	
Net sales/total investment	2.2x	3.1x	6.6x	
Net profit/total investment	—	11.3%	78.7%	
Net sales/inventory	3.5x	4.9x	10.4x	

Florist

A florist shop sells cut flowers and growing plants, but must offer its customers much more. Flower arranging can be considered an art in itself, and a florist provides more service than product.

The business is built around special occasions—weddings, parties and funerals—and special holidays, such as Valentine's Day, Mothers' Day, Memorial Day, and Christmas. All other business probably accounts for less than 20 percent of a florist's annual sales.

Florists are spread out among all types of shopping areas, about one for every 10,000 population. Less than five percent have any national affiliation other than membership in an organization to accommodate out-of-town orders and sales. Inventory spoilage is a big problem, and the common practice of "cleaning out the refrigerator" on funeral arrangements is not a commendable method of combatting the problem.

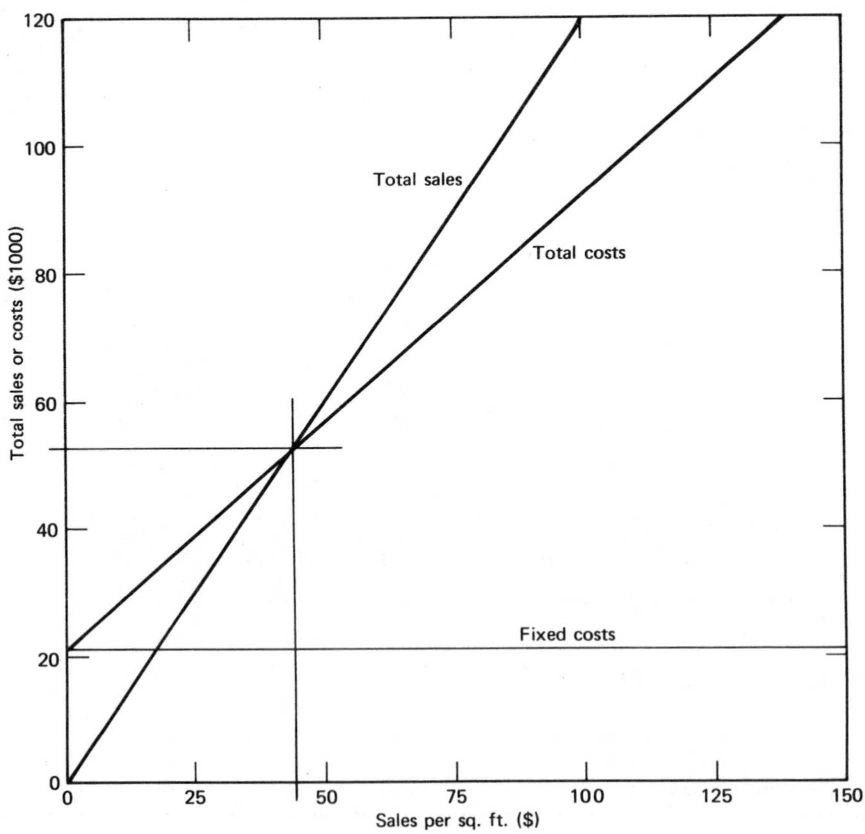

Breakeven chart for 1200 sq. ft. florist shop.

Shops can range in size from less than 100 square feet to as much as 8000 square feet; most are relatively small, between 800 and 2000 square feet.

A typical 1200-square-foot florist shop requires annual sales of $52,800, or about $44 per square foot, to break even. Variable costs, however, are low for a retail business, and any additional volume greatly enhances the profitability.

Economic Characteristics of Retail Florist Shops

Typical size (sq. ft.)		1,200		
Typical investment				
Inventory		11,000		
Depreciable assets		16,000		
All other		9,000		
Total investment		36,000		

	Low	*Typical Operation*	*High*	*Proposed Operation*
Operating Economics				
Sales per square foot	30	50	150	
Net annual sales	36,000	60,000	180,000	
Cost of goods sold	17,900	29,800	89,400	
Gross operating margin	18,100	30,200	90,600	
Fixed operating expenses				
Rent and utilities	9,600	9,600	9,600	
Fixed payroll	8,400	8,400	8,400	
Other fixed expenses	3,000	3,000	3,000	
Total fixed expenses	21,000	21,000	21,000	
Variable operating expenses				
Variable payroll	2,000	3,300	9,900	
Other variable expenses	1,800	3,000	9,000	
Total variable expenses	3,800	6,300	18,900	
Total operating expenses	24,800	27,300	39,900	
Net profit (loss) before taxes	(6,700)	2,900	50,700	
Typical operating ratios				
Net profit/net sales	—	4.8%	28.2%	
Net sales/total investment	1.0x	1.7x	5.0x	
Net profit/total investment	—	8.1%	140.8%	
Net sales/inventory	3.3x	5.5x	16.4x	

Hobbies

Hobby shops share many of the same characteristics and problems as toy stores and arts and crafts shops and may in fact carry many of the same items. Various types of models occupy most of the space in a hobby shop—airplane, automobile, ship and military, and model railroad accessories. Sophisticated electronics may be incorporated in some products such as radio-controlled cars and airplanes, and an extensive selection of model-related tools and equipment is usually available.

The business has been hit hard by competition from discounters, especially in the lower-priced lines, but the independent hobby shop can still offer the knowledgeable sales clerks and technical assistance that discount stores and others lack.

Three-fourths of the hobby shops are located in community and

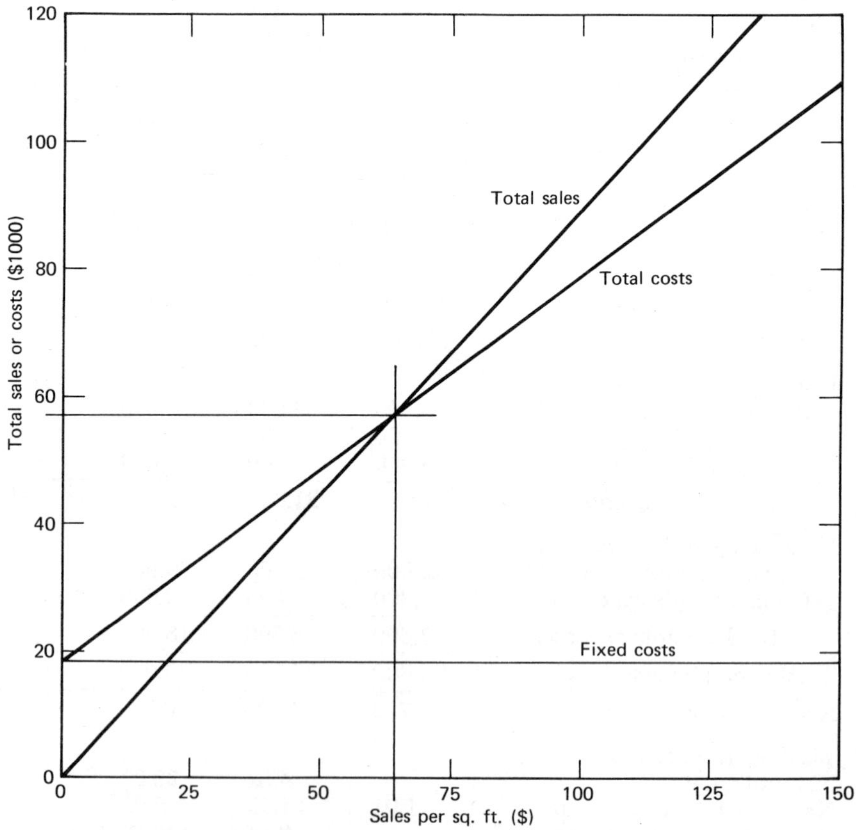

Breakeven chart for 900 sq. ft. hobby shop.

smaller regional shopping centers; 87 percent are independently owned, with about one-fifth of these representing multishop operations under local ownership.

The typical size range for hobby shops is 800 to 2500 square feet. A typical 900-square-foot shop requires annual sales of $57,800, or $64.18 per square foot to break even. Like toy stores, the hobby shop's business is highly seasonal, with most of the year's sales coming in November and December.

Economic Characteristics of Retail Hobby Shops

Typical size (sq. ft.)		900		
Typical investment				
Inventory		14,200		
Depreciable assets		4,700		
All other		7,000		
Total investment		25,900		

	Low	*Typical Operation*	*High*	*Proposed Operation*
Operating Economics				
Sales per square foot	45	70	130	
Net annual sales	40,500	63,000	117,000	
Cost of goods sold	24,600	38,300	71,100	
Gross operating margin	15,900	24,700	45,900	
Fixed operating expenses				
Rent and utilities	9,000	9,000	9,000	
Fixed payroll	7,500	7,500	7,500	
Other fixed expenses	2,100	2,100	2,100	
Total fixed expenses	18,600	18,600	18,600	
Variable operating expenses				
Variable payroll	800	1,300	2,400	
Other variable expenses	2,000	3,100	5,800	
Total variable expenses	2,800	4,400	8,200	
Total operating expenses	21,400	23,000	26,800	
Net profit (loss) before taxes	(5,500)	1,700	19,100	
Typical operating ratios				
Net profit/net sales	—	2.7%	16.3%	
Net sales/total investment	1.6x	3.7x	4.5x	
Net profit/total investment	—	6.6%	73.7%	
Net sales/inventory	2.9x	4.4x	8.2x	

Jewelry

Of all retail businesses, jewelry stores have the highest investment per square foot of floor space, and the type of merchandise carried—small in size but high in value—dictates that store layout and security measures be carefully planned.

The merchandise commonly includes diamonds and other precious stones mounted in precious metals, earrings, bracelets, brooches, sterling and plated silverware, watches, and clocks. Small, expensive gift items may be carried also.

Large discount houses have taken away much of the market that was once held by the small, independent jewelers. As in many other retail fields, the independent businessman simply cannot compete on the basis of price, but must make his advantages to the customer—personal service and guaranteed satisfaction—compensate for his higher merchandise costs and prices.

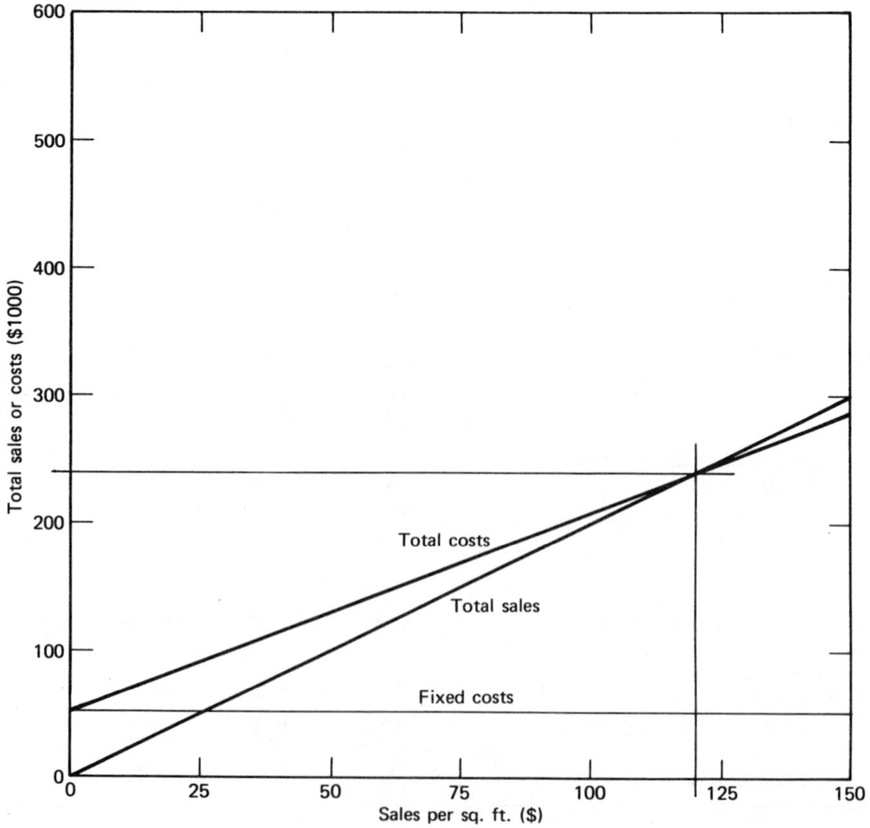

Breakeven chart for 2000 sq. ft. jewelry store.

Two-thirds of the jewelry stores found in shopping centers are locally and independently owned; the other one-third are branches of national chains. Most large regional shopping centers have two or more jewelry stores among their tenants, and almost all jewelry stores are located in community and regional centers. Sales of fine jewelry and watches are heavily oriented toward Christmas; November and December account for 38 percent of annual sales.

Jewelry stores range in size from 500 to 6000 square feet. The typical 2000-square-foot operation breaks even with annual sales of $240,000, or $120 per square foot.

Economic Characteristics of Retail Jewelry Stores

Typical size (sq. ft.)		2,000		
Typical investment				
Inventory		101,600		
Depreciable assets		28,000		
All other		69,200		
Total investment		198,800		
	Low	*Typical Operation*	*High*	*Proposed Operation*
Operating Economics				
Sales per square foot	70	150	300	
Net annual sales	140,000	300,000	600,000	
Cost of goods sold	85,400	183,000	366,000	
Gross operating margin	54,600	117,000	234,000	
Fixed operating expenses				
Rent and utilities	24,000	24,000	24,000	
Fixed payroll	12,000	12,000	12,000	
Other fixed expenses	16,000	16,000	16,000	
Total fixed expenses	52,000	52,000	52,000	
Variable operating expenses				
Variable payroll	17,500	37,000	74,000	
Other variable expenses	7,000	15,000	30,000	
Total variable expenses	24,500	52,000	104,000	
Total operating expenses	76,500	104,000	156,000	
Net profit (loss) before taxes	(21,900)	13,000	78,000	
Typical operating ratios				
Net profit/net sales	—	4.3%	13.0%	
Net sales/total investment	0.7x	1.5x	3.0x	
Net profit/total investment	—	6.5%	39.2%	
Net sales/inventory	1.4x	3.0x	5.9x	

Lawn and Garden Supplies

Retail lawn and garden supply dealers sell trees, shrubs, other plants, seeds, bulbs, mulches, soil conditioners, fertilizers, pesticides, gardening tools, and other lawn and garden supplies. They may offer landscaping services in conjunction with these sales. Most sell only products they purchase from nurseries and others, but some may operate their own greenhouses and nurseries.

Competition comes both from large retailers and mass merchandisers and from their own suppliers, who frequently sell at retail as well as wholesale. Ownership is mostly local; 60 percent of all lawn and garden supply dealers operate single-establishment businesses.

The location must allow for close-in customer parking, with subur-

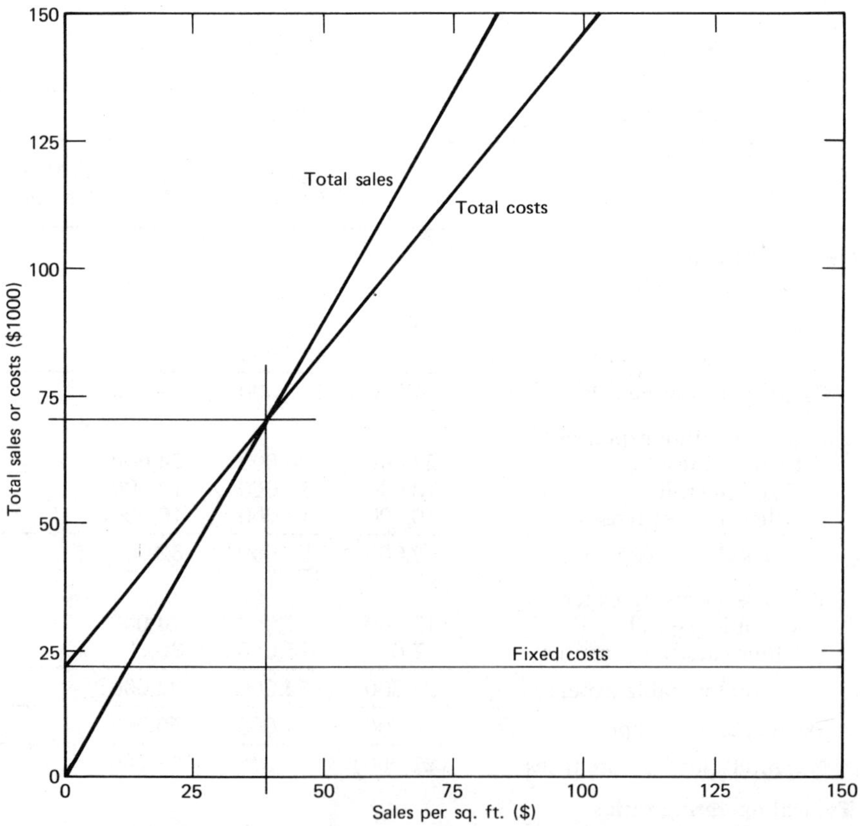

Breakeven chart for 1800 sq. ft. lawn and garden supply store.

ban neighborhoods preferred. The high seasonality of the business requires part-time help during busy periods and a "skeleton" staff at other times.

Sizes may reach 27,000 square feet in a few cases, with the typical operation occupying from 1500 to 3000 square feet. A typical lawn and garden supply dealer with 1800 square feet breaks even at sales of $70,200, or $39.01 per square foot, per year.

Economic Characteristics of Retail Lawn and Garden Supply Stores

Typical size (sq. ft.)		1,800		
Typical investment				
Inventory		10,000		
Depreciable assets		8,000		
All other		10,700		
Total investment		28,700		

	Low	*Typical Operation*	*High*	*Proposed Operation*
Operating Economics				
Sales per square foot	30	45	90	
Net annual sales	54,000	81,000	162,000	
Cost of goods sold	32,600	48,900	97,800	
Gross operating margin	21,400	32,100	64,200	
Fixed operating expenses				
Rent and utilities	9,000	9,000	9,000	
Fixed payroll	11,100	11,100	11,100	
Other fixed expenses	2,300	2,300	2,300	
Total fixed expenses	22,400	22,400	22,400	
Variable operating expenses				
Variable payroll	1,500	2,200	4,400	
Other variable expenses	2,700	4,100	8,400	
Total variable expenses	4,200	6,300	12,800	
Total operating expenses	26,600	28,700	35,200	
Net profit (loss) before taxes	(5,200)	3,400	29,000	
Typical operating ratios				
Net profit/net sales	—	4.2%	17.9%	
Net sales/total investment	1.9x	2.8x	5.6x	
Net profit/total investment	—	11.8%	101.0%	
Net sales/inventory	5.4x	8.1x	16.2x	

Luggage and Leather Goods

Luggage and leather goods shops usually carry only top-quality merchandise in selected lines, since middle- and lower-quality items can be found in most discount and department stores. Some shops, in addition to luggage, brief cases and travel accessories, offer repair services.

The quality and price of the merchandise handled almost dictates a location in a busy, affluent shopping center, and about 80 percent of all luggage shops are found in such centers. About 85 percent are locally owned; these are divided equally between multishop and individual operations.

Shop size can range from less than 100 to more than 5000 square feet,

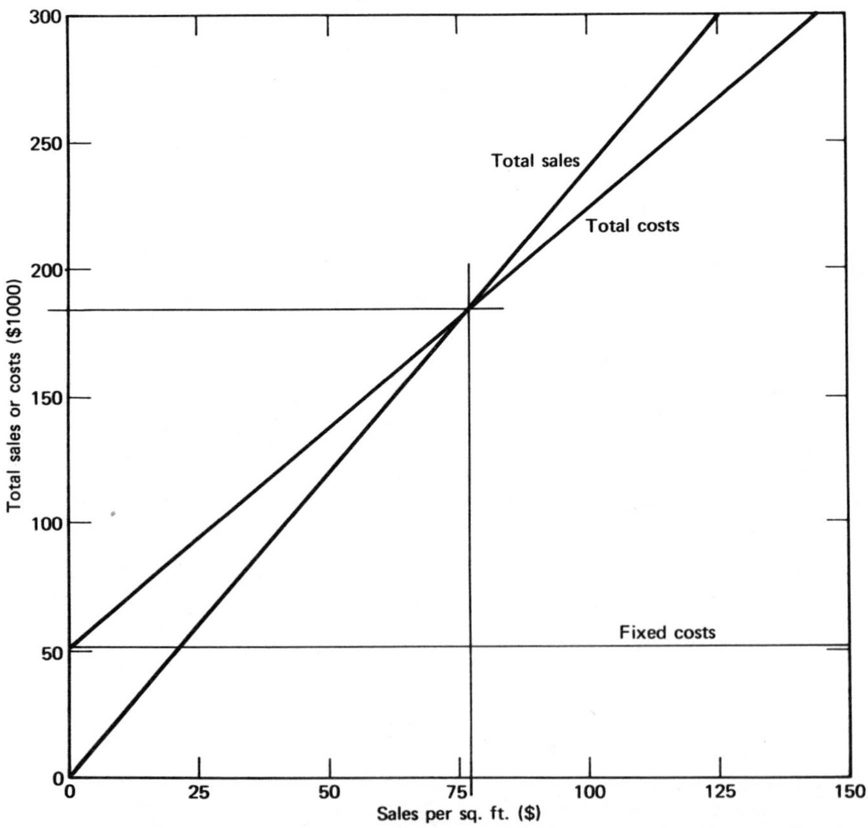

Breakeven chart for 2400 sq. ft. luggage and leather goods store.

typically in the 900 to 3300 square foot range. The business is moderately seasonal, usually with two peak months; 13 percent of the year's business is conducted in May, and December accounts for 14 percent.

A typical 2400 square foot luggage and leather goods shop located in a large regional shopping center needs sales of about $185,000, or $77.17 per square foot, per year to break even.

Economic Characteristics of Retail Luggage and Leather Goods Shops

Typical size (sq. ft.)		2,400		
Typical investment				
Inventory		54,000		
Depreciable assets		22,000		
All other		35,000		
Total investment		111,000		

	Low	*Typical Operation*	*High*	*Proposed Operation*
Operating Economics				
Sales per square foot	50	90	250	
Net annual sales	120,000	216,000	600,000	
Cost of goods sold	70,300	126,500	351,400	
Gross operating margin	49,700	89,500	248,600	
Fixed operating expenses				
Rent and utilities	28,800	28,800	28,800	
Fixed payroll	13,600	13,600	13,600	
Other fixed expenses	8,900	8,900	8,900	
Total fixed expenses	51,300	51,300	51,300	
Variable operating expenses				
Variable payroll	10,400	18,800	52,200	
Other variable expenses	6,000	10,800	30,000	
Total variable expenses	16,400	29,600	82,200	
Total operating expenses	67,700	80,900	133,500	
Net profit (loss) before taxes	(18,000)	8,600	115,100	
Typical operating ratios				
Net profit/net sales	—	4.0%	19.2%	
Net sales/total investment	1.1x	1.9x	5.4x	
Net profit/total investment	—	7.7%	103.7%	
Net sales/inventory	2.2x	4.0x	11.1x	

Musical Instruments

Stores dealing in retail musical instruments may specialize in certain lines such as pianos and/or electronic organs, or they may feature a broad assortment of all types of instruments along with records and tapes, sheet music, and related musical supplies. Stereo equipment is a logical companion line, along with recording systems. Some provision should be made for offering music lessons, and instrument rental/purchase plans should be available. Extended payment is usually necessary on large-ticket items; some stores carry their own accounts receivable, whereas others factor them (sell them at a discount to finance companies).

Ease of customer access, especially students for their lessons, is extremely important. Most musical instrument shops are located in smaller regional and community shopping centers, although some may be found

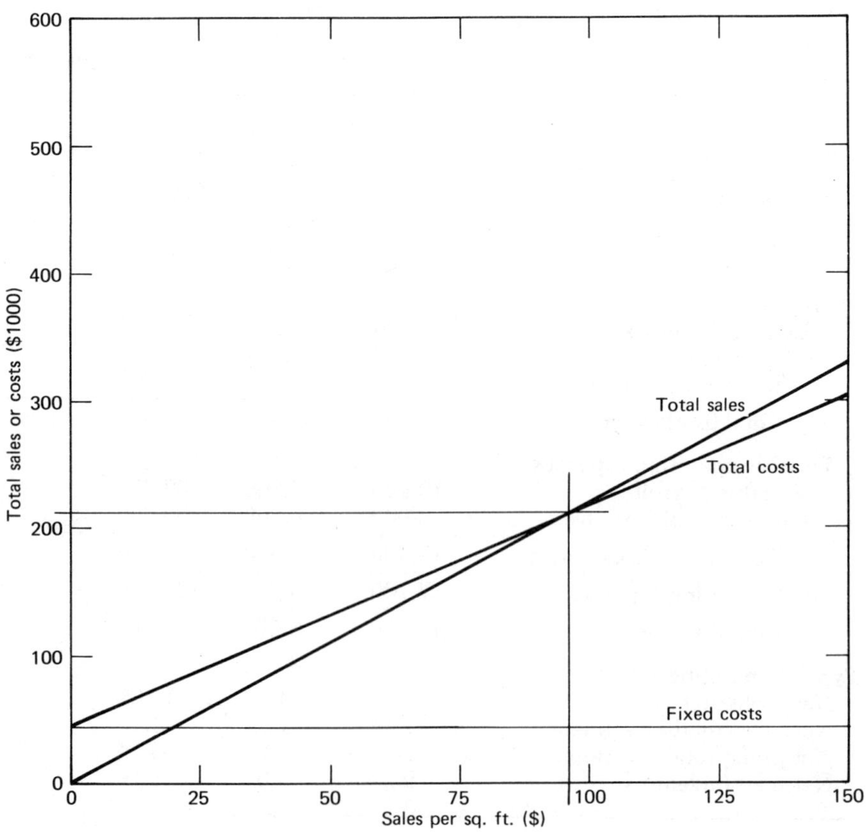

Breakeven chart for 2200 sq. ft. musical instruments store.

in large regional centers, and about 10 percent are in small neighborhood shopping centers. About 84 percent are locally owned, independent operations.

The musical instrument business is highly seasonal; 25 percent of the annual sales come in December and 12 percent in November.

Store sizes are from 400 to 5800 square feet, typically between 1100 and 2600 square feet. A typical store has 2200 square feet and breaks even with annual sales of $212,700, or $96.70 per square foot.

Economic Characteristics of Retail Musical Instrument Stores

Typical size (sq. ft.)		2,200		
Typical investment				
Inventory		70,000		
Depreciable assets		19,000		
All other		53,000		
Total investment		142,000		

	Low	*Typical Operation*	*High*	*Proposed Operation*
Operating Economics				
Sales per square foot	50	120	250	
Net annual sales	110,000	264,000	550,000	
Cost of goods sold	70,700	169,700	353,500	
Gross operating margin	39,300	94,300	196,500	
Fixed operating expenses				
Rent and utilities	20,900	20,900	20,900	
Fixed payroll	12,800	12,800	12,800	
Other fixed expenses	11,400	11,400	11,400	
Total fixed expenses	45,100	45,100	45,100	
Variable operating expenses				
Variable payroll	10,500	10,500	52,500	
Other variable expenses	5,500	13,200	27,500	
Total variable expenses	16,000	38,400	80,000	
Total operating expenses	61,100	83,500	125,100	
Net profit (loss) before taxes	(21,800)	10,800	71,400	
Typical operating ratios				
Net profit/net sales	—	4.1%	13.0%	
Net sales/total investment	0.8x	1.9x	3.9x	
Net profit/total investment	—	7.6%	50.3%	
Net sales/inventory	1.6x	3.8x	7.9x	

Office Supplies and Equipment

The sale of paper and paper products such as accounting and legal forms and stationery supplies makes up a large part of the basic office supplies business. Office equipment sales are also important, covering such items as filing cabinets, book cases, desks and desk accessories, shelving, typewriters, calculators, adding machines, and drafting equipment.

Most of the larger items such as desks and cabinets need not be carried in inventory, although it is advantageous to at least have a sample available. The heavy things can be ordered from manufacturers or distributors and shipped directly to the customer. Small items—paper and other stationery supplies—can be obtained from local office supply distributors, but a good well-balanced inventory is essential nevertheless.

Commercial accounts hold the key to a successful office supply busi-

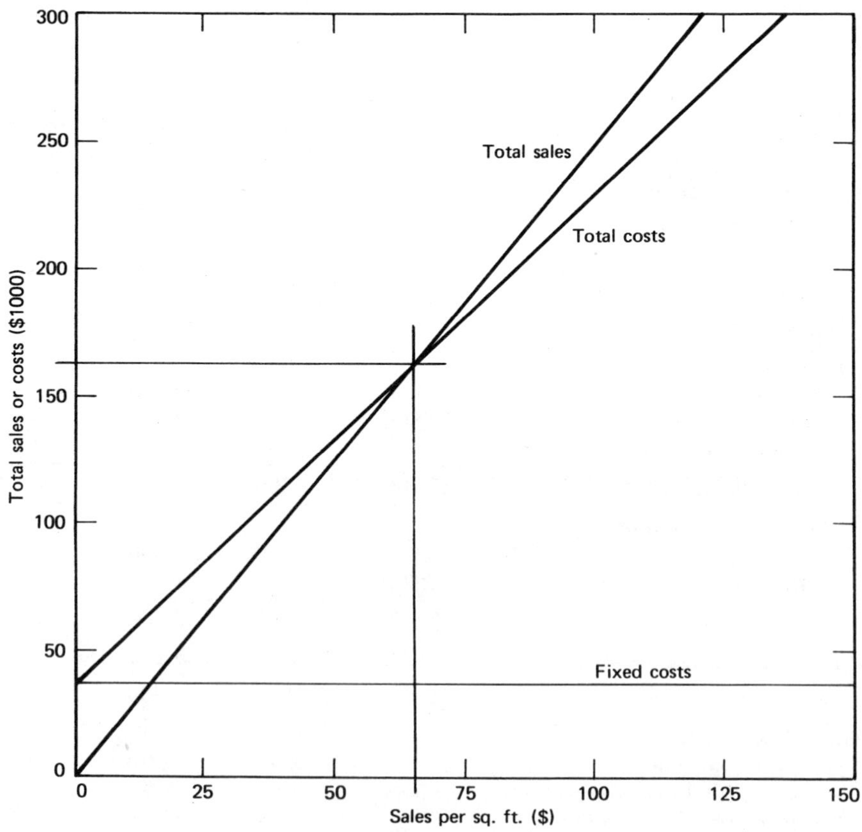

Breakeven chart for 2500 sq. ft. office supply store.

ness; thus promotional efforts must be directed toward acquiring business customers. Because of this emphasis, rapid and reliable sources of supply are necessary.

Office supply stores are almost all independently owned; most are located for easy access to business customers, and delivery service is offered. A sizable investment—over $82,000—is required for the typical 2500-square-foot office supply store, much of which is tied up in accounts receivable. Annual sales of $161,800 ($64.74 per square foot) are required to break even.

Economic Characteristics of Retail Office Supplies and Equipment Stores

Typical size (sq. ft.)		2,500		
Typical investment				
Inventory		37,600		
Depreciable assets		10,100		
All other		34,600		
Total investment		82,300		

	Low	*Typical Operation*	*High*	*Proposed Operation*
Operating Economics				
Sales per square foot	50	80	150	
Net annual sales	125,000	200,000	375,000	
Cost of goods sold	82,800	132,400	248,300	
Gross operating margin	42,200	67,600	126,700	
Fixed operating expenses				
Rent and utilities	16,300	16,300	16,300	
Fixed payroll	14,000	14,000	14,000	
Other fixed expenses	6,600	6,600	6,600	
Total fixed expenses	36,900	36,900	36,900	
Variable operating expenses				
Variable payroll	7,500	12,000	22,500	
Other variable expenses	6,300	10,000	18,800	
Total variable expenses	13,800	22,000	41,300	
Total operating expenses	50,700	58,900	78,200	
Net profit (loss) before taxes	(8,500)	8,700	48,500	
Typical operating ratios				
Net profit/net sales	—	4.4%	12.9%	
Net sales/total investment	1.5x	2.4x	4.6x	
Net profit/total investment	—	10.6%	58.9%	
Net sales/inventory	3.3x	5.3x	10.0x	

Pets

A pet shop is obviously the wrong business for those who believe the adage, "Never invest in anything you have to feed." The inventory must not only be fed, but also cleaned up after, and there is always a threat of disease. Locating good sources of healthy animals may also be a problem; commercial kennels, for example, do not always produce quality stock.

In addition to specialized lines of live pets, the pet shop stocks a variety of related pet supplies involved in their care and housing.

Two-thirds of all pet shops are located in smaller regional and com-

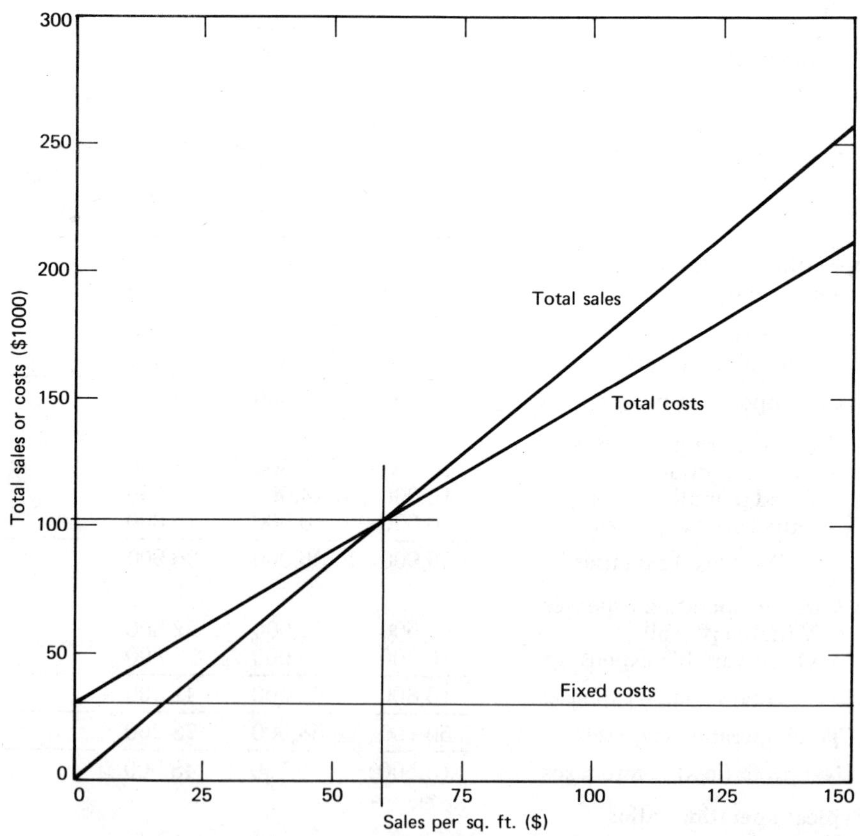

Breakeven chart for 1700 sq. ft. pet shop.

munity shopping centers. More than 80 percent are locally and independently owned.

Sizes range from 500 to 4000 square feet, with most falling in the 1200 to 2500 square foot range. The typical pet shop of 1700-square-feet needs annual sales of $102,200 or $60.14 per square foot, to break even.

Economic Characteristics of Retail Pet Shops

Typical size (sq. ft.)		1,700		
Typical investment				
Inventory		25,000		
Depreciable assets		8,500		
All other		15,000		
Total investment		48,500		
	Low	*Typical Operation*	*High*	*Proposed Operation*
Operating Economics				
Sales per square foot	45	70	100	
Net annual sales	76,500	119,000	170,000	
Cost of goods sold	43,300	67,300	96,100	
Gross operating margin	33,200	51,700	73,900	
Fixed operating expenses				
Rent and utilities	15,300	15,300	15,300	
Fixed payroll	10,700	10,700	10,700	
Other fixed expenses	3,900	3,900	3,900	
Total fixed expenses	29,900	29,900	29,900	
Variable operating expenses				
Variable payroll	7,000	10,900	15,600	
Other variable expenses	3,900	6,000	8,500	
Total variable expenses	10,900	16,900	24,100	
Total operating expenses	40,800	46,800	54,000	
Net profit (loss) before taxes	(7,600)	4,900	19,900	
Typical operating ratios				
Net profit/net sales	—	4.1%	11.7%	
Net sales/total investment	1.6x	2.5x	3.5x	
Net profit/total investment	—	10.1%	41.0%	
Net sales/inventory	3.1x	4.8x	6.8x	

Pipes and Tobacco

In addition to smoking pipes, a pipe shop usually sells imported cigars and cigarettes, smokers' supplies (ashtrays, lighters, humidors, tobacco jars, etc.), and a variety of pipe tobaccos. The pipe tobaccos may be packaged, proprietary blends formulated and packaged at the shop, or custom blends. All the merchandise is of substantially higher quality and price than the products normally found in a drug store's tobacco department.

Investment requirements are not high, but a high-traffic location is important. Almost 90 percent of all pipe and tobacco shops are located in

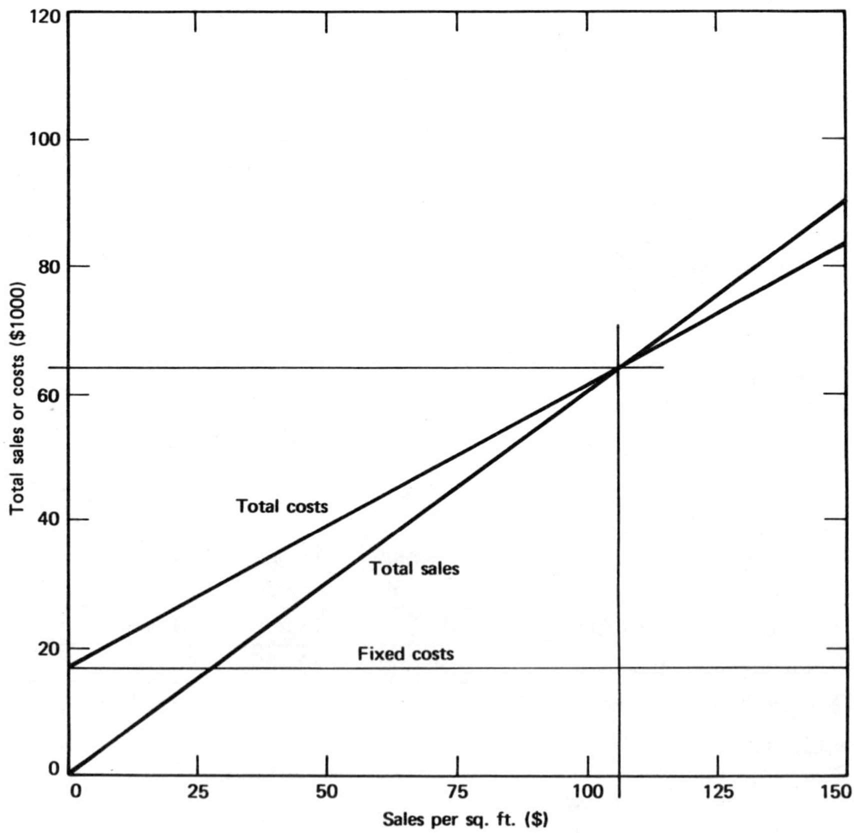

Breakeven chart for 600 sq. ft. pipe and tobacco shop.

large regional shopping centers. About one-third are nationally owned or franchised. Sizes range from 200 to 1500 square feet, with 500 to 900 square feet common.

The typical 600-square-foot shop, located in a busy and affluent regional shopping center, breaks even on gross annual sales of $64,000, or just under $107 per square foot.

Economic Characteristics of Retail Pipe and Tobacco Shops

Typical size (sq. ft.)		600		
Typical investment				
Inventory		9,000		
Depreciable assets		4,800		
All other		8,000		
Total investment		21,800		____
	Low	*Typical Operation*	*High*	*Proposed Operation*
Operating Economics				
Sales per square foot	50	130	200	
Net annual sales	30,000	78,000	120,000	
Cost of goods sold	18,900	49,200	75,700	____
Gross operating margin	11,100	28,800	44,300	
Fixed operating expenses				
Rent and utilities	7,800	7,800	7,800	
Fixed payroll	7,500	7,500	7,500	
Other fixed expenses	1,700	1,700	1,700	____
Total fixed expenses	17,000	17,000	17,000	
Variable operating expenses				
Variable payroll	1,600	4,200	6,500	
Other variable expenses	1,500	3,900	6,000	____
Total variable expenses	3,100	8,100	12,500	____
Total operating expenses	20,100	25,100	29,500	____
Net profit (loss) before taxes	(9,000)	3,700	14,800	
Typical operating ratios				
Net profit/net sales	—	4.7%	12.3%	
Net sales/total investment	1.4x	3.6x	5.5x	
Net profit/total investment	—	17.0%	67.9%	
Net sales/inventory	3.3x	8.7x	13.3x	

Records and Tapes

Stores that sell records and tapes are faced with many of the same problems as book stores: knowing how many of which of the thousands available to carry in stock, and how to divide the inventory and available space between currently popular and stable backstock items.

A record and tape shop is found in almost every large regional shopping center, in about half of the smaller regional centers, and in about one in five community centers. Two-thirds are locally owned independent operations.

The business is highly seasonal, with about one-fourth of the year's sales coming in December and 12 percent in November. Competition from major discounters and mail-order record and tape clubs is strong.

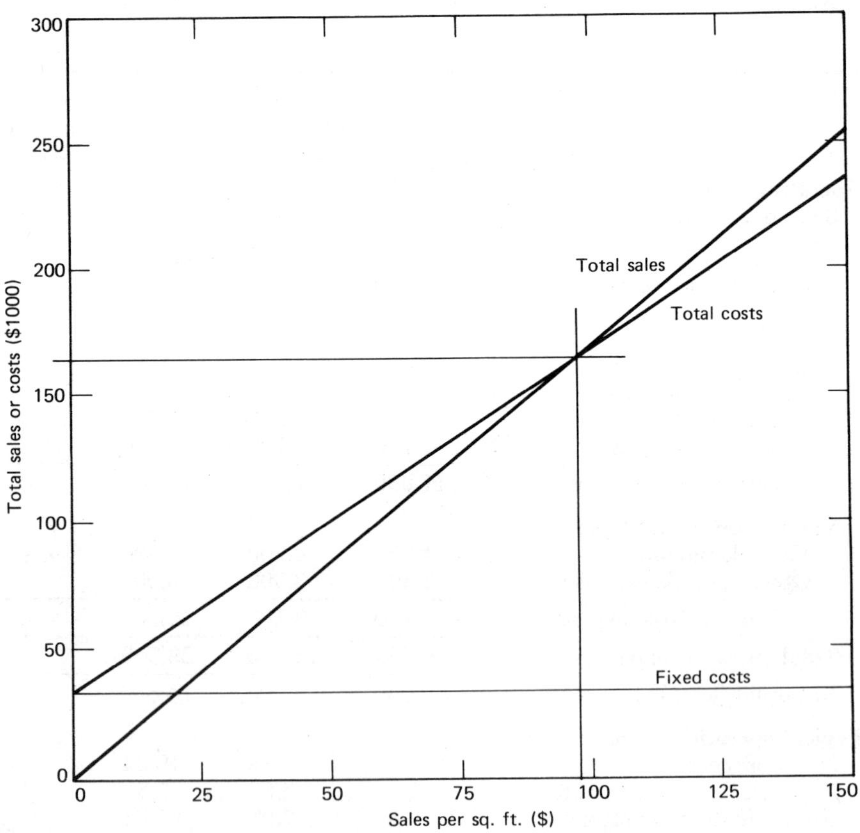

Breakeven chart for 1700 sq. ft. record and tape shop.

Security measures must be kept tight, especially on tapes, to prevent shoplifting. Display cabinets can be employed to minimize this problem, but additional staff may then be necessary to assist customers.

Sizes range from 200 to 5800 square feet for record and tape stores, with 1200 to 2400 square feet typical. The typical 1700-square-foot store breaks even at annual sales of $165,700, or $97.46 per square foot.

Economic Characteristics of Retail Records and Tape Stores

Typical size (sq. ft.)		1,700		
Typical investment				
Inventory		55,700		
Depreciable assets		11,400		
All other		29,100		
Total investment		96,200		

	Low	*Typical Operation*	*High*	*Proposed Operation*
Operating Economics				
Sales per square foot	35	125	170	
Net annual sales	59,500	212,500	289,000	
Cost of goods sold	38,500	137,400	186,900	
Gross operating margin	21,000	75,100	102,100	
Fixed operating expenses				
Rent and utilities	17,000	17,000	17,000	
Fixed payroll	10,700	10,700	10,700	
Other fixed expenses	7,700	7,700	7,700	
Total fixed expenses	35,400	35,400	35,400	
Variable operating expenses				
Variable payroll	5,300	19,100	26,000	
Other variable expenses	3,000	10,600	14,400	
Total variable expenses	8,300	29,700	40,400	
Total operating expenses	43,700	65,100	75,800	
Net profit (loss) before taxes	(22,700)	10,000	26,300	
Typical operating ratios				
Net profit/net sales	—	4.7%	9.1%	
Net sales/total investment	0.6x	2.2x	3.0x	
Net profit/total investment	—	10.4%	27.3%	
Net sales/inventory	1.1x	3.8x	5.2x	

Sewing Machines

Stores that specialize in sewing machine sales generally carry a main line of name-brand merchandise, perhaps a cheaper line for promotional sales, and a variety of used and reconditioned machines obtained through trade-ins. In conjunction with sewing machine sales, the store may offer individual sewing instructions. Replacement parts, accessories, and repair services are all part of the business, and some stores may carry other appliances from the same manufacturers (such as vacuum sweepers). Credit terms are necessary; the store may carry accounts for 30 to 90 days, with longer terms handled through outside firms.

More than 90 percent of the sewing machine sales operations are owned or franchised by national firms. One-half are located in smaller regional shopping centers, with the rest divided between large regional and

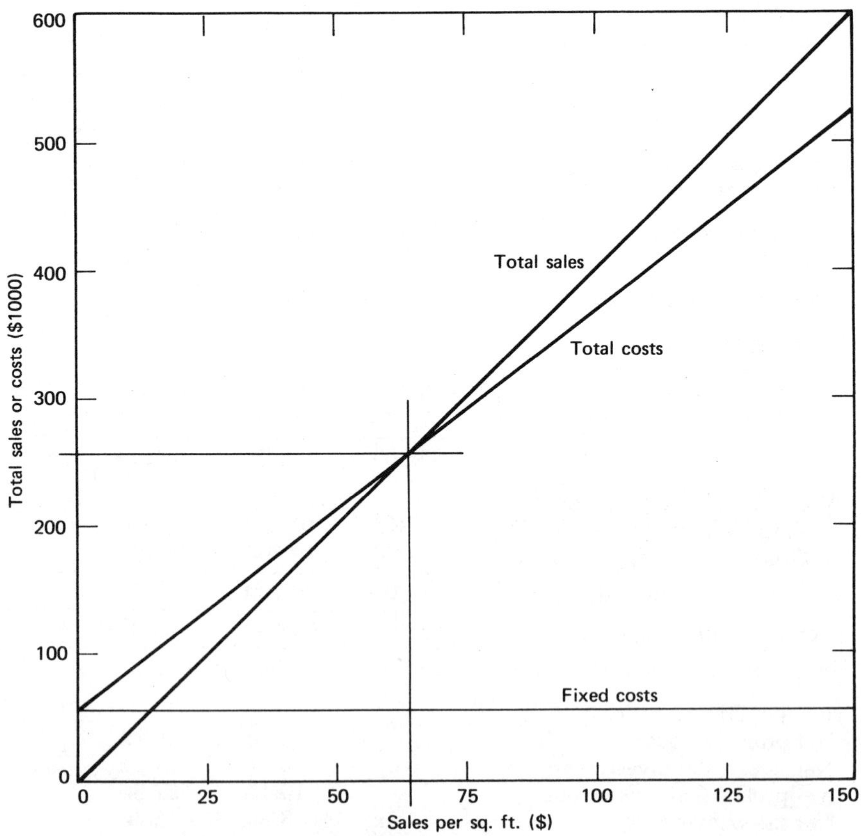

Breakeven chart for 4000 sq. ft. sewing machine store.

community centers. Sewing machines are also available from large department stores and discount merchandisers, but they may be unable to provide the services offered by specialty stores.

Sizes range from 800 to 7000 square feet. Most are between 1000 and 4200 square feet, and 4000 square feet is probably typical. This typical operation requires annual sales of $257,200 or $64.30 per square foot, to break even.

Economic Characteristics of Retail Sewing Machine Stores

Typical size (sq. ft.)		4,000		
Typical investment				
Inventory		82,100		
Depreciable assets		16,700		
All other		43,000		
Total investment		141,800		

	Low	*Typical Operation*	*High*	*Proposed Operation*
Operating Economics				
Sales per square foot	55	78	95	
Net annual sales	220,000	312,000	380,000	
Cost of goods sold	144,900	205,500	250,300	
Gross operating margin	75,100	106,500	129,700	
Fixed operating expenses				
Rent and utilities	24,000	24,000	24,000	
Fixed payroll	20,000	20,000	20,000	
Other fixed expenses	11,300	11,300	11,300	
Total fixed expenses	55,300	55,300	55,300	
Variable operating expenses				
Variable payroll	16,700	23,700	28,900	
Other variable expenses	11,000	15,600	19,000	
Total variable expenses	27,700	39,300	47,900	
Total operating expenses	83,000	94,600	103,200	
Net profit (loss) before taxes	(7,900)	11,900	26,500	
Typical operating ratios				
Net profit/net sales	—	3.8%	7.0%	
Net sales/total investment	1.6x	2.2x	2.7x	
Net profit/total investment	—	8.4%	18.7%	
Net sales/inventory	2.7x	3.8x	4.6x	

Sporting Goods

The full-line sporting goods store is actually a variety store with a mind-boggling array of merchandise for the sports minded. A complete selection of sporting goods is almost impossible; the most common types of merchandise include hunting and fishing equipment, camping equipment and supplies, exercise apparatus, playground equipment, and supplies and equipment for individual sports—bowling, tennis, golf, skiing, baseball, football, basketball, soccer, handball, raquetball, table tennis, billiards, and so on. An increasingly important part of the business is team uniforms, especially for "little league" baseball and football and other locally popular organized sports programs.

Nearly two-thirds of the sporting goods stores are located in large regional shopping centers, with most of the rest found in community cen-

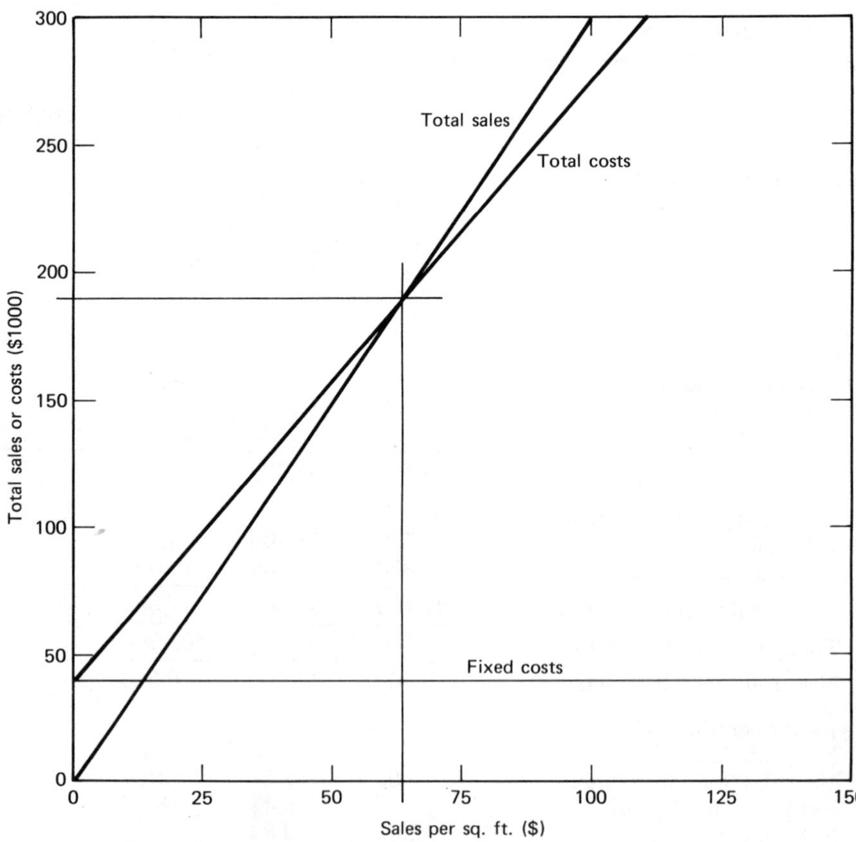

Breakeven chart for 3000 sq. ft. sporting goods store.

ters. About 85 percent of the shops are locally owned independent operations, ranging in size from 500 to 20,000 square feet and averaging from 1400 to 10,800 square feet, depending on the location and depth of coverage. Many are now set up almost on a "boutique" basis, offering complete coverage of a single sport or just a few sports (hunting and fishing, or tennis, golf, and skiing, for example). A typical 3000-square-foot general-line sporting goods store requires about $190,000, or $63.49 per square foot, in annual sales to break even.

Economic Characteristics of Retail Sporting Goods Shops

Typical size (sq. ft.)	3,000	
Typical investment		
Inventory	33,200	
Depreciable assets	10,300	
All other	13,000	
Total investment	56,500	

	Low	*Typical Operation*	*High*	*Proposed Operation*
Operating Economics				
Sales per square foot	40	70	150	
Net annual sales	120,000	210,000	450,000	
Cost of goods sold	83,400	146,000	312,900	
Gross operating margin	36,600	64,000	137,100	
Fixed operating expenses				
Rent and utilities	19,500	19,500	19,500	
Fixed payroll	16,000	16,000	16,000	
Other fixed expenses	4,500	4,500	4,500	
Total fixed expenses	40,000	40,000	40,000	
Variable operating expenses				
Variable payroll	5,400	9,400	20,100	
Other variable expenses	6,000	10,500	22,500	
Total variable expenses	11,400	19,900	42,600	
Total operating expenses	51,400	59,900	82,600	
Net profit (loss) before taxes	(14,800)	4,100	54,500	
Typical operating ratios				
Net profit/net sales	—	2.0%	12.1%	
Net sales/total investment	2.1x	3.7x	8.0x	
Net profit/total investment	—	7.3%	96.5%	
Net sales/inventory	3.6x	6.3x	13.6x	

Toys

Toy stores have probably suffered as much or more than any independent small business from the competition of large discount stores, many of which have erected complete store facilities to handle only toys. A convenient, high-traffic shopping center location is perhaps the toy store's only salvation; even there, variety and department stores get a large part of the toy sales.

The toy business is extremely seasonal; about 60 percent of all toys are sold during the Christmas season, November and December. This situation presents an obvious cash flow problem to a retailer who is open for business on a year-round basis. It is difficult even to cover cash ex-

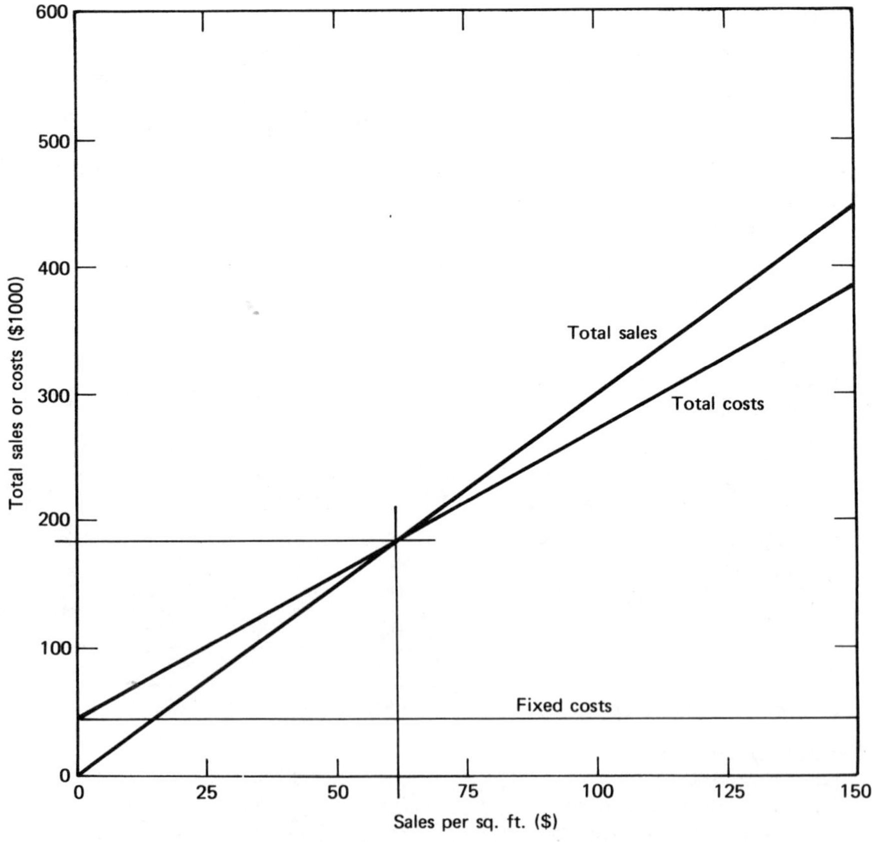

Breakeven chart for 3000 sq. ft. toy store.

penses between January and October, thus necessitating tight budget and inventory controls.

Other problems common to toy stores include breakage, shoplifting, and parents who leave small children in the toy store while they shop elsewhere.

Most toy stores occupy from 1200 to 8800 square feet of floor space. A typical 3000-square-foot store needs yearly sales of $185,800, or $61.93 per square foot, to break even.

Economic Characteristics of Retail Toy Stores

Typical size (sq. ft.)	3,000
Typical investment	
Inventory	31,200
Depreciable assets	10,300
All other	15,300
Total investment	56,800

	Low	*Typical Operation*	*High*	*Proposed Operation*
Operating Economics				
Sales per square foot	25	70	90	
Net annual sales	75,000	210,000	270,000	
Cost of goods sold	48,700	136,300	175,200	
Gross operating margin	26,300	73,700	94,800	
Fixed operating expenses				
Rent and utilities	24,000	24,000	24,000	
Fixed payroll	16,000	16,000	16,000	
Other fixed expenses	4,500	4,500	4,500	
Total fixed expenses	44,500	44,500	44,500	
Variable operating expenses				
Variable payroll	4,800	13,400	17,200	
Other variable expenses	3,700	10,500	13,500	
Total variable expenses	8,500	23,900	30,700	
Total operating expenses	53,000	68,400	75,200	
Net profit (loss) before taxes	(26,700)	5,300	19,600	
Typical operating ratios				
Net profit/net sales	—	2.5%	7.3%	
Net sales/total investment	1.3x	3.7x	4.8x	
Net profit/total investment	—	9.3%	34.5%	
Net sales/inventory	2.4x	6.7x	8.7x	

Variety Store

The variety store—once referred to as the "dime store"—includes a wide range of merchandise in the low and middle price ranges. Everything carried is on open display, and customers select their own merchandise with a minimum of sales help. Sales are usually on a cash-and-carry basis; the stores do not carry their own charge account services, but most accept major bank credit cards. Notions, school supplies, small hardware items, greeting cards, toys and games, housewares, and small appliances are among the staple items usually stocked.

About 70 percent of the variety stores are located in smaller regional and community shopping centers, with the rest divided evenly between large regional and small neighborhood centers. More than 80 percent are parts of national chains (although some of these are locally owned inde-

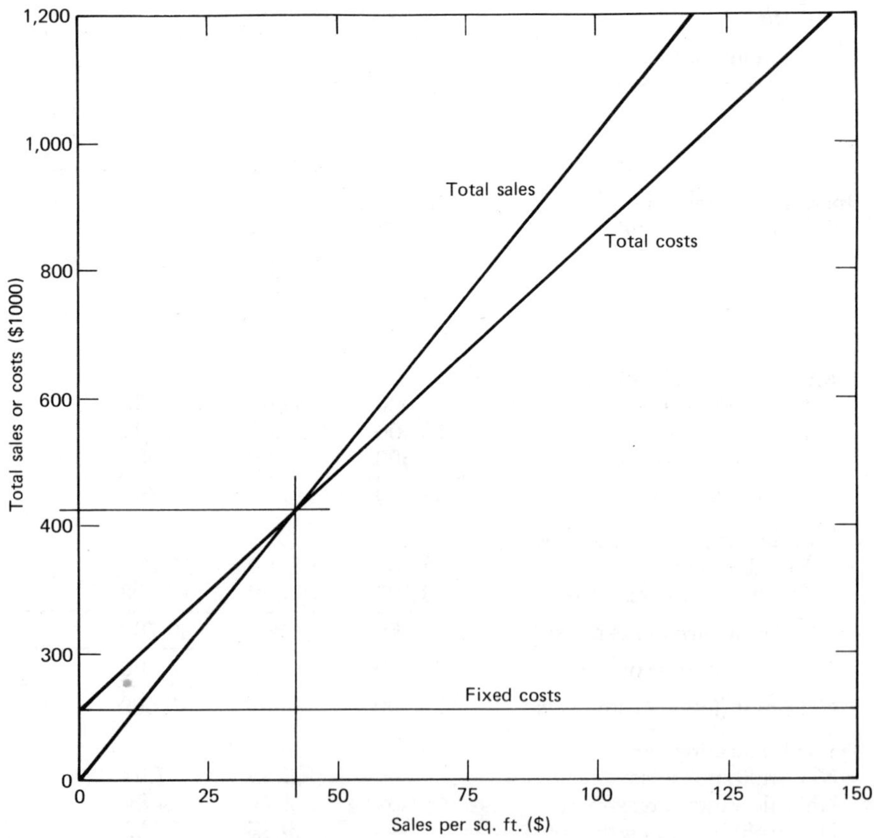

Breakeven chart for 10,000 sq. ft. variety store.

pendents), with unaffiliated independent stores generally limited to the smaller shopping centers.

Most variety stores are between 7000 and 34,000 square feet in size; the independently owned stores are not usually over 15,000 square feet. A typical 10,000-square-foot variety store needs annual sales of about $422,000, or $42.17 per square foot, to break even. Depending on the merchandise mix and location, as much as 30 to 50 percent of the year's sales come in November and December.

Economic Characteristics of Retail Variety Stores

Typical size (sq. ft.)	10,000	
Typical investment		
Inventory	116,000	
Depreciable assets	35,000	
All other	42,000	
Total investment	193,000	______

	Low	*Typical Operation*	*High*	*Proposed Operation*
Operating Economics				
Sales per square foot	30	47	100	
Net annual sales	300,000	470,000	1,000,000	
Cost of goods sold	188,900	296,000	629,800	
Gross operating margin	111,100	174,000	370,200	
Fixed operating expenses				
Rent and utilities	50,000	50,000	50,000	
Fixed payroll	37,500	37,500	37,500	
Other fixed expenses	15,400	15,400	15,400	
Total fixed expenses	102,900	102,900	102,900	
Variable operating expenses				
Variable payroll	23,000	36,000	76,600	
Other variable expenses	15,000	23,500	50,000	
Total variable expenses	38,000	59,500	126,600	
Total operating expenses	140,900	162,400	229,500	
Net profit (loss) before taxes	(29,800)	11,600	140,700	
Typical operating ratios				
Net profit/net sales	—	2.5%	14.1%	
Net sales/total investment	1.6x	2.4x	5.2x	
Net profit/total investment	—	6.0%	72.9%	
Net sales/inventory	2.6x	4.1x	8.6x	

Yard Goods and Fabrics

In addition to yard goods and fabrics, these shops typically sell a wide and complete variety of sewing supplies and needlework accessories. An important promotional sideline for many is conducting classes in tailoring, alterations, and other needlecrafts.

Because of their substantial space requirements for accomodating the relatively bulky merchandise, yard goods and fabrics stores are often found in community and smaller regional shopping centers, and many are located in neighborhood centers. Ownership is split about evenly between national and local operators.

The business as a whole is not highly seasonal, but the market for particular materials is. Woolen yard goods, for example, sell heavily from

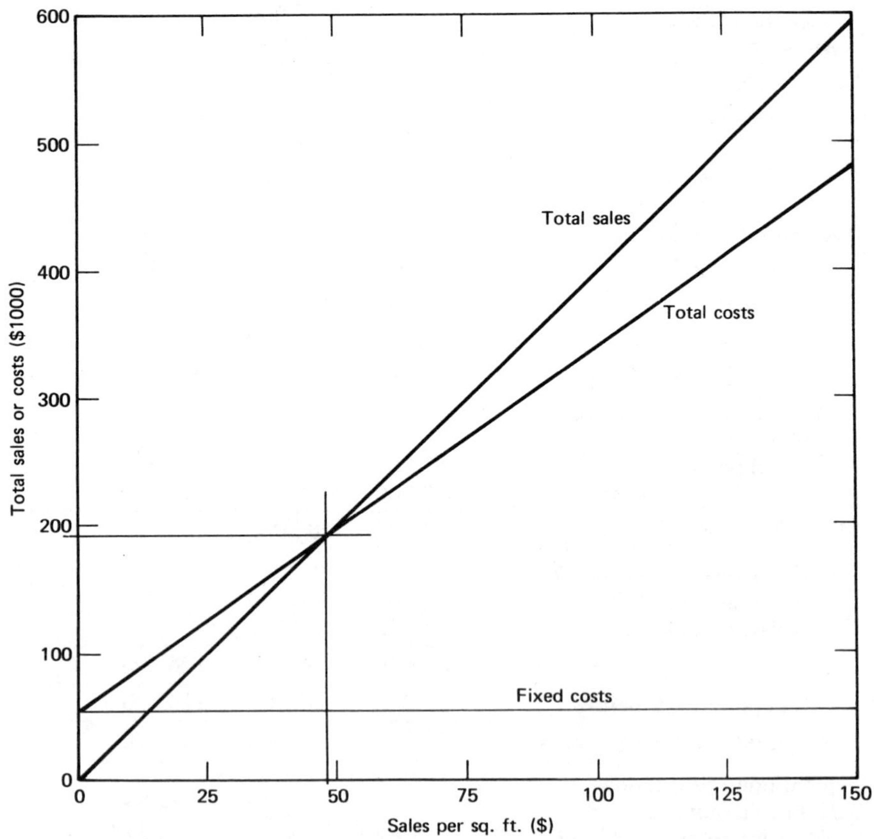

Breakeven chart for 4000 sq. ft. yard goods and fabrics store.

August through December, whereas sales of cotton yard goods reach their peak during the March to June period, and synthetics are steady year-round sellers.

Sizes range up to 20,000 square feet, with 2300 to 4600 square feet the common range. A typical 4000-square-foot store breaks even with annual sales of $191,700, or $47.92 per square foot.

Economic Characteristics of Retail Yard Goods and Fabrics Stores

Typical size (sq. ft.)		4,000		
Typical investment				
Inventory		37,900		
Depreciable assets		11,400		
All other		13,900		
Total investment		63,200		

	Low	*Typical Operation*	*High*	*Proposed Operation*
Operating Economics				
Sales per square foot	25	55	80	
Net annual sales	100,000	220,000	320,000	
Cost of goods sold	64,400	141,600	206,000	
Gross operating margin	35,600	78,400	114,000	
Fixed operating expenses				
Rent and utilities	28,000	28,000	28,000	
Fixed payroll	20,000	20,000	20,000	
Other fixed expenses	5,100	5,100	5,100	
Total fixed expenses	53,100	53,100	53,100	
Variable operating expenses				
Variable payroll	2,900	6,400	9,300	
Other variable expenses	5,000	11,000	16,000	
Total variable expenses	7,900	17,400	25,300	
Total operating expenses	61,000	70,500	78,400	
Net profit (loss) before taxes	(25,400)	7,900	35,600	
Typical operating ratios				
Net profit/net sales	—	3.6%	11.1%	
Net sales/total investment	1.6x	3.5x	5.1x	
Net profit/total investment	—	12.5%	56.3%	
Net sales/inventory	2.6x	5.8x	8.4x	

AMUSEMENTS

Arcades and Amusement Centers
Bowling
Movies

Arcades and Amusement Centers

Arcades and amusement centers offer a broad assortment of coin-operated games and amusement devices. Although customer assistance in playing the games is unnecessary, constant supervision is an absolute must.

The customers are typically teen-aged boys, and some of the games generate considerable excitement and enthusiasm. The customers, too, are unlikely to exercise much care in handling some of the delicate electronic equipment, and many arcades find it desirable to employ off-duty police officers to keep things in hand. Equipment maintenance is a major problem nevertheless.

Since the major shopping centers in most cities have become the fa-

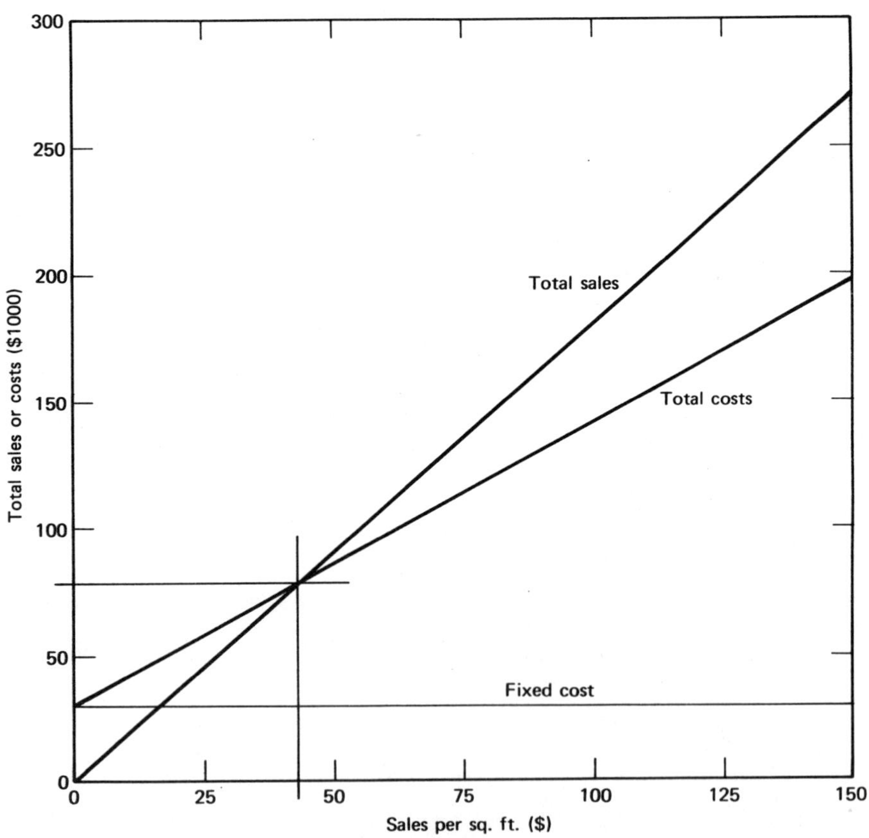

Breakeven chart for 1800 sq. ft. arcade and amusement center.

vorite after-school hangouts for teen-agers, this is where arcades tend to locate. About 80 percent are locally owned, with the other 20 percent nationally franchised. Sizes range from 400 to 20,000 square feet, and are typically from 1100 to 4600 square feet.

A typical 1800-square-foot arcade and amusement center must generate sales of $78,100, or $43.36 per square foot, to break even.

Economic Characteristics of Arcades and Amusement Centers

Typical size (sq. ft.)		1,800		
Typical investment				
Inventory		4,000		
Depreciable assets		28,000		
All other		10,000		
Total investment		42,000		

	Low	*Typical Operation*	*High*	*Proposed Operation*
Operating Economics				
Sales per square foot	20	50	80	
Net annual sales	36,000	90,000	144,000	
Cost of goods sold	16,500	41,300	66,100	
Gross operating margin	19,500	48,700	77,900	
Fixed operating expenses				
Rent and utilities	16,200	16,200	16,200	
Fixed payroll	11,100	11,100	11,100	
Other fixed expenses	3,400	3,400	3,400	
Total fixed expenses	30,700	30,700	30,700	
Variable operating expenses				
Variable payroll	3,500	8,800	14,100	
Other variable expenses	1,800	4,500	7,200	
Total variable expenses	5,300	13,300	21,300	
Total operating expenses	36,000	44,000	52,000	
Net profit (loss) before taxes	(16,500)	4,700	25,900	
Typical operating ratios				
Net profit/net sales	—	5.2%	18.0%	
Net sales/total investment	0.9x	2.1x	3.4x	
Net profit/total investment	—	11.2%	61.7%	
Net sales/inventory	9.0x	22.5x	36.0x	

Bowling

In addition to operating the bowling alleys themselves, most of these establishments also offer eating and drinking facilities along with retail sales of bowling balls, shoes, bags, gloves, and other accessories. Team uniforms, mostly shirts, can also be a profitable sideline.

Because of the size requirements—bowling alleys need at least 9000 square feet and may run as high as 56,000 square feet, with most in the 18,000 to 33,000 square foot range—only about one in 14 major regional shopping centers offer bowling facilities. Most bowling alleys are located near community shopping centers.

Almost two-thirds of all bowling alleys in the United States are independently owned and operated, with the rest divided between local and national chains. A population of around 14,000 should be found in the alley's market area.

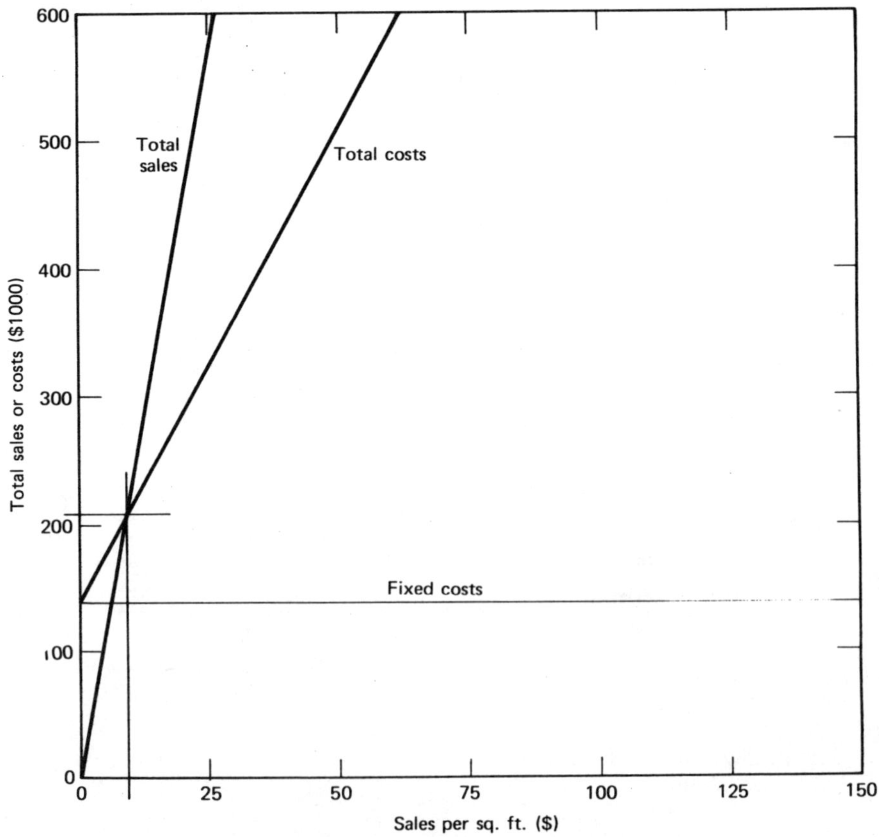

Breakeven chart for 23,000 sq. ft. bowling alley.

A bowling alley is a high investment, high fixed cost, low variable cost business, and, as such, good utilization of the facilities is required to make the operation economically attractive. Regular league play is essential year-round, and promotional efforts should be aimed at developing additional programs for slack (usually afternoon) periods.

The typical 23,000-square-foot bowling alley requires annual sales of $205,400 to break even; good utilization and strong promotion can be highly profitable.

Economic Characteristics of Bowling Alleys

Typical size (sq. ft.)		23,000		
Typical investment				
Inventory		15,700		
Depreciable assets		101,000		
All other		46,700		
Total investment		163,400		
	Low	*Typical Operation*	*High*	*Proposed Operation*
Operating Economics				
Sales per square foot	6	10	20	
Net annual sales	138,000	230,000	460,000	
Cost of goods sold	26,900	44,800	89,600	
Gross operating margin	111,100	185,200	370,400	
Fixed operating expenses				
Rent and utilities	80,500	80,500	80,500	
Fixed payroll	45,000	45,000	45,000	
Other fixed expenses	13,100	13,100	13,100	
Total fixed expenses	138,600	138,600	138,600	
Variable operating expenses				
Variable payroll	11,100	18,500	37,000	
Other variable expenses	6,900	11,500	23,000	
Total variable expenses	18,000	30,000	60,000	
Total operating expenses	156,600	168,600	198,600	
Net profit (loss) before taxes	(45,500)	16,600	171,800	
Typical operating ratios				
Net profit/net sales	—	7.2%	37.3%	
Net sales/total investment	0.8x	1.4x	2.8x	
Net profit/total investment	—	10.2%	105.1%	
Net sales/inventory	8.8x	14.6x	29.3x	

Movies

This category refers only to theaters that are engaged in the indoor exhibition of motion pictures. These theaters are located primarily in large regional shopping centers (about two-thirds of them), with the rest found mostly in community shopping centers. In the large centers, a theater operation may include from two to six separate theaters, each showing different movies.

About one-half of the movie theaters in the United States are affiliated with national chains, and one-third are operated by local chains; only about one in five theaters are independently owned and operated.

The physical size of movie theaters varies from less than 3000 square feet to more than 20,000 square feet. Most range in size between 9000 and 18,000 square feet. It takes a total population of between 15,000 and 20,000 to support a full-scale typical movie theater operation, although

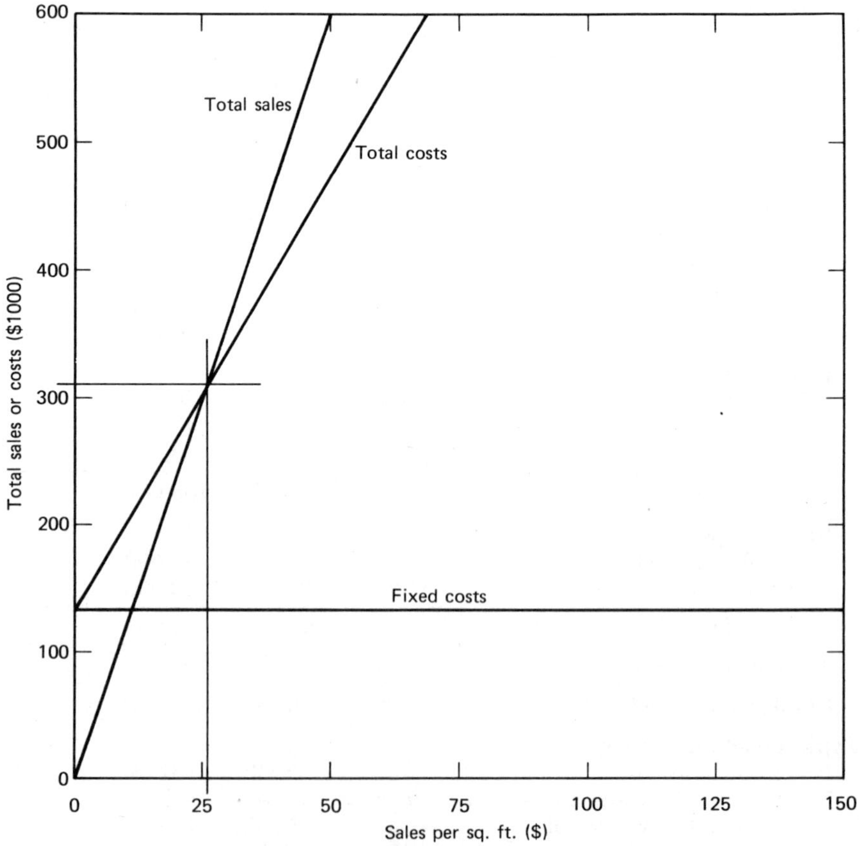

Breakeven chart for 12,000 sq. ft. movie theater.

small-town theaters can function profitably by operating on a limited schedule.

Movie theaters have high fixed costs and require a substantial investment. The breakeven point for a typical 12,000-square-foot theater is $25.93 per square foot, or $311,100, per year; dividing this total by the number of performances annually (usually 800 or more) indicates that high attendance is not necessary to break even. With popular shows and a good location, this can be a highly profitable business.

Economic Characteristics of Movie Theaters

Typical size (sq. ft.)		12,000		
Typical investment				
Inventory		8,200		
Depreciable assets		180,000		
All other		45,000		
Total investment		233,200		

	Low	*Typical Operation*	*High*	*Proposed Operation*
Operating Economics				
Sales per square foot	15	30	60	
Net annual sales	180,000	360,000	720,000	
Cost of goods sold	80,200	160,300	320,600	
Gross operating margin	99,800	199,700	399,400	
Fixed operating expenses				
Rent and utilities	60,000	60,000	60,000	
Fixed payroll	52,500	52,500	52,500	
Other fixed expenses	18,700	18,700	18,700	
Total fixed expenses	131,200	131,200	131,200	
Variable operating expenses				
Variable payroll	15,000	29,900	59,800	
Other variable expenses	9,000	18,000	36,000	
Total variable expenses	24,000	47,900	95,800	
Total operating expenses	155,200	179,100	227,000	
Net profit (loss) before taxes	(55,400)	20,600	172,400	
Typical operating ratios				
Net profit/net sales	—	5.7%	23.9%	
Net sales/total investment	0.8x	1.5x	3.1x	
Net profit/total investment	—	8.8%	73.9%	
Net sales/inventory	22.0x	43.9x	87.8x	

PERSONAL SERVICES

Barber Shop
Beauty Shop
Coin-Operated Laundry
Dry Cleaning
Keys
Photo Studio
Travel Agency

Barber Shop

Many of the old-time hair-cutting establishments have had to change their emphasis with the changing trends in men's hair styles. The shift from haircuts to hair styling has had a significant impact on the business.

Most neighborhood shopping centers still have their barber shop, but most new shops are located in large regional and community shopping centers. About 85 percent of all barber shops are independently owned; the rest are multishop operations, still with local ownership.

Barber shops range in size from 300 square feet to 1600 square feet, with most falling in the 400 to 900 square foot range. There is about one barber shop for every 2100 people in the United States.

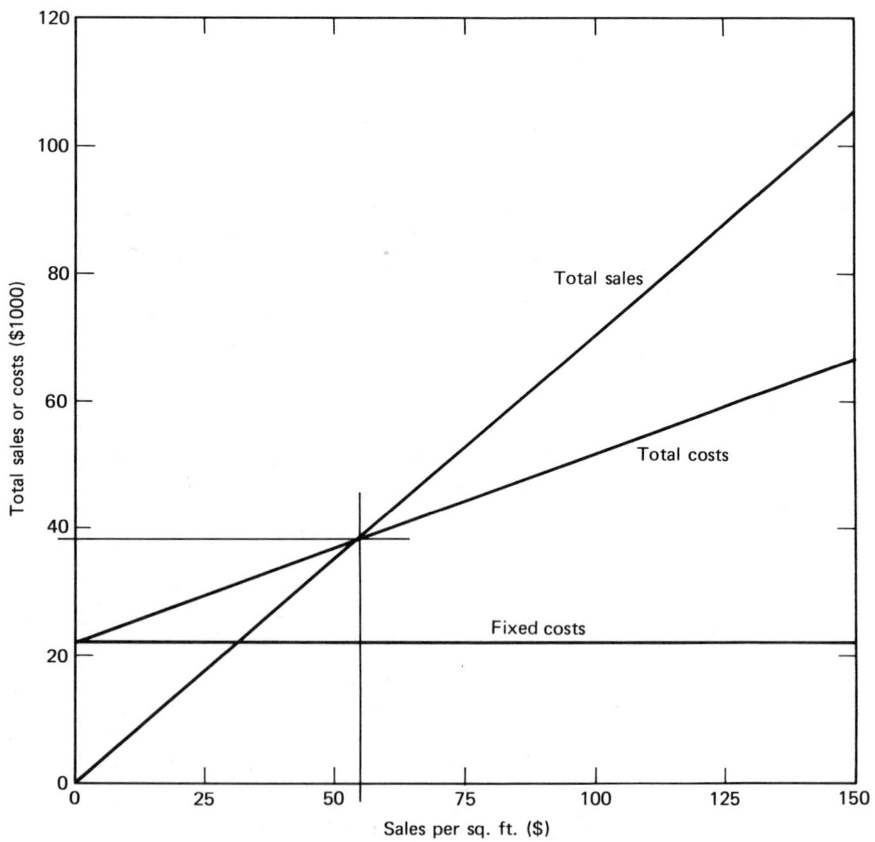

Breakeven chart for 700 sq. ft. barber shop.

The typical barber shop is about 700 square feet in size and requires a total investment of about $18,000. Like most service businesses, its variable costs are low. The typical operation can break even with annual sales of $38,700, or $55.25 per square foot per year.

Economic Characteristics of Barber Shops

Typical size (sq. ft.)		700		
Typical investment				
Inventory		2,400		
Depreciable assets		11,000		
All other		4,900		
Total investment		18,300		
	Low	*Typical Operation*	*High*	*Proposed Operation*
Operating Economics				
Sales per square foot	35	60	90	
Net annual sales	24,500	42,000	63,000	
Cost of goods sold	5,500	9,500	14,300	
Gross operating margin	19,000	32,500	48,700	
Fixed operating expenses				
Rent and utilities	5,600	5,600	5,600	
Fixed payroll	15,000	15,000	15,000	
Other fixed expenses	1,500	1,500	1,500	
Total fixed expenses	22,100	22,100	22,100	
Variable operating expenses				
Variable payroll	3,700	6,400	9,600	
Other variable expenses	1,200	2,100	3,200	
Total variable expenses	4,900	8,500	12,800	
Total operating expenses	27,000	30,600	35,900	
Net profit (loss) before taxes	(8,000)	1,900	13,800	
Typical operating ratios				
Net profit/net sales	—	4.5%	21.9%	
Net sales/total investment	1.3x	2.3x	3.4x	
Net profit/total investment	—	10.4%	75.4%	
Net sales/inventory	10.2x	17.5x	26.3x	

Beauty Shop

In addition to furnishing beauty services, beauty shops usually offer retail sales of beauty products such as cosmetics, hairsprays, hair-treatment products, and shampoos.

At least one beauty shop can be found in almost every regional, community, and neighborhood shopping center. Many major department stores offer beauty shop services, but about 70 percent of all beauty shops are still independently owned and operated. About 20 percent are multi-shop operations of local owners.

Sizes range from 150 to 3000 square feet, although most beauty shops

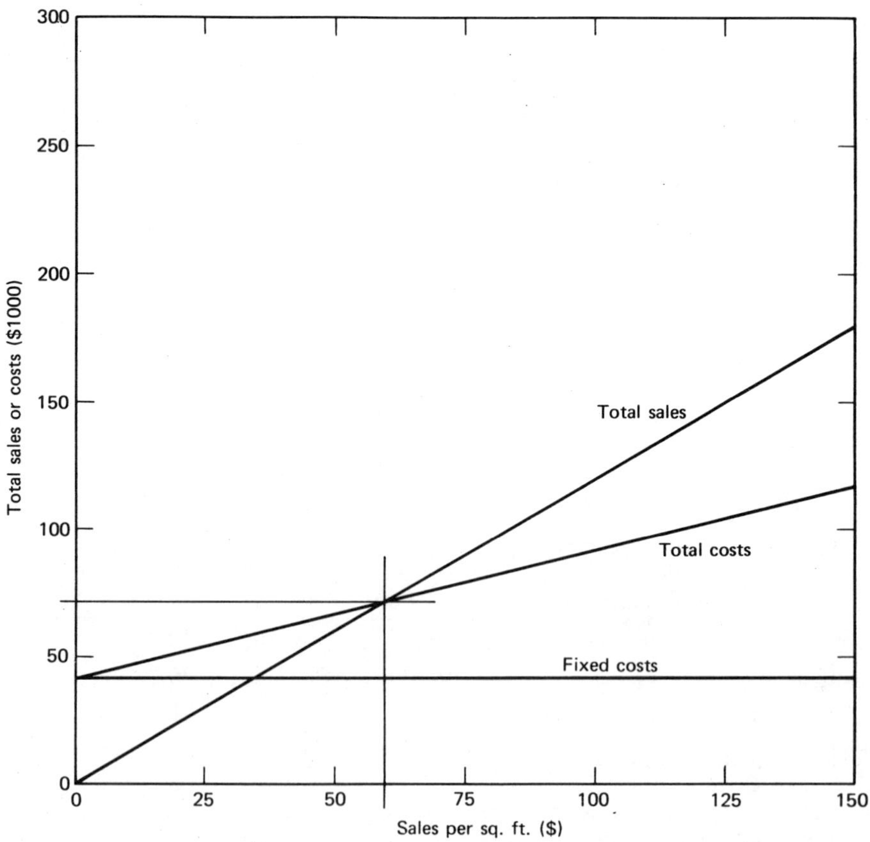

Breakeven chart for 1200 sq. ft. beauty shop.

are from 1000 to 1700 square feet in area. There is about one beauty shop for every 1000 people.

A $37,000 investment is required for a typical 1200-square-foot beauty shop. This operation breaks even with annual sales of $71,600, or $59.68 per square foot per year.

Economic Characteristics of Beauty Shops

Typical size (sq. ft.)		1,200		
Typical investment				
Inventory		4,800		
Depreciable assets		22,800		
All other		9,500		
Total investment		37,100		

	Low	*Typical Operation*	*High*	*Proposed Operation*
Operating Economics				
Sales per square foot	35	65	100	
Net annual sales	42,000	78,000	120,000	
Cost of goods sold	10,700	19,900	30,600	
Gross operating margin	31,300	58,100	89,400	
Fixed operating expenses				
Rent and utilities	9,600	9,600	9,600	
Fixed payroll	30,000	30,000	30,000	
Other fixed expenses	3,000	3,000	3,000	
Total fixed expenses	42,600	42,600	42,600	
Variable operating expenses				
Variable payroll	4,200	7,800	12,000	
Other variable expenses	2,100	3,900	6,000	
Total variable expenses	6,300	11,700	18,000	
Total operating expenses	48,900	54,300	60,600	
Net profit (loss) before taxes	(17,600)	3,800	28,800	
Typical operating ratios				
Net profit/net sales	—	4.9%	24.0%	
Net sales/total investment	1.1x	2.1x	3.2x	
Net profit/total investment	—	10.2%	77.6%	
Net sales/inventory	8.8x	16.3x	25.0x	

Coin-Operated Laundry

Anyone who has experienced problems in keeping his own washing machine in constant working condition should be able to appreciate the coin-op laundry owner's problems in keeping 30 or more machines going. Since these commercial coin-operated machines are sometimes severely abused by customers, maintenance can be a real headache.

There is a coin-op laundry to serve about every 6500 people. They can be located almost anywhere near a large residential population, commonly in community and neighborhood shopping centers. Areas near large apartment complexes and around relatively less affluent neighborhoods in which residents are less likely to own their own equipment appear to be favorite locations.

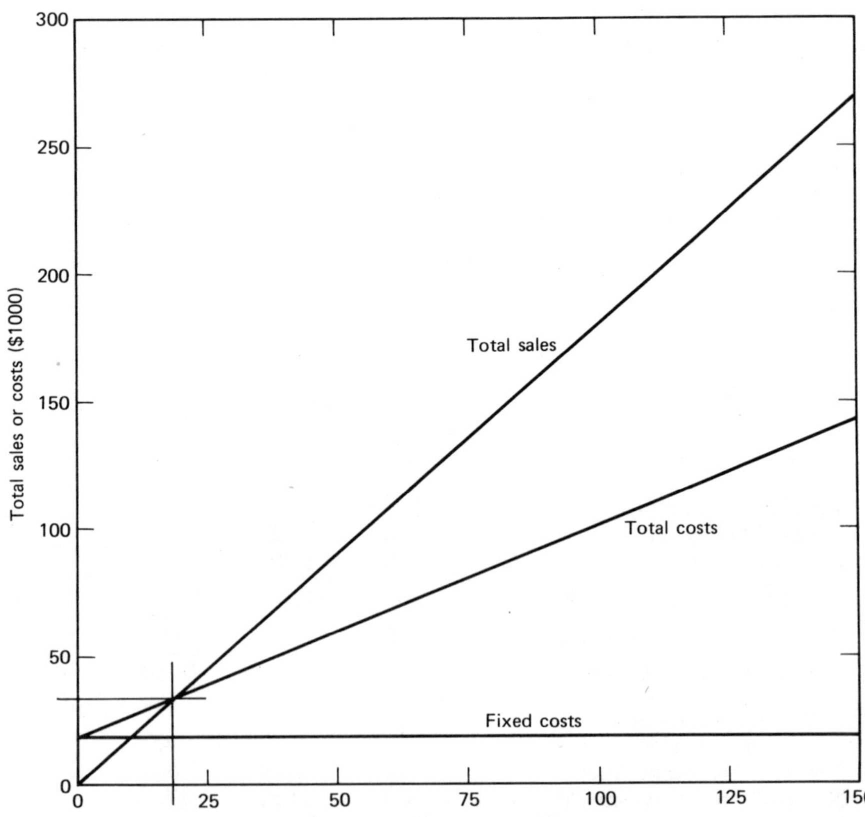

Breakeven chart for 1800 sq. ft. coin-op laundry.

Almost all coin-op laundries are independently or locally owned. Their sizes range from as little as 300 square feet to as much as 12,000 square feet, with most using 1500 to 2000 square feet.

The investment requirement for a typical 1800-square-foot coin-op laundry totals nearly $28,000, with some type of financing available from the equipment manufacturers. It breaks even with annual sales of $33,300, or $18.49 per square foot.

Economic Characteristics of Coin-Op Laundries

Typical size (sq. ft.)		1,800		
Typical investment				
Inventory		3,300		
Depreciable assets		16,600		
All other		7,800		
Total investment		27,700		
	Low	*Typical Operation*	*High*	*Proposed Operation*
Operating Economics				
Sales per square foot	10	20	40	
Net annual sales	18,000	36,000	72,000	
Cost of goods sold	4,600	9,200	18,400	
Gross operating margin	13,400	26,800	53,600	
Fixed operating expenses				
Rent and utilities	9,900	9,900	9,900	
Fixed payroll	7,500	7,500	7,500	
Other fixed expenses	2,200	2,200	2,200	
Total fixed expenses	19,600	19,600	19,600	
Variable operating expenses				
Variable payroll	1,900	3,800	7,500	
Other variable expenses	900	1,800	3,600	
Total variable expenses	2,800	5,600	11,100	
Total operating expenses	22,400	25,200	30,700	
Net profit (loss) before taxes	(9,000)	1,600	22,900	
Typical operating ratios				
Net profit/net sales	—	4.4%	31.8%	
Net sales/total investment	0.6x	1.3x	2.6x	
Net profit/total investment	—	5.8%	82.7%	
Net sales/inventory	5.5x	10.9x	21.8x	

Dry Cleaning

Some dry cleaners have the facilities for doing their dry cleaning and laundry work themselves, but many smaller shops send the work out to be done by others; however, even some small shops may do their own pressing and finish work, perform minor repairs and alterations, and provide storage services for furs and winter wardrobes.

Just over one-half of the dry cleaning establishments are located in community shopping centers, with the rest divided between neighborhood and regional centers. Two-thirds of all dry cleaning shops are independently owned, and an additional 30 percent are parts of locally owned chains; only two percent are nationally franchised.

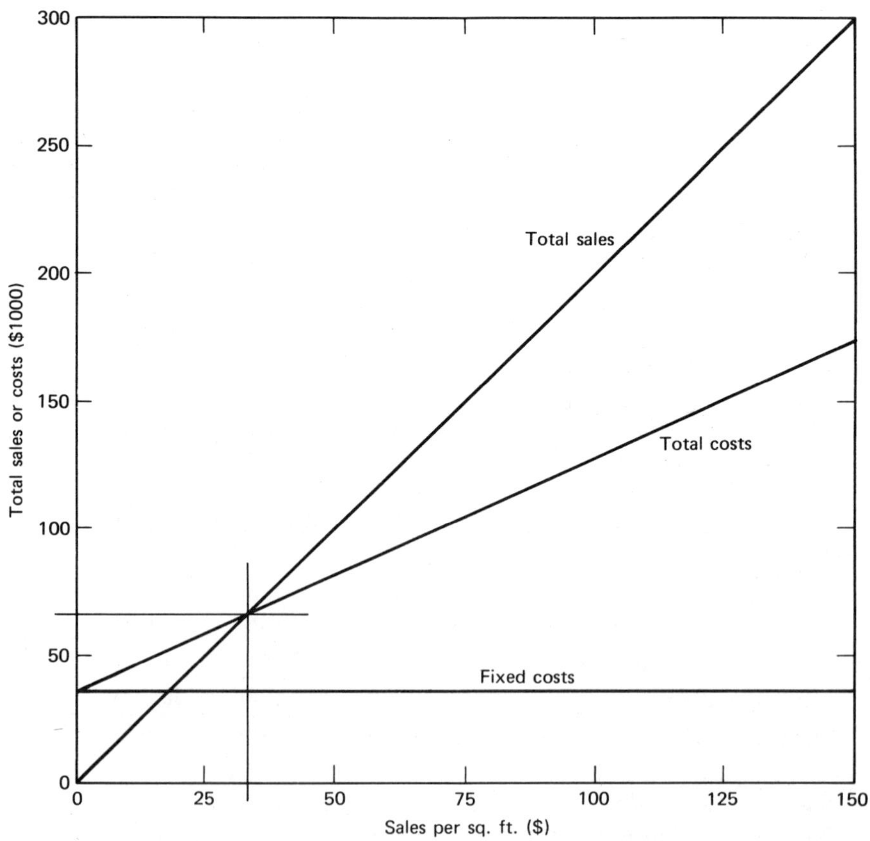

Breakeven chart for 2000 sq. ft. dry cleaning establishment.

Sizes may run from 800 to over 12,000 square feet, with most shops having between 1500 and 2200 square feet.

The typical 2000-square-foot dry cleaning/laundry establishment requires annual sales of $66,700, or $33.34 per square foot, to break even.

Economic Characteristics of Dry Cleaning Shops

Typical size (sq. ft.)		2,000		
Typical investment				
Inventory		5,600		
Depreciable assets		28,500		
All other		12,600		
Total investment		46,700		____

	Low	*Typical Operation*	*High*	*Proposed Operation*
Operating Economics				
Sales per square foot	20	35	65	
Net annual sales	40,000	70,000	130,000	
Cost of goods sold	12,500	21,900	40,700	____
Gross operating margin	27,500	48,100	89,300	
Fixed operating expenses				
Rent and utilities	10,000	10,000	10,000	
Fixed payroll	22,500	22,500	22,500	
Other fixed expenses	3,700	3,700	3,700	____
Total fixed expenses	36,200	36,200	36,200	
Variable operating expenses				
Variable payroll	3,800	6,600	12,300	
Other variable expenses	2,000	3,500	6,500	____
Total variable expenses	5,800	10,100	18,800	____
Total operating expenses	42,000	46,300	55,000	____
Net profit (loss) before taxes	(14,500)	1,800	34,300	
Typical operating ratios				
Net profit/net sales	—	2.6%	26.4%	
Net sales/total investment	0.9x	1.5x	2.8x	
Net profit/total investment	—	3.8%	73.4%	
Net sales/inventory	7.1x	12.5x	23.2x	

Keys

A retail key shop reproduces customer's keys; it does not provide locksmithing services, and it is unlikely to handle any other merchandise except perhaps key chains, holders, and novelties.

This highly specialized operation must compete against dime stores, drug stores, hardware stores, and even department stores, all of which may offer the same services. The key shop must be located in a very high-traffic, convenient location, relying on a large number of small sales to customers whose presence can be attributed to other shopping needs. A small stand in the center of a shopping mall is ideal.

The equipment—a key duplicating machine—is relatively inexpensive and easy to operate, but a good inventory of key blanks is essential.

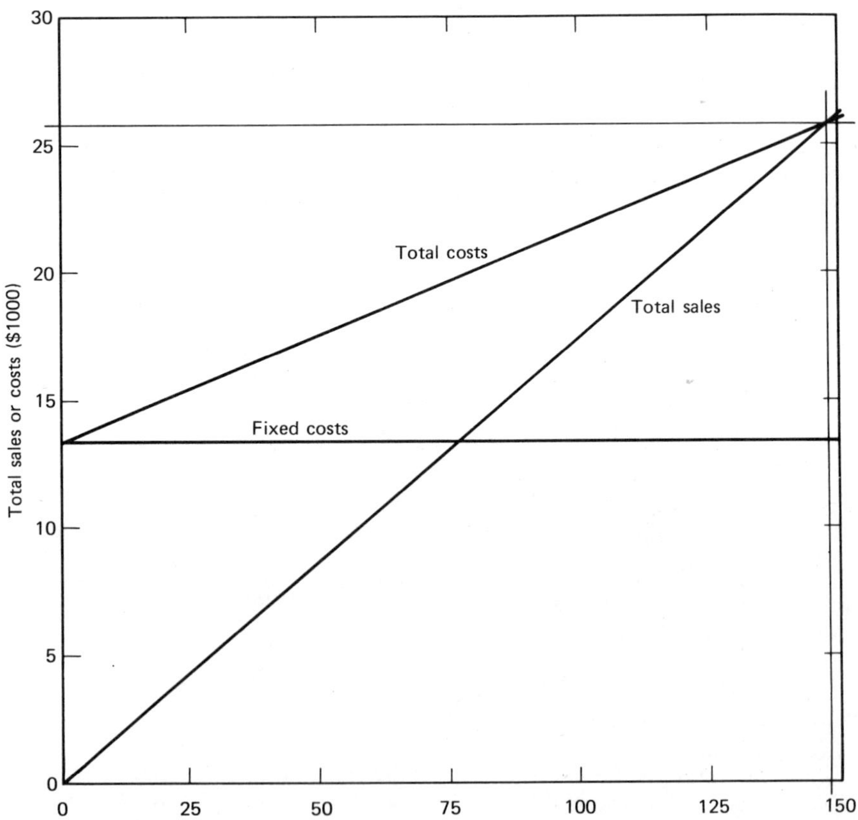

Breakeven chart for 175 sq. ft. key shop.

About one-half of the key shops have some national affiliation, with the other one-half independently operated. Typically, only a very small area is needed—between 150 and 200 square feet is sufficient.

A typical 175-square-foot key shop needs $26,000 worth of business to break even, about $148 per square foot. This breakeven point is high for any retail operation, but still amounts to only around $100 per day. With the right location, this volume can be achieved easily.

Economic Characteristics of Retail Key Shops

Typical size (sq. ft.)		175		
Typical investment				
Inventory		3,500		
Depreciable assets		2,000		
All other		3,000		
Total investment		8,500		
	Low	*Typical Operation*	*High*	*Proposed Operation*
Operating Economics				
Sales per square foot	60	160	270	
Net annual sales	10,500	28,000	47,300	
Cost of goods sold	4,200	11,100	18,700	
Gross operating margin	6,300	16,900	28,600	
Fixed operating expenses				
Rent and utilities	5,300	5,300	5,300	
Fixed payroll	7,500	7,500	7,500	
Other fixed expenses	700	700	700	
Total fixed expenses	13,500	13,500	13,500	
Variable operating expenses				
Variable payroll	300	900	1,500	
Other variable expenses	500	1,400	2,400	
Total variable expenses	800	2,300	3,900	
Total operating expenses	14,300	15,800	17,400	
Net profit (loss) before taxes	(8,000)	1,100	11,200	
Typical operating ratios				
Net profit/net sales	—	3.9%	23.7%	
Net sales/total investment	1.2x	3.3x	5.6x	
Net profit/total investment	—	12.9%	131.8%	
Net sales/inventory	3.0x	8.0x	13.5x	

Photo Studio

Many professional photographers agree that photography is a nice hobby but a difficult business. Certainly, most people do not appreciate the time, skill, and expense that go into producing a good studio portrait. In addition to studio portraits, most photographers also handle out-of-studio work such as weddings and parties. Some get into school portraits and commercial advertising work.

Some three-fourths of all photo studios are located in either regional or community shopping centers, and most of the newer super regional centers have at least one studio. For this type of business, an affluent neighborhood is a definite advantage.

Almost one-half of the photo studios are nationally affiliated, and about one-third are individually owned. Most take up from 200 to 1700

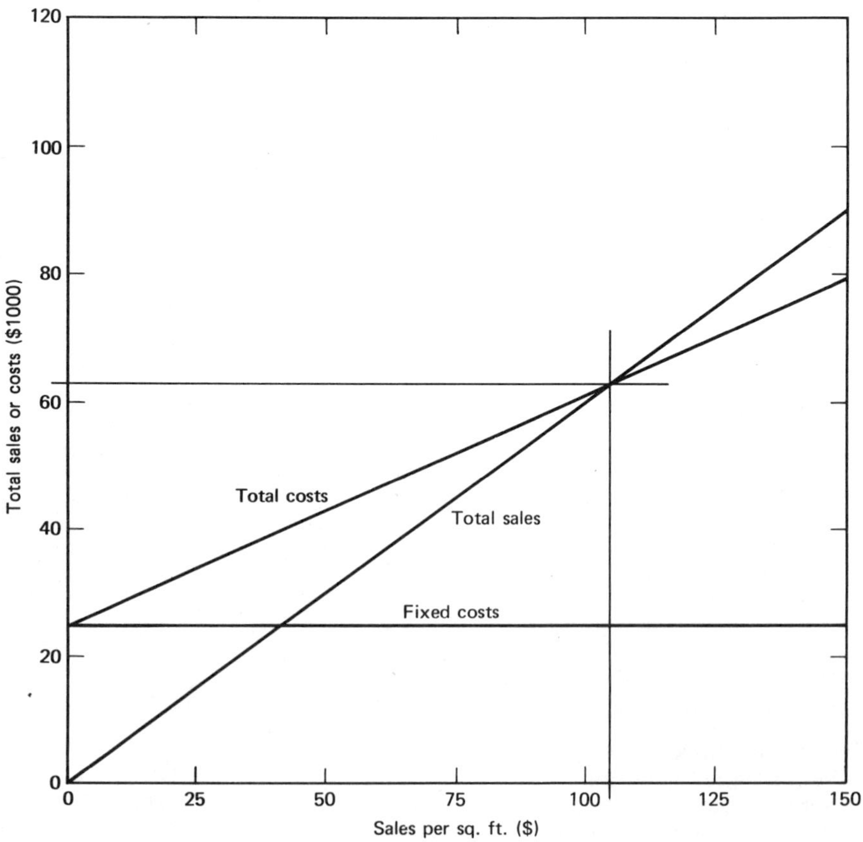

Breakeven chart for 600 sq. ft. photographic studio.

square feet, but some are as small as 80 square feet and a few as large as 10,000 square feet.

Studio portraiture is an art as well as a business, and a studio's success as a business depends heavily on the individual photographer. The typical 600-square-foot photographic studio requires a total investment of $29,000 and needs annual sales of $63,200 ($105.37 per square foot) to break even. There is a photo studio for about every 6000 people.

Economic Characteristics of Photographic Studios

Typical size (sq. ft.)		600		
Typical investment				
Inventory		4,000		
Depreciable assets		18,000		
All other		7,000		
Total investment		29,000		

	Low	*Typical Operation*	*High*	*Proposed Operation*
Operating Economics				
Sales per square foot	50	110	165	
Net annual sales	30,000	66,000	99,000	
Cost of goods sold	14,000	30,800	46,200	
Gross operating margin	16,000	35,200	52,800	
Fixed operating expenses				
Rent and utilities	7,800	7,800	7,800	
Fixed payroll	15,000	15,000	15,000	
Other fixed expenses	2,300	2,300	2,300	
Total fixed expenses	25,100	25,100	25,100	
Variable operating expenses				
Variable payroll	2,600	5,700	8,600	
Other variable expenses	1,500	3,300	5,000	
Total variable expenses	4,100	9,000	13,600	
Total operating expenses	29,200	34,100	38,700	
Net profit (loss) before taxes	(13,200)	1,100	14,100	
Typical operating ratios				
Net profit/net sales	—	1.7%	14.2%	
Net sales/total investment	1.0x	2.3x	3.4x	
Net profit/total investment	—	3.8%	48.6%	
Net sales/inventory	7.5x	16.5x	24.8x	

Travel Agency

Travel agencies provide business travel and vacation planning services, including arrangements for lodging, airline tickets, automobile rentals, entertainment tickets, and travel tours. Their functions, then, range from the very simple to the very complex.

Their regular services are offered to the client at no additional cost, with revenues derived from the commissions paid by airlines, hotels, and others. It is a relatively low-investment business, with a large part of its investment tied up in working capital and accounts receivable. Depending on the specific services offered, the actual cost of providing the services may be from almost nothing up to perhaps 40 percent of sales.

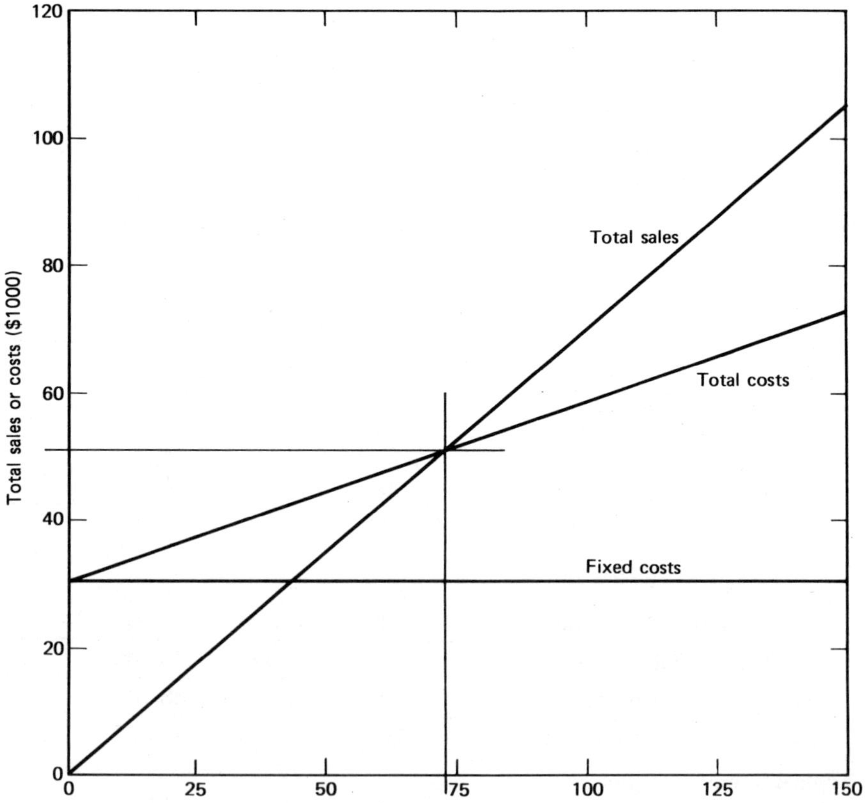

Breakeven chart for 700 sq. ft. travel agency.

The location is important, with 70 percent of the agencies situated in large regional shopping centers. Facilities are not critical; size may vary between 200 and 1800 square feet, with 500 to 1000 square feet most common. About 85 percent are locally owned, independent businesses.

The typical small travel agency, occupying 700 square feet of office space, can break even on annual receipts of $51,500, or $73.61 per square foot.

Economic Characteristics of Travel Agencies

Typical size (sq. ft.)		700		
Typical investment				
Inventory		600		
Depreciable assets		5,400		
All other		14,000		
Total investment		20,000		
	Low	*Typical Operation*	*High*	*Proposed Operation*
Operating Economics				
Sales per square foot	45	80	140	
Net annual sales	31,500	56,000	98,000	
Cost of goods sold	9,500	16,800	29,400	
Gross operating margin	22,000	39,200	68,600	
Fixed operating expenses				
Rent and utilities	7,000	7,000	7,000	
Fixed payroll	22,500	22,500	22,500	
Other fixed expenses	1,600	1,600	1,600	
Total fixed expenses	31,100	31,100	31,100	
Variable operating expenses				
Variable payroll	1,500	2,600	4,600	
Other variable expenses	1,600	2,800	4,900	
Total variable expenses	3,100	5,400	9,500	
Total operating expenses	34,200	36,500	40,600	
Net profit (loss) before taxes	(12,200)	2,700	28,000	
Typical operating ratios				
Net profit/net sales	—	4.8%	28.6%	
Net sales/total investment	1.6x	2.8x	4.9x	
Net profit/total investment	—	13.5%	140.0%	
Net sales/inventory	52.5x	93.3x	163.3x	

AUTOMOTIVE PRODUCTS AND SERVICES

Gasoline Service Station

Recent trends among gasoline service stations seem to be away from service and toward strictly retail gasoline sales. Self-service pumps and minimum services by station personnel greatly reduce the costs of operation and eliminate the need for extensive and expensive service facilities.

The high-volume, minimum-service gasoline stations are generally located along heavily trafficked streets and highways. Other stations, relying heavily on their maintenance and repair services, must compete with the "cut-rate" operations on other than a price-per-gallon basis.

About 90 percent of all gasoline service stations have national affil-

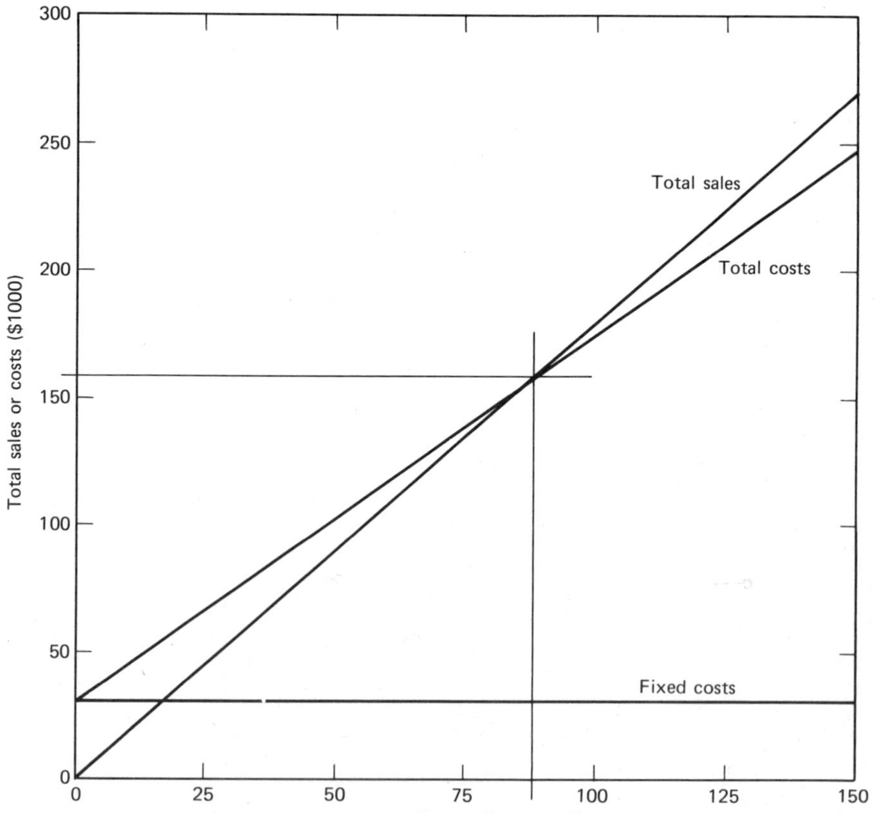

Breakeven chart for 1800 sq. ft. gasoline service station.

iations, although they are almost always operated as independent businesses by local owner/managers.

Sizes of gasoline service stations vary between 900 and 22,500 square feet, with the typical range 1700 to 3000 square feet. A typical 1800-square-foot full-service gasoline station breaks even on annual sales of $158,700 or $88.17 per square foot.

Economic Characteristics of Gasoline Service Stations

Typical size (sq. ft.)		1,800		
Typical investment				
Inventory		14,500		
Depreciable assets		18,000		
All other		12,500		
Total investment		45,000		

	Low	*Typical Operation*	*High*	*Proposed Operation*
Operating Economics				
Sales per square foot	40	100	150	
Net annual sales	72,000	180,000	270,000	
Cost of goods sold	52,500	131,200	196,800	
Gross operating margin	19,500	48,800	73,200	
Fixed operating expenses				
Rent and utilities	12,600	12,600	12,600	
Fixed payroll	15,100	15,100	15,100	
Other fixed expenses	3,600	3,600	3,600	
Total fixed expenses	31,300	31,300	31,300	
Variable operating expenses				
Variable payroll	1,700	4,300	6,500	
Other variable expenses	3,600	9,000	13,500	
Total variable expenses	5,300	13,300	20,000	
Total operating expenses	36,600	44,600	51,300	
Net profit (loss) before taxes	(17,100)	4,200	21,900	
Typical operating ratios				
Net profit/net sales	—	2.3%	8.1%	
Net sales/total investment	1.6x	4.0x	6.0x	
Net profit/total investment	—	9.3%	48.7%	
Net sales/inventory	5.0x	12.4x	18.6x	

Auto Exhaust System Service

"Muffler shops" are engaged in the replacement or, seldom, the repair of anything involved with an automobile exhaust system; this covers everything from the engine exhaust port to the tailpipe, but primarily the exhaust extension, muffler, and tailpipe. Some muffler shops also do brake work and sell and install shock absorbers.

These shops are generally located along shopping strips where new and used car dealers, service stations, and other auto-related businesses tend to congregate. Most are franchised operations.

Despite their advertising claims, most muffler shops find it difficult to cope with anything but popular late-model American-made cars. Even

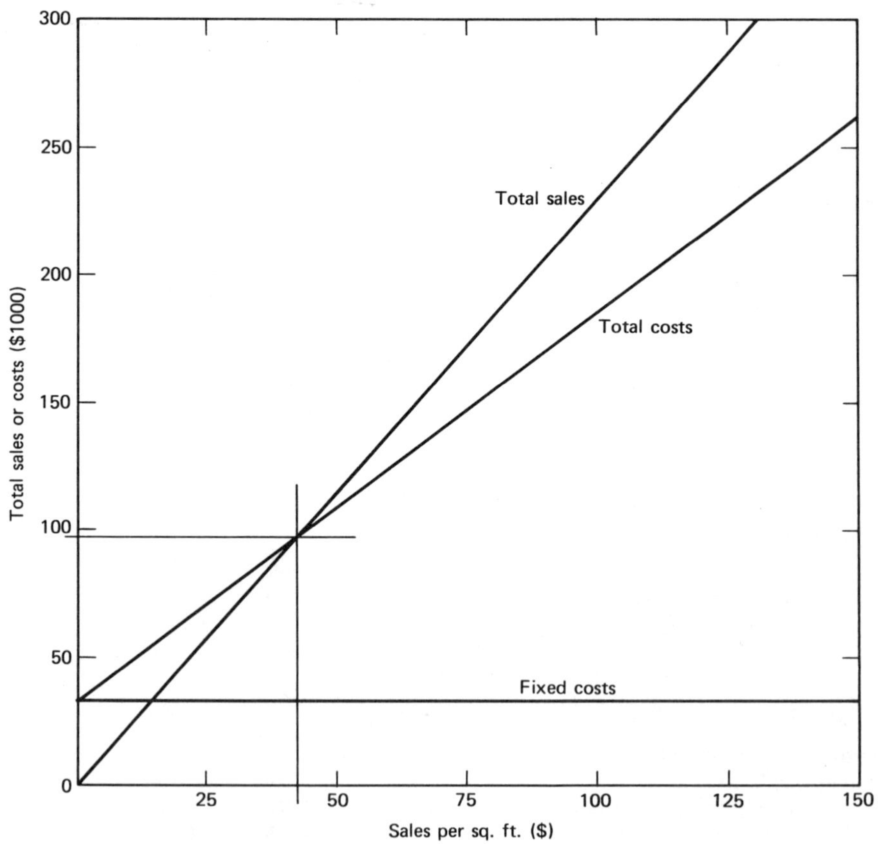

Breakeven chart for 2300 sq. ft. exhaust system service shop.

so, a large inventory of pipes and mufflers is required. Special equipment includes hydraulic lifts, welding and cutting torches, and pipe-bending machines.

A typical 2300-square-foot muffler shop breaks even with annual sales of $97,700, or $42.47 per square foot. This represents a three-bay shop with office and storage facilities.

Economic Characteristics of Exhaust System Service Shops

	Low	Typical Operation	High	Proposed Operation
Typical size (sq. ft.)		2,300		
Typical investment				
Inventory		12,000		
Depreciable assets		15,000		
All other		5,000		
Total investment		32,000		
Operating Economics				
Sales per square foot	40	60	80	
Net annual sales	92,000	138,000	195,500	
Cost of goods sold	47,500	71,200	100,900	
Gross operating margin	44,500	66,800	94,600	
Fixed operating expenses				
Rent and utilities	8,100	8,100	8,100	
Fixed payroll	22,500	22,500	22,500	
Other fixed expenses	2,600	2,600	2,600	
Total fixed expenses	33,200	33,200	33,200	
Variable operating expenses				
Variable payroll	8,700	13,000	18,400	
Other variable expenses	4,600	6,900	9,800	
Total variable expenses	13,300	19,900	28,200	
Total operating expenses	46,500	53,100	61,400	
Net profit (loss) before taxes	(2,000)	13,700	33,200	
Typical operating ratios				
Net profit/net sales	—	9.9%	17.0%	
Net sales/total investment	2.9x	4.3x	6.1x	
Net profit/total investment	—	42.8%	103.8%	
Net sales/inventory	7.7x	11.5x	16.3x	

Auto Painting

In addition to automotive painting and refinishing, auto painting shops may handle minor body repair projects. Some are franchised, offering fast, low-cost, low-quality paint jobs. Good body work and painting is not a fast job, however, and there is a strong market for quality work.

The location is not particularly important if the bulk of the work is performed for commercial accounts such as new and used car dealers, auto rental firms, and companies with large fleets. If the business is to be retail customer oriented, the same locational considerations apply as to other automotive services.

A typical auto painting shop occupies about 1800 square feet. It

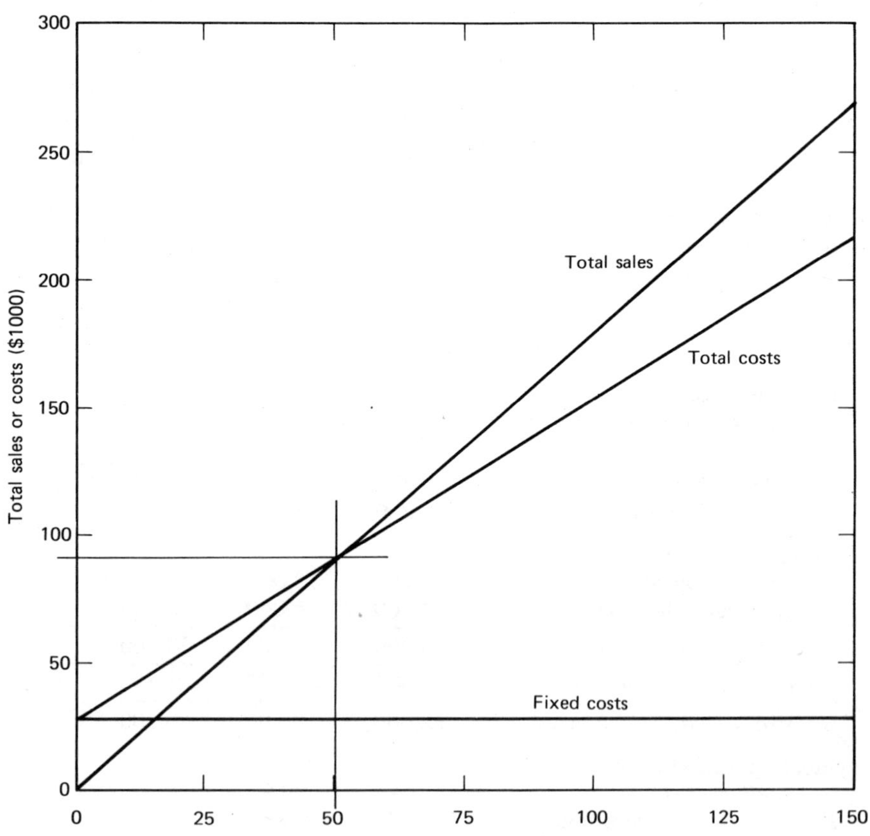

Breakeven chart for 1800 sq. ft. auto painting shop.

breaks even on annual sales of $90,800, or $50.45 per square foot. The required investment is relatively low, and the variable cost rate is substantially higher (0.707) than for most of the other automotive service specialty businesses.

Economic Characteristics of Auto Painting Shops

Typical size (sq. ft.)		1,800		
Typical investment				
Inventory		3,600		
Depreciable assets		9,900		
All other		5,000		
Total investment		18,500		

	Low	*Typical Operation*	*High*	*Proposed Operation*
Operating Economics				
Sales per square foot	35	55	75	
Net annual sales	63,000	99,000	135,000	
Cost of goods sold	32,100	50,500	68,900	
Gross operating margin	30,900	48,500	66,100	
Fixed operating expenses				
Rent and utilities	6,300	6,300	6,300	
Fixed payroll	18,800	18,800	18,800	
Other fixed expenses	1,500	1,500	1,500	
Total fixed expenses	26,600	26,600	26,600	
Variable operating expenses				
Variable payroll	9,200	14,500	19,800	
Other variable expenses	3,200	5,000	6,800	
Total variable expenses	12,400	19,500	26,600	
Total operating expenses	39,000	46,100	53,200	
Net profit (loss) before taxes	(8,100)	2,400	12,900	
Typical operating ratios				
Net profit/net sales	—	2.4%	9.6%	
Net sales/total investment	3.4x	5.4x	7.3x	
Net profit/total investment	—	13.0%	69.7%	
Net sales/inventory	17.5x	27.5x	37.5x	

Auto Transmission Repair

Far more transmissions have been overhauled than have ever needed overhauling, primarily because of the aggressive and sometimes questionable sales techniques of certain franchised transmission repair operations. The courts and Better Business Bureaus have documented many cases of consumer abuse in this area.

Still, automatic transmissions do require service and overhauls, and there is a large market for the service. Ethical, quality work can still sell, as can low-cost, temporary work, as long as it is identified as such. Here, as everywhere else, the customer is entitled to get what he pays for—no more, no less.

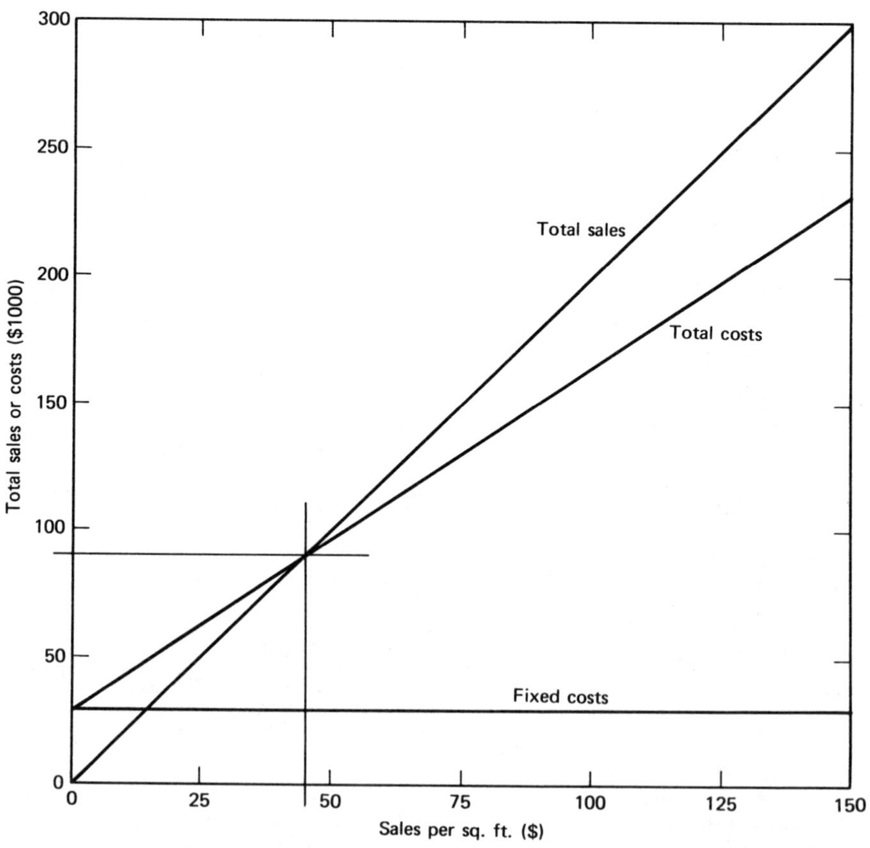

Breakeven chart for 2000 sq. ft. transmission repair shop.

In this field, however, the capable mechanic may operate at a considerable disadvantage in competing with better-known, heavily advertised franchises. The independent operator must develop his business by acquiring commercial accounts from fleet operators and dealers.

The typical 2000-square-foot transmission repair shop needs annual sales of $91,100, or $45.55 per square foot, to break even.

Economic Characteristics of Transmission Repair Shops

Typical size (sq. ft.)		2,000		
Typical investment				
Inventory		7,600		
Depreciable assets		13,100		
All other		5,000		
Total investment		25,700		

	Low	*Typical Operation*	*High*	*Proposed Operation*
Operating Economics				
Sales per square foot	30	50	70	
Net annual sales	60,000	100,000	140,000	
Cost of goods sold	30,100	50,100	70,100	
Gross operating margin	29,900	49,900	69,900	
Fixed operating expenses				
Rent and utilities	7,000	7,000	7,000	
Fixed payroll	20,600	20,600	20,600	
Other fixed expenses	2,100	2,100	2,100	
Total fixed expenses	29,700	29,700	29,700	
Variable operating expenses				
Variable payroll	7,400	12,300	17,200	
Other variable expenses	3,000	5,000	7,000	
Total variable expenses	10,400	17,300	24,200	
Total operating expenses	40,100	47,000	53,900	
Net profit (loss) before taxes	(10,200)	2,900	16,000	
Typical operating ratios				
Net profit/net sales	—	2.9%	11.4%	
Net sales/total investment	2.3x	3.9x	5.4x	
Net profit/total investment	—	11.3%	62.3%	
Net sales/inventory	7.9x	13.2x	18.4x	

Tires, Batteries, and Accessories

The TBA store, in addition to selling tires, batteries, and other automobile-related parts and accessories, may also overlap into several other retail and service fields. Automobile service facilities are necessary for the installation of tires and batteries; thus most shops handle general auto service, maintenance, and repair operations: oil changes, lubes, shock absorber installation, minor tuneups, wheel alignment, brake service, and other service station type jobs. Their retail stores may sell anything from bicycles and hardware to television sets and major appliances.

Three-fourths of the major TBA businesses are located in smaller regional and community shopping centers. When situated at a major shopping area, the TBA operation usually has a separate facility in a remote section of a large parking lot; many are located on busy streets in older shopping areas and in strip areas.

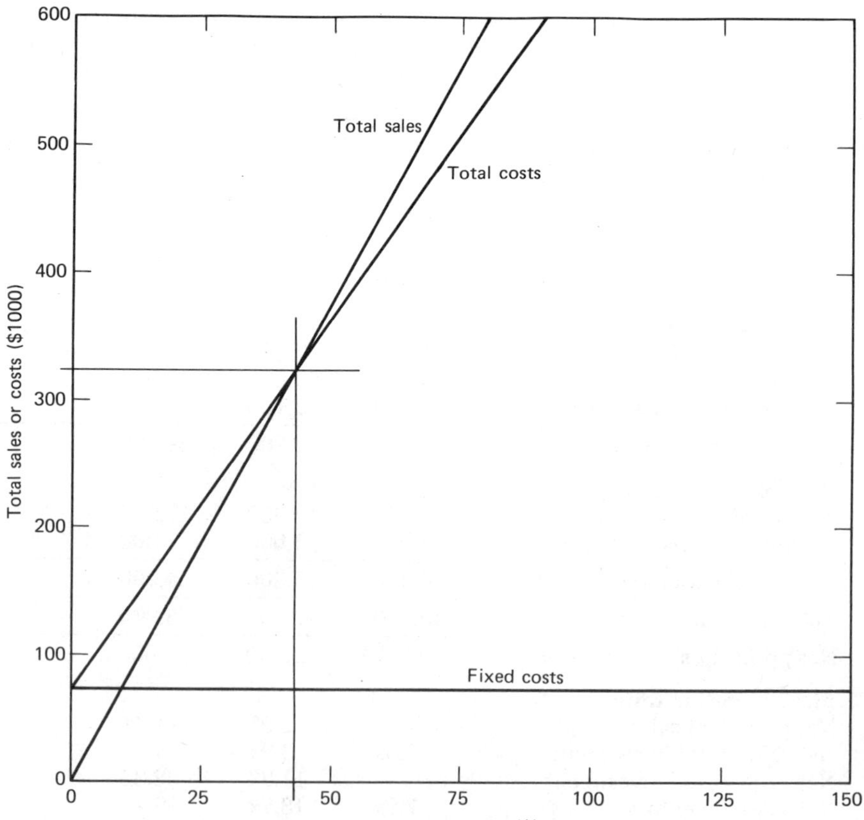

Breakeven chart for 7500 sq. ft. auto tires, batteries, and accessories store.

About 60 percent of the TBA businesses carry nationally recognized names (either tire companies or other national auto-specialty chains), although they may be operated as independent businesses by local franchise owners.

Sizes range from 800 to 22,000 square feet, depending on the scope of merchandise and services offered. Most are between 2000 and 8200 square feet. A typical 7500-square-foot TBA dealer needs annual sales of $324,300 ($43.24 per square foot) to break even.

Economic Characteristics of Retail Auto Tire, Battery, and Accessory Shops

Typical size (sq. ft.)	7,500		
Typical investment			
Inventory	71,200		
Depreciable assets	18,800		
All other	53,500		___
Total investment	143,500		

	Low	*Typical Operation*	*High*	*Proposed Operation*
Operating Economics				
Sales per square foot	35	50	90	
Net annual sales	262,500	375,000	675,000	
Cost of goods sold	173,300	247,500	445,500	___
Gross operating margin	89,200	127,500	229,500	
Fixed operating expenses				
Rent and utilities	30,000	30,000	30,000	
Fixed payroll	30,500	30,500	30,500	
Other fixed expenses	11,500	11,500	11,500	___
Total fixed expenses	72,000	72,000	72,000	
Variable operating expenses				
Variable payroll	17,800	25,400	45,700	
Other variable expenses	13,200	18,800	33,800	___
Total variable expenses	31,000	44,200	79,500	___
Total operating expenses	103,000	116,200	151,500	___
Net profit (loss) before taxes	(13,800)	11,300	78,000	
Typical operating ratios				
Net profit/net sales	—	3.0%	11.6%	
Net sales/total investment	1.8x	2.6x	4.7x	
Net profit/total investment	—	7.9%	54.4%	
Net sales/inventory	3.7x	5.3x	9.5x	

MISCELLANEOUS SERVICES

Small Gasoline Engine Repair
Motel
Fast Printing

Small Gasoline Engine Repair

These shops, usually one- or two-man operations, specialize in the repair of two- and four-cycle gasoline engines, usually under 10 horsepower in size. Such engines are found on lawnmowers, snowblowers, outboard motors, chainsaws, garden tractors, minibikes, and many other types of equipment.

Most of the repair work involves only minor tune-ups and adjustments: replacement of spark plugs, points and condensers, valve grinding and adjustment, carburetor cleaning and adjustment, and gasket replacement. The work is time consuming and highly seasonal. Little is required in the way of special equipment, but a sizable inventory of replacement parts is essential.

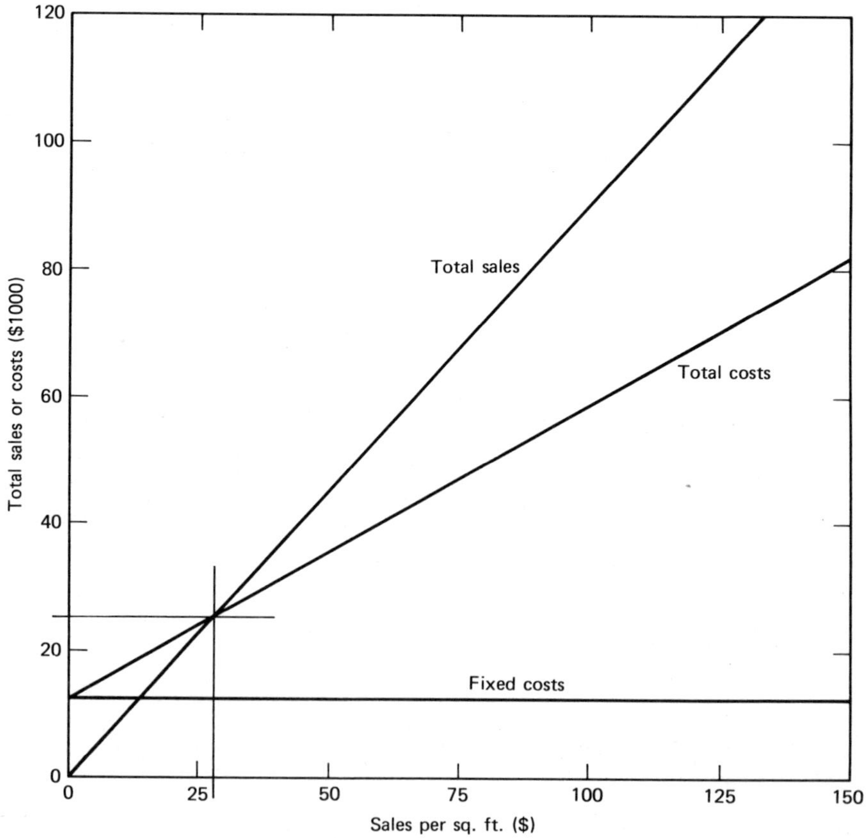

Breakeven chart for 900 sq. ft. small gas engine repair shop.

Businesses of this type are usually located in smaller neighborhood centers. Little working space is needed, but storage space is a necessity.

A typical 900-square-foot small-engine repair shop can break even on annual sales of only $25,400, or $28.17 per square foot. However, because of the man-hours involved and the highly seasonal work load, it is difficult to expand operations without branching into other fields such as equipment sales.

Economic Characteristics of Small Gas Engine Repair Shops

Typical size (sq. ft.)		900		
Typical investment				
Inventory		3,500		
Depreciable assets		2,000		
All other		3,500		
Total investment		9,000		

	Low	*Typical Operation*	*High*	*Proposed Operation*
Operating Economics				
Sales per square foot	20	30	45	
Net annual sales	18,000	27,000	40,500	
Cost of goods sold	5,200	7,800	11,700	
Gross operating margin	12,800	19,200	28,800	
Fixed operating expenses				
Rent and utilities	4,100	4,100	4,100	
Fixed payroll	7,500	7,500	7,500	
Other fixed expenses	700	700	700	
Total fixed expenses	12,300	12,300	12,300	
Variable operating expenses				
Variable payroll	3,100	4,700	7,100	
Other variable expenses	900	1,400	2,100	
Total variable expenses	4,000	6,100	9,200	
Total operating expenses	16,300	18,400	21,500	
Net profit (loss) before taxes	(3,500)	800	7,300	
Typical operating ratios				
Net profit/net sales	—	3.0%	18.0%	
Net sales/total investment	2.0x	3.0x	4.5x	
Net profit/total investment	—	8.9%	81.1%	
Net sales/inventory	5.1x	7.7x	11.6x	

Motel

A small motel provides lodging and a minimum of recreational facilities for the general public. Larger motels may incorporate restaurant facilities and a variety of other services. The largest motels may have convention facilities, golf, tennis, swimming, playgrounds, movies, bowling, shops, and a number of other activities. Probably the minimum, even for a 20-unit motel, is a swimming pool and small playground.

Many motels are franchised operations, whereas many others are loosely affiliated nationally to provide a more effective advance reservation service, even though they are locally owned. In popular resort areas, small motel operations can compete successfully with large ones.

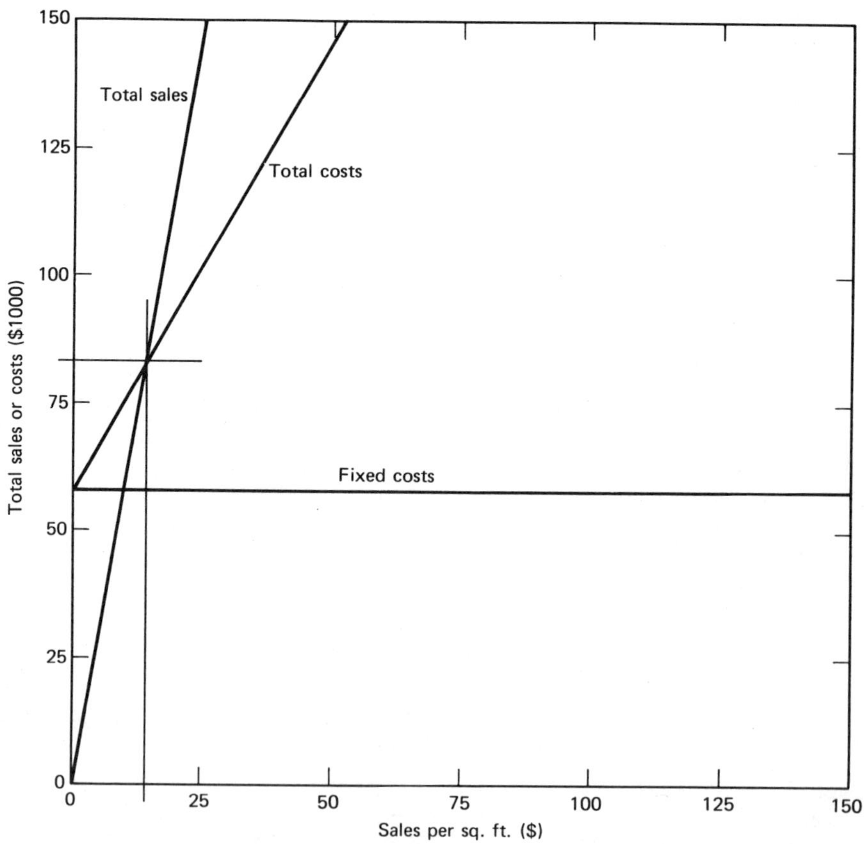

Breakeven chart for 6000 sq. ft. small motel operation.

Variable costs account for only about one-fourth of a motel's receipts, emphasizing the importance of maintaining a healthy occupancy rate. On an overall basis, a 60 percent occupancy rate is desirable; in resort areas, occupancy may run 100 percent during the prime season, and many motels close down their operation during the off season.

A typical small motel (6000 square feet) needs annual receipts of $83,700, or $13.94 per square foot, to break even.

Economic Characteristics of Small Motel Operation

Typical size (sq. ft.)	6,000	
Typical investment		
Inventory	10,000	
Depreciable assets	290,000	
All other	30,000	______
Total investment	330,000	

	Low	*Typical Operation*	*High*	*Proposed Operation*
Operating Economics				
Sales per square foot	10	15	20	
Net annual sales	60,000	90,000	120,000	
Cost of goods sold	4,900	7,300	9,700	______
Gross operating margin	55,100	82,700	110,300	
Fixed operating expenses				
Rent and utilities	18,000	18,000	18,000	
Fixed payroll	18,900	18,900	18,900	
Other fixed expenses	26,400	26,400	26,400	______
Total fixed expenses	63,300	63,300	63,300	
Variable operating expenses				
Variable payroll	6,700	10,100	13,500	
Other variable expenses	3,000	4,500	6,000	______
Total variable expenses	9,700	14,600	19,500	______
Total operating expenses	73,000	77,900	82,800	______
Net profit (loss) before taxes	(17,900)	4,800	27,500	
Typical operating ratios				
Net profit/net sales	—	5.3%	22.9%	
Net sales/total investment	0.2x	0.3x	0.4x	
Net profit/total investment	—	1.5%	8.3%	
Net sales/inventory	6.0x	9.0x	12.0x	

Fast Printing

Fast printing shops have proliferated since the development of suitable reproduction equipment. Working from camera-ready copy supplied by the customer, they can prepare a plate and run 100 copies in just a few minutes, for just a few dollars. They also handle some sizable commercial jobs, running thousands of catalog sheets, brochures, handbills, envelopes, and other material from camera-ready copy. Most shops have copying machines for occasional use, and many offer pickup and delivery service.

Locational characteristics vary widely, depending on the shop's emphasis; they are generally oriented toward small businesses, and the best locations are therefore in areas composed of that type of activity.

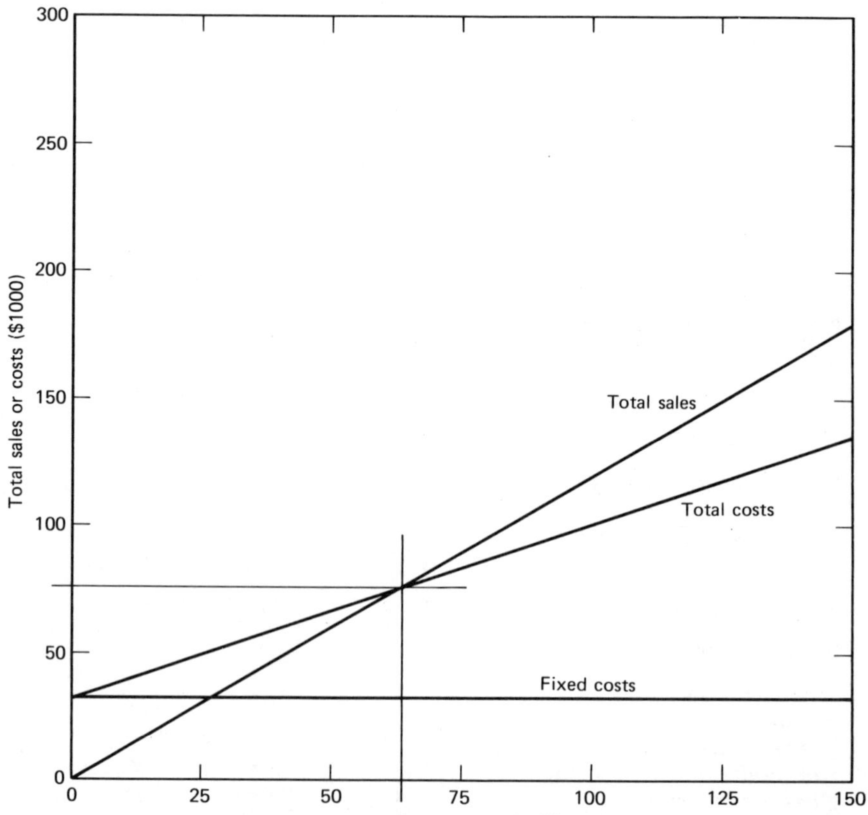

Breakeven chart for 1200 sq. ft. fast printing shop.

Most fast printing shops are franchise-type operations; there are at least a half-dozen major franchisers who offer a complete package including selection of a suitable location and all equipment, plus some sort of training program. All use the same type of equipment, and quality is comparable; there is therefore little customer loyalty to a particular "brand" name, and each shop must develop this loyalty through its service.

The typical shop of 1200 square feet needs annual sales of $77,000, or $64.20 per square foot, to break even.

Economic Characteristics of Fast Printing Shops

Typical size (sq. ft.)		1,200		
Typical investment				
Inventory		6,400		
Depreciable assets		17,100		
All other		23,200		
Total investment		46,700		
	Low	*Typical Operation*	*High*	*Proposed Operation*
Operating Economics				
Sales per square foot	40	70	110	
Net annual sales	48,000	84,000	132,000	
Cost of goods sold	19,400	34,000	53,400	
Gross operating margin	28,600	50,000	78,600	
Fixed operating expenses				
Rent and utilities	9,600	9,600	9,600	
Fixed payroll	18,800	18,800	18,800	
Other fixed expenses	3,700	3,700	3,700	
Total fixed expenses	32,100	32,100	32,100	
Variable operating expenses				
Variable payroll	6,200	10,800	17,000	
Other variable expenses	2,400	4,200	6,600	
Total variable expenses	8,600	15,000	23,600	
Total operating expenses	40,700	47,100	55,700	
Net profit (loss) before taxes	(12,100)	2,900	22,900	
Typical operating ratios				
Net profit/net sales	—	3.4%	20.8%	
Net sales/total investment	1.0x	1.8x	2.8x	
Net profit/total investment	—	5.8%	49.0%	
Net sales/inventory	7.5x	13.1x	20.6x	

Conclusions and Observations

If anything at all is to be learned from all of the economic data presented in this section, it is simply this: there is no sure-fire, guaranteed profitable business that one can get into. Success in business, like success in anything else, can seldom be attained without taking certain risks and without experiencing and overcoming certain difficulties. If being successful were easy, everyone would be successful.

Every business is different, but with a bad location or poor management, any business—no matter how good the product or service—can lose money. With a prime location, yielding high sales per square foot, and alert, informed management, who react quickly and appropriately to the demands of the marketplace, most businesses can become successful and bring in a high return on invested capital.

Breaking even, or losing or making just a little, is not too difficult, which is why there are so many marginally profitable small businesses and so many small business failures. It is much easier to start a business than to keep it going. Once it is going, making it grow and prosper requires a combination of knowledge, skill, and determination: knowledge in knowing what to do, skill in knowing how to do it, and determination in seeing that it actually gets done.

The keys to the profitable operation of a small retail or service business are high sales per square foot and rapid turnover of capital. The way to increase profitability is not to expand the operation in terms of its physical size, but to utilize better the resources at hand.

It is apparent that the typical small business is not particularly attractive as an investment (as indicated by its typically low percentage return on the capital invested in it). Nevertheless, a small business can still provide a good income to the owner-operator who is willing to devote his own time to the venture, and it can become an outstanding investment if the merchandise or service and the market and the management can all be developed to their maximum potential.

Appendix 2
Estimating Retail Store Costs

The estimating guidelines presented here are not intended to be particularly precise, but they do give the general magnitude of costs for store items of particular interest to the small businessman. Using the data presented here, a rough estimate for a new 3000-square-foot retail store might be put together like this:

Carpets, lighting, and interior decoration @ $3/sq. ft.	$ 9,000
Furniture and fixtures: 1000 sq. ft. @ $15/sq. ft.	15,000
Store equipment	3,000
Office equipment	1,000
Miscellaneous store and office supplies	2,000
Total estimated cost	$30,000

The interior decoration applies to the whole store; thus the entire 3000 square feet was charged at $3 per square foot. Furniture and fixtures, however, occupy only a part of the total floor space, usually between 20 and 40 percent, depending on the type of business. Here, one-third of the total space was estimated to contain furniture and fixtures costing $15 per square foot, or $15,000 in total. The other items in the estimate—store and office equipment and supplies—are largely independent of the store size.

If the store size were different from the 3000 square feet shown in the example, the $24,000 allowed for interior decorating, furniture, and fixtures would be expected to change proportionately, whereas the equipment and supplies would remain about the same. A 1000-square-foot store, then, would cost about $14,000 (1/3 × $24,000 + $6000) and a 6000-square-foot operation would run approximately $54,000 (2 × 24,000 + $6000). The total cost per square foot would range from $14 for the small store down to $9 for the larger one.

The prices of individual items listed here reflect a level of quality adequate for typical retail operations. Much more could easily be spent, and bargains in used fixtures or rebuilt equipment can sometimes be found.

Item	*Units*	*Cost (dollars/unit)*
Carpet	Sq. yd.	6–10
Wall mount security case, 48 x 19 x 12″	Each	175
Shallow rim display counter, 48 x 24 x 23″	Each	125
Pegboard spinner, 4 16 x 48″ panels	Each	50
Pegboard merchandiser, 4 x 4.5′	Each	60
Gondola, 8′ x 3′ x 54″	Each	250
Pegboard wall system, 4′ x 7′ x18″	Each	130
Garment display racks and merchandisers	Each	50–600
Showcase, full view, 5′ x 20″ x 37″	Each	225–350
Checkout counter, 5′ x 20″ x 34″	Each	175–450
Stock boxes, plastic, 11 x 15 x 6″	Each	4
Mannequins, full body	Each	100–200
Mannequins, part body	Each	25–75
Folding merchandise table	Each	75
Security mirror, 36″ round	Each	75
Window display package, complete fixtures	Each	400
Sign, outdoor, lighted	Sq. ft.	25–150
Cash register, electronic	Each	1200–1800
Cash register, electromechanical	Each	800–1400
Vacuum cleaner with attachments	Each	200
Imprinting machine	Each	500
Cutting machine	Each	300
Portable register	Each	10–35
Tags, personalized	1000	8–20
Tags, miscellaneous	1000	5–10
Boxes, clothing, plain	100	10–50
Boxes, giftware	100	15–150
Boxes, merchandise, imprinted	100	25–60
Matchbooks, printed	2500	75–90
Self-inking dater	Each	40
Calculator, display	Each	20–50
Calculator, printing	Each	80–200
Time clock	Each	150
Copy machine	Each	150+
Stencil duplicator	Each	150+
Dictating machine	Each	200
Check protector	Each	65
Coffee maker	Each	20–50
Typewriter, electric	Each	150+
Typewriter, standard office	Each	100–200
Shelving, steel utility, 4 x 2 x 8′	Each	75

Item	*Units*	*Cost (dollars/unit)*
File cabinet, 4 drawer steel	Each	70–300
Storage cabinet, 3′ x 18″ x 6′	Each	90
Desk	Each	60–200
Gift bags, imprinted	1000	30–100
Business cards	1000	10–20
Invoice forms, imprinted	1000	15–70
Sales books	100	60–130
Payroll system record book	Each	20
General bookkeeping system record book	Each	20
Combination check writing system book	Each	50
Letterheads	1000	30–40
Envelopes, printed	1000	20–40

References

The best investment a person can make is in the tools of his trade, and books are among the most valuable tools of any trade.

There are many books available that cover virtually all aspects of small business. Some are better than others, but there is something to be learned from every one of them. If the reader gains just one useful idea from a book, the book has been worth far more than its price.

The publications cited here either are in the authors' own reference library or have been found useful in the past.

Books—General

Basic Book of Business, R. Klug. Cahners Books, Boston, 1977.

Basic Retailing, C. M. Larson, R. E. Weigand, and J. S. Write. Prentice-Hall, Englewood Cliffs, NJ, 1976.

Construction Bidding for Profit, W. R. Park. John Wiley & Sons, New York, in preparation.

Cost Engineering Analysis, W. R. Park. John Wiley & Sons, New York, 1973.

Dollars and Cents of Shopping Centers. Urban Land Institute, Washington, DC, annual.

Efficient Accounting and Record-Keeping, D. M. Doyle. McKay, New York, 1977.

Encyclopedia of Business Information Sources. Gale Research Co., Detroit.

Entrepreneur's Manual: Business Start-Ups, Spin-Offs and Innovative Management, R. M. White, Jr. Chilton Book Co., Radnor, PA, 1977.

Financial Guide for the Self-Employed, John Ellis. Regnery, Chicago, 1972.

Gimmicks Make Money in Retailing, Betty J. Minsky. Fairchild Publications, New York.

Guides for Business Analysis and Profit Evaluation. U.S. Department of Commerce, Business and Defense Services Administration, Washington, DC, 1959.

Guides for Profit Planning, B. LaSalle Woelfel. Small Business Administration, Washington, DC, 1960.

Handbook of Home Business Ideas and Plans, staff of Mother Earth News. Bantam Books, New York, 1976.

Handbook of Small Business Finance, R. B. Tower. Small Business Administration, Washington, DC, 1962.

How to Organize and Operate a Small Business, Baumback, Lawyer, and Kelly. Prentice-Hall, Englewood Cliffs, NJ, 1973.

How to Run a Small Business, J. K. Lasser. McGraw-Hill. New York, 1974.

How to Run a Successful Florist and Plant Store, Bram Cavin. McKay, New York, 1977.

How to Run a Successful Restaurant, W. L. Siegel. McKay, New York, 1977.

How to Start and Manage Your Own Business, G. G. Greene. McGraw-Hill, New York, 1975.

How to Start Your Own Business (Vols. 1, 2, 3, 4). Drake Publishers, New York.

Independent Business Operating Techniques—Retail, D. B. Ressler, Jr. American Design Industries, Rochelle Park, NJ, 1976.

Independent Retailing: A Money Making Manual, H. Shaffer and H. Greenwald. Prentice-Hall, Englewood Cliffs, NJ, 1976.

Managing the Independent Business, L. E. Preston (Ed.). Prentice-Hall, Englewood Cliffs, NJ, 1962.

Managing the Small Business, Stegall, Steinmetz, and Kline. Irwin, Homewood, IL, 1976.

Modern Display Techniques, E. M. Mauger. Fairchild Publications, New York.

Money Raising and Planning for the Small Business, D. L. Markstein. Regnery, Chicago, 1974.

New Business Ventures and the Entrepreneur, P. R. Liles. Irwin, Homewood, IL, 1974.

Opening Your Own Retail Store, L. Taetzsch. Regnery, Chicago, 1977.

Practical Bookkeeping for the Small Business, M. L. Dyer. Regnery, Chicago, 1976.

Protecting Your Business, E. W. Loffel. McKay, New York, 1977.

Retail Management: Satisfaction of Consumer Needs, Marquardt, Makens, and Roe. Dryden Press, Hinsdale, IL.

Retailing, G. Pintel and F. Diamond. Prentice-Hall, Englewood Cliffs, NJ, 1977.

Retailing, R. F. Spohn and R. Y. Allen. Reston Publishing Co., Reston, VA, 1977.

Retailing Principles and Practices, G. H. Richert. McGraw-Hill, New York, 1974.

Retailing Strategy, R. J. Gentile. Lebhar-Friedman, New York, 1978.

Small Business Management, Broom and Longenecker. Southwestern Publishing Co., Cincinnati, 1975.

Small Time Operator, B. Kamoroff. Bell Springs Publishing, Laytonville, CA, 1977.

Starting Your Own Business From Scratch, R. D. Young. Knowledge Unlimited, Odin, IL, 1975.

Successful Small Business Management, L. A. Wortman. American Management Association, New York, 1976.

Starting and Succeeding in Your Own Small Business, L. L. Allen. Grosset & Dunlap, New York, 1968.

Tax Planning Opportunities, G. F. Richards. McKay, New York, 1977.

Up Your Own Organization, D. M. Dible. Entrepreneur Press, Santa Clara, CA, 1974.

Woman's Guide to Starting a Business, C. Jessup and G. Chipps. Holt, Rinehart & Winston, New York, 1976.

Annual Statement Studies. Robert Morris Associates, Philadelphia, annual.

Strategy of Contracting for Profit, W. R. Park. Prentice-Hall, Englewood Cliffs, NJ, 1966.

Books—Advertising, Promotion and Sales

Advertising, W. Antrim, McGraw-Hill, New York, 1970.

Advertising, C. A. Kirkpatrick. Houghton Mifflin, Boston.

Advertising: Communications for Management, J. W. Crawford. Allyn & Bacon, Rockleigh, NJ.

Advertising Copywriting, P. W. Burton and J. B. Kreer. Prentice-Hall, Englewood Cliffs, NJ.

Advertising for Modern Retailers, Shirley Milton. Fairchild Publications, New York.

Advertising—How to Write the Kind That Works, D. L. Malickson and J. W. Nason. Scribner's, New York, 1977.

Advertising in the Marketplace, D. Burke. McGraw-Hill, New York, 1973.

Advertising—Its Role in Modern Marketing, S. W. Dunn and A. M. Barban. Dryden Press, Hinsdale, IL.

Advertising Principles and Problems, C. J. Dirksen and A. Kroeger. Irwin, Homewood, IL.

Advertising Techniques and Management, R. V. Zacher. Irwin, Homewood, IL.

Advertising Theory and Practice, Sandage and Fryburger. Irwin, Homewood, IL, 1974.

Businessman's Guide to Advertising and Sales Promotion, H. G. Lewis. McGraw-Hill, New York, 1974.

How and How Much? Advertising for the Small Retailer, J. E. Moyer. University of Illinois, Bureau of Business Management, College of Commerce and Business Administration, Urbana, IL.

How to Get Big Results from a Small Advertising Budget, C. S. Smith. Hawthorn Books, New York, 1973.

Making TV Pay Off, H. P. Abrahams. Fairchild Publications, New York.

Principles of Advertising, Committee on Advertising. Pitman, New York, 1963.

Retail Advertising: A Management Approach, R. J. Gentile. Lebhar-Friedman, New York, 1976.

Retail Advertising and Sales Promotion, C. M. Edwards, Jr. and R. A. Brown. Prentice-Hall, Englewood Cliffs, NJ, 1959.

The Role of Advertising: A Book of Reading, C. H. Dandage. Irwin, Homewood, IL.

Successful Direct Marketing Methods, B. Stone. Crain Books, Chicago, 1975.
The Truth About Selling, S. S. Susser. Eriksson, New York, 1973.
100 Books on Advertising, R. W. Haverfield. University of Missouri, School of Journalism, Columbia, MO.

Books—Directories

The following directories are generally available in the reference section of most libraries.

Business Periodicals Index.
Business Publications Rates and Data.
N. W. Ayer and Son's Directory of Newspapers and Periodicals.
Trade Directories of the World. Croner Publications.
Encyclopedia of Associations. Gale Research Co., Detroit.
National Trade and Professional Associations of the United States and Canada. Columbia Books, Washington, DC.
Trade Names Dictionary. Gale Research Co., Detroit.

U.S. Government Publications

Hundreds of useful publications, covering all phases of small business management, are available from the Government Printing Office in Washington, D.C. or from local offices of the U. S. Department of Commerce or the Small Business Administration. Many of these publications are free, and the rest are inexpensive.

Merchandise Marts

Merchandise marts contain permanent displays and showrooms for all types of retail merchandise. The major merchandise marts are located in Atlanta, Chicago, San Francisco, Dallas, and Los Angeles. Other cities have merchandise shows on a regular basis, and some manufacturers and manufacturers' representatives maintain showrooms for merchandise display on a limited schedule or by special appointment.

Trade, Business, and Commercial Organizations

There are some 3000 different trade, business, and commercial organizations in the United States. The directories of associations should be consulted to locate the organizations active in any particular field of interest. Trade associations can furnish a great deal of useful information to anyone interested in starting or acquiring a new business; they should be one of the first contacts made by the aspiring businessman. In addition to trade associations representing a specific type of business activity, the following organizations offer a broader, more general base:

American Federation of Small Businesses
407 South Dearborn Street
Chicago, IL 60605

Council of Better Business Bureaus
1150 17th Street, N.W.
Washington, DC 20036

Institute for New Enterprise Development
305 Concord Avenue
Belmont, MA 02178

National Business League
4324 Georgia Avenue, N.W.
Washington, DC 20011

National Council for Small Business Management Development
University of Wisconsin Extension
929 North Sixth Avenue
Milwaukee, WI 53203

National Federation of Independent Businesses
150 West 20th Avenue
San Mateo, CA 94403

National Small Business Association
1225 19th Street, N.W.
Washington, DC 20036

Service Corps of Retired Executives
1441 L Street, N.W.
Washington, DC 20416

Smaller Business of America
401 Euclid Avenue
Cleveland, OH 44114

The authors, incidentally, are members of the American Marketing Association, the American Booksellers Association, and several professional societies.

Index